Improving Interagency Collaboration, Innovation and Learning in Criminal Justice Systems

Sarah Hean · Berit Johnsen ·
Anu Kajamaa · Laure Kloetzer
Editors

Improving Interagency Collaboration, Innovation and Learning in Criminal Justice Systems

Supporting Offender Rehabilitation

palgrave
macmillan

Editors
Sarah Hean
Social Work Department
University of Stavanger
Stavanger, Norway

Berit Johnsen
University College of the Norwegian Correctional Service (KRUS)
Lillestrom, Norway

Anu Kajamaa
Faculty of Educational Sciences
University of Helsinki
Helsinki, Finland

Laure Kloetzer
Institute of Psychology and Education
University of Neuchâtel
Neuchâtel, Switzerland

ISBN 978-3-030-70660-9 ISBN 978-3-030-70661-6 (eBook)
https://doi.org/10.1007/978-3-030-70661-6

Cover illustration: Angela Turner-Wilson

This Palgrave Macmillan imprint is published by the registered company Springer Nature Switzerland AG
The registered company address is: Gewerbestrasse 11, 6330 Cham, Switzerland

Acknowledgements

The authors would like to acknowledge all participants who contributed to the project, especially the staff members, volunteers, trustees, mentors and mentees, and other part of Norwegian and Finnish prisons and UK voluntary sector organisations, who participated in this research.

The research in this book was funded by the COLAB project, the EU Commission funded: Horizon 2020 MSCA-RISE project number 734536. The editors contributed equally to the production of this book.

Contents

Notes on Contributors

Marie Aakjær, Ph.D. is an Associated Professor, Centre for Management and Experience Design, University College Absalon, Denmark. She has done qualitative research in the fields of public health and elderly care, the voluntary sector, and correctional services. She specialises in the fields of co-creation, social innovation, and learning and has a background in co-design (participatory design).

Sara Ashencaen Crabtree, Ph.D. is a Professor of Social & Cultural Diversity at Bournemouth University, UK. She has had a wide international academic career and is the bestselling author of *Islam and Social Work* (Policy Press).

Stål Bjørkly, Ph.D. is a Professor in clinical psychology at Molde University College and a Research Consultant at the Centre for Research and Education in Forensic Psychiatry. He has a long clinical career in forensic psychiatry and has published extensively in this field.

Catherine Bullen works as a District Nurse for Wiltshire Health and Care, National Health Service, Salisbury, Wiltshire, UK. She is a qualified Registered General and Mental Health Nurse and has a keen interest in supporting those in marginalised societal groups. Catherine worked as a drug rehabilitation practitioner in a UK prison setting for many years.

Karl Yngvar Dale, Ph.D. is an Associate Professor at Molde University College (MUC) NO. He has clinical and administrative experience from a wide variety of mental health care and substance abuse treatment facilities. As both a specialist in Clinical Psychology and a researcher, Dale has expertise in complicated traumatic stress reactions, violence risk management, community-based mental health work, and healthcare organisation. Dale is currently the leader of the research group in Mental Health Work at the MUC.

Stuart Dearborn works for the Footprints project, a third sector organisation based in Poole, Dorset, UK. Stuart manages, volunteers, and coordinates mentoring services supporting those who are leaving custody and integrating back into society. The recent pandemic has led to more emphasis being placed on online work and staying in contact with outside agencies such as prisons, volunteers, and probation services.

William Dugdale, Ph.D. has a B.Sc. (Hons.) Criminology and Master of Research in Social Science graduate with expertise on the rehabilitation and reintegration of inmates across European prison systems. He worked as a front-line professional for 3 years within the England and Wales prison system at HMP Bure and HMP Norwich, where he was responsible for providing rehabilitative and reintegrative support to inmates. He also undertook a research traineeship at Associazione Antigone in Rome, Italy focusing on de-radicalisation across prison systems in Europe for the European Prison Observatory. William is a COLAB member and has been awarded his Ph.D. at Bournemouth University, UK that explored interprofessional collaborative practice in the Norwegian prison system.

Gunnar Eidhammer, M.Sc. is a Researcher at the Centre for Research and Education in Forensic Psychiatry Oslo University Hospital NO and Nurse Specialist at the Division of Mental Health and Addiction, Vestre Viken Hospital Trust, Vestre Viken HF, NO. He is an Educator in risk assessment and risk management. He is responsible for implementing ERM in Norway and is involved in several ERM projects in Norway.

Terhi Esko, Ph.D. was awarded her Ph.D. by the University of Helsinki, Finland. Her dissertation examines the social impact of academic research in the Educational and Social Sciences. Currently Esko works in the project "Emergence of Health Tech and Life Science Firms in Finland" at Tampere University, Finland. Her research themes include science, technology, and innovation studies and related policy, comparative studies of research organisations, and public service production. She has skills in qualitative content analysis, framing, and narrative methods. She has published in several international journals.

Frans Fluttert, Ph.D. is a Senior Researcher at FPC Dr. S. van Mesdag NL, Associate Professor at Molde University College NO, a Research Supervisor at Centre for Research and Education in Forensic Psychiatry, Oslo University Hospital NO, and an Associate Professor at University of Southern Denmark DK. He is involved in risk management projects across Europe and is member of the EVIPRG. He lectures at universities and publishes internationally within the field of Nursing.

Sarah Hean, Ph.D. is a Professor of Social Work at the University of Stavanger; Norway and a Professor of Social Sciences at the Bournemouth University, England with expertise in interprofessional education and collaborative practice between the mental health and criminal justice systems. She has completed a Marie Curie Sklodowska (MSCA) individual fellowship in interagency practices and is currently principal investigator and coordinator of the COLAB consortium, an MSCA-RISE programme aiming to improve collaborations between criminal justice and welfare services.

Vanessa Heaslip, Ph.D. is an Associate Professor in Nursing at Bournemouth University. Her research interests are in the field of vulnerability and vulnerable groups in society whose voices are not traditionally heard in the academic and professional discourse.

Heli Heikkilä is a Ph.D. candidate in the Faculty of Educational Sciences, University of Helsinki, Finland, and has worked as a Researcher at the Finnish Institute of Occupational Health for over a decade. She has applied developmental work research and its intervention methods in multiple organisations and fields. Her main research interest concerns transformative agency and especially investigating how the individual and collective levels of activity intertwine in changing work.

Richard Heslop, Ph.D. teaches criminology at Bournemouth University and the Open University in the United Kingdom (UK). He also served for 28 years as a police officer in West Yorkshire Police in the UK, before leaving the police in 2016 to become a university academic. Richard holds degrees in sociology, politics, and education. He is a Fulbright Scholar (University of Cincinnati, USA, 2012) and in 2014 he was Visiting Bramshill Scholar at the John Jay College of Criminal Justice in New York. Richard currently serves on the Editorial Board of *Police Practice and Research: An International Journal*, with special responsibilities for police practitioner liaison.

Berit Johnsen, Ph.D. is the Head of research department and a Research Professor in penology at the University College of Norwegian Correctional Service. It is in the interdisciplinary approach and cooperation that characterise her work she finds the potential and inspiration for her research. Johnsen has published papers and articles on a range of penological topics, such as the quality of prison life, resettlement, prison architecture and space, and preventive detention.

Anu Kajamaa, Ph.D. is an Associate Professor and is a Co-leader of the Learning, Culture and Interventions (LECI) research community at the Faculty of Educational Sciences, University of Helsinki, Finland. She has conducted sociocultural and activity-theoretical research and intervention projects in schools, teacher education, health care, social care, and entrepreneurship contexts and published about 60 papers in international journals.

Laure Kloetzer is an Assistant Professor in sociocultural psychology at the Institute of Psychology and Education, University of Neuchâtel (Switzerland). Following Vygotsky's legacy, her expertise is in the field of intervention, developmental methodologies, participatory methods and citizen science, in which she promotes and studies different modes of collaboration between academics and practitioners. She has been researching how to improve dialogue, learning and interprofessional collaboration in the workplace in different fields (in particular, hospitals, factories, schools or lately probation services). Her focus is on doing research "with", and not "on", specific participants.

Päivikki Lahtinen is a Ph.D. candidate at the Faculty of Educational Sciences, University of Helsinki, Finland. She has a master's degree in adult education which consisted of study of organisational learning, development, and change. She also works as an Adviser in the Centre for Entrepreneurship and Social Innovation at University of Agder, Norway. She is a COLAB member and her research interests include co-creation, collaboration, collective learning, and change in which she applies cultural-historical activity theory. Currently she is focusing on different participatory methods related to social innovation and co-creation such as methods of the Change Laboratory and Design Thinking.

Bjørn Kjetil Larsen is a Ph.D. student at Volda University College and an Assistant Professor at Molde University College. His research interests are interprofessional collaboration and interagency collaboration. He has worked as a front-line professional for more than 20 years in the fields of substance abuse treatment, mental health service, correctional service, social service, and child care.

Tine Murphy, Ph.D. is a Senior Lecturer at University College Absalon, Denmark. She has done qualitative research in the fields of health care, the voluntary sector, and correctional services. Her specialty is in the field of management and organisation studies, with a focus on sensemaking theory. She has practical management experience from the financial and healthcare sector.

Søren Walther Nielsen, Ph.D. is an Associate Professor at the University College Absalon, Denmark. He teaches social sciences and conducts research on criminology, including theoretical and methodological reflections on prison activities, emotional discourses, and the researcher's positionality. Other research areas involve policy issues, social work, and public administration. He has published articles on social capital, urban marginality, ethnic minorities, and resocialization processes.

Atle Ødegård, Ph.D. is a Clinical Psychologist and Professor at Molde University College. His research interests are interprofessional collaboration in practice and education, as well as the development of new research methodology in these fields. He is Professor II at Nordland Research Institute, where he focuses specifically on innovation in the public sector.

Eva Pallesen, Ph.D. is a Docent in Centre of Management and Experience Design at University College Absalon, Denmark. Her research focuses on welfare professional work, management, and entrepreneurship in the public sector. She has previously worked as Head of methodology at the Danish Evaluation Institute and as Head of a section in the Danish Ministry of Education.

Jonathan Parker, Ph.D. is a Professor of Society & Social Welfare at Bournemouth University, UK. He is an experienced international scholar of social work policy and education and bestselling author of *Social Work Practice* (Sage).

Paulo Rocha, Ph.D. completed his Ph.D. at the Department of Social Studies at the University of Stavanger, Norway. He received a bachelor's degree in law from Gama Filho University, Brazil and a master's degree in international law from the University of Liverpool. England. He is interested in collaboration and innovation practices in the public sector.

Charlotte Rosenberg, Ph.D. is an Associate Professor at the Centre for Social work and Administration, University College Absalon, Denmark. She has done qualitative research in the field of social work, the voluntary sector, the field of social entrepreneurship and social economy, and correctional services. Her specialty is in the field of social work, with focus on everyday life, people in vulnerable positions, change, and becoming. She has practical experience from the social sector and specifically from the field of development of local communities.

Kristin Røvik is an Assistant Professor at Molde University College. She has many years of practice experience from social work in the field of job inclusion and job rehabilitation, which involves extensive collaboration with other organisations and agencies. Røvik and colleagues have conducted a study focusing inclusion of refugees in Norwegian football clubs and prevention of financial exclusion.

Siv Elin Nord Sæbjørnsen, Ph.D. is an Associate Professor at Molde University College. Sæbjørnsen has many years of experience in the practice field, including child welfare, substance abuse treatment, and mental health care. Her focus areas in research are interprofessional collaboration and service users with complex challenges.

Laura Seppänen, D.Sc. is a Chief Scientist at the Finnish Institute of Occupational Health, and Adjunct Professor at the University of Helsinki. She, has done qualitative research on participatory development of work and workplace learning in multiple domains including social and health care, agri-food systems, rail traffic control, and correctional services. Her practice-based research expertise includes reflection and learning challenges, relational agency and interpretive practice, development and logics of work activities, activity theories, and sustainability. Laura has more than 70 scientific publications.

Liv Jorunn Skippervik has a degree in social work from the University for Stavanger and in law from the University of Bergen, Norway. She works at the department of social work at Stavanger University, teaching amongst other things welfare law and restorative justice. She has special interest in the intersection between law and social work in the practice field. She has practice experience in inclusion of mentally ill patients and prisoners in the labour market, mediation, and has been Head of the regional mediation service.

Caroline Stevens, Ph.D. is the current CEO of Footprints project, a third sector organisation based in Poole, Dorset, UK, having taken over the role in May 2018.

Angela Turner-Wilson, Ph.D. is the Deputy Head of Department for Medical Sciences and Public Health, Bournemouth University, Dorset, UK. She has a keen interest in social inequalities and has worked closely with the criminal justice service. Her current work explores the transient nature of well-being within diverse communities from a local and international perspective.

Jo Wells was a Mentor for the Footprints Project before managing their work in Dorset. After a decade of experience with the project, she began studying for a Ph.D. at Bournemouth University.

Elisabeth Willumsen, Ph.D. is a Professor of Social Work at the Faculty of Health Sciences, University of Stavanger, Norway with a Doctorate in Public Health Science. Her research interests include interprofessional collaboration and social innovation in health and welfare services. Willumsen holds a professor II position at Molde University College, Norway.

Hilkka Ylisassi, Ph.D. (Adult Education), is a Specialist Researcher at the Finnish Institute of Occupational Health. She has extensive work experience in developmental interventions (e.g. Change Laboratory method and its applications) and qualitative research in multiple sectors, e.g. social and health care, rehabilitation, public services, industries, and prison service. Her main theoretical framework bases on cultural-historical activity theory, and interest areas are participatory work development, learning, and transformational agency.

Terminology and Abbreviations

AFR	(*Avdeling for Rusmedisin*) is a department of addictive medicine. It offers treatment and follow-up to people with intoxication and addiction disorders.
BRIK	(*Behovs- og Ressurskartlegging i Kriminalomsorgen*) is a tool for Correctional Services to assess and map the need and resources of the inmate. It assesses if the inmate has problems or issues, e.g. on unemployment, lack of schooling, no place to live, or poor health.
CHAT	Cultural-Historical Activity Theory
CJS	Criminal Justice Services
CLM	Change Laboratory Model
COLAB	An EU-funded project (COLAB-H2020-MSCA-RISE-2016/734536) a partnership of European researchers and practice professionals aimed at improving collaborative practices between criminal justice and welfare-related services.

Contact officer	This is a position in Norwegian prisons similar to that of a prison officer in other European prison contexts. Each prisoner has a nominated prison officer who has the responsibility to engage with the prisoner in supportive, motivational, rehabilitative, and reintegrative work.
Correctional Services/Prisons	These two terms are used interchangeably in this book. Although correctional service has negative connotations in the UK context and we would prefer the use of the term prison, correctional services is the commonly found translation of prison from Norwegian to English when research participants are talking about their experiences.
CSA	The Criminal Sanctions Agency is the governmental organisation responsible for all prison services in Finland.
Developmental task	An innovation or "experiment" that is designed, implemented, and evaluated collaboratively by employees, managers, and researchers.
ERM	Early Recognition Method
HCCE	Human-centred co-evaluation. A method to support employees in their collective efforts to develop work practices by designing and implementing developmental tasks simultaneously with setting goals and finding ways to evaluate and learn from them.
HCR-20^{V3}	The risk management tool: Historical-Clinical-Risk Management-20, Version 3.
IT	Information Technology
KOMPIS	is a central data system which has two internal systems. It provides support for work tasks conducted in prison and delivers notification of imprisonment and release on prisons. KOMPIS is also a management tool. The system interacts with electronic archive within the Correctional Services. It does not interact

	with other systems or agencies of Health Care Services.
Kriminalomsorgen	The Correctional Service in Norway governed by the Ministry of Justice and Public Security, responsible for the implementation and carrying out of custodial and penal sanctions.
L&D	Liaison and Diversion Services in England and Wales
MHS	Mental Health Services
NGO	Non-Governmental Organisations
Object of activity	is an activity-theoretical concept. In activity theory, the distinction between individual *goal*-directed action and collective *object*-oriented activity is of central importance. In the object of the activity, the communal motive is embedded.
Overgangsbolig	A Norwegian transitional residence. These are prisons typically referred to as half-way houses in other prison contexts across Europe. These institutions offer the opportunity for inmates to transition to the final phase of their sentence whilst living at a prison with less restrictive and open conditions.
PINCOM	Perception of Interprofessional Collaboration Model
PINCOM-Q	Perception of Interprofessional Collaboration Model—Questionnaire
SI	Social Innovation
TSO	Third Sector Organisations, used interchangeably with VCS to depict non-state-funded, non-profit organisations with a large component of volunteer staff.
VCS	Voluntary Community Service, used interchangeably with TSO to depict non-state-funded, non-profit organisations with a large component of volunteer staff.
WS	Welfare services: This includes health and social care services.

List of Figures

List of Tables

1

Setting the Scene and Introduction

Sarah Hean, Anu Kajamaa, Berit Johnsen, and Laure Kloetzer

Preparing people for life after prison, resettlement and a life free from crime is a crucial and complex task. Offender rehabilitation is a key strategy employed by prison services internationally to support this.

S. Hean (✉)
Social Work Department, University of Stavanger, Stavanger, Norway
e-mail: sarah.c.hean@uis.no

A. Kajamaa
Faculty of Educational Sciences, University of Helsinki, Helsinki, Finland
e-mail: anu.kajamaa@helsinki.fi

B. Johnsen
University College of the Norwegian Correctional Service (KRUS), Lillestrom, Norway
e-mail: berit.johnsen@krus.no

L. Kloetzer
Institute of Psychology and Education,
University of Neuchâtel, Neuchâtel, Switzerland
e-mail: anu.kajamaa@helsinki.fi

S. Hean et al. (eds.), *Improving Interagency Collaboration, Innovation and Learning in Criminal Justice Systems*,
https://doi.org/10.1007/978-3-030-70661-6_1

Programmes of education, employment, health care and other interventions are typically introduced to aid offenders' rehabilitation, their reintegration into society and reduce the likelihood of recidivism (UK Ministry of Justice, 2013; Skardhamar & Telle, 2012; Armstrong, 2012). These interventions involve an overlap of the work activity of a variety of actors representing professions from welfare (health and social care) and criminal justice services. Good collaboration between these actors, including the prisoner, is required to navigate and better integrate the different interventions and service systems. These latter systems are in an ongoing process of change, struggling to meet effectively the needs of the individual, organisation and the society. Interagency work and collaboration are necessary in this context for continuous learning and innovation creation to take place that address these challenges.

The criminal justice system is a complex environment with many interacting and unpredictable factors. This creates multifaceted challenges for the work activity of the actors involved in prison services and health/welfare services. The complexity of collaborative working in this context can be defined as a "wicked problem" (Rittel & Webber, 1973; Hean et al., 2020). This means the exact problem is often difficult to define; it exists within open systems being influenced by a multitude of interacting influences; professionals may individually be able to come up with multiple solutions dependent on their own experiences but these are each difficult to predict, test or disprove and will vary in effectiveness depending on the context and stakeholders involved. As such, any solution aimed at improving reoffending rates and rehabilitation through optimising interagency collaboration, learning and innovation will often not be consistent with standardised care pathways that promote uniform, one-size-fits-all coordination of care across agencies (Hean et al., 2020).

This book aims to explore some of these wicked problems and challenges to collaboration the prison and penal systems are currently facing and the role of innovation and organisational learning to meeting these challenges. The concepts of interagency collaboration, organisational learning, co-creation and innovation are positioned within a wider debate of prison as a means of welfare versus punishment. The book also discusses the active role of researchers in organisational change, service development and innovation. In this it considers issues of inclusion when it comes to representing the service professional and service user voice in the innovation process. The book hereby provides a resource through which academics, advanced graduate students and professionals/prison administrators interested in prison/criminal research and service development can explore key issues and methods in enhancing collaboration, organisational learning and innovation in this context. The book takes a European focus that the reader may wish to compare and contrast with other international contexts such as North America and Australasia.

There are two sections to the book. The first section presents some of the current collaborative practices and challenges to these in a series of case study criminal justice-related environments. Imprisonment presents an opportunity for the individual to prepare for a life free of crime, and careful coordination of different services, to prepare and support people for release, is often required. This book section has a wider scope than addressing collaboration within the prison alone but covers collaborative practice at several points in an individual's trajectory through a criminal justice system and the roles of a variety of stakeholders including the third sector, state and academic stakeholders within this.

The second section of this book explores strategies and methods available to researchers that can promote collaboration, management and innovation. Action-based participatory research or interventionist approaches to promote innovation and collaboration are introduced as is the role of researchers in these processes. The section examines how researchers can be proactive as agents of organisational change that are often needed to tackle some of the challenges addressed in the first section of this book. Further, risk management strategies to increase quality of integrated care are explored as potential methods and tools for interagency boundary crossing. Means of including multiple voices in service development and innovation are also examined, as is the potential transferability of methods and interventions used in other criminal justice contexts, to successfully promote innovation and organisational learning. This section also provides a resource to promote positive relationships between key actors involved in improving the prisons and penal systems for all involved.

The COLAB Consortium

The content of the book is based on efforts of the COLAB research consortium and its members. COLAB (Horizon 2020 funded CO-LAB MSCA-RISE project number 734536) is a partnership of European researchers and practice professionals comprising 7 Universities and 3 practice organisations related to the criminal justice system from Norway, Finland, UK, the Netherlands, Denmark and Switzerland. The COLAB consortium is a unique community of practice (Wenger, 1998) aimed at building international research capacity and cooperation between a range of complementary disciplines. It is operationalised through a series of inter-sector and international secondments or exchanges between academic and practice partners with the common aim of improving offender rehabilitation and resettlement. The aim of the consortium is to build more effective models of collaboration between health or welfare services and criminal justice services. The longer term intention is to have an impact on the health, welfare and well-being of the prisoner population, whilst securing public safety and reducing reoffending rates. The secondment structure of the project enabled close cooperation between academic and practice partners to develop. This is shown by most of the chapters in the book that have been co-written by a combination of practice and professional partners from COLAB, taking a community of practice stance and learning by working together on this common dissemination goal. The secondment structure also favoured an ethnographic research-informed approach to research with researchers being able to immerse themselves over a period of time in various crimnal justice contexts.

The membership and structure of the COLAB project has meant that the Norwegian prison system has received particular attention here. With the lowest recidivism rates internationally (Fazel & Wolf, 2015; Graunbøl et al., 2010) and noted for their culture of rehabilitation within their prison systems (Pratt, 2008), the Norwegian system provides an interesting backdrop for many of the chapters included. The researchers and authors of the chapters are from a more varied European background, however, and, with the exception of Sepännen and co-authors (Chapter 9), represent a group of international researchers examining the criminal justice system in a national context other than their own. For example, Rocha and Hean (Chapter 6) are a Brazilian and South African, respectively, making sense of a UK liaison and diversion service and Murphy and colleagues (Chapter 4) are Danish researchers making sense of the Norwegian prison sector. This cross-national research enriches our understanding of collaboration in these systems by applying the eye of the external researcher which makes the implicit characteristics of each national context more evident. However, this has limitations also associated with language issues and COLAB members not being familiar with the national context they are exploring.

Cultural-Historical Activity Theory and Change Laboratory Model as a Guiding Framework

As to research-based methods, COLAB, in its inception, drew from an interventionist line underpinned by Cultural-Historical Activity Theory (CHAT) (see e.g. Engeström & Sannino, 2011; Engeström, 2001, 2015; Virkkunen & Newnham, 2013). It made a particular case for implementation of the Change Laboratory Model (CLM) of interagency working and workforce transformation as a potentially more effective means of supporting interagency collaborative practice in this context than current interagency practices. CHAT and the CLM both found favour within the COLAB work because researchers working on the project had previously used these extensively to analyse and facilitate change in collaborations within and between organisations in other fields. However, none of the COLAB project members had applied these in studying collaborations between prison services and mental health services. These have since been proposed as useful tools to provide a holistic understanding of the complex, multifactorial context of collaboration in the field of criminal justice (see Hean et al., 2018). Drawing also on the complementary expertise in the consortium in other models of collaboration, organisational learning and innovation, the consortium had as a primary objective the exploration of the suitability of CHAT and the CLM model, and its adaptation, to the welfare/criminal justice context. The complementary expertise of the consortium is reflected in the content of this book.

In brief, CHAT is rooted in the legacy of Vygotsky, Leont'ev and Luria and it is a multidisciplinary theory, which has gained increasing popularity and relevance amongst researchers in the field of organisation studies (Adler, 2005; Blackler, 2009). CHAT offers a system-level view for researchers and practitioners to analyse work, learning, development and change processes. It provides conceptual and analytical tools, such as the models of activity systems and the methodological cycle of expansive learning. CHAT includes an interventionist methodology, named the Change Laboratory, for enhancing reflection of struggles, competing interests and contradictions in collective activities. Participants in a Change Laboratory are encouraged to reinterpret and discuss their work using video-recordings as a "mirror" reflecting back to them their work place activities. Based on ethnographic data, Nielsen and Kajamaa (Chapter 3) and Kloetzer et al. (Chapter 7) provide examples of these mirror materials. Also, a variety of analytical tools are used to analyse and transform work practices, such as the activity system model, the notion of contradiction and the cycle of expansive learning actions. The role of the researcher is to introduce these tools and to facilitate this process. Sepännen and colleagues (Chapter 9) show us how this learning can be facilitated at several points during a service development intervention including both in the design phase of the innovation process but also during the evaluation of the intervention's outcomes. In these interventions, the end results of learning and change are not predetermined by the interventionist, and the outcomes are designed by the participants as they work out expansive solutions to the contradictions in their activity systems (Virkkunen & Newnham, 2013).

CHAT as a conceptual framework is applied in this book by Rocha and Hean (Chapter 6) to explore the historical development in work activity within Liaison and Diversion Services in the UK. Further, Dugdale and Hean (Chapter 5), Nielsen and Kajamaa (Chapter 3) and Lahtinen and colleagues (Chapter 2) take a CHAT perspective as a means of articulating the collaborative work activities taking place between prison staff and prisoners in Norway. Hean and colleagues (Chapter 8) refer to CHAT as a means through which professionals participating in researcher-facilitated interventions can identify contradictions and use this analysis to make sense of and transform their work activities.

Other Theoretical Lenses and Integration Models

The international and interdisciplinary nature of COLAB members and authors of this book ensures the usage of a breadth of theories other than CHAT in many of the chapters of this book. Murphy and co-authors (Chapter 4) for example by using neo-institutional theory (DiMaggio & Powell, 1991) and sense-making theory (Weick, 1995) show how actors in a Norwegian low-security prison "live with" multiple and potentially conflicting institutional logics.

Many of the chapters of this book refer to service integration models, which can be defined as those methods of funding, administration, organisation, service delivery and care designed to enhance collaboration within and between different services (Kodner & Spreeuwenberg, 2002). Integration models vary in their characteristics and are positioned along a continuum from full integration to full separation of services. The optimal position of one service related to another is usually defined by the organisational context and the needs of the service users (Ahgren & Axelsson, 2005; Lawrence & Lorsch, 1967). Different countries will have diverse ways and models in which health and social care (and especially the mental health services) are integrated with criminal justice (and especially prison) services. These can be located "in the intersection" of different institutional logics of rehabilitation versus control, of punishment versus care.

In this book, because of the predominance of Norwegian prison research in its focus, the Norwegian import model of service integration is the most commonly discussed model of integration, i.e. a model of integration where external public welfare agencies of health, school, library and clerical services deliver their services for people in prison in the same way as they do for other citizens. The following chapters discuss this integration model in relation to how it impacts collaborative practices within prisons and between prisons and external services, see Dugdale and Hean (Chapter 5), Murphy et al. (Chapter 4), Nielsen and Kajamaa (Chapter 3), Lahtinen et al. (Chapter 2). These chapters show how the services vary in where, along the integration continua, each prison and its surrounding services lie and explore how collaboration takes place in these different contexts and levels of integration. Dugdale and Hean (Chapter 5) show how the import model of care provision falls away in a transitional prison/half-way house. Contact and collaboration between prison and external professions are low or non-existent and mediated through the prisoner themselves as they, the prisoner, must actively seek out external service professionals themselves on the outside. Nielsen and Kajamaa (Chapter 3), in their description of a low-security prison in Norway, uncover similar challenges in inter-organisational interactions between specialised mental health services and local prison services. When interagency collaboration between prisons and other services is weak, this makes it difficult for prisoners to navigate between the different services before and after release. Supporting this navigation task can then fall to members of the voluntary sector (see Kloetzer & colleagues, Chapter 7), and processes typically rely on informal procedures, goodwill, imagination, determination and the skills of dedicated individuals.

From an activity-theoretical perspective, the meeting and potential tensions between different institutional logics can be seen as drivers for collective learning and change. In this, the models and practices of integration are crucial as these impact the way institutional logics can eventually coexist. Lahtinen and colleagues (see Chapter 2) provide examples of where the distinct institutional logics of control versus care meet during the conduct of interagency meetings and how these are then resolved.

Similarly, Murphy and Seppänen and colleagues (Chapters 7 and 9, respectively) unravel how institutional logics can exist in parallel and develop a balance that can be described as "dynamic security". From the Finnish context, treatment and control are not seen as separate ends of a philosophical continuum but as preconditions for effective rehabilitation. In an open prison in Norway, Murphy and colleagues find that the prison and health care professionals have developed a range of ways of making sense of their common world, including the use of narratives and metaphors.

Fluttert and colleagues (Chapter 11) analyse collaboration using the concept of "Self" and explore awareness of one's own perceptions as a concept to underpin the communication that occurs between a range of actors. These authors are particularly interested in the awareness of self and dialogue with others in therapeutic situations. They recognise that awareness of self is impacted by, and reacts to, the voices of others. The awareness of self in relation to others is also picked up by Ødegård and Bjorkley (Chapter 10) for whom dialogue is described as a recognition of multiple perspectives and "a move from a perception of reality as absolute to one that is individually and differentially perceived".

Methods for Promoting Social Innovation and Systemic Change

Systems-level integration and individual-level collaborations are not only important for the everyday delivery of correctional and health services but are key to the social innovation process, a process of co-creation between multiple actors that allows for a cross-fertilisation of interprofessional knowledge. In this book, social innovation is perceived as both the process and outcome of taking new knowledge or combining existing knowledge in new ways or applying it to new contexts. It is primarily about creating positive social change, and improving social relations and collaborations to address a social demand (European Commission, 2013; Hean et al., 2015). Furthermore, innovation is essential in the prison environment where prison population demographics and challenges are in a constant state of flux.

An innovation process involves participants engaging in expansive organisational learning (Engeström, 1987/2015), an iterative and cyclical process through which individuals collectively define and redefine their activity. In Chapter 8, Hean and colleagues outline an innovation processes aiming at promoting organisational learning, collaboration and innovation between multiple professionals from participating organisations. The cycles involve participants identifying tensions and contradictions in their work activity, analysing and making sense of these through multiple perspectives, modelling/creating new solutions to these, and locally implementing and experimenting with new forms of activity. Participants, throughout the process, reflect on the outcomes of the intervention and any new tensions that have arisen through this experimentation process before consolidating or upscaling organisational transformations.

Some chapters illustrate how innovation, and the expansive learning processes that underpin these, may develop organically in the prison setting without the interference of the research community. In Rocha and Hean (Chapter 6), practice professionals and policy makers identified the need for a more standardised offering of care provision in Liaison and Diversion services in England and Wales. Taking a historical perspective, the authors describe the expansive learning process that took place, showing how contradictions were identified and solutions to these developed and tested in practice. The chapter by Lahtinen and colleagues (Chapter 2), describes how leaders from different services, when participating in regular interagency meetings in a prison, responded to a lack of prison officer and prisoner voice at these events. They do so by examining during their leadership meetings the use of a mapping tool (BRIK) completed by prison officers with the prisoner. This tool they believed would capture and represent the voice of the prisoner during their leadership meetings. The chapter highlights the tensions that arose in the leaders' examination, experimentation and evaluation of this, their innovative use of BRIK. The tensions included issues of confidentiality of cross-agency information sharing.

Nielsen and Kajamaa (Chapter 3) demonstrate how a prisoner, in his interactions with a service, may also be part of such a cycle of collective learning. They refer to the prisoners' own transformative agency, a concept Sannino et al. (2016, p. 4) describe as "a quality of expansive learning" that "requires breaking away from the given frame of action and taking the initiative to transform it". As the prisoner is involved in their own personal transformation, so too can they be engaged in system-level change and learning.

The Service User's Voice

The inclusion of the service user voice in the innovation and learning process is the central theme of this book, and it is explored in terms of their engagement in change and learning efforts (Hean et al., Chapter 8; Nielsen & Kajamaa, Chapter 3). Ideally, for their voice to be heard accurately, prisoners should actively participate in person in service development efforts. If this is to happen, however, those facilitating such activity should be aware of the need to build mutual trust between prisoners and between prisoners and staff participating in these events. They should recognise and compensate for power asymmetries that may exist between participants (see Hean et al., Chapter 8). Specific skills are needed both in the intervention participants and the facilitator to make constructive dialogue possible in the highly hierarchical prison setting.

Lahtinen and colleagues (Chapter 2) describe how tools, such as BRIK, completed by prisoners and prison officers, brings their voice into leadership interagency meetings even though they do not appear in these meetings in person. Further, the HCR20 and ERM tools (see Ødegård & Bjørkly, Chapter 10 and Flutter et al., Chapter 11), by acting as boundary-crossing tools, can be used to capture the voices of prisoner and other professionals' voices and bring these into the care process. Parker et al. (Chapter 12), and Turner Wilson and colleagues (Chapter 13) explore the value of emic, etic and etemic perspectives. They draw a distinction between the voice of the prisoner as service user (emic) versus the voice of the professional (etic) on what services should look like. Although, including the voice of the prisoner in service development is challenging (Hean et al., Chapter 8), if excluded, it perpetuates the etic perspective alone. Parker et al. call for an etemic view, where both the emic and etic views, each with their own strengths, are combined (Heaslip et al., 2016; Parker et al., Chapter 12). Wilson Turner and colleagues (Chapter 13) provide an illustration of this etemic perspective in presenting a case of a collaboration between a worker and an ex-prisoner. One of these authors, in having multiple identities, acted as a boundary spanner in the COLAB activity and hereby proved to be an invaluable research agent, crossing boundaries of academia, service providers and the service user, simultaneously. Through his etemic perspective he was able to access both professional and service users that the researchers themselves, through cultural differences (national and sector), had previously been denied.

A key issue in including the voice of service users in interventions relate to the vulnerability of the prisoner. Parker and colleagues (Chapter 12) delve more deeply into the concept of vulnerability and reflect, in their discussion of critical ethnography, on how the stigma and labelling of prisoners is problematic. At the level of a discrete intervention, researchers may unconsciously hold biases of prisoners, and for example select certain material representing a particular dimension of the offenders' experience and not others. This may also be manifested in the slant of their analysis, as Wilson Turner and co-authors (Chapter 13) concur. They recognise how they may have consciously or unconsciously prioritised and edited the material they collected, in their jottings, narratives and choice of photos that informed the narrative in their chapter. The discussions of these chapters raise issues of the epistemic violence possibly embedded in the use of data collected by the researchers or professionals in any analysis and interpretation process from which prisoners are absent (Spivak, 1988). Whether influenced by bias or not, the accuracy with which the voice of the prisoner is actually represented in the tools described in Chapters 6, 10 and 11 remains unexamined, however.

Kloetzer and colleagues (Chapter 7) demonstrate how the perspective of the researcher and the professional may be very distinct from each other and from that of the prisoner. Issues relating to the meeting of contrasting perspectives are also observed in Sæbjornesen et al. (Chapter 15) where the implications of contrasting mentor and ex-prisoner perspectives on the rehabilitation prospects of offenders are compared and contrasted. In other words, any research report or intervention is dependent on what the researcher may or may not see as worthy of reporting. Similarly, at a systems level, research ethics committees can be strict in their control over studies that propose to talk directly to offenders. The committee limitations placed on the researcher when they design their studies can discourage researchers from talking to prisoners at all. Although the intention of the committee is to protect the prisoner, and minimise their vulnerability, this also serves to silence the voice of the prisoner (Seppänen et al., Chapter 9). This suggests that, if prisoners are not directly engaged in service development, professionals/researchers may not be in a position to represent the view of the prisoner.

Organisational Multivoicedness

The prisoners' voice is not the only perspective that is in danger of being silenced in research and innovation in the criminal justice environment. Ødegård and Willumsen (Chapter 17) present clear instances where researchers have prejudged the needs and problems of practice institutions. This chapter emphasises the need for approaches to innovation and service development in which problem identification and solutions are created from the bottom up, and a balance is found in the input between the direct and indirect engagement of employees, service users, researchers and policy makers (see Rocha & Hean, Chapter 6 for a discussion of the dangers of top down implementation of policy). This is clearly observed in Kloetzer and colleagues (Chapter 7) when interview data are analysed by first the researcher and then contrasted with the analysis made by staff members from the host organisation themselves participating in the research. Both analyses have utility but their distinctiveness needs to be acknowledged as does, at the end of the day, the priority that must be given, in service development interventions, to what practice see as being the problems at hand and not what the researchers decide the problems to address should be.

Methods of organisational change, innovation and collaboration can involve the unification and comparison of multiple and sometimes contrasting perspectives of participants and facilitators. Theoretically, this process is informed by the concept of multivoicedness utilised in activity theoretical studies, and forming one of the key principles of the Change Laboratory method (Virkkunen & Newnham, 2013; Kerosuo & Engeström, 2003). Multivoicedness is anchored in the theoretical tradition of dialogism (Bakhtin, 1981, 1984, 1986; Markova, 2016) that postulates that the Self and Others are interrelated on ontological, epistemological and ethical levels. The Other is not in opposition to Self, but part of Self (Aveling et al., 2015). From this perspective, collective activity is mediated by the internal and external dialogues in which people participate (with actual or inner voices) representing the diverse communities from which participants are drawn. This relates to Bakhtin's concept of polyphony, a multivoiced reality, "a plurality of independent and unmerged voices and consciousnesses..." (Bakhtin, 1984). Here each utterance made by any one individual in any interaction is anchored in a specific speech context and also beyond to connect to distant others. For Bakhtin, the role of the person being addressed (addressee) during a dialogue between actors is critical. Each utterance is addressed to a postulated addressee, who is present in the mind of the speaker/writer, and whose "active and responsive understanding" is anticipated. Our words are always "half someone else's" (Bakhtin, 1981) and the sense we make of our world is created intersubjectively or collectively by people both present and absent

The concept of multivoicedness is useful not only in workplace interventions involving groups (see Hean et al., Chapter 8), but also in the one-to-one therapeutic situations that Fluttert and colleagues (Chapter 11) describe. In their case, the ERM helps prisoners reflect on the dialogue between self and the voice of internal and external others as a means of managing their risk of violent behaviour within the prison. The prisoner's voice and that of the differing professionals supporting them inter-penetrate.

Whether at the therapeutic or systems level, establishing a dialogue between the actors participating in the learning process is necessary for collective sense-making, shared understanding and learning. Nielsen and Kajamaa (Chapter 3) spell out, however that the expansive learning cycles, and the transformative agency these cycles engender, do not always occur spontaneously and can become blocked. This is illustrated in the poor interactions between external mental health services and prison health staff, in a small Norwegian prison. When the collaborative process is not made explicit and only understood tacitly, then innovations are serendipitous and left to chance rather than a culture of innovation being developed within the criminal justice environment. Explicit methods of innovation promotion are thus required. There is a place for researchers then to take an active role in providing such methods that can facilitate organisational change, service development and innovation. This opens up a discussion about responsibility and accountability more widely in any collaboration and in the innovation process in particular.

Who Has Responsibility for Rehabilitation?

A key dimension of interagency collaboration in service provision is the allocation of roles and responsibilities (Hean et al., 2017). A typical question then is which service provider has the responsibility to support the needs of the prisoner and their rehabilitation? The distribution of responsibility depends on context and is likely to be distributed across multiple actors (Miller, 2001; Hean et al., 2017). Although control of the prisoner clearly lies with the penal system, especially prisons and probation services, who then has responsibility for their rehabilitation?

Prisoners themselves of course have the responsibility to address their own needs and to a certain extent, direct their own lives, but their capacity to do so may be impaired. Professionals working in prison and health/welfare services also have responsibilities allocated based on their capacity/training to support a particular need. This means responsibility is distributed according to the competence of the professionals involved. However, a professional may have the capacity in terms of training but workload and emotional aspects related to this may make offering adequate support impossible (Miller, 2001; Hean et al., 2017). This is illustrated by Nielsen and Kajamaa (Chapter 3) in their reference to the LEON principle (lowest efficient care level) whereby responsibility for treating a prisoner with mental health issues is directed to primary health care providers in the prison in the first instance rather than the less cost-efficient specialised services. Finding a balance between cost and capacity is difficult to achieve and prison primary health providers feel they have a disproportional responsibility for treating mentally ill prisoners when they do not have the capacity/competence for this task.

Miller (2001) also describes responsibility being distributed by virtue of who knows the individual best and is closest to them (communitarian responsibility). In the case of prisoners, the family member may know them best as may the prison officer who engages with the prisoner on a daily basis. Although their capacity to treat the prisoners' needs (e.g. a mental health issue) may be less, the prison officers' proximity to the prisoner suggests they have a responsibility to support them. They will require information from mental health specialists, for example, if they are to take this responsibility, however. Fluttert and colleagues (Chapter 11) discuss how the encouragement of prison officers to engage in the ERM risk assessment may enhance their capacity to support the needs of offenders. Ødegård and Bjørkly (Chapter 10) suggest something similar when exploring how the HCR20 might be used. The question is how prison officers can engage in these joint assessments or access information on the specialised needs of the prisoner more widely bearing in mind the delicacy of information sharing between services. Privacy hinders information sharing between services, and health and prison services struggle with the problem of which knowledge to share, with whom and for which purposes. They need to find a balance between the right to privacy of the prisoner and at the same time improve the holistic management of life, care and treatment.

The perspective on communitarian responsibility may also be broadened to include the role of society in prisoner rehabilitation. In light of the responsibility of the citizen, such as Greta Thunberg in climate change, who and what is the responsibility of the citizen in supporting vulnerable offenders during and after release? Kloetzer et al. (Chapter 7) and Sæbjornesen et al. (Chapters 14 and 15) explore the perspectives and challenges facing volunteers working in a third sector organisation mentoring ex-prisoners. These mentors illustrate an example of average citizens taking responsibility for the rehabilitation process.

Considering the question of allocation of responsibility brings us to reflect on the role and responsibility of university-trained researchers in the offender rehabilitation process. Traditionally, researchers are expected to generate new knowledge and be neutral bystanders. In this book, we take a more active stance, with some fundamental caveats, that researchers have a more active and participatory role and responsibility.

Academic Engagement in Rehabilitation

In their capacity as educating institutions, universities have a responsibility to train health, social care and criminal justice professionals in interprofessional collaboration and innovation competencies, including interagency communication, intercultural competence and what Nielsen and Kajamaa in Chapter 3 refer to as boundary-crossing expertise. Some of these skills are included in national health and social care curricula in many countries but may be bypassed or are referred to only tangentially or theoretically in the training of police and prison officers (Hean et al., 2011; Hean et al., 2014; Hean 2015; Hean et al., 2017). Innovation skills seldom appear. Students from health, social care and criminal justice fields benefit if there are opportunities for them to be exposed to real-life case studies of prisoners, be exposed to prison visits and volunteer in prison and related institutions as part of their professional placements. COLAB had these responsibilities in mind, in its aim to develop resources to promote learning of collaboration and innovation competences. These endeavours are not without their challenges, however, as described in more detail in Ødegård and Willumsen (Chapter 17). They call for training to involve the promotion of a kind of expansive learning process in students, rather than traditional professional training in specified content.

In their capacity as researchers, university staff have a responsibility to describe and hereby potentially disrupt the view of current professional practices. Their analysis can provide an external and alternative lens as an aide to reflection for professionals and other academics, disrupting their current and unexamined views of the collaborative practice status quo and helping them see the familiar as strange (see Hean et al., Chapter 8). This may be a trigger for organisations to take these findings forward to make change and innovation for themselves. Chapters 2–7 and 9 of this book explore some of these potential triggers, exploring collaboration challenges in a variety of Norwegian, Finnish and English criminal justice settings. The chapters focus particularly on the frontline worker perspective of what the challenges are on the ground. These chapters recognise the importance of these workers in terms of their understanding of the local context and their impact on the implementation of policy and organisational change (Lipsky, 2010). It should be noted that with the exception of Kloetzer et al. (Chapter 7) and Sepännen et al. (Chapter 9), that it is generally the researchers' analysis of these triggers that is being presented in these chapters.

Education institutions also have a responsibility to be facilitators of change and innovation by facilitating organisational learning, collaboration and innovation processes. Researchers can take this active role by being innovators themselves as Ødegård and Willumsen (Chapter 17), for example, describe the COLAB consortium as providing "sites for innovation where new relationships for collaboration, different ways of knowledge production and designing/implementing change to improve services for the benefit of service users are created". They explore the development and co-creation process between the university and practice professionals of, what was initially envisaged to be a training programme, developed into a web-based resource to respond to practice needs. It aimed to build the boundary-crossing expertise required and explored in Nielsen and Kajamaa (Chapter 3).

Researchers acting as innovators themselves is also illustrated in chapters exploring the development and utility of tools (such as risk assessment tools) as boundary objects. Murphy et al., in Chapter 4 differentiate between uniprofessional, multi-professional or pan-professional tools that are practice tools used to unify the multiple inputs of engaged agencies and promote dialogue between them. The development of these tools often involves the innovative transfer of knowledge from one discipline into another. Lahitinen and colleagues (Chapter 2) show how prison interagency meetings introduce the digital tool BRIK to serve this function. This is also illustrated by Fluttert et al. (Chapter 11) in their exploration of how the ERM tool may be transferred from the forensic psychiatric institutional context, in which it was initially developed, into the prison setting and be used by prisoners and prison officers together to reflect jointly on what triggers a person's descent into violence. Similarly, Ødegård and Bjørkly in Chapter 10 illustrate the innovation process at work in their novel combination of the HCR20 and PINCOM instruments. They recognise assessment of risk of violence as a substantive area of practice where interprofessional contact between health and prisons, and effective collaboration between the two, is required. The offender may react differently in different contexts and information provided by different professionals on the circumstances that trigger offender violence is invaluable to risk assessment and offender rehabilitation.

A final example of researchers as innovators, and one at the heart, of the COLAB consortium, is the transfer of the Change Laboratory method (CLM) to the new context of the criminal justice system. This also represents a second way in which researchers may take an active role in organisational change by taking responsibility for facilitating the dialogue between stakeholders necessary for innovation. Hean et al. (Chapter 8), describe the theoretical underpinnings of double stimulation and the utility of mirror material as key methods within the Change Laboratory as a means of stimulating meaningful dialogue between actors. Mirror data are representations of practice and work activity that can take the form of extracts from an ethnographic phase of an intervention (e.g. quotes from interviews, videos or photos of observed practices in situ). Participants in a Change Laboratory workshop are encouraged to reinterpret and discuss the mirror material using a variety of cognitive tools, such as a theoretical framework, to make sense of what they see. CHAT is one of these theoretical frameworks. The role of the researcher is to facilitate this process. They present materials to professionals and service users participating in an intervention as a mirror of their everyday work activity. Dialogue comes from them together making sense of this mirror material and identifying where tensions and underlying contradictions in the system lie (Sannino et al., 2016). In Chapter 3, Nielsen and Kajamaa demonstrate how CHAT may be used as a cognitive tool to make sense of the mirror material that could be introduced to a CLM and act as a trigger for expansive learning between participants from different agencies. Kloetzer et al. (Chapter 7) discuss the challenges of bringing mirror material (labelled as micro dramas and dialogical artefacts), that is analysed very differently by researchers and participants, to interventions to stimulate dialogue within a development workshop.

Imaginative, evocative and sensitive ways of representing mirror material may be particularly effective and can draw on the anthropological techniques employed by Turner Wilson et al. (Chapter 13) when using jottings and photos to capture their experiences of the third sector in Norway working with prisoners and ex-prisoners. This has particular relevance to any intervention that might use this material as stimuli in a developmental workshop but in such a way that dialogue can occur in a safe space. The importance of this safe space in social innovation is a topic also addressed by Hean et al. (Chapter 8).

Although we take the stance that researchers have a responsibility to actively engage in organisational change and offender rehabilitation, there are two main caveats. The first is the challenges facing setting up academic–practice partnerships. In Chapter 16, Hean and colleagues explore these challenges more broadly using the experience of four COLAB members and the theoretical lens of the contact hypothesis to reflect on these whilst suggesting strategies through which these relations can be enhanced. Ødegård and Willumsen (Chapter 17) using the lens of social innovation and communities of practice, reflect specifically on the academic–practice relationship when building training opportunities. Whilst these two chapters discuss challenges of academic/practice collaborations, Turner Wilson and colleagues (Chapter 13) take a more positive angle reflecting on the valuable anthropological experiences of three English COLAB members (one researcher and two practice professionals) and their experiences of crossing the academic/professional/national divide.

A second caveat to active academic engagement in organisational change is the vulnerabilities of the people involved. We acknowledge the vulnerability of the researcher, when dealing with complex offenders. The tragic events of university colleagues killed during the London Bridge in the UK in 2019 terrorist attack bring this home (McQuillan, 2019). It raises questions as to the capacity of researchers to actively engage in the offender reintegration process, keeping themselves and others safe whilst doing so. The vulnerability of all participating in organisational change must be acknowledged, and special attention should be paid to researchers that are new to the criminal justice context (see e.g. Jewkes, 2012; Sloan & Wright, 2015).

Final Thoughts and Further Research

This book addresses a gap in the literature of understanding collaboration, innovation and organisational learning in criminal justice systems. The chapters show that collaboration between all actors, including offenders, is required to navigate this system effectively. Otherwise work activiites and services become fragmented or compartmentalised. Information sharing is blocked and this leads to knowledge disparities between agencies and reliance on informal and personal interagency relationships. There is often a lack of contact between agencies and there are structural challenges to collaboration at an intra- and especially the interagency level. There are national policies that are aimed to promote integration and hereby collaboration (e.g. national models of rehabilitation, diversion/liaison in England and the Import Model in Norway) but the implementation of these, at the local level, varies. There is limited time, staff and financial resources leading to a depreciation in the value given to holistic work activity. There are tensions caused by a lack of shared meaning between actors when using workplace tools designed to promote collaboration and there is evidence that workplace structures are not keeping up with a change in prisons from a security/control to a rehabilitation focus. As a consequence, professionals may not have confidence, knowledge or competence to support offenders in achieving their goals of life stability, meaning, hope and the feelings of self-worth they need to manage a future without crime. Despite the problems in collaboration, and hereby innovation and organisational learning, we challenge the idea that security and care are on opposite ends of the continuum and show, in the studies included in this book, new innovative ways in which these can coexist.

The authors also explore and reflect upon the wider responsibilities of the research communities to actively engage in organisational change and discuss the potential of methods that promote organisational collaboration, learning and innovation. A culture of collaboration is important, but we understand little still of how this culture can be created within prisons. Without a culture that is pro-collaboration and innovation, it is unlikely that researchers will be invited into prisons to run bottom change efforts. The book contributes to an understanding of the challenges facing interagency collaborative practice in the criminal justice system, capturing the frontline professional and offender perspective in this context, which was previously poorly understood. It is only the tip of the iceberg, however, and we hope the book serves as the starting point for more detailed studies in other European and international settings. COLAB membership has meant that this book has leant towards particular national settings, theories and interventions but this European and Norwegian focus means there is scope to further explore collaborations in other European and international contexts.

As interagency working is found to be particularly problematic, we recommend future research focus particularly on interagency interactions when criminal justice services and external services are fully segregated from each other on the integration spectrum. There is a need for training in methods of collaboration and innovation in the criminal justice staff but training has timing, resource and logistical implications. Further work is required to clarify the relevance of this type of training for frontline professionals working with offenders in crisis and to develop means that suit the busy and complex lives of the professionals involved.

There is further scope still to explore the methodological challenges of researchers working in prison environments and in international, interdisciplinary milieus. Researchers should pay particular attention to building strong, long-term practice–academic relationships based on trust and logistical ease. We recommend that attention be paid by practice and academia to work on developing a perceived and mutual understanding of the need/demand for organisational change. Our findings suggest that researchers are cogent of the biases they hold of the offender population group and must be prepared to manage the biases of key participants. Building on the current discussions of integration tools and models, and the use of metaphors and narratives, researchers should develop further the use of pan-professional and multi-professional tools, utilised as boundary objects and explore further novel ways of capturing the service user's voice. Researchers should also explore further how boundary spanners, such as one of the authors in Chapter 13, can be better utilised to produce more valid research and useful interventions.

Many of the chapters of this book show that Cultural-Historical Activity Theory (CHAT) has strong potential in the development of criminal justice settings. Theoretically, CHAT can underpin the sense-making that takes place in these settings, but CHAT is naturally not the only sense-making tool and presents only one specific lens. For further studies we recommend a multi-theoretical approach and there is scope for many other perspectives, e.g. institutional theory and negotiation theory, that could be explored in greater depth. There is now also a need to test methods, such as the Change Laboratory in practice, with the permission of the high-security environments in focus in the chapters of this book.

It must be acknowledged that there are ethical issues to be carefully considered and that there is "emotional labour" involved in studying this context and its processes. The chapters in this book have presented evidence of workplace activity conducted mutually but with flexibility and feelings of autonomy. Professionals from different organisations, work together in a hybrid configuration of actors, with different, potentially competing institutional logics, but have often engaged in learning processes leading to actors being able to oscillate between the institutionalised logic of their own profession and a shared logic centred on the needs of the offender. It is thus also important to note that unequal power relations may occur between the participants of change efforts within these contexts. To conclude, we feel that our understanding of interventions in the criminal justice setting is still in its infancy and we will, with great enthusiasm, continue our research and efforts from here.

Acknowledgments The editors contributed equally to the production of this chapter.

References

Adler, P. S. (2005). The evolving object of software development. *Organization, 12*(3), 401–436.

Ahgren, B., & Axelsson, R. (2005, August 31). Evaluating integrated health care: A model for measurement. *International Journal of Integrated Care, 5.*
Armstrong, S. (2012). *Reducing reoffending: Review of selected countries.* SSCJR: Edinburgh.
Aveling, E. L., Gillespie, A., & Cornish, F. (2015). A qualitative method for analysing multivoicedness. *Qualitative Research, 15*(6), 670–687.
Bakhtin, M. M. (1981). *The dialogic imagination: Four essays* (M Holquist, Ed.). Austin, TX: University of Texas Press.
Bakhtin, M. M. (1984). *Problems of Dostoevsky's poetics* (C. Emerson, Ed. and trans.). Minneapolis: University of Minnesota Press.
Bakhtin, M. M. (1986). *Speech genres & other late essays.* Austin, TX: University of Texas Press.
Blackler, F. (2009). Cultural-historical activity theory and organization studies. In A. Sannino, H. Daniels, & K. D. Gutiérrez (Eds.), *Learning and expanding with activity theory* (pp. 19–39). Cambridge: Cambridge University Press.
DiMaggio, P. J., & Powell, W. W. (1991). The Iron cage revisited: Institutional Isomorphism and Collective Rationality. In W. W. Powell & P. DiMaggio (Eds.), *The new institutionalism in organizational analysis.* Chicago, IL: University of Chicago Press.
Engeström, Y. (2001). Expansive learning at work: Toward an activity theoretical reconceptualization. *Journal of Education and Work, 14*(1), 133–156. https://doi.org/10.1080/13639080020028747.
Engeström, Y. (1987/2015). *Learning by expanding: An activity-theoretical approach to developmental research.* Helsinki: Orienta-Konsultit.
Engeström, Y., & Sannino, A. (2011). Discursive manifestations of contradictions in organizational change efforts. *Journal of Organizational Change Management, 24*(3), 368–387.
European Commission. (2013). *Guide to social innovation.* Brussels: EU Commission. Available at https://ec.europa.eu/eip/ageing/library/guide-social-innovation_en. Accessed 1 Aug 2020.
Fazel, S., & Wolf, A. (2015). A systematic review of criminal recidivism rates worldwide: Current difficulties and recommendations for best practice. *PLoS ONE, 10*(6), 1–8.
Graunbøl, H. M., Kielstrup, B., Muiluvuori, M.-L., Tyni, S., Baldursson, E. S., Gudmundsdottir, H., Kristoffersen, R., Krantz, L., & Lindsten, K. (2010). *Retur: En nordisk undersøkelse af recidiv blant klienter i kriminalforsorgen.* Oslo: Kriminalomsorgens utdanningssenter. Available at https://krus.brage.unit.no/krus-xmlui/handle/11250/160672.

Hean, S. (2015). Strengthening the links between practice and education in the development of collaborative competence frameworks. In *Interprofessional education in Europe: Policy and practice* (pp. 9–32). Garant. ISBN 9044133349.

Hean, S., Staddon, S., Clapper, A., Fenge, L. A., Heaslip, V., & Jack, E. (2014). Improving collaborative practice to address offender mental health: Criminal justice and mental health service professionals' attitudes towards interagency training, current training needs and constraints. *Journal of Research in Interprofessional Practice and Education.*

Hean, S., Warr, J., Heaslip, V., & Staddon, S. (2011). Exploring the potential for joint training between legal professionals in the Criminal Justice System and health and social care professionals in the Mental-Health Services. *Journal of Interprofessional Care, 25*(3), 196–202.

Hean, S., Willumsen, E., Ødegård, A., & Bjørkly, S. (2015). Using social innovation as a theoretical framework to guide future thinking on facilitating collaboration between mental health and criminal justice services. *International Journal of Forensic Mental Health, 14*(4), 280–289.

Hean, S., Willumsen, E., & Ødegård, A. (2017). Collaborative practices between correctional and mental health services in Norway: Expanding the roles and responsibility competence domain. *Journal of Interprofessional Care, 31*(1), 18–27.

Hean, S., Willumsen, E., & Ødegård, A. (2018). Making sense of interactions between mental health and criminal justice services: The utility of cultural historical activity systems theory. *International Journal of Prisoner Health, 14*(2), 124–141.

Hean, S., Lahtinen, P., Dugdale, W., Larsen, B. K., & Kajamaa, A. (2020). The Change Laboratory as a tool for collaboration and social innovation. In *Samskaping: sosial innovasjon for helse og velferd* (pp. 207–221). Universitetsforlaget.

Heaslip, V., Hean, S., & Parker, J. (2016). The etemic model of Gypsy Roma Traveller community vulnerability: Is it time to rethink our understanding of vulnerability? *Journal of Clinical Nursing, 27,* 3426–3435.

Jewkes, Y. (2012). Autoethnography and emotions as intellectual resources: Doing prison research differently. *Qualitative Inquiry, 18*(1), 63–75.

Kerosuo, H., & Engeström, Y. (2003). Boundary crossing and learning in creation of new work practice. *Journal of Workbased Learning, 15,* 345–351.

Kodner, D., & Spreeuwenberg, L. C. (2002). Integrated care: Meaning, logic, applications, and implications—A discussion paper. *International Journal of Integrated Care, 2,* 1–6.

Lawrence, P. R., & Lorsch, J. W. (1967). *Organization and environment: Managing differentiation and integration*. Cambridge, MA: Harvard University Press.

Liebling, A., Elliot, C., & Price, D. (1999). Appreciative inquiry and relationships in prisons. *Punishment & Society, 1*(1), 71–98.

Lipsky, M. (2010). *Street-level bureaucracy: Dilemmas of the individual in public service* (30th Annual ed.). New York: Russell Sage Foundation.

Markova, I. (2016). *The dialogical mind: Common sense and ethics*. Cambridge: Cambridge University Press.

McQuillan, M. (2019, December 2). London Bridge attack: Profound questions for higher education. *Research Professional News*. Available at https://www.researchprofessionalnews.com/rr-news-uk-views-of-the-uk-2019-12-london-bridge-attack-profound-questions-for-higher-education/. Accessed Aug 2020.

Miller, D. (2001). Distributing responsibilities*. *The Journal of Political Philosophy, 9*(4), 453–471.

Ministry of Justice, UK. (2013). *Transforming rehabilitation: A strategy for reform transforming rehabilitation: A strategy for reform*. London: Ministry of Justice. Available at https://consult.justice.gov.uk/digital-communications/transformingrehabilitation/results/transforming-rehabilitation-response.pdf. Accessed 1 July 2020.

Pratt, J. (2008). Scandinavian exceptionalism in an era of penal excess: Part I: The nature and roots of Scandinavian exceptionalism. *British Journal of Criminology, 48*(2), 119–137.

Rittel, H. W. J., & Webber, M. M. (1973). Dilemmas in a general theory of planning dilemmas in a general theory of planning. *Policy Planning, 4*, 155–169.

Sannino, A., Engeström, Y., & Lemos, M. (2016). Formative interventions for expansive learning and transformative agency. *Journal of the Learning Sciences, 25*(4), 599–633.

Skardhamar, T., & Telle, K. (2012). Post-release employment and recidivism in Norway. *Journal of Quantitative Criminology, 28*, 629–649.

Sloan, J., & Wright, S. (2015). Going in green: Reflections on the challenges of 'Getting In, Getting On, and Getting Out' for doctoral prison researchers. In D. H. Drake, R. Earle, & J. Sloan (Eds.), *The Palgrave handbook of prison ethnography*. Basingstoke: Palgrave Handbooks.

Spivak, G. C. (1988). Can the subaltern speak? In C. Nelson & L. Grossberg (Eds.), *Marxism and the interpretation of culture* (pp. 271–313). Urbana: University of Illinois Press.

Virkkunen, J., & Newnham, D. S. (2013). *The change laboratory*. CRADLE: Helsinki.
Weick, K. E. (1995). *Sensemaking in organizations*. Thousand Oaks, CA: Sage.
Wenger, E. (1998). *Communities of practice: Learning, meaning and identity*. Cambridge: Cambridge University Press.

Part I

International Contexts of Collaborative Practice in a Variety of Penal Contexts: Substantive Areas for Organisational Innovation and Change—Studies in Norway

This part presents the descriptions of current collaborative practices based on the empirical findings of current research projects describing collaborative practice, innovation and organisational learning within the criminal justice services within a two main European contexts (Norway, England) from the service user and professional perspectives and a variety of contexts including low security prisons, third sector organisations, half way houses and diversion/liaison services. All chapters include some of the key theoretical underpinnings of collaboration, innovation and cross sector organisational learning as situated within the penal system.

2

Interorganisational Collaboration in a Norwegian Prison—Challenges and Opportunities Arising from Interagency Meetings

Päivikki Lahtinen, Anu Kajamaa, Laura Seppänen, Berit Johnsen, Sarah Hean, and Terhi Esko

Introduction

In Norway, prison and health services function as separate agencies, governed by different regulations. In many situations, this separation is managed satisfactorily by efforts of cooperation and mutual respect for

P. Lahtinen (✉) · A. Kajamaa · T. Esko
Faculty of Educational Sciences,
University of Helsinki, Helsinki, Finland
e-mail: paivikki.lahtinen@uia.no

A. Kajamaa
e-mail: anu.kajamaa@helsinki.fi

T. Esko
e-mail: terhi.esko@tuni.fi

L. Seppänen
Finnish Institute of Occupational Health, Helsinki, Finland
e-mail: laura.seppanen@ttl.fi

S. Hean et al. (eds.), *Improving Interagency Collaboration, Innovation and Learning in Criminal Justice Systems*,
https://doi.org/10.1007/978-3-030-70661-6_2

the other's goals, tasks and roles. The different legal and regulatory frameworks of the two agencies often complicate coordination of the services and may hinder collaboration. In the most severe cases, poor coordination between services can lead to diminished health and function for the inmate, and in the longer term an increased likelihood of recidivism.

Efforts to promote collaboration between prison and health services have been emphasised internationally and in Norway (WHO, 2015; Department of Health and Welfare, 2013; Department of Health, 2010). Since the 1970s, the 'Import model' has been the key strategy to promote interagency collaboration. This model makes it a requirement by law for external health care and mental health services to provide care for inmates in the Norwegian prison system (see The Execution of Sentences Act, 2001/2018). This means health care services have an independent role in relation to correctional services and services are provided by external providers brought into the prison. This ensures inmates' right to receive the same care, health, and welfare services as the general population and that the prison is held to account for the care it provides through these independent agencies.

The penal system represents a meeting of punishment and rehabilitation paradigms (Laine, 2011). It manifests in the continuous collaboration needed between both primary and specialised health services (provided by the Regional Health Authority and municipality) and the prison services to improve assessment, diagnosis and treatment of offenders' mental issues, and their associated problems such as substance abuse. Collaboration is also needed to prevent gaps, fragmentation and unnecessary duplications of service provision. This is especially important during the transition of the inmate between departments within the prison, between prisons and then back into society. Successful and

B. Johnsen
University College of Norwegian Correctional Service, Lillestrøm, Norway
e-mail: berit.johnsen@krus.no

S. Hean
Faculty of Social Sciences, University of Stavanger, Stavanger, Norway
e-mail: sarah.c.hean@uis.no

flexible collaboration and integration efforts of services are crucial for improving mental health and the reduction of recidivism rates in the longer term (Bjerkan et al., 2011; Kodner & Spreeuwenberg, 2002).

Imprisonment and treatment of the mentally ill offender occur in tandem and require collaborative efforts between Norwegian prison and mental health services. Challenges that arise here are linked to strong boundaries between the services, the service providers' different conceptualisations of issues, such as confidentiality, commitment and knowledge sharing between the distinct service providers (Lahtinen et al., 2018; Hean et al., 2017a, 2017b, 2018). Limited resources, distinct work practices, differing attitudes towards the inmates and logistical challenges related to the long distances between service providers and the prison also add to the complexity (Langeveld & Melhus, 2004; Hean et al., 2017a, 2017b).

In this chapter, we describe how one Norwegian prison has met this contradictory demand between punishment and treatment in their development of *interagency meetings*. The interagency meeting is an arena for collaboration between the distinct service providers. At the meetings, professionals work together to find a potential and effective solution for tackling inmates' substance abuse. However, the decision-making at the meeting has become more challenging because of the increased substance abuse and complexity of inmates' life. In order to meet this challenge, the professional at the meeting must create a broader picture of inmates' life-view, needs and resources. Through three examples from interagency meetings, we have explored how the contradiction between mental health well-being (or rehabilitation) and punishment (or control) is present at interagency meeting discussions. Our analysis focuses on interactions between distinct professionals at the meetings and how the actors employ distinct tools to develop an overall perspective of an inmate's needs and resources, and shared understanding of an issue at hand. To identify challenges and to develop interprofessional collaboration further, we have provided an applicable and modifiable model which can be used in prison systems and more broadly, in social and health care contexts and in other complex organisations. With this chapter, our contribution is to research on studying collaboration in complex organisational settings.

The Norwegian Prison Under Study

We present a case study of a high-security prison in the west of Norway in which interagency meetings are held to enhance interaction between those responsible for the management of prison and health services. The interagency meetings have been created specially to tackle the increased substance abuse of the inmates, and the needs this creates for collaboration between the prison and the health services. The prison has established bimonthly interagency meetings to manage the multiple tasks and to align and combine the diverse tasks, roles, goals and expertise of the range of professionals working with the inmates. The meetings are part of a comprehensive treatment plan defining how the inmate's rehabilitation needs are to be addressed before, during and after their detention. The group consists of prison inspectors (at least two, from the closed and open sections of the prison), two social workers, a psychiatrist, a resettlement coordinator and internal health care professionals (the manager or deputy head of the prison health unit), a leader of a regional department of addictive medicine (an external expert on substance abuse treatment in prison) and a nurse from the prison's internal substance abuse treatment unit. The meetings are officially led by a psychiatrist and an expert from the department of addictive medicine (hereafter AFR). The organisations involved in the interagency meeting are identified in Fig. 2.1.

The aim of the meetings is defined in the terms of reference for the interagency meetings that were co-authored by representatives of prisons and department of addictive medicine. The aim is to discuss the needs and requests of the inmates, to gain an overall perspective of their situation, to address their problems and to support them. The needs of all inmates of the Norwegian prison in question may be discussed during these meetings. Members of the interagency meeting are mostly representatives of management from the different services or specialists. Frontline prison officers and inmates are not present.

During the meetings, the participants discuss and assess an inmate's situation by using specific plans and tools, as a means for re-integration and rehabilitation. In the next section, we will describe these tools in

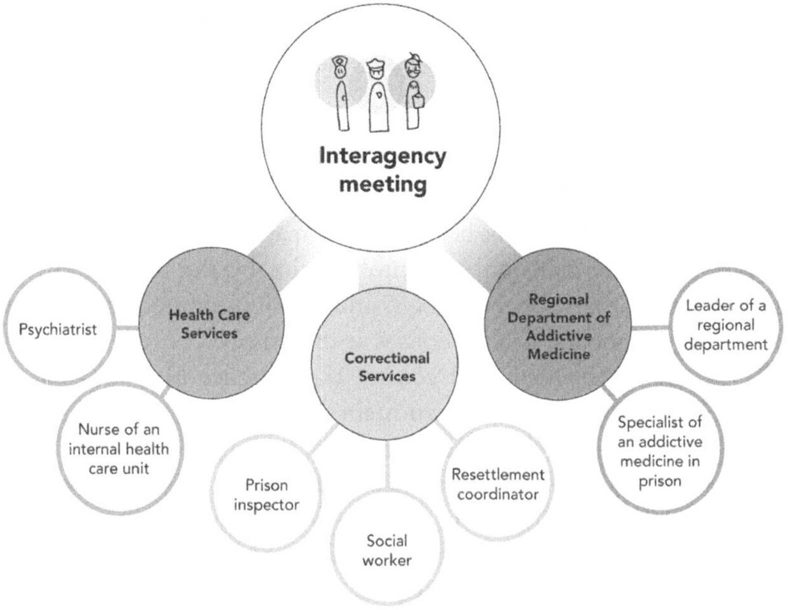

Fig. 2.1 Organisations and professionals in the interagency meeting

more detail and plans which are used in correctional services and health services.

Tools Used in Prison

The activity of prison with inmates is guided by two main plans, namely the sentence plan and the individual (care) plan. The content of sentence is determined by the Norwegian Correctional Service within the limits set by the court in its judgement. The intention is to clarify the expectations of the offender and to provide predictability during the sentence. The sentence plan is individually composed in consultation with the convicted person. The core of the individual care plan on the other hand is based on the individual rights of all Norwegian citizens. It is an important tool for contributing and coordinating individual cases across care, health and welfare services. The individual plan is developed for people with a need for long-term and coordinated health and care services. The municipality has primary responsible for preparing the plan (Helse- og omsorgsdepartementet, 2018).

The assessments and decisions made at each of the interagency meetings are incorporated into the sentence plan and the individual care plan. Both plans are updated continuously, applying further information collected during interactions between the inmate and the frontline prison professionals. The plans are put into practice by the inmate with the prison contact officers, social workers and health professionals in primary and specialised mental health services at the prison.

In order to implement and control the sentence plan implementation in Correctional Services, two main digital tools (called BRIK and KOMPIS) are in use. The BRIK (*Behovs- og ressurskartlegging i Kriminalomsorgen*) has been in use since 2016 in all prisons in Norway (Kriminalomsorgen, 2017, p. 11). It is an assessment tool used in systematically planning the work of prison services and for mapping the needs and resources of the inmates. BRIK is filled in by the inmate and the contact officer who is a prison officer with special responsibility for following up with individual prisoners during their imprisonment. BRIK covers questions about the inmate's education, family situation and living and health conditions. Its aim is to secure the inmate's rights to get treatment from health and social care services personnel. For systematic coordination of the sentence plan, prison service personnel use a digital system called the KOMPIS. KOMPIS is a Correctional Service central data system and covers every prison in Norway to report on actions carried out with the inmates during their sentence. It is also an electronic archive and management tool of work duties for the Correctional Service.

In Health Care Services, there is another core digital tool called a medical case summary, for controlling the implementation of the individual plan. In a medical case summary, health care providers present important information about an inmate's health, regardless of where the treatment is received. It is related to the Individual plan of Health Care Services (Helse- og omsorgsdepartementet, 2018). The digital systems of Correctional Services and Health Care Services do not interact with each other.

The summary of plans and digital tools is described in Table 2.1. In addition to these digital tools of prison and health care services, the frontline professionals, such as contact officers and nurses, also meet inmates at informal gatherings. These informal discussions between the frontline workers can be seen as an arena/tool for knowledge creation for Correctional Services and Health Care Services. These informal discussions take place during the informal gatherings, such as during the dinners or when escorting the inmates to school or a workplace.

Table 2.1 Summary of tools in use in the prison

Tools for the health care services in prison	
Individual plan	• based on individual rights of all Norwegian citizens • is compiled on the consent of the patient or the user • a tool for contributing and coordinating health and welfare services for a patient
Medical case summary	• a digital tool for following the individual plan • present information about a person's or inmate's health, procedures and measurements, regardless of where the treatment is received
Tools for the correctional services	
Sentence plan	• is individually composed in consultation with the inmate • the content is determined by the Norwegian Correctional Service and Law
KOMPIS	• is a central data system, which has two internal systems • provides information and tasks conducted in prison • delivers notification of imprisonment and release on prisons • is an electronic archive and management tool for Correctional Services
BRIK	• a digital system for mapping the needs and resources of the inmates • covers information of inmate's education, work situation, welfare and health conditions and family situation

Theoretical Framework

In this study, we applied an activity-theoretical framework to analyse the interagency meeting interaction. In activity theory, the activity within the interagency meeting is conceptualised as collective, cultural, deeply contextual and historically derived. From an activity-theoretical view, the activity taking place in the interagency meeting is driven by a shared object-related motive (Leont'ev, 1978) and artefacts (such as tools, signs and language). In the prison, these artefacts take the form of the diverse tools and plans, such as the sentence plan, individual plan, BRIK and KOMPIS.

The overall object, or purpose, of the interagency meeting, is to discuss the needs and requests of the inmates, to gain an overall perspective of their situation, to address their problems and to support them. The sense and meaning of the actions of participants in the interagency meeting will be driven by this object of their collective activity (Vygotsky, 1978). The object of the activity is constantly moulded, shaped and kept moving by the participants as they interact with each other (Engeström & Blackler, 2005). Participants may hold their own individual objects under this broader object. In the prison context, for example, health care professionals focus on the well-being of the inmates from a physical and mental point of view. On the other hand, prison professionals focus on the security and control of the inmates and their observations of the inmates' everyday life situations.

Actors/subjects are not always aware of the object of their activity, which creates gaps, tensions and challenges in service provision. Contradictions may manifest locally as ruptures, obstacles and other problematic issues in the working of the organisation, which are connected to the historical development and transformation of work and production and to larger societal contradictions (Engeström & Sannino, 2011). From an activity-theoretical view, tensions or contradictions in organisations have the potential to be turned into drivers for learning and change (Engeström, 2015). In a prison, obstacles and tensions may arise when knowledge needs to be shared between the professional groups, but knowledge sharing is restricted and fails. This tension may trigger collective reflection and the development of new innovative practices and solutions, some potentially leading to changes in working practices.

Artefacts mediate the activity between subjects/actors (members of the interagency meeting) and their objects. The artefacts within the interagency meeting are tools that mediate activity within the interagency meeting and can include internal/cognitive representations such as mental models or external physical/practical tools such as care plans (Engeström, 2005, p. 320). In this chapter, we have explored how participants in the interagency meetings used these artefacts collaboratively when working towards their main and personal objects. It highlights dialogical processes in which different perspectives and voices merge and collide (Engeström, 1995). By so doing, we gain a better understanding of how the artefacts are typically used in meetings and how they can be used in a broader manner in future. For example, a conceptual model may work as a diagnostic tool, but it may also become a frozen definition to identify and classify the phenomena (Engeström, 2005 p. 320).

Prison as a Research Site and Methodological Challenges

Ethnographic research in a closed prison is challenging, especially for a researcher entering a prison for the first time (Sloan & Wright, 2015), as there are many issues that must be considered. For safety and security reasons, access to the prison required providing an assessment of the researcher's background. The data collection methods were evaluated by the Correctional Service and the Norwegian Centre for Research Data, NSD authorities. The first author of this chapter met with the Regional Prison Service Authority to explain the study and clear security screening to access the prison. Finally, written permission to conduct the research was obtained from the prison.

The timing of entering the prison was crucial and had to be adjusted to meet the daily life in the prison, which may vary despite strict daily routines. Some days are busier than others and security incidents arise unpredictably. From the prison perspective, additional security risks need to be mitigated because of the researcher working in this closed environment. It required extra planning, and hence resources, to secure the researcher while they continued with their daily routines. The researcher (the first author of this paper) was actively in contact with the prison inspector with whom the visit was planned, and who provided updated information on the daily living conditions of the prison. By doing so, the working lives of frontline workers were taken into consideration. The close collaboration with frontline workers and prison authorities enabled the researcher to approach data collection in a flexible way and minimize the disruption she caused. Participation in the research was voluntary and could be ended at any time. The researchers' respect of the participants' anonymity and privacy was essential, and the anonymised data collection method had to be planned in a way that secured the inmate's privacy and considered their vulnerability.

Data Collection and Observing the Interagency Meetings

Studying the service collaboration and interaction between distinct services, we used ethnographic methodology for the investigation of local activities in the prison context (see Amit, 2000; Falzon, 2009; Kajamaa, 2011).

The data for this chapter comprised observations of three interagency meetings at the prison. The meetings averaged two hours in length. In the meetings, the participants follow an agenda, providing a stepwise script for the meetings, discussing 2–3 offenders' cases at every meeting. Each participant takes a well-defined role in the meeting: for example, a psychiatrist leads the meeting, the social worker presents the inmate's request for medication and the prison manager informs the group of how well the inmate is complying with prison regulations.

The study is part of a larger research project (the COLAB project) in which we applied multi-site ethnography (see Marcus, 1995; 1998) as a research method for empirical data collection and focused on multiple sites of the prison and mental health services. Multi-site ethnography extends the ethnographic method from observation conducted in a situationally and temporally bounded field to a multi-temporal and historically situated field (Marcus, 1995). Observation involves participation and interaction and is a collaborative process between the observer and participants (Angrosino & Pérez, 2000). In this project, our dataset was gathered during 2017–2018 including audio-recorded interviews with prison and mental health professionals, interviews with the inmates, observations, field notes, multiple documents and photographs.

In our ethnographical data collection, the researcher sent a request to attend an interagency meeting, accompanied by a summary of the objectives for conducting the investigation. At the first meeting, members agreed that the researcher could be present at the meetings and make observations in the prison ward when agreed in advance with the prison inspector. For the purpose of data collection, the researcher had to consider two factors: a tight meeting schedule and preparation of data collection set up in the facilities that could not be accessed in advance. Recording and field notes could not be done on a computer or mobile phone, so the investigator used manual tools such as paper and pens and an mp3 recorder to record the activity of the interagency meetings. All the tools which had possible access to Internet connections were prohibited because of prison regulations.

Analysis

Our analytic approach was abductive, involving repeated iterations between theory and data (Van Maanen et al., 2007). Our analysis of the three interagency meetings applied the techniques provided by Jordan and Henderson (1995, p. 57) to depict the nature and context of the activity taking place in the meetings, the unit of our analysis. During the analysis, we inductively depicted the dynamics of interaction in the meetings and participants' social activity during the interagency meetings, forming overarching categories of the main types of collaboration. We then focused our attention on the tensions and the conceptualisation of the object of the activity held by the participants.

Findings

The multiple professional groups working with the inmates represent historically distinct goals, tools, rules, knowledge, expertise, divisions of labour and values. During their daily work, they thus focus on profession-specific tasks and usually do not desire nor are provided with opportunities for joint reflection on their individual and collective activity. However, the interagency meetings provide an 'opportunity space' for reflection and construction of new forms of collaborative practice. In our view, these meetings ideally enhance "a process of shared construction of an object, a mobilization of the necessary and complementary cultural resources as well as a process of mutual learning" (Miettinen, 2006, p. 176; see also Miettinen, 1996).

Next, illustrative empirical examples from the interagency meetings are presented, to demonstrate how the professional groups interact in these. At the first meeting we attended, the interaction proceeded per the meeting agenda. Due to the time of the meeting (end of December 2017) and the researcher's first visit to prison, the meeting focused mainly on the researcher's visit and conducting the research in prison. They also updated the next year meeting schedule. However, the challenges and opportunities arose in the second and third meetings.

Example 1: Transcending professional distinctions to enhance collaboration

At the second interagency meeting, the interaction first proceeded per the meeting agenda. The meeting was led by the psychiatrist and the external department of addictive medicine (AFR) leader. The social worker presented the inmate's case. However, in the middle of the meeting, the AFR leader suggested the need for inclusion and cooperation of prison officers, to get a better overall view of the motives behind an inmate's request for increasing substance medication.

A note from the research diary:

> *In the middle of the meeting, the discussion got a bit heated when the AFR focusing on substance abuse issues highlighted* ***the responsibility of the officers to talk with the inmates about their motives and needs****. According to the AFR, this makes a difference so that they [members of interagency meeting]* ***can get a good overall picture of the inmate, and of what kind of treatment or medication is needed. Getting the overall picture is also important for understanding what motives lie behind the inmate's requests****. Often the medical case summary (which is used in the meetings) does not cover this. In these meetings, the participants do not use information systems that prison workers use that would include information about the inmates.*

The AFR leader then suggested the need 'to get a good overall picture of the inmate' by which the AFR leader referred to getting broader understanding of the inmate's needs and motivation. For the leader of the AFR, the knowledge of the inmate's motivation is a tool to manage the substance abuse medication and subsequent rehabilitation. However, this knowledge production is dependent on the contact prison officers' and the inmates' interaction. Even though neither the inmates nor the contact officers are involved in the interagency meetings, the actors collectively agreed this need for a more holistic view. They then began to combine the knowledge of the actors present about this inmate, but the motivation behind the inmate's requests still remained unclear. In order to enhance a holistic view, the participants turned to BRIK, a digital assessment tool used to assess the inmate's needs and resources, and especially to sections that might reveal his/her motivational issues (e.g. a motivation to sell the medication to other inmates), completed by prison officers. The BRIK provided an opportunity to include contact officers' voices and in-depth knowledge of the inmate, and the inmate's own view of his/her needs and resources, even though they were not present at the interagency meeting.

Regulations related to patient consent and confidentiality governed the use of tools within this exemplar interagency interaction. This is because inmates must give written consent for their personal information from the different systems to be shared (e.g. information from the medical case summary from health services, the central data system of the prison service [KOMPIS] and from BRIK).

Example 2: Challenges in the usage of a new digital tool to enhance collaboration

The topic of having a holistic view of an offender continued at the third interagency meeting. This time, the actors at the meeting clearly specified from where they wanted to get this necessary knowledge. To provide a holistic view of the inmate's motivation behind a request, the participants indicated that knowledge written in the digital assessment tool (BRIK) is indeed important, but the tool also brings challenges.

A note from the research diary:

> *The AFR representative says that BRIK has a lot of useful information that could be used. Social worker A says that not everyone sees the value of BRIK, so updating BRIK is a challenge. A participant from the Open Prison says that the meaning of BRIK comes up at the end of the sentence when the inmate transfers to the open department. […] Social worker B explains that using the system is a problem in their department. Not every employee knows how to use it.*

During the meeting, the AFR suggested that sharing knowledge between prison and health services, documented in the BRIK, would be especially useful and important to develop the practices in the interagency meeting. The participants at the interagency meeting also agreed that the constant updating of the BRIK is crucial as it widens the knowledge and the understanding of the inmates' needs during their sentence. It is also an important 'boundary crossing tool' (see Star & Griesemer, 1989) at the end of sentence when the inmate is transferred to the Open Prison department.

A continuation of note from the research diary:

> *The resettlement coordinator continues that BRIK should be updated in a simple way but AFR says it needs to be updated continuously. The prison inspector points out that the quality of updates should be good.*

As shown by the note, it became obvious that the practices for updating the content of the BRIK are not clear nor shared among the contact officers. The updating practices varied from department to department from a quite superficial procedure to a broader description of the inmates' needs. Also, as the social worker reminded the group, the sharing of information is not for them to decide but is dependent on the consent of the inmate.

Example 3: The Reconciliation of the Different Needs

At the third meeting, the example is an inquiry from the specialised health care sector in which it was recommended that an inmate with mental health issues needed further care in an external institution. The AFR gave the following brief introduction to the prisoner's situation. The inmate had previously been treated for a mental illness and the professionals suggested continuing the rehabilitation outside the prison. The AFR leader indicated that the inmate's psychologist from the AFR department, who was not present at the meeting, had been in contact with the local health care unit based within the prison, to negotiate about how they should proceed. The case was complex because the treatment plan had to be intertwined with the sentence plan and required treatment from an external specialised institution. This was also the wish of the inmate. Before the participants began the discussion, the AFR leader reminded those present that they need to make a joint decision for the inmate's near future before they can promise anything to the inmate. The aim of this meeting was clear; they needed to construct a shared plan between health care services and prison services in order to promote this inmate's health and well-being.

Quote from the meeting:

> *... today, during this meeting, will we begin to do a treatment plan and a sentence plan for [the inmate]. Everyone who is here will know what we all think [...] I think it's important that we take one step at a time here so...* (AFR leader)

The discussion continued around the promotion of the inmate's mental health issues. The AFR leader had been in contact with the psychologist from the department of addictive medicine, who suggested that in this case, the inmate would benefit if he/she could have care and rehabilitation in the specialised institute outside of the prison. For the mental health services, the aim is to offer the care suggested for the patient. The prison services aim to ensure completion of the sentence. And for the inmate, the concern is his/her personal needs and wishes about their own future life. Even though the inmate was reluctant to move to the recommended institute because of its significant distance from the prison, the AFR leader suggested that this care pathway should still be considered.

Before implementing the care plan, the mental health care services needed to know the prison services' perspective and how the care plan could be fitted into the sentence plan. The key question was timing. The length of the care in the institution was not known in advance, and to ensure effective care, the inmate should not be sent back from the rehabilitation institution to the prison prematurely. To comply with the sentence plan, the challenge was to decide the stage at which the inmate should be transferred to the rehabilitation institution. The members of the meeting agreed that updating the sentence plan was needed, to fit with the needs related to the mental health problems of the inmate. The AFR leader pointed out that even though members of the meeting were making this joint decision, the inmate should be made aware that he/she could influence this decision and have some control over his/her own life during imprisonment. The meeting participants wanted the inmate to be made aware that they had started to coordinate the process for his/her request, but that this would take time. The prison inspector promised to take responsibility for talking with the inmate.

This meeting allowed the mental health service representatives to present the need for rehabilitation of an inmate that required coordination with and contribution from the prison services. The meeting offered an important arena for the different actors to construct options for a new direction for their action, and for promoting the inmate's health and well-being. During the meeting, an aim emerged in which both plans, the individual health care plan and the prison services' sentence plan, would be reconciled. The interactions between the actors meant that the perspectives and the tools employed about and around the inmate's life in the prison were now intertwined and partially redesigned.

Various Professional Perspectives in the Interagency Meetings

In sum, through these three examples, it can be noted that the representatives of the professional groups, namely the prison inspectors, social workers, psychologist, psychiatrist, a resettlement coordinator, leader of department of addictive medicine and an internal health care professional, conceptualised the object of their work activity (i.e. the patient-inmate) in many and different ways. From the health professionals' viewpoint, for example, the central object of the activity is the offender's physical and mental suffering and its diagnosis and care. For prison staff, the objective is the successful and secure completion of the prison sentence. We have also presented how the professional groups discuss and utilise different plans as tools to support the inmates in interagency meetings in a Norwegian prison context.

Moreover, from the prison personnel's viewpoint, the focus is on controlling and implementing the offender's sentence plan and preventing new crimes. Further, the participants in the interagency meeting, use specific artefacts, models and tools, (e.g. KOMPIS), to ensure that the daily life of the inmates runs as smoothly as possible.

The decisions made in the interagency meeting are related to the inmate by the social worker or a prison inspector. They keep the inmate informed of the process of his/her proceedings if decision-making requires further investigation with other instances such as being moved to an external treatment institution. For the inmates, the decisions affect their own life goals and experiences and they may have little interest in the tools being employed by the meeting members.

Contradiction is prompted because prison officers, who do not attend the interagency meetings, do not necessarily know the importance of the information they record in BRIK, or elsewhere. Instead, it is seen as a duty alongside controlling the sentence. For the members of the interagency meetings, the outcomes and contents of a digital tool such as BRIK are relevant for decision-making. This information, however, would benefit the participants of the interagency meetings and might enhance the prison's practices and activities.

Discussion

The interagency meeting is a cooperative arrangement with various agencies coming together to jointly discuss, reflect on and further improve the existing and future services of the inmates. An analysis of the groups' terms of reference shows the aim of the group to be the promotion of collaboration between the actors at the meeting and hereby maintain treatment for the prisoner as they complete their sentence. In so doing, the prison and the health services aim to ensure that every inmate at the prison will get high-quality care. The findings of our study show that interagency meetings enabled articulation and sharing of different professional views about an inmate's problems and needs.

Our examples show how the interagency meetings can also reveal the unexpected issues and complexities of prison life experienced differently by the participants around the same table. These can potentially serve as a springboard for finding good, tailored solutions for complex needs and situations. During the observed meetings, the professionals met a need to develop a more holistic picture of the inmates. The development of a holistic approach called for a new understanding of the underlying challenges and contradictions and the mapping of future opportunities at the level of the entire service system. In order to align the various objects, and to create a more holistic approach on behalf of the inmate at the interagency meeting, the discussions observed within the interagency meetings revealed a need to gain more information from the frontline workers such as prison officers who work closely with offenders on a daily basis. The officers have a key role in bringing up issues pertaining to individual inmates and implementing decisions made by the interagency meeting. However, the officers' viewpoint is missing, because the officers did not attend interagency meetings. Another way to gain a missing part for a more holistic view of the inmate is to capture the inmate's articulation of his/her own motivation to rectify criminal behaviour or substance abuse. They are also missing from these meetings and professionals acknowledged this prevented a better overall picture of the inmate being gained.

The BRIK digital assessment tool was suggested as a means to bridge the gap between the knowledge of the different actors and provide the information needed. A contradiction arose, however, when the same collaborative tool, BRIK, had different meanings for different practitioners in the activity. Further, the policy for filling and updating BRIK has varied from one department to another in the prison. Therefore, the relevance and quality of information stored within the tool are dependent on how the individual prison officers updated the BRIK system.

The voice and motivation of the inmate are partially presented through the request presented by the social worker and documented in the BRIK or a medical care summary. Yet, more detailed information concerning the demands and needs of an inmate is constructed in informal discussions between contact officers and inmates in their daily encounters. However, transforming this orally articulated information into a recognisable written form such as to BRIK or to any other form of report is demanding and some of the orally expressed needs of patients or inmates are lost during this process (see Berkenkotter & Ravotas, 1997). Further tensions arise regarding information protection and the legal rights of the inmate to allow or forbid different actors from using his/her information during the interagency meeting that have been shared informally in this way.

Our analysis indicated that in the observed prison, collaborative tools had a powerful potential for linking different professionals and the inmates together and for integrating the prison and mental health care services in a multi-voiced collective constellation of activities. Yet, it is important to bear in mind that the different professionals have different perceptions and aims, often even when using the same tool, and these perceptions guide their individual actions. The value of dealing with the contradictions in interagency meeting was fundamentally developmental, not only to create better plans for the inmates, but also for improving prison practices that would improve collaboration and information flow between different professional groups. The instruments mediating information transmission are crucial in enabling and stabilising interprofessional collaboration, but our examples show that they are not enough: work practices in the prison needed to be improved further to optimise their utility.

Inspired by the prison in our study, we have formulated a model which can be applied and modified for identifying challenges and developing interprofessional collaboration in prison systems and more broadly in social and health care contexts and in other complex organisations. We suggest that interorganisational collaboration in prisons can be illustrated and promoted via our tool, presented in Fig. 2.2. This model of collaboration is inspired by cultural-historical activity theory (e.g. Engeström, 1987; Kajamaa & Lahtinen, 2016), viewing human activity as object-oriented, artefact-mediated and socio-culturally constructed system. The model (Fig. 2.2) provides an overall perspective of the actors involved in providing health care services in the prison and the core tools in use. It emphasises inmate involvement, which is a crucial, yet undervalued, ingredient in the joint service provision of the parties. In practical application, the model may be used as an analytical device in the inter-agency meetings and as a way for the parties to plan and develop service processes collectively. Furthermore, it can potentially become a useful model of collaboration for prison and health care services with a specific focus on the inmate's situation and problems, aiding the alignment of their tasks, goals, roles and expertise to support the inmate's imprisonment and rehabilitation (Kajamaa, 2010).

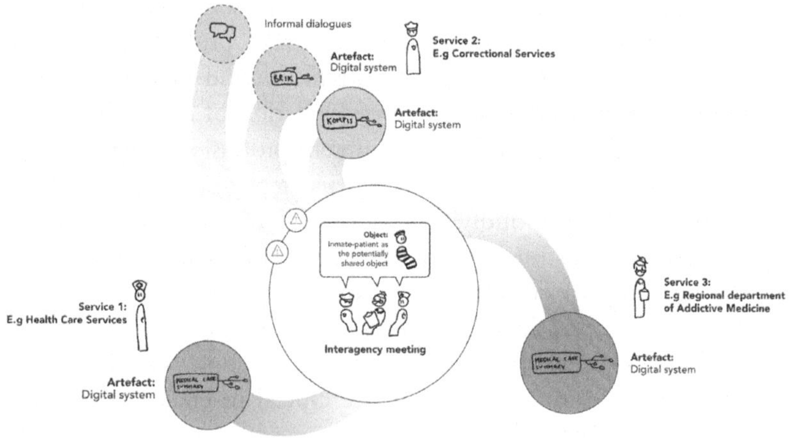

Fig. 2.2 The conceptual model of collaboration for prison and health care services

In Fig. 2.2, the service organisations that are collaborating are illustrated with distinct colours and human representatives. They are representatives of management from the different services or specialists and are present at the meeting. In the interagency meeting, the object of activity, the inmate-patient, is not present. However, his/her personal information is shared, after obtaining his consent, and is the basis of the discussion around the necessary care actions to be taken. The information is transferred to interagency meetings via artefacts. Artefacts are illustrated with circles, which in this observed case, were each services' own digital systems, BRIK, KOMPIS or medical case summaries. Both the general health care service and department of addictive medicine used the medical care summary as a tool to bring their information to the interagency meeting. The Correctional Service, on the other hand, used BRIK and KOMPIS digital systems, as their sources of inmate's information.

In Fig. 2.2 'informal dialogues' are presented in the model as another possible source for building a holistic view of an offender's motives. These take place when contact officers meet with prisoners informally in different settings during a day. However, both parties involved in these informal discussions (i.e. the contact officer and inmate) are not present at the meeting. The dashed lines around both BRIK and the 'informal dialogues' in the figure represent instances where the inmate's voice is heard.

Contradictions are illustrated as red triangles. In the studied case, one of the contradictions was the distinct meanings BRIK had for prison workers versus those held by participants in the interagency meeting. Another contradiction is the information flow from informal dialogues to interagency meeting. Here the issue lies in the difficulty to articulate orally shared knowledge from informal discussion and the restrictions for doing so because of the confidentiality of such private discussions.

Conclusion

Interpreting the interagency meeting through an activity theory lens highlights the emergent shared object of the participants within the interagency meetings at the prison, namely the *planning of the comprehensive rehabilitative sentence pathway* for an inmate. The comprehensiveness of the plan the participants create together expands the object of the interagency meeting beyond the artefacts of any one of the professional groups engaged. An activity-theoretical aspect offers a view in which opposing forces within the meeting, such as treatment versus punishment paradigms, are not perceived as radically reversed categories or universal logical oppositions, but as strong dialectical tensions which exist and are experienced and interpreted as tensions and juxtapositions in organisational life. These act as triggers that may be then collectively transcended (Kajamaa, 2011).

From an activity-theoretical perspective, once the object of the activity expands or changes as a response to these triggers, then the mediating artefacts and tools also need to be renewed or changed to deal with and to manage the transformed object. In our empirical examples, the tools used in the interagency meetings were not originally created to promote collaboration between prison and health services. However, through the joint discussions between the distinct professional groups, the tools had started to have a multifunctional purpose, as the professionals began to use them to develop a more holistic view of inmates. In the first and second examples, the interagency meetings introduced BRIK as a tool to enhance collaboration, despite it having initially been designed for the purposes and use of the prison service only.

The artefacts used in service provision, such as the individual plan and the sentence plan, are tools for the social and health services and the correctional service to plan and document possible treatments or activities during the sentence time. BRIK was brought in as an additional tool for the creation of an holistic view of the offender's resources and needs. These tools are made from the perspective of the institutions, and their focus is to provide welfare services for 'formal problems' such as treatment of drug addictions, substance abuse problems, the need for therapeutic interventions, etc., and to prevent an offender's likelihood of reoffending. However, the use of these tools is connected to the work duties of either the authority or care personnel who are actively involved in documenting or filling in the forms. In its current form, the tools are mandatory tasks to be fulfilled for inmates and contact officers. This led to the purpose of BRIK being interpreted differently by the latter and the participants of the interagency meeting.

To promote integrated service provision for the inmates, it would be a benefit to introduce a practice-based collaboration tool in which all actors could get an overall understanding of the service provision as a whole, and in which the inmate's own life experiences and his/her agentive acts would be placed at the centre (Cole, 1996). Moreover, a model, such as the one we developed and presented in Fig. 2.2, may be used as a boundary object (Star & Griesemer, 1989) that mediates negotiation, reduces fragmentation and enhances coherence, learning and understanding among the actors.

A further step could be also to create novel forms of collaboration, which promote knowledge sharing in ways that consider both the confidentiality of private discussions between prison officers and the offender, and the need to understand the motivation behind an inmate's request at the interagency meeting. Contact officers and inmates can be seen as users of interorganisational collaboration services, and as resources on decision-making which are provided during the interagency meeting. Including users' voices, such as those of the contact officers' and inmates' own voices, in interagency meetings, could promote collaboration and in a direction in which no single actor has the sole, fixed authority (Engeström, 2004; Kajamaa & Lahtinen, 2016). Multiple professionals and the inmates could become real "partners" in service provision and its use. In sum, the interagency meetings potentially align the objects and the tools of the different participants. Further alignment is still needed between different services and between the several departments within this prison.

Acknowledgments We warmly thank Theodor Andreas Aas Henriksen at the Centre for Entrepreneurship and Social Innovation, University of Agder, Norway for his help in creating the figures for this chapter.

References

Amit, V. (2000). *Constructing the field, ethnographic fieldwork in the contemporary world*. London and New York, NY: Routledge.

Angrosino, M. V., & Pérez, K. A. (2000). Rethinking observation: From method to context. In N. K. Denzin & Y. S. Lincoln (Eds.), *Handbook of qualitative research* (pp. 673–702). London: Sage.

Berkenkotter, C., & Ravotas, D. (1997). Genre as tool in the transmission of practice over time and across professional boundaries. *Mind, Culture, and Activity, 4*(4), 256–274. https://doi.org/10.1207/s15327884mca0404_4.

Bjerkan, J., Richter, M., Grimsmo, A., Hellesø, R., & Brender, J. (2011). Integrated care in Norway: The state of affairs years after regulation by law. *International Journal of Integrated Care, 11*(1). https://doi.org/10.5334/ijic.530.

Cole, M. (1996). *Cultural psychology. A once and future discipline*. Cambridge, Massachusetts, and London, England: The Belknap Press of Harvard University Press.

Department of Health. (2010). *Equity and excellence: Liberating the NHS* (Vol. 7881). The Stationery Office.

Department of Health and Welfare. (2013). *Morgendagens omsorg: Norwegian government* (White Paper No. 29). Norway: Helse og Omsorg Departement.

Engeström, Y. (1987). *Learning by expanding. An activity-theoretical approach to developmental research*. Helsinki: Orienta-konsultit.

Engeström, R. (1995). Voice as communicative action. *Mind, Culture, and Activity, 2*, 192–214.

Engeström, Y. (2004). New forms of learning in co-configuration work. *Journal of Workplace Learning, 16*(1/2), 11–21.

Engeström, Y. (2005). Developmental work research: Expanding activity theory in practice (Vol. 12). In G. Rückriem (Ed.) Lehmans Media. Berlin.

Engeström, Y. (2015). *Learning by expanding: An activity-theoretical approach to developmental research*. New York, NY: Cambridge University Press.

Engeström, Y., & Blackler, F. (2005). On the life of the object. *Organization, 12*(3), 307–330.

Engeström, Y., & Sannino, A. (2011). Discursive manifestations of contradictions in organizational change efforts: A methodological framework. *Journal of Organizational Change Management, 24*(3), 368–387.

Falzon, M.-A. (Ed). (2009). Introduction: Multi-sited ethnography: Theory, praxis and locality in contemporary research. In M.-A. Falzon (Ed.), *Multi-sited ethnography: Theory, praxis and locality in contemporary research* (pp. 1–25). Farnham: Ashgate.

Hean, S., Willumsen, E., & Ødegård, A. (2017a). Collaborative practices between correctional and mental health services in Norway: Expanding the roles and responsibility competence domain. *Journal of Interprofessional Care*, 31(1), 18–27.

Hean, S., Ødegård, A., & Willumsen, E. (2017b). Improving collaboration between professionals supporting mentally ill offenders. *International Journal of Prisoner Health, 13*(2), 91–104.

Hean, S., Willumsen, E., & Ødegård, A. (2018). Making sense of interactions between mental health and criminal justice services: The utility of cultural historical activity systems theory. *International Journal of Prisoner Health, 14*(2), 124–141.

Helse- og omsorgsdepartementet. (2018). *Sentrale forskrifter. Forskrift om habilitering og rehabilitering, individuell plan og koordinator* [The central regulations: Regulation for habilitation and rehabilitation, individual plan and coordination.]. Retrieved from https://lovdata.no/dokument/SF/forskrift/2011-12-16-1256/.

Jordan, B., & Henderson, A. (1995). Interaction analysis: Foundations and practice. *The Journal of the Learning Sciences, 4*, 39–103. https://doi.org/10.1207/s15327809jls0401_2.

Kajamaa, A. (2010). Expanding care pathways–towards interplay of multiple care objects. *International Journal for Public Sector Management, 23*(4), 392–402.

Kajamaa, A. (2011). *Unraveling the helix of change: An activity-theoretical study of health care change efforts and their consequences*. Helsinki: Unigrafi.

Kajamaa, A., & Lahtinen, P. (2016). Carnivalization as a new mode of collaboration. *Journal of Workplace Learning, 28*(4), 188–205. https://doi.org/10.1108/JWL-11-2015-0084.

Kodner, D., & Spreeuwenberg, L. C. (2002). Integrated care: Meaning, logic, applications, and implications—A discussion paper. *International Journal of Integrated Care, 2*(4), 1–6.

Kriminalomsorgen. (2017). *Årsrapport 2017 for kriminalomsorgen* [Annual report of 2017 for Correctional Services].

Lahtinen, P., Esko, T., Kajamaa, A., Johnsen, B., Seppänen, L., & Hean, S. (2018). *Addressing reoffending through addressing offender mental health:*

Exploring the viability of the Change Laboratory method as means of promoting social innovation in the delivery of integrated mental health care offenders in prison services. Project Report. Stavanger: University of Stavanger. Retrieved from http://eprints.bournemouth.ac.uk/31548/1/20181210_FINAL_ko-krus%20report_%28PL%2CSH%2CTE%29.pdf.

Laine, M. (2011). Rankaisu ja kuntoutus [Punishment and rehabilitation]. In R. Lavikkala & H. Linderborg (Eds.), *Rikosseuraamustyön kehittämisen kysymyksiä* (pp. 13–40). Tampere: Rikosseuraamusalan koulutuskeskus 2/2011.

Langeveld, H., & Melhus H. (2004). Are psychiatric disorders identified and treated by in-prison health services? *Tidsskrift for den Norske Lægeforening: Tidsskrift for Praktisk Medicin, ny Række, 124*(16), 2094–2097.

Leont'ev, A. N. (1978). *Activity, consciousness and personality*. Englewood Cliffs, NJ: Prentice-Hall.

Marcus, G. E. (1995). Ethnography in/of the world system: The emergence of multi-sited ethnography. *Annual Review of Anthropology, 24*(1), 95–117.

Marcus, G. E. (1998). *Ethnography through thick and thin*. Princeton, NJ: Princeton University Press.

Miettinen, R. (1996). Theories of invention and an industrial innovation. *Science Studies, 9*(2), 34–48.

Miettinen, R. (2006). The sources of novelty: A cultural and systemic view of distributed creativity. *Journal Compilation, 15*(2), 173–181.

Sloan, J., & Wright, S. (2015). Going in green: Reflection of the challenges and 'getting in, getting on, and getting out' for doctoral prison researchers. In D. H. Drake, R. Earle, & J. Sloan (Eds.), *The Palgrave handbook of prison ethnography* (pp. 143–163). Basingstoke: Palgrave Macmillan.

Star, S. L., & Griesemer, J. R. (1989). 'Institutional ecology', 'translations' and boundary objects: Amateurs and professionals in Berkeley's Museum of Vertebrate Zoology 1907–39. In M. Biagioli (Ed.), *The science studies reader* (pp. 503–524). London: Routledge.

The Execution of Sentences Act (2001/2018). Retrieved from https://lovdata.no/dokument/NLE/lov/2001-05-18-21.

Van Maanen, J., Sørensen, J. B., & Terence, R. M. (2007). The interplay between theory and method. *Academy of Management Review, 32*(4), 1145–1154.

Vygotsky, L. S. (1978). *Mind in society: The development of higher psychological processes*. Cambridge, MA: Harvard University Press.

World Health Organisation. (2015). *Global strategy on people-centred and integrated health services*. Retrieved from http://www.who.int/servicedeliverysafety/areas/people-centred-care/en/.

3

Mirrors of Prison Life—From Compartmentalised Practice Towards Boundary Crossing Expertise

Søren Walther Nielsen and Anu Kajamaa

Introduction

The prevailing high rate of recidivism among ex-offenders, many with mental health problems, is indicative of the fragile nature of resocialisation processes and the challenges faced in the interactions between the two distinct institutions of "punishment" and "treatment". It is a fact that a much higher proportion of the inmates in prisons have mental disorders compared with the population outside prison (Cramer, 2016). To support the mentally ill inmates, and reinforce their capacity of resocialisation, it is crucial that the staff of different service providing institutions (e.g. specialised mental health and prison services) engage in

S. W. Nielsen (✉)
University College Absalon, Roskilde, Denmark
e-mail: snie@pha.dk

A. Kajamaa
Faculty of Educational Sciences, University of Helsinki, Helsinki, Finland
e-mail: anu.kajamaa@helsinki.fi

S. Hean et al. (eds.), *Improving Interagency Collaboration, Innovation and Learning in Criminal Justice Systems*,
https://doi.org/10.1007/978-3-030-70661-6_3

interagency collaboration to gain proper knowledge about the inmates' livelihoods, life situations and health problems (Lehtmets & Pont, 2014; Helsedirektoratet, 2016; Bjørngaard et al., 2009). However, the complexity and unpredictability of interagency collaboration and knowledge management create a need to shed light on the challenges faced by the professionals working with inmates with mental health problems. As a consequence, calls for more effective models of collaboration have been made (Fenge et al., 2014; Hean et al., 2017).

In this chapter, we take an activity-theoretical approach to identify the boundaries and collaboration and integration needs between different service providers. The activity-theoretical approach has been chosen as it helps identify the tensions which can act as triggers for future organisational change (Engeström, 2008; Kajamaa, 2011; Engeström & Kärkkäinen, 1995). We pay special attention to compartmentalisation of practices by which we mean the work that takes place in separated, isolated compartments, which invariably results in poor coordination and problems in service provision. While acknowledging the contradictory dynamics of organisational life, we aim to uncover challenges manifested in the interaction between the specialised mental health service outside the prison, the primary health service located in the prison, and the prison services, including the inmates as subjects of our study.

Theoretical–Methodological Framework

Cultural-historical activity theory (Leont'ev, 1978; Engeström et al., 1999; Sannino et al., 2009; Engeström & Sannino, 2010; Engeström, 2015), applied in this chapter, perceives tensions in work practices as manifestations of historically accumulated, systemic contradictions (Engeström & Sannino, 2011; Engeström, 2000). Contradictions are considered to be products of the socio-economic activities in which they are embedded. Further, "contradictions act as driving forces of change as they generate tensions, disturbances and innovative attempts for development in social action" (Kerosuo et al., 2010, p. 115). Activity theory helps us to construct a contextualised view in which social activities are carried out by a multitude of interacting individuals, groups and networks. The participants in each of these have their own worldviews, that may conflict with or be complementary to the other voices and opinions represented (Sannino et al., 2016; Engeström, 2016).

Our focus in this chapter is on the compartmentalisation of service provision practices for the inmates. According to the Cambridge Dictionary, compartmentalisation means: "to separate something into parts and not allow those parts to mix together". Using this definition as an entry point, "*compartmentalised practice*" is here understood as those challenges that emerge when information, meanings, awareness, facts, etc., are being separated into isolated psychological or physical compartments. Compartmentalisation is likely to complicate the everyday interactions between the mentally ill inmates and different service providers connected to the prison setting. From an activity-theoretical perspective, compartmentalisation causes tensions and poor coordination of the activity between the different systems, likely leading to fragmentation of the overall object of their collective activity, that is the rehabilitation and better quality of life of the mentally ill inmates.

"*Compartmentalised expertise*" can be seen as historically shaped and transferred through an apprentice-like relationship between a particular profession and those learning this profession (Engeström, 2018). In addition to the development of one's own expertise, a professional must work with partners from other disciplines. To do so, interagency work is needed, and it requires collaborative and transformative competencies developed in response to the ever-changing conditions of professional and organisational life. These competencies are "...inherently heterogeneous and increasingly dependent on crossing boundaries, generating hybrids, and forming alliances across contexts and domains. There is no universally valid, homogenous, self-sufficient expertise" (Engeström, 2018, p. 14). The notion of this "*boundary crossing expertise*" is here positioned within a collective object-oriented activity, which flexibly transcends both professional and organisational boundaries (Edwards & Kinti, 2010; Engeström, 2018).

Most of the data analysed for this chapter were collected by carrying out ethnographic fieldwork in a low-security prison in South-Eastern Norway. The data were collected by interviewing and observing inmates and prison staff, and primary health service staff located in the prison.[1]Other informants related to this local field of inquiry were a physician working part-time in the prison and a first-line prison psychiatrist working in a high-security prison situated nearby. Some of the data were collected from a local community mental health centre by interviewing various staff of that institution. The aim of our data collection was to gather insider perspectives on what goes on, who or what is involved, and why, to see issues from the standpoint of the informant.

The ethnographic data of the informants were assembled as an "extended" case study constructed on the basis of a series of connected cases occurring within prison life (Gluckman, 2006; Mitchell, 2006). In our analysis, we have applied the activity theory (Engeström, 2015. See Chapters 1 and 8 for an explanation of this conceptual framework) and a narrative approach (Mishler, 1986; Czarniawska, 2007). The data for each case were organised into "mirrors of prison life". A mirror can be seen as a critical account, or explanation of a concrete activity, a situation or a cluster of activities, included in our ethnographic data, and analysed and interpreted by us in terms of activity systems, their tensions and organisational learning.

On this basis, we have presented our findings in four sections. The first section is based on an account given by a frontline psychiatrist working in a high-security prison. Her narrative describes the shortage of psychiatric beds and the lack of specialised psychiatric knowledge about mentally ill inmates. The second section focuses on the low-security prison and depicts how an inmate, who was an addict and suffered from an antisocial personality disorder when imprisoned, negotiates the challenges of prison life and enacts different forms of resocialisation. The third section is concerned with the prison staff and the primary health staff located in the low-security setting. It illustrates their views on tensions about interagency collaboration with the local community

[1] The primary health service located in the prison is a result of reorganisation of prison services that has been taking place in Norway since 1969. According to the ideology of reorganisation, whenever possible, inmates should receive the same level of service as citizens living outside the prison. Consequently, the primary health service of the municipality was "imported" into the prison where it constitutes a separate service unit organised and financed by the municipality and collaborating closely with other prison services on a daily basis (Fridhov & Langelid, 2017).

mental health centre (in Norwegian: Distriktspsykiatrisk Senter (DPS)). The fourth section presents the problems of collaboration as described by the staff of the DPS.

First Mirror: The Psychiatrist

During interviewing we used snowballing techniques in which each informant was asked to name two to three other people in the same professional network. These other people were then included in the interview sample, the human landscape of ethnographic research stretching well beyond the local field site. Several informants named an experienced first-line psychiatrist working in a high-security prison, who had formerly risk-assessed many of the inmates presently populating the low-security prison in which we carried out fieldwork. The informants pointed out that this psychiatrist had extensive knowledge about the mental illnesses of inmates and the collaboration with the psychiatric system outside the prison. Thus, the psychiatrist was interviewed, and she turned out to have strong ties to the research setting and was an informant providing vital contextualisation (see also Gluckman, 2006). When asked about the collaboration between the prison service and the mental health service she explained:

> *Inmates can also be psychotic and then we have a problem. It is the health service in the prison that makes the referral to the community mental health centre. According to my experience, if the mentally ill inmate perhaps is admitted to that centre, the staff show little interest in our category of patients. I have spent years getting inmates with a treatment need hospitalised. Recently, we filed a complaint in the regional court (Fylkesmannen) about mistreatment of a mentally ill inmate. He has been diagnosed with chronic schizophrenia. In the past, he was hospitalised several times but every time the therapists assessed his symptoms to be simulations (...) I think there are several reasons for these conditions. Firstly, there are few places in psychiatry where they work a lot with inmates and therefore have the necessary knowledge about prison conditions. I also think that there exists a basic capacity problem in psychiatry. There are not enough beds. Think about this: in 1960 there were 18,000*

psychiatric beds in the whole country; today that figure is down to 3,500 beds. (Interview with psychiatrist, 20 October 2017)

This excerpt identifies an interface riddled by tensions, in particular regarding what should have been the shared object of activity of the specialised mental health service and the primary health service located in the prison: the treatment of the prisoner. The psychiatrist accounts for the consequences of compartmentalised division of labour as follows. She describes the vast amount of resources, sometimes used in vain, to get inmates hospitalised and the mistreatment of mentally ill inmates, in situations lacking interagency collaboration. Officially, the collaboration between primary health service located in the prison and the specialised mental health service is regulated by formal agreements between institutions but the operationalisation of these is less clear-cut. The psychiatrist calls for better treatment of mentally ill inmates and her account comprises several constraining factors of interagency collaboration, including the lack of psychiatric beds and a deficiency of psychiatric knowledge about prisons and inmates.

In this mirror, the psychiatrist describes how different rationalities clash when the specialised mental health service and the primary health service located in the prison attempt to deal with the object of rehabilitation: the troubled inmate with a mental disorder. The lack of expertise in the specialised mental health service when it comes to working with prisoners hinders object-oriented care provision, blocking the admission to the psychiatric hospital ward. If admission *is* eventually granted, their lack of expertise in dealing with prisoners impacts on the care they receive while in hospital. According to the psychiatrist, the lack of boundary crossing knowledge in the specialised mental health services and the lack of collaboration with the primary health service located in the prison makes the likelihood of the inmate's recovery uncertain. Figure 3.1 presents elements of the psychiatrist's activity system. In the figure, the narrated disturbances are indicated with lightning arrows between the elements of this activity system.

The tensions analysed in the activity system (in Fig. 3.1) are indicative of compartmentalised psychiatric expertise. It seems counterproductive inasmuch as it closes in on itself, and the psychiatrist cannot reach out to

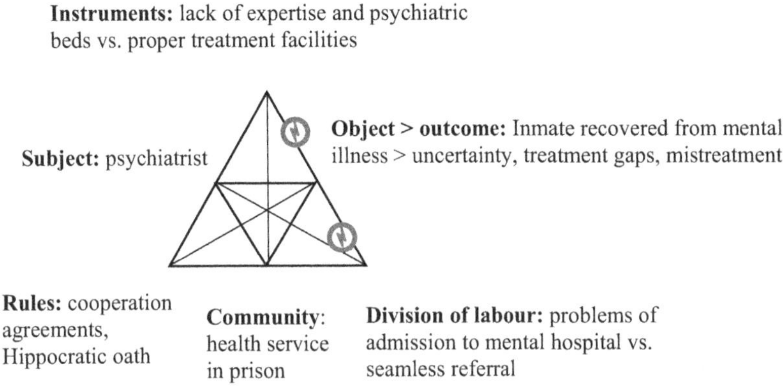

Fig. 3.1 The disturbances recounted by the first-line prison psychiatrist

other actors knowledgeable on the inmate's situation (e.g. a psychiatrist reaching out to a prison officer in order to incorporate into a care plan his expertise on individual inmates with mental disorders). In this context, the compartmentalised practices produce mismatches which invariably result in poor communication and mistakes, not least because of the blocked coordination and information flow. The constrained interagency collaboration presumably creates frustrations, confusion and discoordination on both sides, among staff of the prison and the staff of the mental hospital.

The lack of psychiatric beds illustrates a lack of resources. However, it is something which can be reduced (but not eliminated) by improved organisational collaboration, e.g. if more inmates receive psychiatric treatment in the prison. Similarly, if the specialised mental health services lack qualified personnel due to economic constraints, the shortage of staff cannot be balanced entirely by improvements between the prison and mental health service collaborations. Despite the collaboration intentions, lack of resources will continue to limit the system's treatment capacity, and indirectly its institutional "willingness" to admit mentally ill inmates. In fact, resource shortages may limit collaboration efforts in the first place as the compartmentalisation of treatment and work practices of the mental health service often emerge when the psychiatric system is pressured to meet the cost-efficiency requirements of the health care sector. In this light, policy analysis made by the Norwegian Medical Association (NMA) shows how certain patient groups may be prioritised when budget cuts are made (Den norske legeforening, 2018) and the prison population, supposedly because of social stigma, is unlikely to be one of the priority groups.

Second Mirror: The Inmate

Exploring how inmates make sense of the world around them, give meaning to it and socialise with others requires some reflections on our ethnographic research process. Collecting information on mentally vulnerable inmates is naturally a sensitive issue. Prison staff members were not permitted to pass information to us on the inmates, so it was difficult for us to identify the interviewees, and get in contact with them. To overcome these difficulties, a member of our research team became an apprentice in the prison storage and was trained by a supervisor-inmate. It allowed him to follow the daily routines of prison life, and via the combined role of an apprentice-researcher, staying in the field for a prolonged period (Downey et al., 2015). The apprenticeship meant that the researcher's presence gained legitimacy and generated trust. Then, the inmates began to exchange information with him on their life course experiences, including mental vulnerability.

We have created the following mirror by selecting one of the interviewed inmate's narrative for an in-depth analysis. The narrative is based on participant observations and several interviews with the inmate who had a double diagnosis (drug addiction and antisocial personality disorder) when he began serving his sentence for having committed a homicide. Besides showing the common connection between crime, drug abuse and mental health problems (Friestad & Kjelsberg, 2009; Cramer, 2016), these ethnographic data demonstrate how an individual inmate can experience problems related to the poor collaboration between the prison services and the mental health services.

In his mirror, the inmate emphasised the good relationship he established with a prison officer and a nurse from the primary health service located in the prison. Both professionals were therapeutically trained and supported him with his much-needed reflective therapy through weekly conversations (Andersen, 1987, 2005; Anderson, 2003; Wagner, 2009). During the first part of imprisonment, the inmate had not had any contact with his family, including his children. The reflective therapy helped him to ease his anxiety, and his fears related to being reunited with his family. To restore the relationship with his family, the inmate made a phone call to his mother and his experience of this first call was one of success. Afterwards, while on leave from the prison, he made several family visits to his hometown and managed to reactivate his family bonds. We asked him if the visits also reactivated contacts with his former criminal friends, to which he responded in the following way:

> *No, not at all. Several things have happened to my old environment. First, most of these friends come from a city not located in the region where my mother lives. Second, many of my former friends died of an overdose, have committed suicide or are imprisoned. Third, other friends have been through a change process similar to mine. That is good. Anyhow, I have a family and all family members have been so caring and helpful. I am very lucky in that regard.* (Interview with inmate, 6 October 2017)

This excerpt shows how the inmate was trying to create distance between himself and his criminal past by recounting the unpleasant destinies of former accomplices. It also illustrates the importance of family relations to him. Furthermore, during the interview the inmate explained how renewal of family ties supported him in dealing with some of his mental problems, such as the guilt about the terrible things he had done, and the shame generated by his bad self-image. He recounted how he had expressed remorse and apologised to his family and children. They forgave him and the process contributed to repairing the damage he had caused. In terms of resocialisation, his reconfigured social identity as a son, a brother and a father, added important aspects to his personality and later became vital elements of his recovery.

The inmate's gradual recovery, psychologically and socially, was also supported by his vocational development when he started as an apprentice in the prison's mechanical workshop. His learning curve was quite steep because most metalwork had to be made within a margin of one-tenth of a millimetre. He performed his work according to the instructions given by the workshop manager. However, the guidance provided by teachers and required considerable cognitive efforts for him. The workshop activities involved cognitive exercises like experimentation, modelling, problem-solving and testing through maintaining the vehicles. The work to ensure the functionality and reliability of the engines, including their mechanical, hydraulic and electrical systems, also demanded theoretical knowledge (contained in drawings and manuals) to be used through the operation of welding equipment as well as lathes and drilling and milling machines. Consequently, the inmate's participation in the prison's education and work activities was stimulating and productive, enabling him to become a skilled and certified motorcycle (MC) mechanic.

The inmate's new status of being a skilled mechanic gave him the prospect of resocialisation. The change in the inmate's occupational status, relative to his previous position as an unskilled worker, can possibly lead to a higher social stratum in the future, and he might become an employed worker. Presumably, the inmate hoped to convert this new "social mobility" into a higher degree of commitment to civilian life. Moreover, the inmate explained that he had a job arrangement with an employer that would allow him to commence wage labour in a mechanical workshop following his release from prison. He had organised this employment plan himself, without support from the public jobcentre and it shows us something about the inmate's vigour and determination.

In his resocialisation, attention needs to be drawn to the relationship between personal and vocational learning, in other words, how his social identity and work identity had become interlinked. The inmate's resocialisation meant that he was learning new vocational skills. Via these skills, he adapted norms, values and attitudes that would ease his reintegration into the labour market and the private sphere. These processes of resocialisation are both sociocultural *and* material (Engeström, 2016), as they enhance the individual's capacity to handle psychological challenges as well as material objects and practical work activities. Analytically, participation in activities of the prison workshop had encouraged the inmate to embark on new cycles of resocialisation covering the distance between his actual imprisonment and the societal prospect of reintegration into civil society.

For multiple reasons, the case of this inmate also illustrates a tension-laden journey, with some tensions being created by his need to overcome his own drug addiction. The treatment of drug addiction was a core aim written into the premises of his homicide sentence. However, as the inmate pointed out in an interview, it was difficult to be admitted into the drug treatment programme. The staff of the primary health service located in the prison supported the inmate with a medical referral focusing on the inmate's urgent need for the drug treatment (only available outside prison), but the admission turned out to be an issue of long-term planning. It took four years for the inmate and the primary health staff located in the prison to get the referral through to the specialised psychiatric hospital ward outside the prison. To manage the crisis caused by lack of admission, the inmate showed a high degree of willpower, for example, when he continuously insisted on implementing the premises of his sentence, instructing him to embark on a detox programme, as demonstrated here:

> *In my opinion, there should be talks on drugs and rehabilitation, it is so important. I would recommend that inmates stand up for themselves and are outspoken, you do not achieve anything by sitting down and not saying anything. I am very satisfied that I did it because it led me on the right way, so stand up for yourself!* (Interview with inmate, 6 October 2017)

During the waiting period before getting treatment at the specialised hospital ward, the inmate tried to give up drugs on his own and steadily regained his motivation to rehabilitate, e.g. when he woke up one morning without withdrawal symptoms and a screaming nervous system. Despite the self-initiated change, he was still struggling with the effects of depression and questions of how to handle the risk of relapse in situations in which he was in contact with drug addicts in prison. He still needed to find ways/tools with which to hold onto his new "clean, crime free" identity and exert self-control that would help transformation from his old patterns of drug user identity and behaviour.

When after years of waiting the inmate eventually met a specialised consultant in the psychiatric hospital ward outside prison, he was told that it was unusual for them to treat a patient who was not an active drug user. The consultant, nevertheless, agreed to offer twelve consultations allowing the inmate to bring up topics on his own initiative. In the final evaluation, the consultant noted that the patient was motivated and had achieved good emotional control. The consultant recommended further conversational treatment in prison to facilitate transition to civilian life (Interview with inmate, 6 October 2017). Figure 3.2 presents the elements of the inmate's activity system. The challenges within this system are indicated with a lightning arrow.

Although the inmate had to wait four years for the treatment of his drug addiction and mental illness, the period became a source of change. The long wait spurred both the inmate and the primary health staff located in the prison into collaborating with each other. Their collaboration included the reflective therapy carried out in the prison in the interim, and it reduced and at last dissolved his antisocial personality disorder. It had expanded the inmate's resocialisation and reflective capability to make plans and independent decisions. It contributed not only

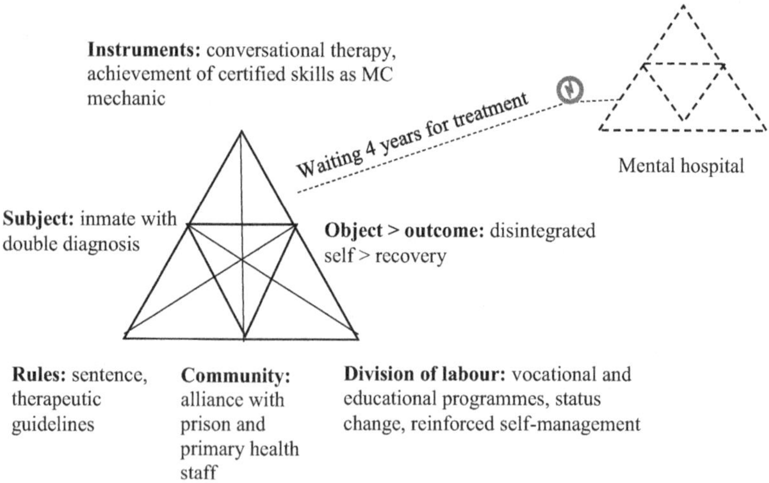

Fig. 3.2 The strengths and vulnerabilities experienced by the inmate

to his mental rehabilitation but also enabled him to be more self-directed and successful in his future drug treatment.

According to the inmate, it was the trust shown to him by the prison officer and the primary health nurse (who supported him with reflective therapy), which paved the way for the development of his life skills. For example, the inmate narrated how their trust enabled him to distance himself from the subculture of drug trade and the hyper-masculine hierarchy, the latter known as a general feature of prison life (see also Abrahamsen, 2017; Ricciardelli et al., 2015; Viggiani, 2012). By freeing himself from the social group pressure, usually forcing inmates to follow a given frame of criminal norms of loyalty and toughness (see also Ricciardelli, 2015), the inmate demonstrated individuality and used his acquired knowledge and skills to navigate towards being a citizen with a normal livelihood. Through this process of individuation and change, the difficult situation of being imprisoned gained a new meaning embedded in a collectively generated vision, the societal discourse on resocialisation outlining a possible future outside the prison. However, had the inmate chosen to follow the existing and risk-prone prison subculture, this narrative would certainly have been very different, likely with negative outcomes.

Third Mirror: The Prison Authority and the Primary Health Staff

Staff are important members of the prison community and we chose two informants from our sample, a deputy head and a primary health nurse. The interview strategy we employed in the prison involved formal interviews based on a semi-structured questionnaire. Whenever needed, the formal interview schedule was supplemented with informal conversations, follow-up interviews and e-mail correspondence. Besides participant observation, for example, at interagency meetings, interviewing was supplemented with other forms of human communication (Jorgensen, 1989), including document analysis of work programmes, minutes of meetings, evaluation of inmates, etc. In this way, fieldwork generated a vast amount of information, from which we selected the most illuminating data and analysed it with the help of the activity system model.

Our ethnographic research in the prison enjoyed the support of the local deputy head who in many ways helped us to establish an overview and get in contact with staff and inmates. Questioned about the prison population's mental illnesses, he explained that although they rarely suffer from psychosis, they are often diagnosed with other mental disorders. Furthermore, we invited the deputy head to comment on the problems of interagency collaboration with the specialised psychiatric system outside the prison, previously narrated by the first-line psychiatrist working in a high-security prison. From the deputy head's standpoint, the collaborative problems he experiences are of another kind. Still, both the deputy head, and later the primary health nurse, described interagency collaboration with the specialised psychiatric sector as difficult. It seems that the deputy head and the primary health nurse working in the prison shared day-to-day experiences concerning cooperation between the different service providers. Here the issue of collaboration is elaborated by the primary health nurse:

> *What we as health service staff experience is the big difference in how the DPS treats the patients after a white paper reform was carried out a couple of years ago. Prior to the reform, more inmates were admitted for polyclinical treatment at DPS. Presently, our experience is that the specialised psychiatric service is occupied with patient assessment and diagnosis while actual treatment is expected to be carried out by the primary health service of the municipality, in our case the health service of the prison. We do not feel competent and qualified to handle the more difficult cases of mental disorder occurring in the prison. Although the DPS is responsible for providing the primary health service with guidance, our need for supervision, methods and tools is hardly ever met.* (Mail correspondence with nurse, 2 August 2018)

The reported problems are indications of compartmentalised practice at the interface between the primary health service located in the prison and the DPS. The aim of the governmental white paper reform referred to by the nurse, was to improve collaborative interaction between public sectors and institutions. The regulative policy has been termed the "LEON" principle. It specifies that treatment must be carried out at the lowest possible level of effective care. Accordingly, it is not the diagnosis that determines where the patient receives treatment. Instead, priority is given to factors such as the patient's clinical condition, the treatment needed and qualifications of the available therapist (Social- og helsedirektoratet, 2006, p. 9). The "LEON" principle is associated with other parts of the health legislation and regional cooperation agreements.

Yet, in some circumstances, as articulated by the primary health nurse working in the prison, the regulative policy has produced coordination problems and treatment gaps. For example, reversal of an inmate's referral to the primary health service in the prison is met with resentment among the health staff, since they do not possess the necessary expertise and instruments. In this light, the LEON principle does not seem to reduce the compartmentalisation of psychiatric expertise, and the present state of affairs blocks potential efforts to share, through procedures of exchange and distribution, the specialised psychiatric knowledge and treatment methods. The primary health nurse's statements and the challenges within this system are summarised in Fig. 3.3.

The nurse's viewpoint is formed by her experiences of adverse effects of compartmentalisation, for example the unmet need for guidance and

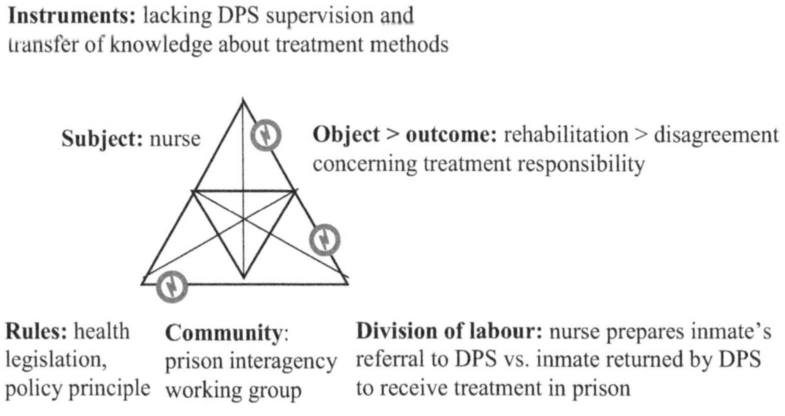

Fig. 3.3 Tensions narrated by the primary health nurse located in the prison

knowledge sharing. Shortage of material resources and facilities necessary for psychiatric treatment might add another range of tensions to the relationship between the primary health service located in the prison and the DPS. Adverse effects might also create unintended consequences, as illustrated in a follow-up interview. Here the prison's primary health nurse explained how she sometimes requested that the DPS carry out a risk assessment of a mentally ill inmate. The reason for the request could be that the inmate was violent or otherwise dangerous to himself and his surroundings. However, such requests were often denied by the DPS. Without a risk assessment, the prison authority had to relocate the inmate by transferring him to a high-security prison possessing the necessary means to pacify that type of unruly behaviour. The example demonstrates stakeholders' experiences generated through the struggle for access to assessment capacity of the DPS, and the situation illustrates a latent need to develop interagency collaboration and boundary-crossing expertise.

Fourth Mirror: The DPS' Staff

To capture the psychiatric health care provider's standpoints and gather more information on the multiple perspectives, we now describe the DPS' organisational setup and experiences expressed by some staff members. It was not without challenges to get in contact with the relevant staff at DPS. When doing fieldwork in the prison, our research team tried to identify the primary health service's contacts at the DPS. It turned out to be difficult to get the names, perhaps due to confusion as to whom the actual contact persons were. The situation conveyed an impression of a messy "interaction order". On second thought, this could also be a sign of misunderstandings, due to the limited knowledge of newly employed staff or failure on our behalf to establish the necessary rapport. In this light, arbitrariness and contingent conditions can affect the gathering of accurate information, which we tried to handle by building trust and cooperation as well as cross-validating data. The incident also shows how difficult it is for outsiders, say researchers, to navigate through unknown interconnected networks and arenas (Glaeser, 2006).

Regarding the organisation of DPS, it is regulated according to law and government guidelines of specialised health services (Helsedirektoratet, 2014). The organisation is divided into several teams covering outpatient clinics, outreach teams and inpatient treatment. Health personnel consists of various professionals, such as a psychologist, psychiatrist, physiotherapist, social worker and specialised nurse. The staff occupy a range of administrative and medical positions and function as the psychiatric system's gatekeepers. Their main responsibilities include assessment of multiple patient-needs and diagnostic work. In addition, they provide services to and cooperate with regional hospitals and various institutions at the local level. The DPS' own summary of the organisational challenges comprises better access to specialised services, recruitment of professional staff qualified to handle given tasks and responsibilities, improvement of cooperation with external partners and strengthening of the professional medical expertise (Social- og helsedirektoratet, 2006).

A psychologist and a specialised nurse from two different teams at the DPS explained the present collaboration with the primary health service located in the prison by recalling positive experiences and the good job done by the health staff. However, they also recalled some inadequacies. The shortcomings involve imprecise information contained in the referral of mentally ill inmates and too few joint meetings and shared goals of treatment. Both informants suggested that collaboration could be improved by exchanges of information and the development of a better-shared understanding of the mental health problem (Interview with psychologist, 22 November 2017; interview with nurse, 24 November 2017). A physician (GP), working part-time in the primary health service located in the prison, added to the picture by stating that participation in follow-up meetings at DPS sometimes were irregular due to logistical difficulties (Interview with GP, 22. November 2017). Figure 3.4 presents our activity-theoretical interpretation of the interviews with the psychologist and the specialised nurse, and the problems of collaboration they expressed.

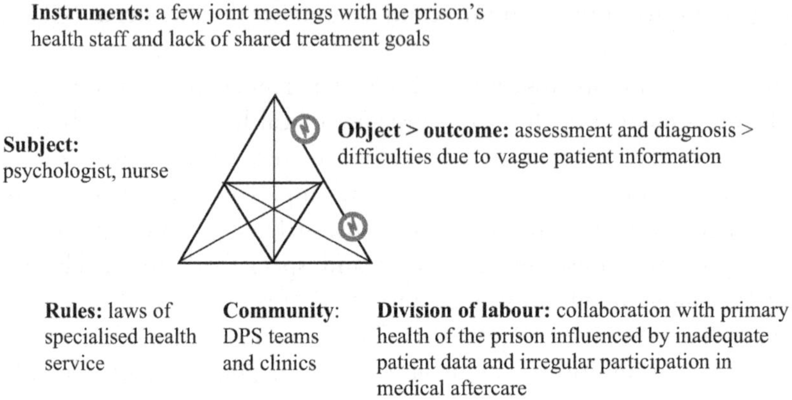

Fig. 3.4 The troubles of collaboration expressed by the DPS' staff

There are several reasons behind the troublesome interagency collaboration. A mismatch of insufficient information about the patient seemingly affects the psychiatric assessment capacity. Inadequate documentation at several levels as well as irregular participation by various primary health staff constitute other factors of constraint. The critical topics of too few joint meetings and the shortage of common treatment goals indicate that some instruments of collaboration are missing. In terms of analysis, the criss-crossing, flux and interweaving of tensions frame a situation in which organisational cohesion exists side by side with drivers of organisational transformation. We traced a possible new pattern of interaction through asking questions about the solutions to the troubles described. When asked about how the relationship between the primary health service located in the prison and the DPS could be developed in the future, the psychologist said:

> *Yes, one thing is collaboration. In my opinion we could establish an arena, a meeting place between [name of prison] and the psychiatry…I think that therapists from [DPS] polyclinic and the emergency team would be interested in participating. The prison staff could benefit from communications with the therapists of the psychiatry and receive education…in criminal psychology, how to talk to patients with psychiatric problems, I think.* (Interview with psychologist, 22. November 2017)

In these excerpts, the psychologist articulates a new scenario. In our interpretation, he presents the seeds of change by calling for more refined collaboration to overcome the compartmentalised practices. In the proposal put forward by the DPS psychologist, we sense a need for the development of interagency expertise that explores opportunities and reorganises the collaboration between the two service providers. Establishment of a boundary crossing meeting place could be realised through network activities and adhoccratic modes of working. Such a collaborative endeavour would be characterised by flexible arrangements and the ability to handle unexpected things. The organisational platform deviates from a professional bureaucracy and is closer to an innovative organisation with decentralised decision making and tasks continuously redefined and adjusted according to the ever changing needs. Presumably, coproduction within this context might bring about a high level of conflict but the conflicts are seen as useful, or even desirable, and act as sources of development. Exactly how this type of boundary crossing knowledge exchange and reorganisation (Engeström, 2018) should be enacted is difficult to predict. Questioning and problematising the current work practices maybe seen as the first step towards this direction.

Discussion

From an activity-theoretical standpoint, Fig. 3.5 addresses the key topics of compartmentalisation and boundary-crossing expertise by illustrating the interacting activity systems of the service providers involved, the primary health service located in the prison in alliance with the prison authority, and the specialised mental health service, DPS. The activity systems of the inmate and the first-line psychiatrist working in a high-security prison are not included, but they remain important cases for cross-references and background knowledge. Figure 3.5 highlights the inadequacy of the existing methods and instruments for sharing information across services, which then complicates the distribution of treatment responsibility between the two services. For example, the staff of the primary health service located in the prison lack treatment guidelines and treatment competencies, skills "belonging" to actors of the activity

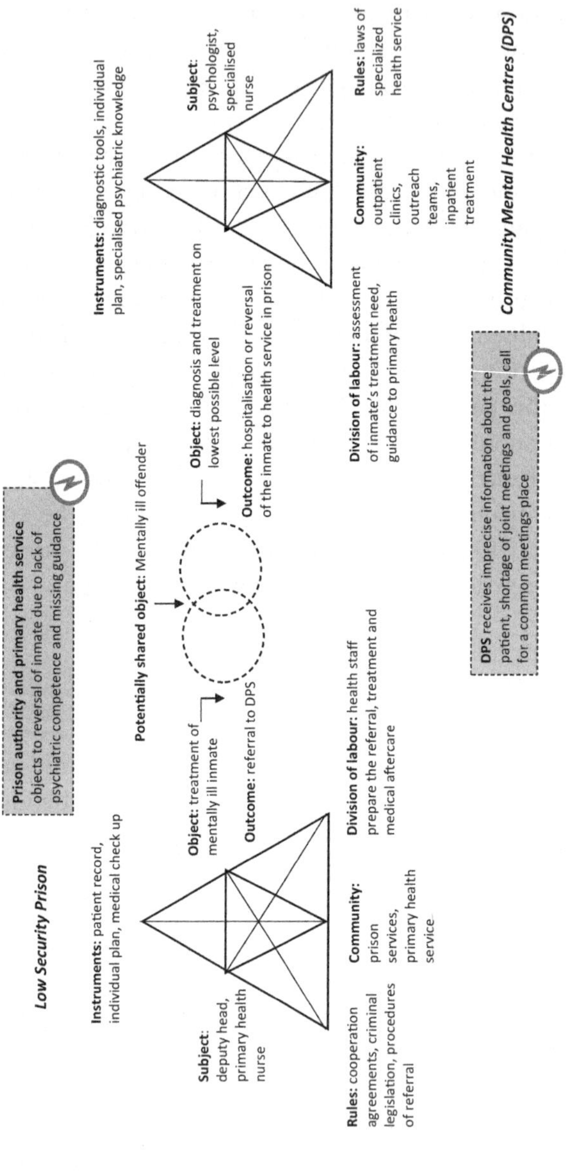

Fig. 3.5 Tension between the primary health service in the prison and the DPS

system of the DPS. Moreover, what could have been shared tools, such as medical referrals, are not always an issue of collaboration between the activity systems. Similarly, there does not seem to be a well-defined division of labour and the unclear interface often hinders collaboration.

Our research team had the opportunity to discuss the findings presented in the figure with the involved informants on three occasions: one seminar at which the prison staff and the staff of the primary health service were present, and two workshops, held in the prison, at which staff of the DPS also participated. On all occasions, the participants validated the ethnographic data and the way we had "mirrored" their interviews reflecting troubles of collaboration. The participants did not try to blame the professional groups "in the other camp" for the problems. For example, the prison staff did not articulate the problem of collaboration as one belonging to the municipality because that institution organises the primary health service located in the prison. In fact, all practitioners acknowledged the interagency tensions as a shared problematic not confined to a particular institution or sector. They expressed a professional sense of social responsibility reaching beyond their own confinements in order to solve the problem.

In general, the practitioners' feedback on the seminar and workshops corroborated our research results, saying that the interagency tensions seemed not to arise from the wrong activity (or inactivity) of individual actors or professions. Neither are they the result of miss-matching expectations. Primarily, they are the accumulated constraints caused by organisational compartmentalisation and lack of boundary-crossing expertise. It is problematic that the primary health service located in the prison and DPS function as two separate compartments, not having a shared understanding of the object of collective activity (the treatment of the mentally ill inmate with the aim of enhancing the quality of life). In the worst-case scenario, the inmate falls "between" the two institutions without receiving qualified treatment. This compartmentalisation and predicament then leaves some individual inmates in a stalemate characterised by ambiguity and uncertainty.

In terms of theoretical application, our research findings on constrained processes support a long-standing ethnographic proposition concerning two mechanisms underlying the development of social systems and organisations, namely one of fission and one of fusion (Gluckman, 1958). It should be noted that the compartmentalised expertise of both the specialised psychiatric service and the primary health service located in the prison yields certain benefits alongside the abovementioned constraints. Professional actors convey strong vocational identities, and the meaningfulness of their daily work and feelings of belongingness, loyalty and commitment are embedded in the practices customary to their own profession and location. Further, the compartmentalised expertise often accommodates different interests and objects within the organisation and tends to produce in-group norms and legitimacy of the workplace—thereby creating effects of fusion. At the same time, however, the professionals may underestimate the need for collaboration and information sharing with those representing other institutions and professional perspectives. For this reason, the more compartmentalised an organisation is, the more difficult the interagency collaboration will be because it limits the interaction of the practitioners. In our view, this pattern shows effects of fission which tend to rupture collaborative efforts and organisational integration (Showers et al., 2004; Amiot et al., 2017).

Conclusions

In this chapter, we have provided multiple "mirrors" expressed by various informants related to the area of prison life. The mirrors have focused on organisational compartmentalisation and its negative consequences, such as the tensions in collaboration between the primary health service located in the prison and the specialised mental health service of DPS. The compartmentalisation is often related to hierarchical and bureaucratic modes of working, such as the privileging of knowledge exchanges between accredited professionals and institutions accorded with recognised authority and status. At the practical level, however, the compartmentalisation of work practices and knowledge disparities may cause problems, such as imprecise referrals information, lack of transfer of psychiatric guidance, rejected risk assessment of mentally ill inmates etc.

Finding powerful solutions to organisational tensions and contradictions requires collective explication and analysis (Engeström, 2018). We have attempted this by constructing "mirrors". These mirrors potentially facilitate organisational change and learning because we hope that the analysis depicted in these will help other researchers and practitioners to understand better the issues of boundaries, collaboration and expertise at the interfaces of prison, primary health service located in the prison and the mental health service at DPS.

From a developmental perspective, the tensions and disturbances identified in the ethnographic data may function as triggers for organisational change and learning, and the production of new ways of working (Engeström, 2008). The articulated need of a power-shift from professional bureaucracy to adhocracy, including multiciplinary teams consisting of primary health staff and DPS staff, exemplifies the future prospects. In this regard, the mirrors could be used as stimuli in participatory development workshops, such as the Change Laboratory, to facilitate dialogue and collaborative learning (see Virkkunen & Newnham, 2013; Hean et al., 2020, Chapters 1 and 8).

In boundary-crossing interventions of this kind, the individual inmate's self-knowledge and personal resources need to be included among other stakeholder voices and interests. In other words, such concerted efforts may engender the interagency competencies and reorganisation that are needed. They may also create an opportunity for emancipatory projects to emerge from below, such as "ad hoc alliances" through which mentally ill inmates are provided with an opportunity to participate as an expert in their own treatment and decision-making processes related to recovery and resocialisation. This type of expansive learning process might create innovative practices and support flexible collaboration.

References

Abrahamsen, M. H. (2017). Duften af frihed I det åbne fængsel. *Nordisk tidsskrift for kriminalvidenskab, Nr., 3,* 318–339.

Amiot, C., Doucerain, M., & Louis, W. (2017). The pathway to accepting derogatory ingroup norms: The roles of compartmentalization and legitimacy. *Psychology of Sport and Exercise, 32*(2017), 58–66.
Andersen, T. (1987). The reflecting team: Dialogue and meta-dialogue in clinical work. *Family Proccess, 26,* 415–428.
Andersen, T. (2005). *Reflekterende processer—Samtaler og samtaler om samtalerne.* København: Dansk Psykologisk Forlag.
Anderson, H. (2003). *Samtale, Sprog og Terapi—Et postmoderne perspektiv.* København: Hans Reitzels Forlag.
Bjørngaard, J., Rustad, Å., & Kjelsberg, E. (2009). The prisoner as patient—A health service satisfaction survey. *BMC Health Service Research, 2009*(9), 176.
Cramer, V. (2016). *The prevalence of mental disorders among convicted inmates in Norwegian prisons.* The Centre for Research and Education ibn Forensic Psychiatry. Project Report 2016-2. Oslo University Hospital.
Czarniawska, B. (2007). Narrative inquiry in and about organizations. In J. Clandinin (Ed.), *Handbook of narrative inquiry: Mapping a methodology* (pp. 383–404). Newbury Park, CA: Sage.
Den norske legeforening. (2018). *Samfunnspolitisk afdeling. Pressemeddelelse. Statsbudgettet: halvhjertet for helse.* http://legeforeningen.no/Nyheter/2018/Statsbudsjettet-Halvhjertet-for-helse.
Downey, G., Dalidowicz, M., & Mason, P. (2015). Apprenticeship as a method: Embodied learning in ethnographic practice. *Qualitative Research, 15*(2), 183–200.
Edwards, A., & Kinti, I. (2010). Working relationally at organisational boundaries: Negotiating expertise and identity. In H. Daniels, A. Edwards, Y. Engeström, T. Gallagher, & S. Ludvigsen (Eds.), *Activity theory in practise—Promoting learning across boundaries and agencies.* London: Routledge.
Engeström, Y. (2000). Activity theory and the social construction of knowledge: A story of four umpires. *Organization, 7*(2), 301–310.
Engeström, Y. (2008). *From teams to knots—Activity-theoretical studies of collaboration and learning at work.* Cambridge: Cambridge University Press.
Engeström, Y. (2015). *Learning by expanding—An activity-theoretical approach to developmental research.* New York, NY: Cambridge University Press.
Engeström, Y. (2016). *Studies in expansive learning—Learning what is not yet there.* New York, NY: Cambridge University Press.
Engeström, Y. (2018). *Expertise in transition—Expansive learning in medical work.* New York, NY: Cambridge University Press.

Engeström, Y., Miettinen, R., & Punamäki, R.-L. (Eds.). (1999). *Perspectives on activity theory*. Cambridge: Cambridge University Press.

Engeström, Y., & Sannino A. (2010). Studies of expansive learning: Foundations, findings and future challenges. *Educational Research Review*. https://doi.org/10.1016/j.edurev.2009.12.002:1-24.

Engeström, Y., & Sannino, A. (2011). Discursive manifestations of contradictions in organisational change efforts—A methodological framework. *Journal of Organizational Change Management, 24*(3), 368–387.

Engeström, Y., & Kärkkäinen, M. (1995). Polycontextuality and boundary crossing in expert cognition: Learning and problem-solving min complex work activities. *Learning and Instruction, 5*, 319–336.

Fenge, L., Hean, S., Staddon, S., Clapper, A., Heaslip, V., & Jack, E. (2014). Mental health and the criminal justice system: The role of interagency training to promote practitioner understanding of the diversion agenda. *Journal of Social Welfare and Family Law, 36*(1), 36–46.

Friestad, C., & Kjelsberg, E. (2009). Drug use and mental health problems among prison inmates—Results from a nation-wide prison population study. *Nordic Journal of Psychiatry, 63*(3), 237–245.

Fridhov, I. M., & Langelid, T. (2017). Importmodellen i norsk fengselsvesen. *Nordisk Tidsskrift for Kriminalvidenskab*, december 2017, 104. årgang, Nr. 3, 259–288.

Glaeser, A. (2006). The ontology for the ethnographic analysis of social processes. In T. M. S. Evens & D. Handleman (Eds.), *Manchester school—Practice and ethnographic praxis in anthropology* (pp. 64–93). New York, NY: Berghahn Books.

Gluckman, M. (1958). *Analysis of a social situation in modern Zululand*. Manchester: Manchester University Press.

Gluckman, M. (2006). Ethnographic data in British social anthropology. In T. M. S. Evens & D. Handleman (Eds.), *Manchester school—Practice and ethnographic praxis in anthropology* (pp. 13–22). New York, NY: Berghahn Books.

Hean, S., Ødegård, A., & Willumsen, E. (2017, June 12). Improving collaboration between professionals supporting mentally ill offenders. *International Journal of Prison Health, 13*(2): 91–104.

Hean, S., Lahtinen, P., Dugdale, W., Larsen, B., & Kajamaa, A. (2020). The change laboratory as a tool for collaboration and social innovation. In E. Willumsen & A. Ødegård (Eds.), *Samskaping: Sosial innovasjon for helse og velferd* (pp. 207–221). Oslo: Universitetsforlaget.

Helsedirektoratet. (2014). Organisering og praksis i ambulante akutteam ved distriktspsykiatriske sentre (DPS). *Rapport*. Avdeling psykisk helsevern og rus. Oslo.

Helsedirektoratet. (2016). Helse—g omsorgstjenester til innsatte I fengsel. *Veileder*. Opdateret desember 2016. Helsedirektoratet. Avdeling minoritetshelse og rehabilitering.

Jorgensen, D. L. (1989). *Participant observation*. New York, NY: Sage.

Kajamaa, A. (2011). Boundary breaking in a hospital: Expansive learning between the worlds of evaluation and frontline work. *The Learning Organization, 18*(4), 361–377.

Kerosuo, H., Kajamaa, A., & Engeström, Y. (2010, June). Promoting innovation and learning through change: An Example from Finnish health care. *Central European Journal of Public Policy, 4*(1), 210–231.

Lehtmets, A., & Pont, J. (2014). *Prison health care and medical ethics—A manual for health-care workers and other prison staff with responsibility for prisoners' well-being*. Report. Bruxelles: Council of Europe.

Leont'ev, A. N. (1978). *Activity, consciousness and Personality*. Englewood Cliffs, NJ: Prentice-Hall.

Mishler, E. (1986). *Research interviewing: Context and narrative*. Cambridge, MA: Harvard University Press.

Mitchell, J. C. (2006). Case and situation analysis. In T. M. S. Evens & D. Handleman (Eds.), *Manchester School—Practice and ethnographic praxis in anthropology* (pp. 23–42). New York, NY: Berghahn Books.

Ricciardelli, R. (2015). Establishing and asserting masculinity in Canadian penitentiaries. *Journal of Gender Studies, 24*(2), 170–191.

Ricciardelli, R., Maier, K., & Hannah-Moffat, K. (2015). Strategic masculinities: Vulnerabilities, risk and the production of prison masculinities. *Theoretical Criminology, 19*(4), 491–513.

Sannino, A., Daniels, H., & Gutierrez, K. (2009). *Learning and expanding with activity theory*. Cambridge: Cambridge University Press.

Sannino, A., Engeström, Y., & Lemos, M. (2016). Formative interventions for expansive learning and transformative agency. *Journal of the Learning Sciences, 25*(4), 599–633.

Showers, C., Limke, A., & Ziegler-Hill, V. (2004). Self-structure and self-change: Applications to psychological treatment. *Behavior Therapy, 2004*, 167–184.

Social- og helsedirektoratet. (2006). Distriktspsykiatriske sentre—med blikket vendt mod kommunerne og spesialiserte sygehusfunksjoner i ryggen. *Veileder*, 15–1388.

Viggiani, N. (2012). Trying to be something you are not: Masculine performances within a prison setting. *Men and Masculinities, 15*(3), 271–291.
Virkkunen, J., & Newnham, D. S. (2013). *The change laboratory—A tool for collaborative development of work and education.* Rotterdam: Sense Publishers.
Wagner, J. (2009). Reflections on reflecting processes in a Swedish prison. *International Journal of Collaborative Practices, 1*(1), 18–30.

4

"Living with" Interagency Collaboration—Three Sustaining Practices

Tine Murphy, Marie Aakjær, Eva Pallesen, and Charlotte Rosenberg

Background

Cross-professional collaboration is increasingly prevalent in welfare contexts due to the current pressure for integrating different professional domains around desired effects on citizens' life, well-being and participation. In the context of this demand for greater cross-professional

T. Murphy (✉) · M. Aakjær · E. Pallesen · C. Rosenberg
Centre for Management and Experience Design,
University College Absalon, Roskilde, Denmark
e-mail: timu@pha.dk

M. Aakjær
e-mail: maaa@pha.dk

E. Pallesen
e-mail: evpa@pha.dk

C. Rosenberg
e-mail: chro@pha.dk

S. Hean et al. (eds.), *Improving Interagency Collaboration, Innovation and Learning in Criminal Justice Systems*,
https://doi.org/10.1007/978-3-030-70661-6_4

collaboration, it becomes important to understand the specific practices, which can sustain this.

This chapter explores how collaboration can take place between actors who are simultaneously affected by social processes in different arenas. These actors' norms and regulations do not just develop within the prison where they interact, they also develop in other arenas. These other arenas can be different professions, institutional fields, sectors, or even organisations. Based on this reasoning we will use the terms cross-professional, cross-institutional, cross-sectoral, and cross-organisational as interchangeable. Our assertion is that the insights from the chapter are equally relevant to all of the above types of collaboration.

Based on empirical data produced as part of the COLAB project (see Chapter 1 of this volume), this chapter explores how the staff and management of a low-security prison and professionals, engaged in work activity related to the inmates' education, health care, sports & leisure, faith and social services, collaborate. In particular, the chapter explores which practices can support the cross-organisational collaboration afforded by the Norwegian import model. The chapter identifies some of the key features of these local practices which underpin this process seen through the lens of sensemaking theory (Weick, 1995; Weick et al., 2005).

Drawing on a combination of neo-institutional theory (DiMaggio & Powell, 1991) and sensemaking theory, we investigate an example of how "the Norwegian import model" enables actors to make sense of their work in a way that facilitates collaboration. This is not a new ambition; other scholars have called for a greater attention to how different institutional logics integrate in daily practice (Pache & Santos, 2013). To the extent that neo-institutional studies have been undertaken, they have focused on how a contradiction between logics is addressed, either by keeping logics separate or by some form of compromise or reconciliation between these (Tracey et al., 2011). Our analysis, however, finds that the encounters in the prison can better be understood as a "living with" different professional logics (Austin et al., 2018). We find that the professionals in the prison—rather than keeping logics separate or attempting to unify or compromise logics internally—have developed a number of practices in which logics can live with each other. Notably, while compromising requires the confrontation of the differences between institutional logics and ultimately changing the respective professional logics, "living with" does not imply modifying the respective professional logics. Rather it implies nurturing an openness of each professional towards the possibility that "the key" for solving problems around the inmates may lie in unexpected places and may require the problem to be framed in another professional domain. We suggest that a condition for this "living with" is that professional logics are not primarily made sense in relation to each other but in parallel, which leaves space for a non-hierarchical configuration, where one logic does not dominate the other. We outline three types of practices within the prison that enable actors, in this case, to sidestep and collaborate with actors from other institutional fields.

Theoretical Framework

Institutional Logics

"Institutional logics" is a theoretical construct that helps us grasp the organising principles for a field (Friedland & Alford, 1991), the taken-for-granted rules that guide the behaviour of professionals—or the "belief systems and related practices that predominate in an organisational field" (Scott, 2001, referred in Reay & Hinings, 2009, p. 529).

According to DiMaggio and Powell (1991), we would expect organisations straddling several institutional fields to be exposed to conflicting institutional isomorphic forces. Isomorphic forces push organisations within the same field into becoming more homogenous in order to be perceived as legitimate (ibid.).

In this chapter, we will use the lens of sensemaking theory to explore how the local processes of organising are affected by different institutional pressures. Institutional fields and local sensemaking processes can be understood as mutually constitutive. On the one hand, institutional fields may provide overarching ideas, which actors in a local context may enact as relevant to organising their interactions. On the other hand, sense made through local interactions may spread and become institutionalised, as "sensemaking is the feedstock for institutionalization" (Weick, 1995, p. 36).

Organisational Sensemaking and Collaboration

Sensemaking theory examines the ongoing movement of actions and meanings (Weick 1969/1979, 1995, 2001; Sandberg & Tsoukas, 2015). The analysis of the three practices we observed in the prison context draws on Weick's concept of the *processes of organising* which emphasies how actions shape meaning and thus the way services are organised. We are interested in the link between joint action/collaboration in the organisational setting of the prison and meaning made there. Weick (1995) suggests that these are linked by the concept of organising: "Organising happens when meaning created through one interaction is generalised and used to make sense of another specific situation" (Murphy, 2015, p 154 own translation summarising Weick, 1995 inspired by Wiley, 1988, Weick, 2004, Weick et al., 2005). We will examine practices through which actors in the prison made sense of their professional work while being exposed to the overlap of multiple institutional logics that the import model of Norwegian prison care provision had created.

Empirical Case: The Norwegian Import Model in the Rehabilitation Prison

The empirical context of the present study is a Norwegian low-security rehabilitation prison. The prison houses approximately 60 prisoners serving longer sentences of an average of 3–7 years.

The overall task of the Norwegian prison service is to "ensure a proper execution of remand and prison sentences, with due regard to the security of all citizens" and simultaneously "prevent recidivism by enabling the offenders, through their own initiatives, to change their criminal behaviour".[1] Hence, the prison service works with a dual focus of implementation of detention and punishment on the one hand and in the long term achieving security for society by preventing criminal acts now and in the future. To accomplish this, the prison service collaborates closely with regional and local public agencies to create the conditions for prisoners to change their life trajectory; i.e. changes related to the inmates' education, socio-economic status and health.

The prevalent way of securing collaboration between Norwegian prison and welfare services is through the Norwegian Import model (Fridhov & Langelid, 2017). It involves two (or more) formally separate organisations weaving together in terms of daily practice at a specific location by means of a practical arrangement, where a desk from one organisation (e.g. the health services) is physically placed in another (the prison services).

The chosen empirical delimitation of the studied group of actors is the physical location of the prison. It corresponds to the "we" frequently used by the professionals in the study and includes actors who share daily practices. This "we" includes a number of actors who work part of the week at the prison, but who are employed by other formal organisations located elsewhere. That is, they are hired, paid and can be fired by managers not employed by the local prison. By focusing the empirical study on interaction undertaken on a specific local prison we revert to a classical definition of "the organisation" similar to the one used by Taylor (1916/2011) and Roethlisberger and Dickson (1939). They implicitly define the organisation as the "plant"—encompassing actors undertaking activities at a specific location.

Data Collection and Ethical Considerations

The empirical basis for this paper stems from qualitative interviews conducted with prison officers ($n = 3$), general health care service professionals ($n = 3$), mental health care professionals ($n = 3$), a teacher, priest and social worker, workshop mangers and prison management ($n = 4$),

[1] http://www.kriminalomsorgen.no/information-in-english.265199.no.html.

supplemented with observations and informal conversations emerging during the research team's stay in the prison. In addition, interviews with prisoners were carried out ($n = 5$). Interviews of an average duration of 45–60 min were recorded and transcribed afterwards. All interviews were conducted as semi-structured interviews, investigating the work practices of professionals and the intersections between these.

Conducting research in a prison context requires careful deliberation with regard to ethical considerations. Whether the researcher is present as an interviewer or as an observer, it requires ethical considerations since both are essentially participatory (Czarniawska-Joerges, 2007) in the sense that they invariably affect local interaction. A central concern in conducting the research, both in the interviews and the numerous informal conversations between researchers and participants, has been to respect the potential vulnerability of both the prisoners as well as the officers. Activities were conducted in accordance with the rules outlined by the Norwegian Data Protection Agency. Participants have been informed about the purpose of the study and how the material would be used, i.e. that only the researchers would have access, and that data was only gathered for the purpose of the research project.

Analysis

The study was part of the COLAB project, the objective of which was to explore the relevance of the Change Laboratory model (Engeström, et al., 1996), as an intervention framework through which researchers could facilitate organisational learning in the prison, driven by interaction and learning together with "others", within the criminal justice setting. The idea is that the mirroring and reflection on disturbances and shared analysis of contradictions between distinct activity systems can facilitate expansive learning (see Chapter 8 of this volume). However, what struck us as we spent time on site in the Norwegian prison was the extent to which actors at the prison were capable of overcoming conflicts and difficulties in interagency collaboration by themselves. So, the emphasis of our focus shifted, and we were increasingly curious about the practices that had emerged locally to manage cross-professional collaborations and what they had already learnt to do. The following questions arose: *Do they engage in continuous conflicts over institutional logics? Do they avoid conflicts by decoupling practices and sensemaking about them? Do they negotiate compromises between multiple institutional logics?*

Initially we performed an analysis informed by the grounded theory approach (Glaser & Straus, 2017) of the transcribed interviews and field notes from observations. We examined cross-professional interaction and ways of talking about them. We were looking for indications of compromise, decoupling, or other ways of bending professional logics towards each other. The analysis will show that we mainly found something else which we have called "living with". This led us to ask the following question: *Through which practices of sensemaking is this "living with" allowed to exist*? Hence, our research focus in the analysis became:

Which practices are pivotal in underpinning shared sensemaking processes that enable actors to collaborate despite different institutional logics?

We found a number of aspects of the practice that the actors have developed and we group these aspects into three types of mutually constitutive or interrelated practices (Fig. 4.1):

1. Narrative practices; including a modular vision, the practice of double vision and the use of translatable/pliable metaphors. 2. Practices around tools & documents. 3. Patterns of cross-professional meetings.

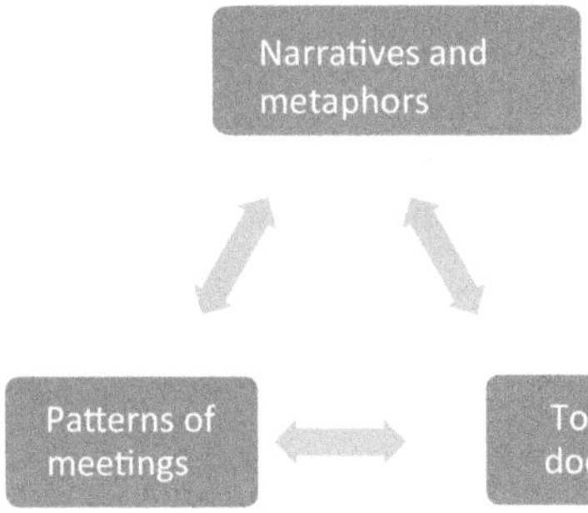

Fig. 4.1 Illustration of the relationship between the three types of practices sustaining cross-professional practice

In the following, we explore how these three types of practices are mutually constitutive. When combined, these underpin the collaboration and enable professionals to "live with" professional logics that are not primarily made sense of in relation to each other but in parallel, leaving space for a non-hierarchical configuration.

Narratives and Metaphors

The analysis shows that there are three aspects of narrative practices, which are pivotal to the collaboration across multiple institutional logics. First, a modular vision (the term is explained below) functions as an umbrella for and leveller of the various professions. Secondly, for some actors this shared modular vision is a vehicle for "living with" competing logics by the practice of double vision. Thirdly, there is widespread use of pliable metaphors for the shared activities, which lend themselves to translations into multiple logics.

A Modular Vision

In the studied prison, the actors from diverse professions, formal organisations, and institutional fields and their different institutional logics "live with each other" through the development of a narrative practice that render all activities and actors equally important. We suggest that this may be called a "modular" narrative. When we look up definitions of the word modular the following comes up:

> *Something, as a house or piece of furniture, built or organised in self-contained units or sections.* (http://www.dictionary.com/browse/modular)

> *Consisting of separate modules; especially where each module performs or fulfils some specified function and could be replaced by a similar module for the same function, independently of the other modules.* (https://en.wiktionary.org/wiki/modular)

From the various observations and interviews, we found that the actor who had the most central role in making sense of the collaboration in the prison was the local manager of the prison. He was responsible for managing the rehabilitation within the prison. The regional manager, who had also his office at the prison, could also have had a significant role in the sensemaking process. However, the vision, which the local manager narrated, was the one that was widely quoted and drawn on when other actors made sense of their shared activities. Furthermore, the local manager had a frequent interaction with the actors at the local prison, which was far greater than the more sporadic interaction of the regional manager. Therefore, in the analysis below, we concentrate on the local manager's version of the vision for the prison.

The local manager saw it as his job to narrate the vision for the prison repeatedly in interaction with all actors and inmates on site. He was explicit about his job as sense giver, or "culture cultivator" as he conceptualised it. He states that

> *culture is a perishable good; we have to work to recreate it all the time* (Interview with local manager)

> It is the primary vision for the rehabilitation in the prison that they *The most important task of the prison is to reintroduce inmates back into society in a proper way. So that they have a platform to start from and can experience a safe release... We have a local vision that says: "apprenticeship to better life-mastering" (oplæring til bedre livsmestring). The cooperation between areas where the inmate experiences mastering, which we can use in several arenas... It is the sum of all efforts and the process, which the inmate has been in... it can be in relation to his crime, it can be in relation to network, it can be in relation to his private finances. Really, many, many different... arenas.* (Interview with local manager)

It is the primary vision for the rehabilitation in the prison that they achieve their goal through work in the many arenas. This seems to be uncontested and widely shared. Subsequent interviews with a range of actors working on site and the regional manager reveal a remarkably homogeneous view of the vision—all interviewees repeat more or less the same vision. They are all able to expand on the vision and relate it to their own day-to-day activities. Therefore, the vision does seem to organise (Weick, 1995; Murphy, 2015) activities and sensemaking for all professions irrespective of their different institutional logics.

A modular narrative is unusual. Consider narratives of how a large hospital functions. It is likely that the narrative would narrate a hierarchy placing for example a diagnostic laboratory like radiology below the ones performing treatments such as surgical departments.

The conceptualisation of working in many different arenas is key here. The metaphor that inmates travel through a number of arenas creates a modular image. It is easy to see each arena as having different sub-goals, as working through different tools with different logics. Hence, the modular metaphor lends itself to making sense of collaboration across multiple institutional narratives.

Importantly, the arenas are narrated as concurrent and not sequenced. There is not one of the arenas, which is emphasised as taking precedence over another. The narrative relates the arenas to each other by emphasising that the inmate's development to freedom may start by mastering any of the arenas, and that progress in one arena will help progress in others.

The arenas are also narrated as being self-contained. They are not seen as being independent, but the professionals emphasise that the inmate can master one and not another arena independently. From this, it follows that the approaches and logics in one arena do not need to be coordinated with the logics in another in order to co-exist, i.e. the narrative vehicle allows the professional logics to exist side by side.

The modular narrative reflects no desire to create compromises between arenas or merge them into one. On the contrary, prisoners focusing on mastering different life arenas is assumed to work precisely *because* of their self-contained nature, which ensures that the inmate will meet a range of different approaches to rehabilitation. If one arena doesn't work, there is a good chance that another will. It is the diversity of logics and practices that is thought to be the virtue of the system. This also means that the exact methods employed by the health care workers can be replaced and decided locally by them. It does not need to be agreed upon and coordinated with actors associated with other arenas. The overall effect is that the modular vision creates a tolerance for and reproduction of institutional diversity. The shared modular vision is centred on the citizen, in this case, the inmate, in a way that does not position one profession as being more important to another.

The Use of Double Vision

The question arises as how actors in the prison then make sense of their work, drawing on both their own specific professional logic *and* the shared modular vision. Austin et al. (2018) studied the mechanism through which actors who operate in contexts with multiple institutional logic cope. They identified a number of different scenarios:

- Conflict: Actors will engage in conflicts with each other over whose logic is most appropriate.
- Compromise: Actors can create a compromise, a new local logic blended from different institutional logics. The compromise then replaces the mono-professional logics.
- Decoupling: Actors can decouple their logics by hiding and not drawing on their own professional logic but adhering to the dominant logic of the organisation.

We found that in this study case, actors create a fourth option: they develop "double vision" which enables them to "live with" multiple logics simultaneously. Everybody seems to have made an effort over time to create meaning that bridges a variety of institutional logics with a shared modular vision. One of the ways of doing this was to position the shared vision (the rehabilitation of the offender) as the primary goal. The dictates of the institutional logic are a parallel goal. The prison therefore operates with a double vision. This is what the local manager is doing in the quote below:

> *... and then of course that the execution of the punishment which we have here is undertaken in a safe and responsible way.* (Interview with local manager)

When he says: "*…and then of course…*", this is his way of acknowledging that the administration of punishment and ensuring the security of the public and prison staff is also a goal of the prison.

One of the ways these multiple goals are able to co-exist is by a double vision working through an uneven distribution of attention to the multiple goals. Punishment and ensuring the security of the public are not given much attention in the interviews. Neither employees nor management draws on the punitive vision to make sense of their own activities. They draw on a resocialisation vision. Their focus is on facilitating a development process that leads to the inmates' mastering of more areas of their lives in preparation for their release.

An aspect of this that enables the co-existence of logics is *not* using the single professional logic as a resource in sensemaking about the job and organisation, but instead drawing on the shared vision. If the local manager primarily used the institutional logic of the prison service as a narrative resource or cue in his sensemaking, he would be expanding on his identity as someone who keeps society safe. He emphasises control when making sense of his actions and when asked about a challenge he is particularly proud of handling, it related to punishment and security. In parallel, however, he is able to help inmates master life skills. We found a similar pattern of double vision and "living with" multiple logics among the other professions.

Pliable Metaphors

Another narrative mechanism which feeds sensemaking processes that can sustain cross-institutional collaboration is the use of pliable metaphors. The metaphors are pliable in the sense that they can be moulded and appropriated into different logics. An example of a pliable metaphor is "finding the key".

> *… Sometimes we struggle to find that key." Interviewer: "Yes, and what can it be, that key?" Local manager: "No, well it can be very different things.*

> *Because it is, what I sometimes think is a strength, because that* - pause – *sometimes it is leisure time or it is the prison ward who finds it. Sometimes it is the school, sometimes it is the car workshop or* (the name of the social worker), *right?* (Interview with local manager)

The metaphor "finding the key" can easily be appropriated into a number of logics. It basically means to succeed or make progress on whatever terms are dominant in that institutional field, the same as the expression "to master". Actors from different professions also use the metaphor "family" and position themselves as "parents". The metaphors are pliable since they lend themselves to being translated into something meaningful in many different logics. As long as actors do not emphasise details about what the key is or exactly how the inmates show that they "master" an arena, or exactly what a "parent" does, they are able to feel like a unit.

The modular vision, double vision, and the use of pliable metaphors are all parts of the narrative practice that enables different professionals working in the prison regularly together to make sense of their collaboration.

Tools, Documents and Related Practices

Tools and documents appeared to be central to the practices, which underpinned cross-institutional collaboration. We identified a number of different types of tools and documents used in the prison context. These included written guidelines or concepts developed as tools for various interventions into the development of the inmate. These included screening tools to be used for example in risk assessment (see Chapters 10 and 11 of this volume), tools for documenting the development of the inmate on various parameters, and "structuring" documents laying out guidelines, e.g. for meetings.

We make a distinction between three types of tools enacted as being (1) uni-professional (for exclusive use by one profession), (2) multi-professional (laying out a number of professions fulfilling each their role) or (3) pan-professional (not associated exclusively with any one profession or institutional logic). The two later tools are described in more detail below since they are particularly interesting in regard to enabling cross-professional practice.

Multi-professional Structuring Documents

The cross-institutional collaboration in the prison was structured by a number of documents. One key document sets out the framework of the Responsibility Group Meeting (RGM). The purpose of these meetings is explained in the quote from the document below.

> *"Agenda for Responsibility Group" Meetings (RGM)*
> *The RGMs are the inmate's meetings and are held to support the inmate and his rehabilitation process. The goal of the meeting is to give the RGM a better insight into the situation of the inmate, and a good understanding of his goals. It structures the work, and improves cooperation internally and externally."*

The shared vision for the prison, as mentioned above, is to help inmates master the different arenas of their lives. The RGMs are enacted as being important events where progress on prisoners' set goals are discussed and plans for future progress made. The meetings are held approximately a month after arrival, before the release, and every three months during the inmates' time at the prison.

Each prison officer functions as contact for four inmates. The written instructions for the RGMs states that these "contact officers" chair the meetings for their inmates. He or she invites key stakeholders to the meeting, sets the agenda together with the inmate and writes minutes from the meetings. Our observations and interviews indicated that the practice at the RGMs generally did reflect these instructions. According to the RGM framework document, the participants invited by the contact officer are: The inmate, a representative from the prison workshop where the inmate works, the school, leisure, health care, a social worker and other relevant parties. The document also outlines that all of those areas should be given consideration at the meeting. It is therefore a multi-professional structuring document.

The document structures collaboration in two ways: (1) it ensures that a variety of professions meet regularly and (2) it outlines that they all have something equally important to contribute.

We found another example of a multi-professional structuring document in the shape of the admissions form. This form is the basis for deciding whether to allow a transfer of an inmate from a higher security prison to the lower security rehabilitation prison.

Pan-Professional Tools

We observed an occasion of a nurse and a social worker pouring over a new guide to intervention conversations with inmates who had slipped back into at least one instance of substance abuse. The written guide itself was not associated with a specific profession, and these two local actors did not recognise it as such. This tool was thus enacted as a pan-professional tool for intervention.

The analysis above leads us to believe that the use of multi- and pan-professional tools and documents can underpin sustained collaboration to a higher extent than tools and documents, which are enacted uniprofessionally. Further research into this area should be encouraged.

We are using the term "being enacted as" rather than "being" to emphasise that the effect of drawing on a tool or document is not given by the physical attributes of the artefact in itself but is produced through the social process of enacting the attributes of the artefact. Consider for example the tool of introducing meetings with prisoners where they reflect on their needs and plans (so-called intervention conversations). These could be enacted by nursing staff alone, as a mono-professional tool, the outcome of which could be shared with social workers, for instance, but to which the latter could make no contribution or challenge. However, the same tool was instead enacted as a pan-professional tool in which social workers, nurses and the offender worker together during these interventions, which became a key element of their shared collaborative practice.

Is it enacted as a pan-professional tool or as a mono-professional tool? This can of course be explicitly stated on the artefact, but we would still contend that the key practice is the enactment of the tool.

Pattern of Meetings

We have already touched upon the patterns of interaction in the analysis above. In this section, we examine further this third aspect of the shared practice: Who meets whom and how often?

Actors with different professional backgrounds met frequently: They have desks at the prison, often in the same building. They eat lunch together. They participate in social activities together with each other and with the inmates. They meet in clusters as ordered by the perceived needs of the inmates in connection with the RGMs. They have "faggruppemøter", which are cross-professional meetings held at the production workshops where prisoners worked during the day. Farming, auto mechanics, the kitchen, professionals from the school, and the social services get together on a weekly basis and discuss each inmate's situation and progress. They have Monday morning meetings. The local manager explains that there is a representative from each department at these meetings. Formally, Monday morning meetings do not include employees not employed and paid by the prison. However, representatives from the imported services—such as the school and health services—are also present. This indicates that besides the formal organisational chart, there is a "ghost"-chart which includes and integrates the imported functions and in effect organises the work at the prison.

The Prisoner Forum is another multi-professional meeting. It is a closed forum meeting that impacts the other shared practices in the prison, in that it is a primary formal and actual decision-making forum. Actors do not take ownership of the decisions of this forum. They just treat them as *fait-a-complis*. The forum decides on prisoners' requests for early release, leave and other permissions.

Overall there is much and frequent interaction across the many professions who work in the prison. School advisors/teachers, health care services (nurses) and the prison officers seem to be the ones who are the most integrated into patterns of interaction. This in spite of the codes of confidentiality under which health care operate. The priest is also quite integrated and is for example sometimes invited to RGMs by the inmate. He has a desk in the prison, but also operates under comprehensive codes of confidentiality that restricts the communication about the prisoners with other professionals. The priest is a less frequent participant in meetings. The doctor is far less integrated in the patterns of interaction although he works in the prison on a regular basis. This may be due to his higher wage and the time constraints that shape his workday. The librarian also has a desk in the prison and is employed elsewhere, but he or she does not appear in any of our data.

So, the pattern of interaction is characterised by widespread and frequent interaction across professional boundaries. The following notes are from the Sunday coffee chat with the advisor from the school:

> *School advisor*: *We have worked at it since I started in '95–96. We bring each other on trips with the inmates all the time. We have respect and knowledge about each other's areas of expertise. ...*
>
> *Interviewer*: *Well, I think that you need shared experiences, to develop a shared culture.*
>
> *School advisor*: *Exactly! We go on trips together all the time. And we see each other SO often. We have Christmas lunch together as we did last week, we "hygger" (have a cosy time together). We do so much together, and we talk so much across all employees. And then we have all these meetings together. The RGMs are really important. That is where we hear each other's thoughts about the inmate. We have "faggruppemøter" every day where I go in turn to one of the four different workshops with one of the social workers. There we talk about the inmates who work there. That means that we get to talk about all the inmates once a week. Then we agree on what we say to the inmates. They get the same message regardless of whether they go to their contact officer or to a health care worker or to the workshop foreman or to me at the school (Interview with educational advisor).*

Their pattern of interaction is in part aimed at sharing information about the inmates and ensuring a unified strategy and response towards the inmate across professions. The meaning they attach to the importance of an unified response to the inmates is twofold: first it is to ensure that they apply pressure and support in an unified way to be able to reach the inmate as much as possible. But, second, it is also to avoid that the inmates "divide and rule" by playing actors out against each other.

Discussion

The analysis has identified three shared practices (Fig. 4.1), which have been central to sustaining collaboration within the prison. One is the narrative practice of reproducing a modular vision, the use of double vision and pliable metaphors, which lend themselves to translation into multiple institutional logics. The second is a use of pan-professional tools and documents that are not explicitly linked to any singular profession, and the use of multi-professional tools and documents, which are explicitly linked to a range of different professions. The third is the pattern of shared meetings. These three practices have not emerged in isolation, and they are not sustained in isolation. They are all mutually constitutive meaning these practices mutually shape each other in essential ways.

The sensemaking perspective helps us be more attentive to how the three practices shape each other. This is illustrated by the double arrows in Fig. 4.1. The first arrow is between meetings and narratives/metaphors. The pliable metaphors and modular narratives create a sense that we, as professionals, are in this together. This legitimises spending time and resources on a pattern of frequent shared cross-professional meetings. The pattern of shared meetings is not only sustained by the shared metaphors and narratives but in turn, the meetings also sustain these shared narratives. This happens through the mechanism of actions driving meaning (Weick, 1995). In this case, repeated shared actions (e.g. meetings) are places where shared retrospective and prospective sensemaking about collaboration take place and where being a "we" is expressed through the metaphors and narratives.

The second arrow is between the pattern of meetings and the tools and documents. The tools and documents are used to order the pattern of meetings. They outline which professions are expected to contribute at which meeting and how. Conversely, the tools and documents only affect actions if they are enacted (followed) and not ignored at meetings. So the actions at meetings affect the status and importance of documents and tools.

The last double arrow is between narratives and tools/documents. The meaning attached to the tools and documents is shaped by and through the shared language (narratives and metaphors). Conversely, the tools and documents also affect the narratives because they act as indicators of the nature of the cooperation between professions. In this manner, the three practices are continuously shaped and reshaped by each other in an ongoing process. There is not any single factor, which precedes and decisively shapes the others.

The purpose of the analysis was to examine which practices enable the dual process of sensemaking and collaborating across institutional logics. We found three mutually co-constituting aspects of the practice developed in the prison, which together provide a way to straddle multiple institutional logics.

As already indicated, we suggest that the practice developed is characterised by multiple institutional logics "living with each other" rather than being a compromise or negotiated blending. As emphasised by Austin et al. (2018), in many approaches to organisational analysis, different logics need to be resolved, perhaps by one prevailing over the other (Eikhof & Haunschild, 2007). However, Austin et al. propose that an open attitude towards rendering conflicting influences "conversant" (i.e. co-existing without resorting to compromise), is more productive than attempting to resolve the conflict. To be "conversant" is to include another's work as part of one's own. This is very different from compromise, they stress, since the latter resolves conflict by modifying (usually, reducing) one's own objective in order to allow that the other might also attempt to realise a diminished version of his or her objective. "Other" and "own" are overcome in the ensemble (Austin et al., 2018, p. 1515).

We find that the way the practices identified in the prison "live with each other" in some respects resonate with Austin et al.'s findings on how different logics may become conversant. However, there are also important differences: When analysing the mechanisms through which the two logics of economy and aesthetics can live with each other in the same organisation, Austin et al. suggest that this happens through a shared insistence that no one owns the work, that roles given to the representatives are not confining and that actors speak on behalf of each other. There should further be a shared commitment to frequent, shared conversations and parity of status between actors and that any outcomes of cooperation/negotiation between the parties maintain the values/qualities that are deemed important by the respective logics. Hereby conflicting logics meet in conversation without either being dulled or compromised. Each contributes a special point of view, together creating a new vision. This is the equivalent of an orchestra, the symphony they create being the product of the contribution of each individual musician and their instrument.

However, in the prison, it was not a conscious strategy for the actors in our case to avoid being confined by roles. There just seemed to be a dynamic in their interaction that allowed them to oscillate in and out of their own and others' institutionalised roles. They did share ownership of the joint outcome with each other and the inmate and they showed a commitment to shared conversations just as they narrated that all arenas were of equal importance. However, they did not seek, nurture or value conflict between different perspectives. In the prison, we did not find much explicit sensemaking about conflict or observe actual conflict. There can be a number of reasons for this, one of which may be that the professionals consciously seek unity in their response to the inmates.

Providing support that ensures an inmate's life, well-being and participation, requires the integration of many different professional domains. This organising principle means professionals employed by different organisations, each with different institutional logics, will work at the same physical location with the same citizens and with the same overall purpose. In the context of demand for greater interagency collaboration between professional groups, it becomes important to understand the specific practices, which may underpin such collaboration. To do this, in this chapter, we explored specifically which practices in the Norwegian prison setting, are pivotal in underpinning the shared sensemaking processes that enabled actors to collaborate despite different institutional logics.

We identified three aspects of the shared practice through which different and potentially competing institutional logics live together in the prison—without resorting to compromise or conflict. These include a modular narrative, use of pliable metaphors, pan- and multi-professional artefacts, and frequent and widespread interaction.

We suggest that the shared practices in the prison function through a sensemaking process, where professionals in the prison have become able to oscillate between the institutionalised logic of their profession and a shared logic centred on the inmate (the citizen). Lastly, we found that they had developed a pattern of frequent interaction between the multiple professions who work at the prison—interactions that were both work related as well as social. We suggest that the practices of the studied prison can be seen as a case of different institutional logics "living with" each other rather than a case of compromising or resolving contradictions. However, it is a "living with" which gives conflict another role than the one in the practices of "living with" identified by Austin et al. (2018). We have here emphasised the meta-nature of the shared narrative, the use of metaphors and the role of the tools and documents.

References

Austin, R., Hjorth, D., & Hessel, S. (2018). How aesthetics and economy become conversant in creative firms. *Organization Studies, 39*(11), 1501–1519.

Czarniawska-Joerges, B. (2007). *Shadowing: And other techniques for doing fieldwork in modern societies.* Copenhagen Business School Press DK.

DiMaggio, P. J., & Powell, W. W. (1991). The iron cage revisited: Institutional isomorphism and collective rationality. In W. W. Powell & P. DiMaggio (Eds.), *The new institutionalism in organizational analysis.* Chicago, IL: University of Chicago Press.

Eikhof, D. R., & Haunschild, A. (2007). For art's sake! Artistic and economic logics in creative production. *Journal of Organizational Behavior, 28,* 523–538.

Engeström, Y., Virkkunen, J., Helle, M., Pihlaja, J., & Poikela, R. (1996). The change laboratory as a tool for transforming work. *Lifelong Learning in Europe, 1*(2), 10–17.

Fridhov, I. M., & Langelid, T. (2017). Importmodellen i norsk fengselsvesen. *Nordisk Tidsskrift for Kriminalvidenskab, 104*(3), 259–288.

Friedland, R., & Alford, R. R. (1991) Bringing society back in: Symbols, practices, and institutional contradictions. In W. W. Powell & P. DiMaggio (Eds.), *The new institutionalism in organizational analysis* (pp. 232–263). Chicago: University of Chicago Press.

Glaser, B. G., & Straus, A. L. (2017). *Discovery of grounded theory: Strategies for qualitative research*. New York: Routledge.

Murphy, T. (2015). *Sensemaking - Introduktion til Karl Weick*. København: Hans Reitzels Forlag.

Pache, A. C., & Santos, F. (2013). Inside the hybrid organization: Selective coupling as a response to competing institutional logics. *Academy of Management Journal, 56*(4), 972–1001.

Reay, T., & Hinings, C. R. (2009). Managing the rivalry of competing institutional logics. *Organization Studies.*

Roethlisberger, F. J., & Dickson, W. J. (1939). *Management and the Worker*. Bristol: Thoemmes.

Sandberg, J., & Tsoukas, H. (2015). Making sense of the sensemaking perspective: Its constituents, limitations, and opportunities for further development. *Journal of Organizational Behavior, 36,* 6–32.

Taylor, F. W. (2011/1916). The principles of scientific management. In J. M. Shafritz, J. S. Ott, & Y. S. Jang (pp. 65–76). New York: Wadsworth Cengage Learning.

Tracey, P., Phillips, N., & Jarvis, O. (2011). Bridging institutional entrepreneurship and the creation of new organizational forms: A multilevel model. *Organization Science*: orsc.1090.0522.

Weick K.E. (1969/1979). *The social psychology of organizing*. Reading, MA: Addison-Wesley.

Weick, K. E. (1995). *Sensemaking in organizations.* Thousand Oaks, CA: Sage.

Weick, K. E. (2001). *Making sense of the organization.* Blackwell Business, MA: Malden.

Weick, K. E. (2004). A bias for conversation: Acting discursively in organizations. In D. Grant, C. Hardy, C. Oswick, & L. Putnam (red.), *The SAGE handbook of organizational discourse.* London: Sage.

Weick, K. E., Sutcliffe, K. M., & Obstfeld, D. (2005). Organizing and the process of sensemaking. *Organization Science, 16*(4), 409–421.

5

The Application of Norwegian Humane Ideals by Front-Line Workers When Collaboratively Reintegrating Inmates Back into Society

William Dugdale and Sarah Hean

Introduction

Traditionally, prison systems and their administrations have a strong focus upon the principles of punishment to ensure prisoners are effectively held accountable for their actions. This is balanced by the belief that prison may also serve as a site for rehabilitation (Maruna & Immarigeon, 2004). The argument over the delivery of prisoner rehabilitation has been a long-standing issue within criminology: the *What Works* debate questions the effectiveness of this, exploring the methods used to address a prisoner's needs and thereby reduce rates of reoffending (McGuire, 1995; Ward & Maruna, 2007). In order to successfully reduce

W. Dugdale (✉) · S. Hean
Bournemouth University, Bournemouth, UK
e-mail: wdugdale@bournemouth.ac.uk

S. Hean
University of Stavanger, Stavanger, Norway
e-mail: Sarah.c.hean@uis.no

S. Hean et al. (eds.), *Improving Interagency Collaboration, Innovation and Learning in Criminal Justice Systems*,
https://doi.org/10.1007/978-3-030-70661-6_5

reoffending, empirical evidence has increasingly supported the view that rehabilitation and reintegration ought to be the prime focus for front-line staff working with inmates rather than merely punishment (Andrews & Bonta, 2010).

In comparative criminology, Nordic countries, including Norway, are consistently portrayed as exceptions to the global move towards growing rates of imprisonment and *tough on crime* polices with less welfare-orientation (Pratt, 2008a, 2008b). A balance of control versus rehabilitation is typified in the Norwegian prison system (Ugelvik, 2016), where policy aims to create conditions that seek to minimise prisoner deprivation, fear and suffering (Pratt & Eriksson, 2011). The Norwegian prison system is widely regarded worldwide for its focus on prisoner treatment, rehabilitation and successful reintegration in the society with low reoffending rates of 20%, in contrast with other European countries such as England and Wales that have a reoffending rate of 45% (Fazel & Wolf, 2015; Pakes & Holt, 2017). Although Norwegian prisons, the well-known Halden and Bastøy for example, are said to refrain from inflicting further punishment upon prisoners, nevertheless, Jewkes (2020) calls for prison sociologists to subject prisons in Norway to rigorous empirical scrutiny.

Prisoner rehabilitation and reintegration requires careful interprofessional collaborative practice, provided by multiple key workers from different professional backgrounds and organisations (World Health Organization, 2010). Collaborative practice serves as an effective strategy to cope with the pressures within the prison environment and through group effort, improve the capacity for organisational personnel to work together (Bond & Gittell, 2010; Wolff et al., 2013). Effective interprofessional collaboration generally is recognised as an active way of improving outcomes and the cost-effectiveness of care, but contributions are required from a range of professionals' competencies and skills across various services. Professionals, working with the complex care needs of a population and resource shortages, must therefore be able to work collaboratively in interprofessional teams/groups to mitigate challenges and ensure consistent, continuous, and reliable care (Bainbridge et al., 2010; WHO, 2010). It is also necessary to expand opportunities for innovation between these services. Studies on interprofessional practice enable an analysis of the drivers and barriers of collaboration with the practices among services being examined (Sørensen & Torfing, 2011). Research has shown the importance of collaboration within prisons (Wolff et al., 2013) and Hean, Ødegård, et al. (2017), Hean, Willumsen, et al. (2017), Hean et al. (2018) have called for expanding knowledge on how this collaboration manifests and functions in this context. However, the processes of collaboration in this context are underexplored and requires field analysis of professional practice. There is a need for clarity in these collaboration processes across services as a mismatch in expectations creates unclear or disjoined working activity. Disparity can also blur the line of responsibility for resource provision. Research is therefore required to explore how services work collaboratively together.

This chapter explores interprofessional collaborative practice in the Norwegian prison context. It discusses findings from two immersive case studies (Yin, 2014) in eastern Norway, that explored specifically the perspectives of collaborative practices held by front-line professionals working in a particular Norwegian prison context, the transitional residence (*overgangbolig*). The chapter explores specifically one key issue that arose from this analysis, namely how the humane traditions that underpin the Norwegian prison system were manifested at the ground-level by front-line professionals, promoting their collaborative practices while working together towards prisoner reintegration. It contributes to debate on how the foundational policies of differing European prison systems underpin front-line prison practice. We discuss how the contrasting punitive and rehabilitative/reintegrative ideals manifest, particularly in the daily work and interactions with each other and with prisoners. In other words, we explore how the humane traditions of the Norwegian system impact prison-based practices and the implications for front-line personnel and the collaborative nature of their work.

Humane Traditions in Norway

Nordic countries are considered to maintain more humane prison regimes because of their distinctive welfare state models. In Norway, for example, this model is rooted in strong cultures of equality, social solidarity and cohesion (Pratt & Eriksson, 2011). As a welfare state, the main goals of the Norwegian state is to give members of society the best possible conditions to maximise their own potential while remaining free to control him/herself and administer their own freedom (Foucault, 2007). Various services and front-line staff operationalise this goal of the welfare state when working together in prison on the common objective of rehabilitation and reintegration (Ugelvik, 2012, 2016; Smith & Ugelvik, 2017).

Norwegian prison officer training and practice emphasises the humanistic side of the prison establishment (Bruhn et al., 2017) and organisational penal policy, such as the Norwegian government White Paper no. 37 (2008) *Criminal punishment—Less crime—Safer society*, outlines the key principles of security, rehabilitation, and reintegration. In this policy, rehabilitative and reintegrative work is considered central components of the prison sentence. It spells out explicitly that the professional practice within prisons is founded on a humanistic view that prisoners deserve equal treatment to that of the general population and that their debt to society has been paid once the sentence is completed. It takes the stance that reoffending rates may be reduced through the rehabilitation work of the Prison Service and that life within prison and out in community have to be as similar as possible. If the sentence is to work, the reintegration of a person must be planned and cared for in a good way to ensure the goal of a successful return to society is achieved. The humanist principles and values of the Norwegian prison system are also enforced in the Norwegian government White Paper no. 12 (2014) *Development plan for capacity in the correctional care.* The document recognises that prisoners should be seen as equal, have self-worth, be given choices and express creativity and that a convicted person must take responsibility for their own life and actions both during and after completion of a sentence.

The values enshrined into the above documents, and in the Norwegian prison system overall, can be summarised by four key principles: the principles of justice, normality, progression, and proximity (Norwegian government White Paper no. 37, 2008). The *principle of justice* indicates that it is in fact the detention itself which is the punishment, thus the convicted person should not lose other civil rights. The *principle of normality* implies that a person's existence during a sentence shall be as equal as possible to life elsewhere in society, while the *principle of progression* is one that means during a sentence the conditions of confinement should gradually become less strict for a convicted person. This means the prisoner gains more freedom the closer the prisoner is to the completion of a sentence. Lastly, the *principle of proximity* indicates that convicted persons should be held in prisons as close to their home location as possible with the purpose to prevent social isolation and enable contact with family and the local community during their sentence. These humane principles written into the Norwegian penal policy direct professional practice in such a way to reduce the negative influences of a person's sentence (e.g. institutionalisation).

In operationalising these humane traditions, greater demands have been placed on prison service personnel to collaborate with outside health and welfare services to obtain proper housing, work, training, or other measures that can contribute to a lawful life for the inmates after release (Execution of Sentences Act, 2002; Kriminalomsorgen, 2005; Norwegian Ministry of Justice and Public Security, 2017). Supporting inmates in this way has been listed as a shared responsibility between agencies necessitating collaborative interprofessional relationships. The prison becomes part of a network of government agencies, volunteer organisations, and other services that together support change in the individual prisoner. Effective collaboration between all relevant bodies is essential if the rehabilitative and reintegration process is to be successful. The importance of cross-agency and management cooperation is recognised in the Norwegian penal code (Execution of Sentences Act, 2002), in the Kriminalomsorgen (2005) *Occupational Guidelines for Correctional Care* and manifested in the national educational curriculum of prison officers (Bruhn et al., 2017), cooperation agreements and joint instructions between agencies.

Despite the necessity for collaboration outlined above, the way collaborative practice may actually contribute or arise from the humane prison traditions and the link of this to the debated success of the Norwegian system are largely underexplored. This chapter therefore explores the impact of these traditions on prison practices and the implications for collaborative practice.

A focus on front-line staff is important first because of their close contact with the prisoner. At the front-line level, prison officers in their daily work are expected to guard, help, care for, and motivate those sent to prison, a fact that promotes a need for close collaboration to work with other service providers including health and welfare agencies (Smith & Ugelvik, 2017). Front-line staff are also those individuals who in their occupational role implement the aims and policies of government. As such they dictate how the values and principles written in policy documents are implemented in the prison system (Bruhn et al., 2017). Fundamentally, front-line professionals are the crucial individuals, known by Lipsky (2010) as the street-level bureaucrats in public service employment, who perform their day-to-day work under certain structured conditions. These are the individuals who experience and undertake the critical roles that constitute the services recommended by the state. At the ground level, the public service workers interact directly with citizens in the course of their jobs with personal authority and discretion in how they deliver government policy. These front-line personnel have a considerable impact on people's lives. The work undertaken by front-line staff therefore mediates the relationship between citizens and the state (Lipsky, 2010), and their actions, including their collaborative actions, will ultimately dictate the effectiveness of prisoner rehabilitation and reintegration.

Transitional Residences

In line with the principle of progression in the Norwegian prison system, prisoners move from a high or low security (open) prison to a half-way house, also referred to as a transitional residence, to serve the final part of their sentence before being released back into the community (Johnsen & Fridhov, 2018). Known of as an *Overgangsbolig*, a transitional residence or half-way house is still a prison with clear control protocols. These prisons are typically perceived as less restrictive than other prisons with open conditions allowing inmates to have more freedom to attend work or education and live in the community as normally as possible. For an inmate to be transferred here it must be appropriate for the promotion of positive development and to reduce reoffending. Typically, an inmate has between three and eighteen months remaining of their prison sentence to be eligible to stay in the residence. The timeframe allows professionals an extended period to work with an inmate on their needs for living, work, and training. While residing at the prison, inmates must pay rent and agree to partake in either work or education outside the prison during the completion of their sentence. Through this process, collaboration with other services and professionals should take place to help rehabilitate inmates and plan for release and reintegration into society.

The transitional prison is a useful context in which to study collaborative practice because the provision of services at the transitional residence opposes the more commonplace service integration model, typically referred to as the *Import Model*, employed in prisons in Norway.

The Import Model was introduced into criminal justice policy and implemented in Norwegian prisons (Christie, 1970). It dictated that health and welfare services offered by the prisons are provided by the municipality in which the prison is located and not the prison itself (Bjørngaard et al., 2009). Ordinary authorities such as education and health services take responsibility for providing welfare and care in prison. Preceding this, services provided by doctors, nurses, and others were employed directly by the prison system. The intention of the Import Model is that by providing external health/welfare professionals, prison services are held to account by the external scrutiny of outside services and also that prisoners receive the same service as that provided by the general population.

In transitional prisons the Import Model falls away due to the freer conditions of the prisoners and the need to get prisoners more able to access external services for themselves in the community (Dugdale, 2020). Staff from other Norwegian prisons, health services such as the DPS (specialised psychiatric outpatient service) or NAV (the labour and welfare service) do not enter the transitional residences. Exploring collaborative practices in this context makes an interesting contrast to the study for collaborative practices elsewhere in Norway in high-security prisons (Hean, Ødegård, et al., 2017; Hean, Willumsen, et al., 2017) where the Import Model is in place. To develop collaborative working, there is a need to understand and assess organisational level effects of collaboration to further inform and innovate future practice and policy (Hean et al., 2011). Through examining organisational work, the key features of learning can be identified in work settings to promote and develop new forms of collaborative provision (Warmington et al., 2004). Cultural-Historical Activity Theory (CHAT) is considered particularly useful in this context by focusing on issues such as complex interactions, relationships, and their challenges to widen understanding of issues such as organisational learning, change, and collective knowledge creation (Engeström et al., 2007; Allen et al., 2011). In this penal context, CHAT is viewed as a constructive lens to theorise organisations through the activity systems model to identify the participants, their motivation, roles, and actions (Foot, 2014). As a theoretical framework, CHAT has been applied in organisational research to articulate the activity systems in which people collaborate the practical activities and their social origins (Blackler, 1993, 1995, 2009). This theoretical framework has been employed to gain an organisational view of collaborative practice as we consider the humane traditions and norms of the Norwegian prison system as a key mediating factor of professionals' ideals, and consequently the collaborative nature of their work.

Underpinning the research questions of this study (see Dugdale, 2020), CHAT has been used to analyse and describe the elements of organisational work being undertaken by the specific individuals of interest in the activity (Engeström, 1987, 1999, 2000, 2001). The core components of the activity system model, namely the object, tools, subject, community, rules, and division of labour, have been employed as analytical lenses to explore the interactions between these components and theorise the nature of collaboration practice. As the prime inquiry in this chapter, we consider the main findings from the subjects in this context to detail their agency and the applied ideals in the daily work with prisoners before they are released. The importance of the subjects' agency is that it is understood as the ability to construct and transform an individual's own work activity. An individual's agency is seen to depend not only on their own individual capabilities, but it is devised by other external factors such as the social norms of collaboration in the activity (Virkkunen, 2006). To account for the collaborative practices at the transitional residences in Norway, we have used CHAT to explore the link between the humane traditions/norms of this prison system which are clearly applied through the ideals of these front-line workers.

Methods

A case study approach (Yin, 2014) was employed as a form of inquiry and relied on multiple sources of data collection to collect rich and in-depth descriptive data at two sites, namely the transitional residence. Immersive methods of data collection within prison-oriented research such as observations, shadowing, and semi-structured interviews. These were employed as they have proved to be important tools to build descriptive detail and uncovering the truth about the work undertaken within prisons (Liebling et al., 1999; Drake et al., 2015). To build an effective account of the prison system, a review of policy documentation released by the Norwegian government and the criminal justice system (*Kriminalomsorgen*) was conducted. This highlighted the key values and principles guiding staff.

Front-line professionals, such as prison officers, were a focus as they are the key individuals in undertaking daily prison practice. Employed by the Correctional Service, the purposeful sample of front-line staff were predominantly from a social work or prison-based background. The front-line professionals of the first case study encompassed six contact prison officers (equitable to prison officers in other European contexts), four social workers, and a nurse with pharmaceutical training to handle and manage the medication within the prison. The second case study incorporated six prison contact officers and five social workers.

The empirical data was collected through two months of immersive and observational fieldwork at each transitional residence, and specifically the front-line staff, including observations, shadowing a contact officer and social worker at each site, and semi-structured interviews with front-line staff. Observations and interviews were informed by the CHAT framework. Although data was collected on all dimensions of the activity system, we present specifically the findings that relate to the subjects' ideals.

As part of the fieldwork procedure, researchers participated and immersed themselves into the cultural web of the prison, becoming a part of it as much as possible. Similarly, the process was for the researcher to think, act, communicate, and feel as someone positioned in the web and needs to be emotionally, intellectually, and physically present (Ugelvik, 2014). To analyse the data, Template Analysis (King, 2004, 2012) was utilised as it has been demonstrated to be a clearly defined and flexible analytical method that refers to a group of techniques for thematically organising and analysing textual data. The key features which typify it are its flexibility of the coding structure, lack of prescription regarding levels of hierarchical coding, the use of a priori themes, and the iterative development and use of an initial template. A full description of the theoretical framework, empirical material, and iterative process of the analysis is presented elsewhere (see Dugdale, 2020).

Both case studies had 11 front-line professionals employed at each transitional residence, with space for 16 male and female inmates at the first case site, and 20 male inmates at the second. The prison leader and management were influential figures reinforcing the working principles at both prison sites and valuing the front-liners' autonomy, discretion, and input. Notably, the convicted persons at these prisons are formally considered inmates, yet both sets of professionals referred to them as clients or residents to reduce stigma and aid their transition back into community. To account for the sensitivity of the professionals' terminology in these findings, the term client will be referred to in place of inmate or prisoner. In both cases, each client was allocated one or two prison professionals as a contact officer to support their reintegration needs.

Front-Line Reintegrative Practice

The following section displays the centrality of front-line practice at the two prisons studied. The "*objects*" of the practices of staff observed here highlight the premise and key goals of the work undertaken by them at the two sites: the professionals' aim to socialise the clients and assist them access community-based services.

Referring firstly to socialisation, the clients had spent several years, and in some examples more than 10–15 years in prison. Therefore a prime aim of the professionals was to continue or begin the process of socially training the clients to live back in society. They did so through continuously re-evaluating and monitoring the prisoners' needs or lifestyle by becoming familiar with each client's routines, their problems, and daily happenings in their life. By working closely with each client, the staff ensured they were collectively familiar with the clients' well-being and their daily activities through regular interactions, such as informal conversations or one-to-one meetings. Similarly, these efforts were also about providing tailored one-to-one support based on the different needs and lifestyles of each client, required while living at the residence and planning for their return to the community (e.g. welfare including accommodation and finances, employment, education, physical, and mental health). Supportive relationships between offender/client and professional were therefore essential to develop openness and trust between the two parties. These relations were crucial to promote the clients' empowerment, reflect on the options available, and ensure the clients were taking primary responsibility for their daily activities. As a process, socialisation involved staff responding to the clients' needs, encouraging positive action or behaviour at the residence, and replicating a lifestyle that facilitated the prisoners' reintegration back into society.

Recognising the second main object, the staff at these residences also ensured that the clients were accessing services which were based externally from the prison. The staff worked closely with each client to support access to the differing services in the community such as the welfare service NAV. However, it was primarily the responsibility of each client themselves to obtain the necessary specialised care or assistance in society as it would be a process they would be maintaining independently upon release. The staff distinguished between clients that were able to access services themselves, whereas others either did not have the knowledge or confidence to do so and therefore a professional would step up to assist such as making phone calls or attending appointments. We now consider the subjects at both transitional residences which articulated the professional ideals that underpin their daily tasks and were operationalised into practice.

Professional Ideals

Case Study One

At the *first case study*, the front-line professionals—the contact officers, social workers, and the nurse—had shared values of attempting to normalise the lives of clients. They provided a normal as possible structure for clients to aid their return to society and prevent them from returning to prison in the future. In pursing this, professionals envisaged themselves as motivational roles models:

> *that they believe in themselves, I try to make them believe in them self. To look at things easier.* (contact officer one)

Each staff member wanted to do their best for the client as the long-term vision was to normalise their lives by having proactive routines such as having a job, educational course, or completing other domestic tasks. There was a collective consciousness with very little differentiation between the working ideals despite their contrasting educational/professional backgrounds. The focus was to be a person that the clients were able to look up to and be motivated by to change for the better. By actively reaching out, a professional would get to know each client's difficulties or flaws and attempt to influence positive behaviour or action. A key motivation for the professionals was that they wanted to work directly with people to provide "*love and care*" (social worker one) rather than excessively exerting punishment upon them while being in prison.

> *that we do our best to make, to help people become their best, becoming someone's neighbour, going back into society and you don't do that by punishing obviously but by helping in some way.* (contact officer two)

Professionals viewed themselves as influential figures for the clients to live normally at the transitional residence and encourage a positive change for their future life in the community,

> *we also have better possibility to influence them, to maybe do some positive things for themselves.* (contact officer three)

They articulated their work as being extremely meaningful as they were able to help individuals from difficult backgrounds to motivate and harness a meaningful life. The staff did not intend to harass or treat clients as if they were being watched, but to create a harmonious atmosphere that allowed the clients to live with increased autonomy to upkeep their own daily routines. Collectively, these outlooks emphasised the personable and responsive approach with each client rather than being overly controlling or exerting authority upon them. As part of daily life at the prison, the staff put humane treatment at the forefront of their work activity through manifesting a mutual respect and a sense of equality which built strong bonds between the staff and clients, "*I think it's more of the personality and how we treat people*" (nurse).

The professional work activity in the organisation was a balancing act of support and control at the prison. However, broadly speaking, security procedures and incidents were limited at the prison. It was seen as a time to build relations, interact and work closely with each client. Rather than being a restrictive place to live, the prison sentence itself was viewed as the punishment and professionals therefore wanted that clients get the most out of the remainder of their sentence. Professionals tried as much as possible to normalise the clients' lives, giving them peace of mind and tranquillity before shortly returning to society:

> *I mean the point is to normalise everything, you can't just have the prison thinking all the time, you have to get the other side too.* (social worker two)

In summary, the ideals of the professionals at the first case study were collectively to normalise the clients' lives to motivate and support them while they progressed from finishing their prison sentence towards living back in the community. Although the normalisation principle in penal policy in Norway is strictly about normalising the services and living conditions in prison, here normalisation was about normalising the convicted persons' lives at the transitional residence.

Case Study Two

At the *second case study*, the professionals employed at the transitional residence were a balance of contact officers and social workers. The ideals of their work were one of reparation by wanting to repair the damage being in prison may have caused the clients. The collective outlooks of the staff was to give clients a second chance despite the crimes they had committed. The collective motivation was therefore to treat the clients respectfully and be impartial to the severity of their offences and give them an opportunity of a new life in the community:

> *Everyone deserves another chance. I think it's important, I also have in the back of my head I also think there is a reason for what everyone, everything happens for a reason.* (contact officer two)

Staff spoke of not intending to judge them for their crimes as they wanted to treat them equally as normal citizens,

> *[Everyone] deserves respect as equal to yourself*. (social worker one)

A portion of the clients was known to have committed sex offences and the staff expressed a friendly approach to their work as they wanted to do their best for the clients and treat them equally regardless of the stigma associated with these crimes and sentences. The intentions were neither to judge nor to exert innocence or guilt upon the clients. Moreover, the collective emphasis was about working with people and their difficulties to offer a second chance of life and making amends for their mistakes,

> *I like working with people, I like to help people, I think that even the people who have done bad things they deserve a second chance.* (social worker four)

Although several clients maintained their innocence, the intent of the workers were to be impartial and hear their thoughts rather than judge them for it, including critically discussing the position of the victim and maintaining an open thought process. The staff treated the clients respectfully as any other citizen to refrain from merely reading their sentence information and having a preconceived perception about an individual.

These key workers recognised the difficult and complex backgrounds of people in prison and acknowledged the narratives of each client and their complex upbringings or lives. The professionals had extensive experience in the prison system having worked with a wide range of clients serving sentences for murder, violence, drugs, and sex offences. Despite this, the time spent at the residence was an opportunity to offer clients a second chance in life to understand their perspectives and personal challenges. Similarly, recognition was also that the reason for being in prison did not necessarily have to malicious and the clients can still be supported to be good friends, fathers, and husbands.

> *the reason behind all of it doesn't need to be evil. It could be many reasons behind it, the reason doesn't need to be the most obvious reason. It would be something else that other people didn't think or didn't know about.* (contact officer two)

Comparatively to the first case, staff expressed the importance of balancing both security and support at the prison to ensure they always kept in mind the prison principles and supportive nature of their work,

> *we should have a nice balance of security and nice a balance of the good relationship we have.* (contact officer one)

The front-liners reflected on their work experiences in other closed institutions and the importance of implementing some form of security at the residence, but that rehabilitation was the prominent focus,

> *It's mostly rehabilitation. Security, of course I have security in the back of my head because I worked 16 years in high security prison.* (contact officer two)

Balancing these principles was to ensure that the clients have an element of structure or control, but also having supportive provisions to make amends for the extensive time in a closed prison and their own difficulties. The transitional residence was also seen as a place of tranquillity and harmony to focus on rehabilitation and the clients' ensuing reintegration, but still keeping in mind the security as this was an integral part of their education or work experience that upholds the safety of prison, staff, prisoners, and the public:

> *the social side is more important now I would say, but of course we have to always have in mind that we work in a prison and that's what I always say to my colleagues.* (social worker one)

The professionals regularly reflected on their experiences at other institutions and the heightened focus on security. The increased control at closed establishments meant they were not able to spend extended periods of time alone with prisoners as it was not considered an essential or ordinary part of their work, along with always having staff safety in mind. The professionals now valued how they are able to have explicit focus on the supportive nature of their work at the transitional residence. Mutually, the ideals of the contact officers and social workers at this second case were to support the clients to make amends for their mistakes, foster their own personal development, and progress towards a life back in society.

Discussion

Beginning this discussion, these findings demonstrate the compatibility and application of the professionals' humane ideals across the two transitional residences in Norway that were translated into practice. Earlier in this chapter we presented the humane traditions/norms of the prison system that have been encapsulated into the policy and training. Thus, we consider the link between the humane traditions/norms in Norway that have been expressed in the ideals at each case study site to discuss how these ideals manifest the collaborative practices that were observed.

In line with Lipsky (2010), we have viewed how government policy is played out at the front-line in which the diverse occupations of public service personnel may entail improvisation and responsiveness to individual cases, but they are said to be embodied by an essential paradox that is highly scripted to perform and achieve relatively clear objectives derived from the political culture. Irrespective of the differing professions at the two prison sites, the application of these professional ideals reframed from having fragmented or separated service personnel. Thus, the shared welfare-orientated and humane outlooks encouraged the multi-voiced professionals at each transitional residence to reintegrate inmates back into society. In CHAT terms, the mediation between the traditions/norms of the prison system and the key front-line subjects play an important role in shaping and informing the work activity based on the origin of the subjects' social needs. This holds importance as the subjects' motivation can evolve and is viewed as a directed action towards the emerging priorities and objects (action and goals) of the activity (Miettinen, 2005).

Prisons in Norway are said to belong to a humane tradition and culture with an underpinning value of penal welfare, together with a long reputation and tradition for pursuing humanistic prison policies that embrace rehabilitation within prisons (Pratt & Eriksson, 2013). As front-line professionals are considered the key individuals who transform the aims and policies of the government and the prison system into practice (Bruhn et al. 2017), greater demands have been placed on the Correctional Service and the ideals of front-line personnel in prisons to work collaboratively. This position reflects the traditions in the Norwegian penal code to implement agreements and joint instructions to contribute towards co-creating effective positive solutions for inmates before, during, and after a sentence. These traditions illuminate the fundamental values of the prison system and the growth of collaboration between prison staff to refrain from merely punishing inmates (Execution of Sentences Act, 2002; Kriminalomsorgen, 2005). In this case, the emerging ideals at the front-line are viewed as key contributors that mediated collaborative practice at the transitional residences.

Transforming the government policies into practice is seen to not only mediate the emerging ideals of public service personnel, but also has implications for collaborative practice. As prison systems are said to amalgamate working cultures into their penal policies, local variations in the interpretation and implementation of practice can still occur possibly due to the wide array of organisations and complex working environment in prisons (Rudes & Magnuson, 2019). The work undertaken in prisons can represent challenges due to conflicting ideals to punish convicted persons, protect citizens from criminals, and rehabilitate prisoners to ensure that they desist from committing further crime upon release from prison (Griffin, 2002). The effectiveness of prisons can be inhibited by administrations that overtly focus on other punitive measures such as control. It is argued that the punitive philosophy of prison work has a detrimental effect on the performance of the organisational goals of staff within prisons. Strategies that are heavily autocratic can also undermine the social cohesion and rehabilitative work undertaken by staff in prisons (Craig, 2004). Explicitly, empirical studies in criminology and sociology have therefore increasingly supported the philosophy of rehabilitating inmates rather than merely punishing them to reduce reoffending (Ward & Maruna, 2007). As seen in these two case studies, the underpinning policies of a system can play an important part in facilitating and supporting front-line staff to manifest common outlooks while working with inmates. Consequently, the underpinning traditions/norms of the Norwegian prison system informed the professionals' shared ideals, which in turn, stimulated collaborative practice among the workforces.

Bruhn et al. (2017) discuss the daily regimes that involve interactions 24 hours a day with prisoners while constantly guarding, helping, caring, and motivating those sent to prison, the dilemmas of prison work therefore stem from the need to find a balance between security procedures and rehabilitative work in everyday practice. The ongoing occupational development and professionalisation of prison officers is said to run consistent with the central aims of Norwegian prison policy, developing the humanistic side of the prison establishment with a focus on openness, respect, and professionalism. The development of prison staff has also been structured around different interprofessional fields such as security and safety, social work and reintegration rather than merely traditional security disciplines, outlining the goal of having well-developed collaborative relationship between prison officers, other staff, and prisoners. In Norway, humanistic prison policy and training have changed a prison officers' role from simply a guard role to one which encompasses the motivation and rehabilitation of prisoners (Bruhn et al., 2017). The professional development of prison staff is important as poor quality and inexperienced workforce with problematic training undermines the safety and well-being or prisoners and staff (Crewe et al., 2011). Front-line prison staff in Norway are expected to guard, help, care for and motivate those sent to prison, a fact that promotes close collaboration to work with other professional colleagues (Smith & Ugelvik, 2017).

Differentiating between the official tasks listed in policy and training (the job description of prison staff), and the activity (what staff actually undertake), the staff at the overgangsbolig centralise the collaborative rehabilitative and reintegrative work with prisoners, rather than disproportionately employing their authority or security measures. At the heart of prison life, the professionalism of staff is seen as critical for authority to be used legitimately and being good at not using force, but to still be in control and things still getting done (Liebling, 2011). High levels of staff professionalism which are a matter of craft, skill, and fairness, are necessary to assure high-quality services that reflect an organised and professionalised ethos (Crewe et al., 2015). The professionalism is viewed as key to determine the quality of prison life as it mediates the attitudes of prison staff and their ability to initiate routines that are fair, safe, respectful, reliable, and responsive (Rynne et al., 2008). Staff that value the peaceful coexistence with prisoners evoke mutual respect, human dignity, sharing of resources, and the development of individual potential (Crewe & Liebling, 2012). The professionalism in Norway is an important consideration that evoked the collaborative attitudes at the overgangsbolig. Similarly, these humanistic ideals are said to reinforce the idea that smaller prisons in Norway demonstrate a collaborative ethos between not only other staff, but also prisoners for prison life to run smoothly (Johnsen & Granheim, 2012). Opposed to having differing professional outlooks, these ideals as seen as important to be operationalised collaboratively into practice while working with prisoners prior to release.

To problematise these findings, there is little consideration for prisoners who have an increased level of need and require more specialised support. Dilemmas may be present at these sites as the staff view prisoners idealistically and there may be less opportunities for these individuals characterised as excessively "*needy*" to reside at these prisons. Prioritising persons who already hold a certain level of capabilities to live in the community may be considered beneficial here, but individuals that have experienced extensive institutionalisation require further attention (see Wolff et al., 2012). Moreover, individuals' encountering an increasing level of need resemble a challenge for staff at the reintegrative phase of a prison sentence to effectively transition them from prison to society.

To reiterate the key argument, the traditions in Norway has positioned professionals in prisons to have a humanistic view of prisoners deserving equal treatment to that of the general population, self-worth, creativity, and that convicted persons have made up for the penalty of a crime once the sentence is completed. Reoffending rates should be reduced through the rehabilitation and reintegrative work of the Correctional Service with life within prison and out in community having as little difference as possible to ease reintegration. A rehabilitative and reintegrative emphasis are considered central components of the prison sentence and if the sentence is to work, the reintegration of an inmate must be planned and cared for in a good way to ensure that the goal of successfully returning to society is achieved. Recognition is that individuals have the right to make their own choices and take responsibility for the consequences of the actions taken during their prison sentence. A convicted person must therefore have empowerment in their own life, both during and after completion of a sentence to ease the transition from prison to the community.

In Norway, the underpinning penal policies have aimed to uphold traditions that direct staff and promote redemption, learning, training, healing, and the commitment to normalisation in prisons (Pratt & Eriksson, 2011). Compared to the rehabilitation and reintegrative strategies of other countries, the Norwegian approach is deemed to be a good one as many prisoners receive the help to manage and establish a life without crime (Johnsen & Fridhov, 2018). Suggestions from this study are that the underpinning humane traditions which focus on the welfare of inmates such as their rehabilitation and reintegration took precedence over other principles such as punishment at the transitional residences. These traditions are considered important for practice to reinforce the shared ideals across the multidisciplinary personnel and to conduct collaborative practice as they reintegrate inmates back into society.

While expanding knowledge at the front-line of the Norwegian prison system, the key message demonstrates the underpinning traditions of penal policy and the link between how these are operationalised and collaboratively translated into practice through the shared ideals of front-line staff. Indications are that there is compatibility between the humane traditions that underpin the prison system, and the ideals applied by the front-line professionals. The shared humane ideals were found to stimulate collaborative practice among the staff while working with inmates' needs before they were released from the transitional residences and to reintegrate them back into society. Recommendations are for future research across European prison systems to expand knowledge of the contrasting traditions that underpin systems/policies and the implications upon prison administrations, institutions, front-line staff, and across the progressive phases of a convicted person's sentence. These traditions are considered influential to reinforce the conceptions of front-line staff that guide the collaborative practices in prisons. Evaluating current educational and training programmes of front-line staff, most notably prison officers and other service personnel in prisons is also a key consideration. Understanding the current education of prison-based staff is seen as critical to map the needs, obstacles, and challenges of different personnel, which in turn provides an opportunity to inform future interprofessional education and develop collaborative practice that effectively reduces reoffending.

Conclusion

Through expanding knowledge of organisational prison policy and practice in the Norwegian prison system, the research demonstrates the humane traditions that underpin this system and were applied by front-line personnel at two transitional residences. Irrespective of the differing professions at these sites, the shared humane ideals of front-line staff suggest that a welfare embedded approach prioritising rehabilitation and reintegration take precedence over punishment in the final stages of an inmate's sentence. These ideals are noteworthy if contrasting principles and values are at odds with each other and may have implications for collaborative practice to occur across professions. Rather than creating division and disparity between different professional groups, the Norwegian prison staff outlined their common ideological capacity to encourage working as a collaborative workforce at the two transitional residences. Consequently, this study finds that there seems to be compatibility between the humane traditions that underpin the Norwegian prison system and the shared ideals applied within front-line practice. These ideals are noteworthy at the final phase of the prison system to encourage collaborative practice among front-line professionals to reintegrate inmates back into society.

References

Allen, D. K., Karanasios, S., & Slavova, M. (2011). Working with activity theory: Context, technology, and information behavior. *Journal of the Association for Information Science and Technology, 62*(4), 776–788.

Andrews, D. A., & Bonta, J. (2010). Rehabilitating criminal justice policy and practice. *Psychology, Public Policy, and Law, 16*(1), 39–55.

Bainbridge, L., Nasmith, L., Orchard, C., & Wood, V. (2010). Competencies for interprofessional collaboration. *Journal of Physical Therapy Education, 24*(1), 6–11.

Bjørngaard, J. H., Rustad, A. B., & Kjelsberg, E. (2009). The prisoner as patient—A health services satisfaction survey. *BMC Health Services Research, 9*(176), 1–9.

Blackler, F. (1993). Knowledge and the theory of organizations: Organizations as activity systems and the reframing of management. *Journal of Management Studies, 30*(6), 863–884.

Blackler, F. (1995). Knowledge, knowledge work and organizations: An overview and interpretation. *Organization Studies, 16*(6), 1021–1046.

Blackler, F. (2009). Cultural-historical activity theory and organization studies. In A. L. Sannino., H. Daniels., & K. D. Gutierrez (Eds.), *Learning and expanding with activity theory* (pp. 19–39). New York: Cambridge University Press.

Bond, B. J., & Gittell, J. H. (2010). Cross-agency coordination of offender reentry: Testing collaboration outcomes. *Journal of Criminal Justice, 38*(2), 118–129.

Bruhn, A., Nylander, P. Å., & Johnsen, B. (2017). From prison guards to... what? Occupational development of prison officers in Sweden and Norway. *Journal of Scandinavian Studies in Criminology and Crime Prevention, 18*(1), 68–83.

Christie, N. (1970). Modeller for en fengselorganisasjon. In R. Østensen (Ed.), *I stedet for fengsel*. Oslo: Pax Forlag.

Craig, S. (2004). Rehabilitation versus control: An organizational theory of prison management. *Prison Journal, 84*(4), 92–114.

Crewe, B., & Liebling, A. (2012). Are liberal-humanitarian penal values and practices exceptional? In T. Ugelvik, & J. Dullum (Eds.), *Penal exceptionalism? Nordic prison policy and practice* (pp. 175–198). London: Routledge.

Crewe, B., Liebling, A., & Hulley, S. (2011). Staff culture, use of authority and prisoner quality of life in public and private sector prisons. *Australian & New Zealand Journal of Criminology, 44*(1), 94–115.

Crewe, B., Liebling, A., & Hulley, S. (2015). Staff-prisoner relationships, staff professionalism, and the use of authority in public- and private-sector prisons. *Law & Social Inquiry, 40*(2), 309–344.

Drake, D. H., Earle, R., & Sloan, J. (2015). General introduction: What ethnography tells us about prisons and what prisons tell us about ethnography. In D. H. Drake, R. Earle, & J. Sloan (Eds.), *Palgrave handbook of prison ethnography* (pp. 1–16). Basingstoke: Palgrave Mcmillan.

Dugdale, W. (2020). *Interprofessional collaborative practice in the Norwegian prison system: A case study exploration of front-line professionals at two transitional residences reintegrating inmates back into society* (Published doctoral thesis). Bournemouth, UK: Bournemouth University.

Engeström, Y. (1987). *Learning by expanding*. Helsinki: Orienta-Konsultit Oy.

Engeström, Y. (1999). Activity theory and individual and social transformation. In Y. Engeström., R. Miettinen., & R. L. Punamäki (Eds.), *Perspectives on activity theory* (pp. 19–38). Cambridge: University Press.

Engeström, Y. (2000). Activity theory as a framework for analyzing and redesigning. *Ergonomics, 43*(7), 960–974.

Engeström, Y. (2001). Expansive learning at work: Toward an activity theoretical reconceptualization. *Journal of Education and Work, 14*(1), 133–156.

Engeström, Y., Kerosuo, H., & Kajamaa, A. (2007). Beyond discontinuity: Expansive organizational learning remembered. *Management Learning, 38*(3), 319–336.

Fazel, S., & Wolf, A. (2015). A systematic review of criminal recidivism rates worldwide: Current difficulties and recommendations for best practice. *PLoS ONE, 10*(6), 1–8.

Foot, K. A. (2014). Cultural-historical activity theory: Exploring a theory to inform practice and research. *Journal of Human Behavior in the Social Environment, 24*(3), 329–347.

Foucault, M. (2007). *Security, territory, population.* New York: Palgrave Macmillan.

Griffin, M. L. (2002). The influence of professional orientation on detention officers' attitudes toward the use of force. *Criminal Justice and Behavior, 29*(3), 250–277.

Hean, S., Heaslip, V., Warr, J., & Staddon, S. (2011). Exploring the potential for joint training between legal professionals in the criminal justice system and health and social care professionals in the mental-health services. *Journal of Interprofessional Care, 25*(3), 196–202.

Hean, S., Ødegård, A., & Willumsen, E. (2017). Improving collaboration between professionals supporting mentally ill offenders. *International Journal of Prisoner Health, 13*(2), 91–104.

Hean, S., Willumsen, E., & Ødegård, A. (2017). Collaborative practices between correctional and mental health services in Norway: Expanding the roles and responsibility competence domain. *Journal of Interprofessional Care, 31*(1), 18–27.

Hean, S., Willumsen, E., & Ødegård, A. (2018). Making sense of interactions between mental health and criminal justice services: the utility of cultural historical activity systems theory. *International Journal of Prisoner Health, 14*(2), 124–141.

Jewkes, Y. (2020). "An Iron Fist in a Silk Glove": The pains of Halden Prison. In B. Crewe, A. Goldsmith, & M. Halsey (Eds.), *Power and authority in the modern prison: Revisiting the society of captives.* Oxford: Clarendon Press.

Johnsen, B., & Fridhov, I. M. (2018). Offender resettlement in Norway: Positive principles—Challenging practices. In F. Dünkel, I. Pruin, A. Storgaard, & J. Weber (Eds.), *Prisoner resettlement in Europe* (pp. 249–262). London: Routledge.

Johnsen, B., & Granheim, P. K. (2012). Prison size and quality of life in Norwegian closed prisons in late modernity. In T. Ugelvik, & J. Dullum (Eds.), *Penal exceptionalism? Nordic prison policy and practice* (pp. 199–214). London: Routledge.

King, N. (2004). Using templates in the thematic analysis of text. In C. Cassell & G. Symon (Eds.), *Essential guide to qualitative methods in organizational research* (pp. 256–270). London: Sage.

King, N. (2012). Doing template analysis. In G. Symon, & C. Cassell (Eds.), *Qualitative organizational research: Core methods and current challenges.* (pp. 426–450). London: Sage.

Kriminalomsorgen. (2005). *Yrkesetiske retningslinjer for kriminalomsorgen (Occupational guidelines for the correctional care)* (2nd ed.). Oslo: Kriminalomsorgens sentrale forvaltning.

Liebling, A. (2011). Distinctions and distinctiveness in the work of prison officers: Legitimacy and authority revisited. *European Journal of Criminology, 8*(6), 484–499.

Liebling, A., Elliot, C., & Price, D. (1999). Appreciative inquiry and relationships in prisons. *Punishment & Society, 1*(1), 71–98.

Lipsky, M. (2010). *Street-level bureaucracy: Dilemmas of the individual in public service* (30th Ann ed.). New York: Russell Sage Foundation.

Maruna, S., & Immarigeon, R. (2004). *After crime and punishment: Pathways to offender reintegration.* Cullompton: Willan Publishing.

McGuire, J. (1995). *What works: Reducing reoffending. Guidelines from research and practice.* Chichester: John Wiley & Sons Ltd.

Miettinen, R. (2005). Object of activity and individual motivation. *Mind, Culture, and Activity, 12*(1), 52–69.

Norwegian Government White Paper no. 12 (2014). *Utviklingsplan for kapasitet I kriminalomsorgen (Development plan for capacity in the correctional care).* Oslo: Departementenes sikkerhets- og serviceorganisasjon.

Norwegian Government White Paper no. 37 (2008). *Straff som virker – mindre kriminalitet – tryggere samfunn (Criminal punishment—Less crime—Safer society).* Oslo: Departementenes servicesenter.

Norwegian Ministry of Justice and Public Security. *The Execution of Sentences Act 2002.*

Norwegian Ministry of Justice and Public Security. (2017). *Redusert tilbakefall til ny kriminalitet: Nasjonal strategi for samordnet tilbakeføring etter gjennomført straff 2017–2021.* Oslo: Justis- og beredskapsdepartementet.

Pakes, F., & Holt, K. (2017). Crimmigration and the prison: Comparing trends in prison policy and practice in England & Wales and Norway. *European Journal of Criminology, 14*(1), 63–77.

Pratt, J. (2008a). Scandinavian exceptionalism in an era of penal excess: Part I: The nature and roots of Scandinavian Exceptionalism. *British Journal of Criminology, 48*(2), 119–137.

Pratt, J. (2008b). Scandinavian exceptionalism in an era of penal excess: Part II: Does Scandinavian exceptionalism have a future? *British Journal of Criminology, 48*(3), 275–292.

Pratt, J., & Eriksson, A. (2011). "Mr. Larsson is walking out again". The origins and development of Scandinavian prison systems. *Australian & New Zealand Journal of Criminology, 44*(1), 7–23.

Pratt, J., & Eriksson, A. (2013). *Contrasts in punishment: An explanation of Anglophone excess and Nordic exceptionalism.* London: Routledge.

Rudes, D. S., & Magnuson, S. (2019). Scapegoating culture: Misunderstanding organizational culture as the problem in carceral institutions and beyond. *Sociology Compass, 13*(2), 1–12.

Rynne, J., Harding, R., & Wortley, R. (2008). Market testing and prison riots: How public-sector commercialization contributed to a prison riot. *Criminology and Public Policy, 7*(1), 117–142.

Smith, P. S., & Ugelvik, T. (2017). *Scandinavian penal history, culture and prison practice: Embraced by the welfare state?* London: Palgrave Macmillan.

Sørensen, E., & Torfing, J. (2011). Enhancing collaborative innovation in the public sector. *Administration & Society, 43*(8), 842–868.

Ugelvik, T. (2012). The dark side of a culture of equality: Reimagining communities in a Norwegian remand prison. In T. Ugelvik & J. Dullum (Eds.), *Penal exceptionalism? Nordic prison policy and practice* (pp. 121–138). London: Routledge.

Ugelvik, T. (2014). Prison ethnography as lived experience: Notes from the diaries of a beginner let loose in Oslo Prison. *Qualitative Inquiry, 20*(4), 471–480.

Ugelvik, T. (2016). Prisons as welfare institutions? Punishment and the Nordic model. In J. Bennett, Y. Jewkes, & B. Crewe (Eds.), *Handbook on prisons* (pp. 388–402). London: Routledge.

Virkkunen, J. (2006). Hybrid agency in co-configuration work. *Outlines. Critical Practice Studies, 8*(1), 61–75.

Ward, T., & Maruna, S. (2007). *Rehabilitation: Beyond the risk paradigm.* London: Routledge.

Warmington, P., Daniels, H., Edwards, A., Brown, S., Leadbetter, J., Martin, D., et al. (2004). *Interagency Collaboration: A review of the literature*. Bath: Learning in and for Interagency Working Project.

Wolff, N., Frueh, B. C., Huening, J., Shi, J., Epperson, M. W., Morgan, R., et al. (2013). Practice informs the next generation of behavioral health and criminal justice interventions. *International Journal of Law and Psychiatry, 36*(1), 1–10.

Wolff, N., Shi, J., & Schumann, B. E. (2012). Reentry preparedness among soon-to-be-released inmates and the role of time served. *Journal of Criminal Justice, 40*(5), 379–385.

World Health Organization. (2010). *Framework for action on interprofessional education & collaborative practice*. Geneva: Health Professions Network Nursing and Midwifery Office.

Yin, R. K. (2014). *Case study research: Design and methods* (5th ed.). Los Angeles: Sage.

Part II

International Contexts of Collaborative Practice in a Variety of Penal Contexts: Substantive Areas for Organisational Innovation and Change—Studies in England

6

Tracing the Historical Development of a Service Model for Interagency Collaboration: Contradictions as Barriers and Potential Drivers for Change

Paulo Rocha and Sarah Hean

Introduction

The average person entering the criminal justice system (CJS) grapples with mental health problems (Fazel & Danesh, 2002). These disenfranchised individuals are also prone to substance misuse problems and other social difficulties such as unemployment, debt and homelessness (World Health Organisation, 2015), which increases their proclivity to offend/reoffend (Hare, 2002). To that end, effective rehabilitation strategies need to tackle clusters of correlated risk factors and provide multifaceted solutions in order to decrease reoffending rates (Andrews & Bonta, 2016).

P. Rocha (✉)
Department of Social Studies, University of Stavanger, Stavanger, Norway
e-mail: paulo.t.bastosrocha@uis.no

S. Hean
Social Work Department, University of Stavanger, Stavanger, Norway
e-mail: sarah.c.hean@uis.no

S. Hean et al. (eds.), *Improving Interagency Collaboration, Innovation and Learning in Criminal Justice Systems*,
https://doi.org/10.1007/978-3-030-70661-6_6

By and large, rehabilitation strategies tend to be rolled out in prison by the state. However, the suboptimal conditions that exist in the prison system limit the rehabilitation efforts deployed (Farrington, 2006; Skeem & Peterson, 2012). This means the concomitant deployment of rehabilitation programmes in the community are vital. Indeed, the importance of through-of-the-gate support is well recognised in the United Kingdom and care, enabled through collaboration between criminal justice (CJS) and welfare systems (WS), is considered to be key to success (Ministry of Justice UK, 2013). However, collaboration often collapses due to incompatible agendas of the different agencies and philosophical differences among professionals (Stone, 2003).

In England and Wales, Criminal Justice Liaison and Diversion (L&D) services work specifically with vulnerable people when they are first in contact with the criminal justice system (NHS England Liaison and Diversion Programme, 2014). These services first identify vulnerable individuals entering the criminal justice system and refer them to appropriate care. Additionally, L&D services ensure that data about service users arrive at decision-makers in the criminal justice system (e.g. courts and police) to inform their choices (e.g. in sentencing or providing treatment) (Reed, 1992).

Initially L&D services were managed and funded locally. This meant that not all areas nationally had L&D services available and, among those that had, there was considerable variation in the nature of service (Disley et al., 2016). Responsive to this challenge, the government in England commissioned a study to review the conditions of people with mental health problems or learning disabilities in the criminal justice system. The findings of the review recommended there should be an expansion of L&D services (Bradley, 2009) and this galvanised the development of a national model across England to standardise L&D practices nationwide (NHS England Liaison and Diversion Programme, 2014).

The model posited that vulnerabilities should be identified as soon as the individuals entered the criminal justice system, which meant having L&D workers placed in court and police stations to assist in the screening, assessment and signposting of offenders to the relevant care as required. The model also instructed L&D workers to, if appropriate, divert the offender out of criminal justice altogether and into care (NHS England Liaison and Diversion Programme, 2014). The national government had a goal to reduce duplication of effort and resolve complications in collaboration between agencies. They aimed to enable criminal justice and welfare systems to work together in tandem and avoid silo working that could otherwise be pernicious to service users (Rogers & Ormston, 2016).

Ten sites across six areas in England (North, Midlands, East, London, South East and South West) were forerunners in the trial of the new model in 2014 (Disley et al., 2016). The results demonstrated that L&D efforts had a substantial impact on decreasing the number of arrests (Bonkiewicz et al., 2014) and increasing positive outcomes for primary health care (Earl et al., 2015). However, organisational aspects behind L&D's influence were underexplored (Pakes & Winstone, 2009, 2010). This book chapter addresses this shortfall by grappling with L&D's organisational processes and work activity. The focus is on the perspective of professionals working directly with clients within both L&D and its neighbouring services. To that end, the chapter constructs a historical perspective of L&D activity providing a timeline whereby tensions and potential contradictions within and between L&D, and neighbouring services activity systems are identified before, during and after the process of implementation of the national model. The development of a historical understanding, by tracing contradictions back to their origins, is paramount if these are to be resolved and the service developed further.

Cultural-Historical Activity Theory as a Means of Exploring the Implementation of the National L&D Model

Cultural-historical activity theory (CHAT) is a multidisciplinary model which has gained increasing popularity and relevance among researchers in the fields of education and organisation studies (see e.g. Engeström, 1987; Engeström et al., 1999; Adler, 2005; Sannino et al., 2009). It has, for example, been adopted as an analytical tool in organisational studies

(Blackler, 1993, 2009), human resource development and management practices (Ardichvili, 2003; Fenwick, 2006; Gvaramadze, 2008), and organisational and individual learning (Engeström et al., 2007; Schulz & Geithner, 2010). However, it has not been yet widely applied to the study of collaborative practices in offender rehabilitation settings.

CHAT is an object or goal-oriented approach that promotes the study of work activity from the standpoint of a chosen subject (a front-line worker, for example). It investigates how the subject and their collaborative community carry out a specific object/goal engrossed in an overall work activity through the mediation of artefacts, rules and division of labour (Engeström, 1987). The mediation tends to be two-directional. Initially, culturally produced artefacts and tools are internalised by the subjects engaged in the activity and this shapes their consciousness. Subsequently, the same artefacts and tools give the subject the leverage to shape the activity in which they were produced in the first place, which is a process called externalisation (Daniels, 2001). Simply put, the tool shapes the subject who in turn shapes the world through using the tool (Cole, 1996). Different agencies may be engaged in different work activities, each described in terms of a separate activity system. Nonetheless, together they represent a community of separate—but interconnected—activity systems that may or may not share common goals/objects, as represented in Fig. 6.1.

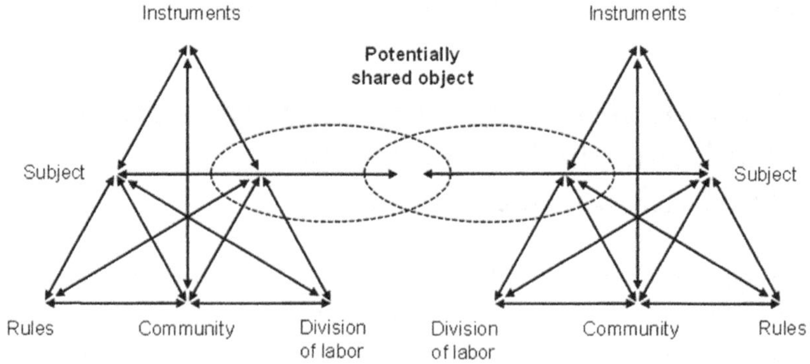

Fig. 6.1 Activity as a dynamic model of interlinked activity systems (see Engeström, 2000, p. 306)

Activity systems develop over time and across cultures through resolution of the contradictions lurking within and/or between each of the nodes of the triangle or even between activity systems (Engeström, 1987). This premise can be traced back to Vygotsky's lessons which predicated human consciousness being determined by their activity (Daniels, 2001). In this vein, the work routines devised by professionals at the several L&D sites are an embodiment of their consciousness, which takes place through their activities predicated on local contingencies. In the analysis of these local practices, it is critical to take into account the cultural and historical circumstances of each L&D site in order to avoid overly simplistic models of explanation. In other words, CHAT is used as an analytical tool because its epistemological approach combines both historical and cultural dimensions of social phenomena to make sense of activities, i.e. CHAT has utility as an exploratory tool because it allows the study of collaboration at a systems level and accounts for the multiple factors that mediate collective work activity (Engeström, 1999). In the offender rehabilitation context, these systems might be two adjacent services that have separate but also some common goals: working together on the same piece of rehabilitation strategy, for example, police custody officers collaborate with L&D workers to screen and assess individuals for vulnerabilities (their shared object of activity) when they enter the criminal justice system.

When participants within or between activity systems encounter tensions, obstacles and challenges that stem from contradictions in their work activity, this may prevent or limit the actors from achieving their goal/object and the desired outcome (Engeström & Sannino, 2011). Nonetheless, the historically evolved and systemic contradictions ought not to be perceived as elusive inconveniences, but rather as central "sources of change and development" (Engeström, 2001, p. 137). They have the potential to become influential factors that force the system to reconfigure through a process of 'expansive learning' (Engeström, 2001) (see Chapters 1 and 8 for a more detailed description of expansive learning).

An Activity Theoretical Case Study of Liaison and Diversion Services

Study Description

The chosen case study L&D site was forerunner in the implementation of the national model since its outset in 2014 ('wave one'). The L&D team consists of four administration staff, eight Support, Time and Recovery workers, eight mental health practitioners, two team leaders and one service manager. Due to the small size of the staff, the team leaders and the service manager also function as mental health practitioners when necessary, which transforms them into front-line workers for the effects of this study. In 2017, the service assessed 2365 adults and numbers increase yearly (Williams et al., 2019).

In addition to the entire front-line staff of the L&D service, participants from neighbouring organisations were also involved in the research. Including the perspective of professionals from other agencies such as, for example, police and community mental health teams, contributed to the depiction of the different activity systems interacting with L&D. The aim of study reflected in this paper was to respond the over-arching question: *How is interagency collaboration between L&D and neighbouring services perceived by street-level L&D workers after the introduction of a new national model for Liaison & Diversion?*

The paper dwells specifically on the historical dimension of the L&D services and provides a perspective of L&D practice both prior, during and after the implementation of the new national model. A qualitative case study approach (Yin, 2009) was used to explore collaborative practice carried out by the front-line staff of an L&D site located in England. The case study reported here is part of a wider project that aims to improve collaboration between agencies in the criminal justice system and welfare services (Horizon 2020 funded CO-LAB MSCA-RISE project number 734536). The first phase of the study collected background information on the L&D through document analysis, followed by second phase of observations and interviews with professionals from both L&D, criminal justice and welfare systems. Data collection took place between 2017 and 2019. Table 6.1 summarises these data collection points.

Table 6.1 Data collection procedure summary

Data	Sources	Procedure
Background document analysis	Materials were available at the investigated L&D scheme, which provided an overview of the transition period the scheme went through between being a locally managed organisation to being a 'wave-one' site following the new L&D model. The dataset included internal documents describing the process of implementation of the L&D national model (n = 27) and statistical reports on the number of clients being screened and assessed in custody and court upon the rollout (n = 12)	Read all the materials and documented any descriptive statistics related to the impact the new L&D model had on the performance/work routine of the investigated scheme
Semi-structured interviews	Front-line workers at both the criminal justice system (n = 2), the welfare services (n = 7) and the L&D (n = 19)	Audio recorded semi-structured Interviews, transcribed and thematically analysed
Observations	Observed participants' interactions with other services and the tools available to facilitate communication within and between agencies	Detailed field notes of observations

Sample

Interview participants were divided into two groups. A first group included the entire L&D front-line staff and the second group included front-line workers from other services in both the criminal justice (the Police) and welfare systems (a Community Mental Health Team, an Assertive Outreach Team, a Homeless Health Service unity and a mental health/peer support service). To be considered a front-line worker, they had to fall within the following categories (a) being a worker who interacts directly with the public he/she serves, and (b) not having work pertaining only to administrative tasks.

Out of the 28 participants, 11 were male and 17 female. All of them were British, but two of them had an immigrant background. The vast majority had a university degree in health-related field or were in the process of obtaining one. Their work experience varied greatly. While the majority had several years or even decades of experience (although not necessarily working at the same organisation), there were a few ($n = 3$) who were just starting their professional lives with no more one year of experience.

Analysis

A template analysis was applied to data, and a coding 'template' developed to capture themes emerging from the data set and organise them in a meaningful and useful manner (King, 2012). The analysis engendered a final template consisting of one meta-theme, one theme, three subthemes, four categories and three sub-categories, which was applied to the entire dataset and served as the basis for interpretation of the data and writing up of the findings. We used activity theory (Engeström, 1987; Engeström & Sannino, 2011) to interpret these themes, the activity systems and the contradictions these uncovered as these emerged historically. The method allowed for open coding at the outset of the analytical process, which enabled an unconstrained exploration of various aspects of the data. However, the method also suggests the production of an a priori template to guide later stages of the analytical process. At this point, CHAT's principles were paramount in the attempt to reconcile open codes with structured templates. This paper draws upon findings of one of the three subthemes namely "Contradictions between the national model's instructions and working conditions at the street-level". Hereinafter, we present and discuss the findings of how L&D front-line workers have dealt with the instructions of the new national model and how (if) they have been implemented in practice.

Results of the Case Study: Historical Phases of the L&D Work Activity

Front-line professionals, in examining the work activity of the L&D service, described three historical dimensions/phases: (a) before the rollout of the L&D national model, (b) during the rollout of the L&D national model, and (c) after the rollout of the L&D national model. As the case study L&D site started its operation in their current working model in 2008, data on the historical phases are presented from that point on. We used both document analysis and interviewees' accounts to trace a historical arch or trajectory of the service's development (Table 6.2).

The timeline illustrates the documents collected on the working model of the L&D service between 2008 and 2019. These were all public documents mostly issued by the government, associated organisations or research institutions. Interviews and observations began in mid-2017, although interviews were retrospective, referring both to current and previous ways in which L&D had functioned and developed.

The First Phase: The L&D Service Prior to the Rollout of a New National Model

A review of service documentation before the rollout of the national model (Table 6.2 documents between 2008 and 2014) showed that L&D services across the country up to 2014 were funded and managed locally with wide variation in resourcing and methods of delivery in the

Table 6.2 Timeline of data collected

Background documents

2008	2009	2011	2012	2013	2014	2015	2016	2017	2018	2019
• A report on the use of section 136 of the Mental Health Act 1983 at the location of the study with recommendations for development	• Lord Bradley Review	• Invitation letter from the National L&D Development Network (NLDDN) for the site to participate in their network and evaluation study • Report by (OHRN) Offender Health Research Network	• Definition of the consortia responsible for the NLDDN and its functions. • Invitation of the studied site to join the NLDDN • Agreement between the local police and the local Healthcare system NHS University Foundation Trust • Commencement of the Custody L&D service at the site: A report on the service's goals, background and method of data collection • Report on the L&D stats for the period of Oct. to Dec. 2012 • Business Case Local L&D Application to rollout the National Model	• Briefing of the Offender Health Collaborative adapting the European Foundation for Quality Management. • Report by the Independent Commission on Mental Health and Policing • Report on the L&D stats for the period of Jan. to Dec. 2013 • Standard contract for L&D service between the local L&D service and NHS	• Implementation of a locally commissioned mental health street triage pilot by the local Healthcare University Foundation Trust Criminal Justice Liaison and Diversion Service. • 2014 Annual L&D service activity report • Liaison & Diversion Operating Model 2013/14	• 2015 Annual L&D service activity report • Terms of Reference for L&D	• 2016 Annual L&D service activity report • Evaluation of the Offender Liaison & Diversion Trial Schemes conducted by RAND Europe	• 2017 Annual L&D service activity report • Outcome Evaluation of Liaison and Diversion Services – Progress Report 1	• 2018 Annual L&D service activity report • Outcome Evaluation of Liaison and Diversion Services – Progress Report 1	• Health and Justice Characteristics of Local Liaison & Diversion Population • Data Inventory Report of the Health and Justice Characteristics of Local Liaison & Diversion Population (2019)

Interviews/Observations

individual L&D services. The rules and tools governing the activity of each of the L&D services were tailored for local circumstances. While one location would be staffed with mental health practitioners and support workers, others would have only health practitioners. Some locations would operate seven days a week, others would operate only from Monday to Friday. The variation in rules and available tools led to varied outcomes for the different L&D sites. Figure 6.2 represents the contradictions existent within this phase of the L&D activity.

There were two main tensions (see Fig. 6.2) during the work activity of the L&D at this time, as follows:

(a) There was a tension between tools of the individual activity systems of each local L&D service as a consequence of local rules catering to particular circumstances. Each L&D site would operate with tools specific to their local context (e.g. local computer systems were not shared by other L&D schemes and work routines were specific to a given context). Each site operated with different staff composition, working hours did not match, databases were not shared and communication tools varied. In light of the compartmentalised

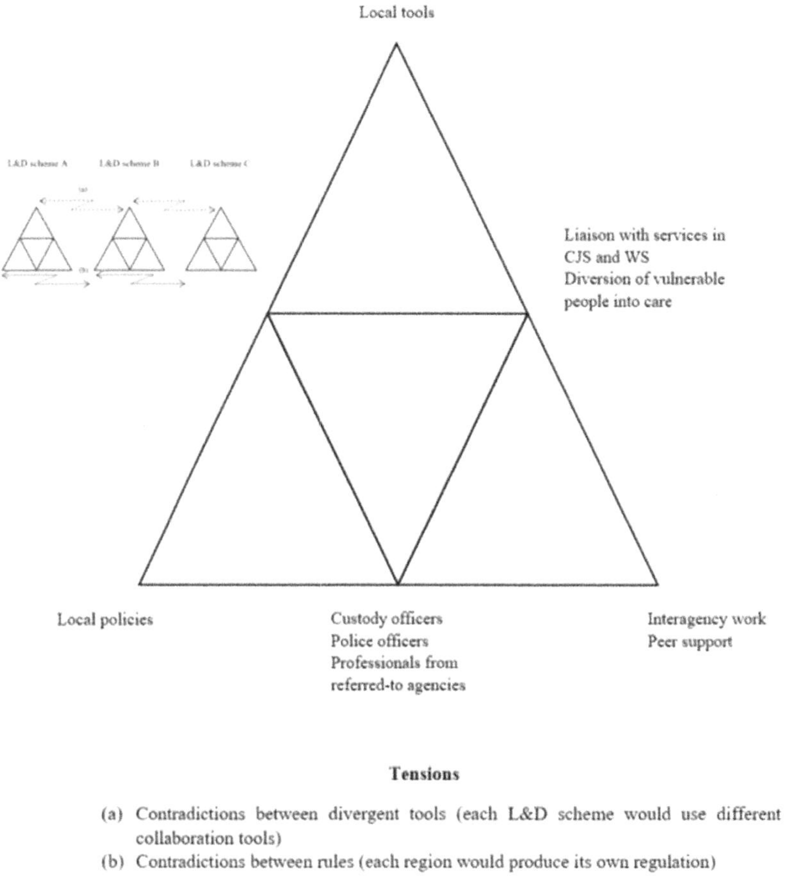

Fig. 6.2 The first phase—before the rollout of the L&D national model and the contradictions within the element 'subject' of the L&D activity system

characteristics of the service back then, these tools were not interconnected between sites and any attempt to collaborate between L&D services was troublesome. These conditions forced sites into isolation, information from one L&D site not being shared with others, and a comparison of outcomes across sites being impossible.

(b) There was also a tension between the rules of the individual activity systems of each local L&D service. Rules were devised by and for local L&D services, which meant a high degree of variation between sites. In this sense, having organisations operate under the L&D's umbrella was not a guarantee of similar practices being implemented: local contingencies had a strong impact on the rules governing the service.

These tensions identified were repeatedly mentioned by interviewees and substantiated by the analysis of documents between 2008 and 2014, more specifically documents such as the Bradley review (2009), the Report by the Offender Health Research Network (2011) and the Report by the Independent Commission on Mental Health and Policing (2013), which reported on the discrepancy between work routines at different L&D sites.

L&D services deal typically with vulnerable people who have no fixed residence, no permanent job and a chaotic lifestyle. They may move around the country and come into contact with criminal justice services in different areas. Information sharing between L&D sites is key if the service is to avoid unnecessary repetition and overlap in treatment. In this sense, the tensions illustrated in Fig. 6.2, pre roll out of the national model, were an impediment to optimal service performance. The difficult communication between L&D sites limited information sharing and each location ended up treating service users as if it was their first contact with the service. That was a resource-consuming practice. Despite a need for collaboration across sites because of clients' mobility, there was minimal support for local L&D services trying to collaborate and this forced them to operate in isolation. Moreover, any attempt to compare outcomes between locations failed because of the diverse peculiarities of each region.

In an attempt to transcend these tensions, the government in England and Wales intervened. Their aim was to ensure that vulnerable people who were in contact with the criminal justice system would be endowed with homogeneous and commensurate support. This lead to the commissioning of the Lord Bradley Review (Bradley, 2009) and the development of a national L&D model to standardise the rules, tools and objectives applied to L&D services across the country as well as to expand the number of locations in which L&D services were available.

The Second Phase: The L&D Services During the Rollout of a New National Model

Our document analysis—more precisely, documents such as the Invitation Letter from the National Liaison and Diversion Development Network (2011)—pointed out that in 2011, the Department of Health in England invited 54 liaison and diversion sites across the country to join a newly created network that would inform Lord Bradley's Review (Bradley, 2009) and advocate for the development of the L&D national model focused on standardising practice across the country and ensuring equal conditions at all locations (Department of Health, 2011).

The national model was largely developed based on the evidence produced by the aforementioned Bradley review and aimed to clarify and standardise several points that were previously managed locally (NHS England Liaison and Diversion Programme, 2014). The model recommended, for example, the provision of support workers as part of the L&D service (NHS England Liaison and Diversion Programme, 2014, p. 24), the need for partnership with services in criminal justice and welfare systems (by placing L&D workers in police stations and courts) (NHS England Liaison and Diversion Programme, 2014, p. 21), and 24/7 coverage for L&D services (NHS England Liaison and Diversion Programme, 2014, p. 5). Furthermore, the model proposed that all the L&D sites across the country should pursue the same goals, namely: improved access to healthcare and support services for vulnerable individuals; diversion of individuals, where suitable; the delivery of efficiencies; and an overall reduction of reoffending (NHS England Liaison and Diversion Programme, 2014, p. 10).

The national model for L&D services represents the outcome of the expansive learning engaged in by policymakers and service developers in response to the tensions that local services had been experiencing historically. The response was a new or expanded L&D activity system (Fig. 6.3). With the new national policy in place, local L&D sites were then expected to transition from their locally-based management approach to a new one that incorporated the standard instructions of the national model. Here, however, new tensions arose. As reported by

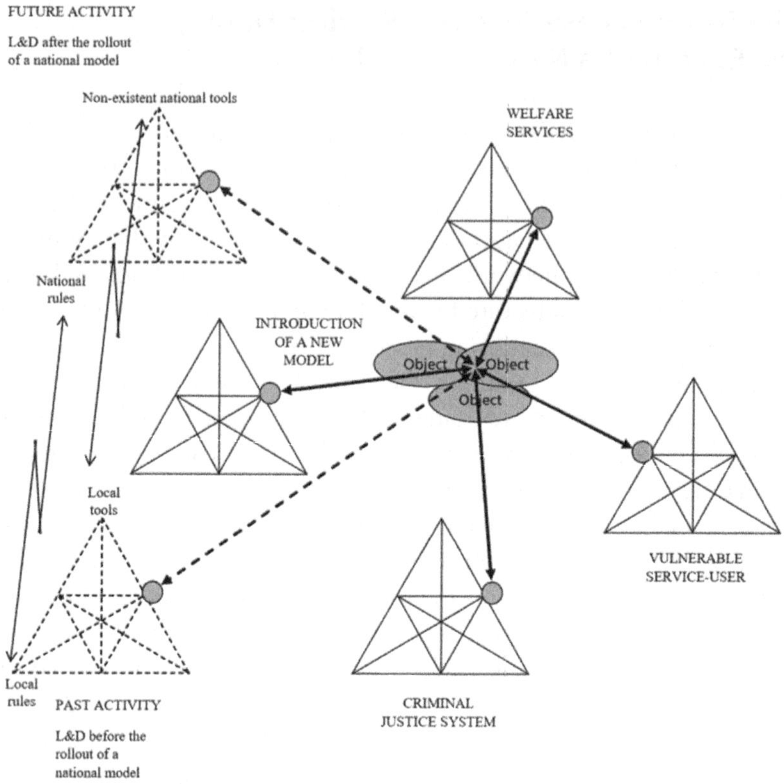

Fig. 6.3 The Second Phase—during the rollout of the L&D national model. A contradiction between an old and a new improved L&D activity system

participants, the national model did not take into account local contingencies and applying the national standardised model uniformly across various L&D sites proved impossible.

In this scenario, tensions between the local L&D services (each one representing an independent activity system governed by local rules in the historical pre-national model) and the new standard policy (where all L&D sites would have to follow the instructions of the national model) started to occur. This historically evolved contradiction stems from tensions that happened between an old and a new activity system after an intervention, or organisational change has taken place (Engeström, 1987).

The contradiction illustrated in Fig. 6.3 developed because the new model, while unifying the rules being applied across sites, did not take into account the presence of local tools and operational aspects of the L&D service. Nevertheless, a review of the 'wave one' sites (Disley et al., 2016) demonstrated that the new national model had had a positive impact on service outcomes (e.g. an increase in the number of vulnerable cases identified in custody, an increase in the number of referrals to welfare services, improved access to information by court professionals). The caveat is that the review did not look into the organisational stability of the various L&D sites and the context under which they operated, which was the focus of our study. In the end, reviewing L&D through an activity theoretical lens showed that although the new model introduced new rules and championed standardised outcomes, it did not provide L&D services with new tools to promote liaison with other agencies. In this sense, we were not able to produce evidence that dovetails with the positive impact on service outcomes reported (Disley et al., 2016) and the introduction of the new model.

The Third Phase: The L&D Service After the Rollout of a New National Model

Figure 6.4 represents the L&D activity systems after the rollout of the national model (current practice). The national model (Rule) has now begun to influence the way the service is funded and has managed to introduce standardised outcomes (NHS England Liaison and Diversion Programme, 2014) against which sites have their performance equally judged (indeed an expansion of the original L&D activity systems). Diverse locations are still operating using old tools, however, to apply these new rules of the national model to their local circumstances.

Interviewees who had participated in the implementation of the new model, and who are still working for L&D described other tensions during this phase. Now, contradictions seem to occur not only between L&D sites but also between the L&D and other criminal justice and

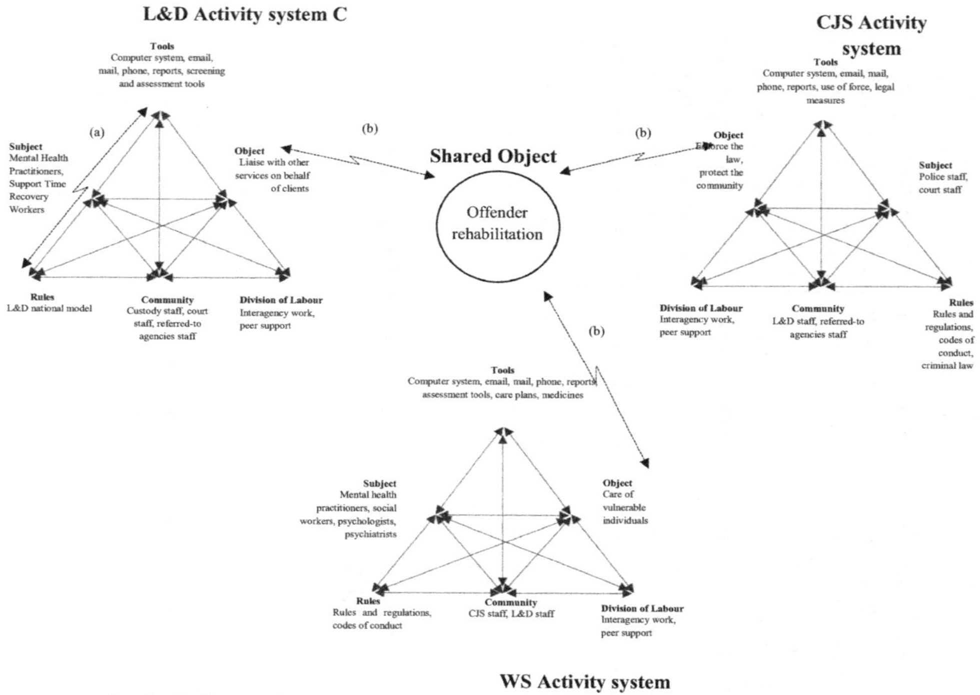

Contradictions

(a) New rules vs. old tools

(b) Object of liaison vs. object of law enforcement vs object of care

Fig. 6.4 The Third Phase—after the rollout of the L&D national model. Contradictions within the L&D activity system and with other services

welfare services. That is to say that the national model was not able to significantly transform interagency collaborative practice as had been expected. Professionals from the L&D, the criminal justice and welfare systems work together in an interdisciplinary network surrounding vulnerable service-users. Interviewees mentioned how IT systems are the default communication tool between professionals, but reported that technology-related activities are still confined within the boundaries of each organisation. In these conditions, they described information sharing to support communication between services as insufficient. These tensions might have been already present prior to the new model but are particularly salient in the current climate. There were exceptions, however, to this compartmentalisation of IT systems. For example, services funded by the National Health Service (L&D, community mental health teams, assertive outreach teams) used the same software and were, therefore, able to exchange information through it. Nevertheless, even in such cases, the interconnection between agencies was geographically limited, as intercommunication was bound to the limits of each county.

When asked whether having access to other organisation's system would facilitate their work, professionals explained that such a solution would still have tensions associated with it, as it would require professionals across organisations to share the same skillset in order to fathom the information on each other's systems. An example was that L&D while operating in custody had access to the police's IT system, but the police did not have access to L&D's IT system at all. As it was clarified by participants, access was offered to the police, but the organisation declined as they felt police officers would not be able to understand the information on the system.

Participants also mentioned a conundrum amid organisations as to each other's roles, responsibilities and level of influence. While on the one hand, welfare organisations assumed it was in the police capacity and influence to deal with vulnerable people, on the other hand, the police assumed the same about welfare services. An example of such situation was given by an interviewee who explained that some welfare organisations assumed the police performed welfare checks when in fact that was a task of another crisis team in a welfare service providing assistance to individuals having a mental health crisis in the community. In the interviewee's opinion, this assumption may lead to individuals falling through the service net. That was not an isolated account. Overall, participants agreed that allocation of responsibilities by organisation was not clear. They acknowledged a need for more clarity about care pathways and saw the L&D as having the task of bridging criminal justice and welfare services.

In summary, front-line professionals, when asked to speculate on the historical development of the system, highlighted that despite the introduction of the national model in an attempt to standardise L&D provision, different locations still operate through old communication tools that vary from site to site and tensions between L&D services remain. This tension between a new rule (the national model) being implemented and the use of old tools of communication (fragmented IT systems) reverberates out into the interactions between the activity systems of L&D and its neighbouring services in criminal justice and welfare systems. This contradiction between the activity systems of different agencies impacts on their collaborative relationships and hinders the construction of the shared object (the support and rehabilitation of the vulnerable client).

Discussion and Conclusions

The results of this study traced the development of the L&D activity system over time. First, L&D sites were locally managed and there was a great deal of performance variation between them. Then, during the implementation of a national model for L&D, the government focused on replacing heterogeneity with homogeneous practice across the country. However, it tried to do so by overlooking local communication tools and strategies. The result was that local L&D services were operationalising the new model through old tools and continued to adapt the policy to their local circumstances. This has meant that the implementation of the national model has not galvanised improved collaboration between L&D sites, and between L&D and neighbouring services in criminal justice and welfare systems, as envisaged.

The L&D case exemplifies a top-down attempt to address an existent shortcoming in the service, namely the lack of communication across L&D sites that led to heterogeneous practice. In CHAT, this sort of contradiction cannot be resolved through a forceful adaptation of practice to a unilaterally developed solution. Contradictions do trigger an expansive learning process in which stakeholders begin to question current routines, leading eventually to a resolution. But this requires a co-reconceptualisation of practice by all those involved (Kajamaa & Schulz, 2018). Routines are the reification of ready-made solutions to recurring problems and their persistence keeps organisational evolution at bay. Therefore, it is paramount to square routines and innovative initiatives.

As we could observe in our study, the process of implementation of the new national model policy resulted in the occurrence of new contradictions, which lay between the actors as well as between the new rule being introduced and its intended use in practice. Herein, we suggest that the stratified hierarchy of interest comprising decision-makers and policymakers at the top, followed by middle-level managers and finally front-line professionals at the bottom might have been part of the reason for a subpar roll out of the national model for L&D services. Under a Coalition government prevailing in the UK from 2010 to 2015, policymakers prioritised top-down performance-based commissioning in different areas of government, including welfare-to-work programmes, public health budgets and criminal justice system (Bochel & Powell, 2016). Middle-level managers strived to reconcile the new political agenda with the contingencies existent at lower levels of the government. Front-line workers felt downtrodden, as they were expected to square novel expectations introduced top-down on the one hand with sparse resources on the other.

The diversity of motives amid the different strata of the service created challenges for the implementation of the L&D new model (an abstract concept) into concrete practice. As pointed out by Kajamaa and Schulz (2018, p. 3), "the consequences of implementation processes, however, cannot always be predicted and the efforts may lead to undesired adaptations and unanticipated outcomes", which was what we could observe in our study. Different L&D sites adapted the national model to their own local circumstances and the national government's attempt to innovate did not pan out as expected at the street-level, which was most likely not accounted for at the moment of the enactment of the new policy.

The literature has already highlighted the importance of front-line workers in street-level policy implementation (Lipsky, 1980). They are crucial in the generation, coercive adoption, and bottom-up adaptation of process and social innovations (Volberda et al., 2014). Nevertheless, in the public administration, there is a proclivity to carry out innovation as a top-down process and front-line workers are in a weak position of being mere legitimisers (Elkjaer, 2002). We see dialectics between the actors of an activity system as crucial to the negotiation, design and reconceptualisation of an activity, which tends to result in a more efficient implementation process and appropriate innovation in their local context. Our study views the adaptation of the new L&D model to local contexts as an innovation process. However, this innovation process in which L&D services are currently engaged seems to lack a consistent and rigorous approach. It would benefit from a dialogue between all stakeholders and one that flattens out the current stratified hierarchical structure. To that end, we see opportunity for some sort of intervention that facilitates communication between these strata: between policy-makers, management and front-line professionals for a description of some of these interventions, e.g., Change Laboratory Model (see e.g. Kerosuo & Engeström, 2003; Tolviainen, 2007).

In the end, the historical development of the L&D service described in this study originated from an identified problem of service isolation and lack of standardisation and information sharing between agencies (Bradley, 2009). It represents an expansive learning cycle that has been ongoing over the past few decades, in which contradictions within the L&D system and also between L&D, criminal justice and welfare services activity systems have triggered new ways of functioning being constructed to resolve these challenges (Engeström, 1987). The introduction of the national L&D model as a solution being implemented and experimented with in practice (see Chapter 8 for a wider discussion of the expansive learning cycle and innovation) represented the first iteration of these learning cycles. However, not all relevant stakeholders (especially the front-line worker) were included in the learning process and the reconceptualisation of the L&D model. Evidence suggests that future iterations of a more inclusive expansive learning cycle are required.

References

Adler, P. (2005). The evolving object of software development. *Organization, 12*(3), 401–435.

Andrews, D., & Bonta, J. (2016). *The psychology of criminal conduct.* Routledge.

Ardichvili, A. (2003). Constructing socially situated learning experiences in human resource development: An activity theory perspective. *Human Resource Development International, 6*(5), 310–325.

Blackler, F. (1993). Knowledge and the theory of organizations: Organizations as activity systems and the reframing of management. *Journal of Management Studies, 30*(6), 863–884.

Blackler, F. (2009). Cultural-historical activity theory and organization studies. In A. Sannino, H. Daniels, & K. Gutierrez (Eds.), *Learning and expanding with activity theory* (pp. 19–39). New York: Cambridge University Press.

Bochel, H., & Powell, M. (2016). Tre transformation of the welfare state? The Conservative-Liberal Democrat coalition government and social policy. In H. Bochel & M. Powell (Eds.), *The coalition government and social policy: Restructuring the welfare state* (pp. 1–25). Bristol: Policy Press.

Bonkiewicz, L., Green, A., Moyer, K., & Wright, J. (2014). Left alone when the cops go home: Evaluating a post-mental health crisis assistance program. *Policing: An International Journal of Police Strategies & Management, 37*(4), 762–778.

Bradley, L. (2009). The Bradley report. *Department of Health.* http://www.dh.gov.uk/prod_consum_dh/groups/dh_digitalassets/documents/digitalasset/dh_098698.pdf.

Cole, M. (1996). *Cultural psychology.* Cambridge, MA: The Belknap Press of Harvard University Press.

Daniels, H. (2001). *Vygotsky and pedagogy.* London: Routledge.

Department of Health. (2011). *National liaison and diversion programme—Development network and evaluation study.* London.

Disley, E., et al. (2016). *Evaluation of the offender liaison and diversion trial schemes.* Cambridge: RAND.

Earl, F., Cocksedge, K., Rheeder, B., Morgan, J., & Palmer, J. (2015). Neighbourhood outreach: A novel approach to liaison and diversion. *The Journal of Forensic Psychiatry & Psychology, 26*(5), 573–585.

Elkjaer, B. (2002). The learning organization: An undelivered promise. *Management Learning, 32*(4), 437–452.

Engeström, Y. (1987). *Learning by expanding: An activity-theoretical approach to developmental research.* Helsinki: Orienta-Konsultit.

Engeström, Y. (1999). Activity theory and individual and social transformation. In Y. Engeström, R. Miettinen, & R. Punamaki (Eds.), *Perspectives on activity theory.* Cambridge: Cambridge University Press.

Engeström, Y. (2000). A story of four umpires. *Organization, 7*(2), 301–310.

Engeström, Y. (2001). Expansive learning at work: Toward an activity theoretical reconceptualization. *Journal of Education and Work, 14*(1), 133–156.

Engeström, Y., & Sannino, A. (2011). Discursive manifestations of contradictions in organizational change efforts. *Journal of Organizational Change Management, 24*(3), 368–387.

Engeström, Y., Kerosuo, H., & Kajamaa, A. (2007). Beyond Discontinuity Expansive Organizational Learning Remembered. *Management Learning, 38*(3), 319–336.

Engeström, Y., Miettinen, R., & Punamäki, R. (1999). *Perspectives on activity theory.* Cambridge: Cambridge University Press.

Farrington, D. P. (2006). Reducing crime. In A. Perry, C. McDougall, & D. P. Farrington (Eds.), *Reducing crime: The effectiveness of criminal justice interventions* (pp. 1–11). West Sussex: Wiley.

Fazel, S., & Danesh, J. (2002). Serious mental disorder in 23 000 prisoners: A systematic review of 62 surveys. *The lancet, 359*(9306), 545–550.

Fenwick, T. (2006). Toward enriched conceptions of work learning: Participation expansion, and translation among individuals with/in activity. *Human Resource Development Review, 5*(3), 285–302.

Gvaramadze, I. (2008). Human resource development practice: The paradox of empowerment and individualization. *Human Resource Development International, 11*(5), 465–477.

Hare, R. (2002). Psichopathy and risk for recidivism and violence. In N. Gray, J. Laing, & L. Moaks (Eds.), *Criminal justice, mental health and politics of risk.* London: Cavendish.

Independent Commission on Mental Health and Policing. (2013). *The independent commission on mental health and policing report.* Available https://www.basw.co.uk/system/files/resources/basw_22916-3_0.pdf. Accessed 1 Aug 2020.

Kajamaa, A., & Schulz, K. (2018). From the abstract to the concrete—Implementation of an innovative tool in home care. *Health Services Management Research, 31*(1), 2–10.

Kerosuo, H., & Engeström, Y. (2003). Boundary crossing and learning in creation of new work practice. *Journal of Workplace Learning, 15*, 345–351.

King, N. (2012). Doing template analysis. In G. Symon & C. Cassell (Eds.), *Qualitative organizational research: Core methods and current challenges* (pp. 426–450). London: Sage.

Lipsky, M. (1980). *Street-level bureaucracy: Dilemmas of the individual in public services*. New York: Russell Sage.

Ministry of Justice UK. (2013). *Transforming rehabilitation: A revolution in the way we manage offenders*. London: The Stationery Office.

NHS England Liaison and Diversion Programme. (2014). *Liaison and diversion operation model 2013/14*. London: The NHS Constitution.

Offender Health Research Network. (2011). *Liaison and diversion services: Current practices and future directions.*

Pakes, F., & Winstone, J. (2010). A site visit survey of 101 mental health liaison and diversion schemes in England. *The Journal of Forensic Psychiatry & Psychology, 21*(6), 873–886.

Pakes, F., & Winstone, J. (2009). Effective practice in mental health diversion and liaison. *The Howard Journal of Criminal Justice, 48*(2), 158–171.

Reed, J. (1992). Review of health and social services for mentally disordered offenders and those requiring similar services. In *Department of Health/Home Office*. London: HMSO.

Rogers, L., & Ormston, G. (2016). Successful strategies for working with mentally disordered offenders within a complex multi-agency environment. In J. Winstone (Ed.), *Mental health, crime and criminal justice: Responses and reforms* (pp. 218–241). London: Palgrave Macmillan.

Sannino, A., Daniels, H., & Gutierrez, K. (2009). Activity theory between historical engagement and future-making practice. In A. Sannino, H. Daniels, & K. Gutierrez (Eds.), *Learning and expanding with activity theory* (pp. 1–18). New York: Cambridge University Press.

Schulz, K., & Geithner, S. (2010). Individual and organizational development as interplay: An activity oriented approach. *German Journal of Research in Human Resource Management, 24*(2), 130–151.

Skeem, J. L., & Peterson, J. K. (2012). Identifying, treating, and reducing risk for offenders with mental illness. In J. Petersilia & K. Reitz (Eds.), *The Oxford handbook of sentencing and corrections*. Oxford: Oxford Handbooks Online.

Stone, N. (2003). *A companion guide to mentally disordered offenders.* Crayford: Shaw and Sons.

Tolviainen, H. (2007). Interorganisational leaning across levels: An object orientate approach. *Journal of Workplace Learning, 19*(6), 343–358.

Volberda, H., Van Den Bosch, F., & Mihalache, O. (2014). Advancing management innovation: Synthesizing processes, levels of analysis and change agents. *Organization Studies, 35*(9), 1245–1264.

Williams, N., Sadler, S., Durcan, G., & Mayers, A. (2019). *Health and justice characteristics of Dorset's liaison and diversion population.* Unpublished manuscript.

World Health Organisation. (2015). *Global strategy on people-centred and integrated health services.* Geneva: WHO.

Yin, R. (2009). *Case study research and applications: Design and methods.* London: Sage.

7

Mentoring in Practice: Rebuilding Dialogue with Mentees' Stories

Laure Kloetzer, Jo Wells, Laura Seppänen, and Sarah Hean

Introduction

This chapter reports on an intervention in organisational learning and innovation conducted in 2019 with a Voluntary and Community

L. Kloetzer (✉)
Institute of Psychology and Education, University of Neuchâtel, Neuchâtel, Switzerland
e-mail: laure.kloetzer@unine.ch

J. Wells
Bournemouth University, Poole, England, UK
e-mail: wellsj@bournemouth.ac.uk

L. Seppänen
University of Helsinki, Helsinki, Finland
e-mail: laura.seppanen@ttl.fi

S. Hean
University of Stavanger, Stavanger, Norway
e-mail: sarah.c.hean@uis.no

S. Hean et al. (eds.), *Improving Interagency Collaboration, Innovation and Learning in Criminal Justice Systems*,
https://doi.org/10.1007/978-3-030-70661-6_7

Sector (VCS) organisation in the South of England, active since 2005 mentoring ex-prisoners to support their (re)integration back into society. This intervention aimed at analysing the VCS activity and (re)building dialogue within the team. The organisation was seen by its staff as in a context of crisis. This was largely attributed to the uncertainties on funding and changing expectations of the role of the VCS within the Criminal Justice System in the UK. To support the (re)building of dialogue, the intervention hybridised the practices and methodologies of *Change Lab* and *Clinic of Activity* methods. The chapter first introduces the context of the intervention, secondly some methodological aspects of the intervention and thirdly the main findings of the researcher's empirical analysis of mentoring in practice. It will then discuss how these research data were used in a developmental workshop to support dialogue and reflection amongst staff members of the charity. The concepts of dialogical artefacts and micro-dramas will be used to analyse the dynamics at stake. We show that the researcher and practice participants have taken very different angles to make sense of the dialogical artefacts and micro-dramas presented to them. We finally discuss when and who should conduct the analysis of the research data collected from the workplace organisation, and drive problem identification required as a driver for future innovation.

In some research-led and more traditional interventions, the researcher conducts the analysis of research data and presents their findings to key stakeholders engaged in organisational learning, change and innovation activities—see for example design approaches (Penuel, 2014). They hope their analysis of the data will trigger dialogue between participants leading to cocreation and innovation. However, Sannino et al. (2016) claim that it is not for the researcher to make this analysis and hereby identify the problem embedded within the raw data collected from practice but the workers participating in the intervention themselves. This is at the heart of formative interventions such as Clinic of Activity and Change Laboratories, where mirror data selected from interviews and observations are brought to the developmental workshop. Here participants, in cooperation with the researcher and perhaps with the use of analytical tools such as theoretical frameworks, analyse the mirror data and draw their own conclusions of where problems in practice lie. In this chapter, we present evidence of this in a narrative in which the empirical analysis of the researcher and the later analysis of practice professionals engaged in a developmental workshop took very different turns. This contrast highlights the limits of researcher driven rather than researcher facilitated analysis of workplace data in the work development process.

The Involvement of the Voluntary Community Sector in Criminal Justice

The VCS has a long and well-established history of supporting prisoners and ex-prisoners in the criminal justice systems of Britain and the USA (Bryans et al., 2002; Epstein, 2009; Hughes, 2016) and VCS organisations have been piloting projects to support individuals in the community "at risk of reoffending" since the 1970s. These have ranged in scope from radical projects such as the Newham Alternatives Project (Dronfield, 1979) to "Community Chaplaincy" interventions (Whitehead, 2011). In the 1990s, the VCS became viewed as key partners in the core business of crime reduction (Tomczak, 2016). Clinks (an infrastructure organisation supporting voluntary organisations in the criminal justice system in England and Wales) was established in 1998 to support, promote and represent the involvement of the VCS in the criminal justice system (Gojkovic et al., 2011). Such projects raised questions about the efficacy and gaps within public sector offender rehabilitation. It has been argued that the VCS filled a particular gap left in England when probation services moved away from their traditional values of "advise, assist and befriend" towards a more "managerialist" and risk-driven agenda (Robinson & McNeill, 2013; Hucklesby & Wincup, 2014). In 2013, the Ministry of Justice announced a "Rehabilitation Revolution" which promised support to "anyone who had spent a day or more in prison", commissioning services from a competitive pool of commercial and VCS organisations. The *Transforming Rehabilitation Act* came into force in 2014 (Ministry of Justice, 2013). Whilst smaller organisations expected funding from the state as a result of this legislation, most were in fact almost side-lined, when large contracts were divided out across the country between the bigger charities and private companies called CRCs (Community Rehabilitation Companies). Following a number of reports on the limits of this system, National Probation Services are to take back the supervision of all offenders from December 2020.

Benefits and Risks of Through-the-Gate Mentoring Schemes

The VCS offers mentoring schemes, amongst other services, across England and Wales, mainly helping those leaving custody to resettle back into the community (Hinde & White, 2019; McNeill, 2019). Mentoring encompasses a range of different activities occurring in different contexts. A consensual definition describes mentoring as a "one-to-one relationship which is freely entered into and based upon trust and confidentiality. Mentoring is distinct from befriending in that it involves working to clearly defined goals and within set time frames" (Hucklesby & Wincup, 2014, p. 376). In the UK, mentoring has become routine criminal justice practice, despite some lack of demonstrated outcomes in reducing reoffending (Newburn & Shiner, 2006), and is a strategic priority in policy aimed at reducing reoffending (HM Government, 2019).

The increase in VCS mentoring schemes, and other offender-related services, are argued to be a response to public sector "austerity cuts" and marketisation agenda (Hucklesby & Wincup, 2014, p. 374). According to Hucklesby and Wincup, current mentoring policy "brings a group not currently subject to supervision under the gaze of the state" (ibidem, p. 375). They conclude with "the paradox inherent in using mentoring within the criminal justice: on the one hand, it (mentoring) might assist offenders to deal with long-standing problems but on the other hand, it provides a vehicle through which the formal criminal justice system can deepen its involvement in offenders' lives" (p. 375).

In summary, mentoring schemes, and VCS organisations across the UK, face a complex working environment, one in which they need to learn, innovate and develop to respond to the current demands and challenges placed upon them. In this chapter we present the potential of interventions designed to promote these processes.

Intervening in a Context of Crisis

This intervention took place within a VCS organisation in England, which had extensive experience in mentoring ex-prisoners, with complex issues locally. Prior to the *Transforming Rehabilitation* agenda, this organisation had a memorandum of understanding with local prisons allowing staff and volunteers to take referrals from prison, assess prisoner's needs and support their preparation for release. Typically, volunteers would meet people at the prison gate and accompany them in the days, weeks and months following release. The organisation's beneficiaries were often of low socio-economic status, with limited work qualifications and employment history. Many of their beneficiaries reported childhood neglect, abuse and being expelled from school. Many had never owned a home, or even held a tenancy. A majority had serious substance misuse issues, many were physically dependent on alcohol or opiates. At least half of them had health problems, either mental or physical, often both. The mental health issues included autism, personality disorders, severe trauma and Post Traumatic Stress Disorder. These were further compounded by learning disabilities—typically dyslexia—or behavioural disorders such as ADHD.

Since its beginnings, the financial situation of this VCS organisation had been uncertain, due to the lack of regular funding for its mentoring activity. They continued to support their clients, whilst simultaneously seeking to develop and innovate, imagining new projects for the future and finding ways to find its place in the landscape created by the Transforming Rehabilitation agenda. The context of mentoring was changing, from mentoring independently from any institution on a volunteer basis, to diverse mentoring schemes in diversion or community sentence schemes. These changes of context for mentoring created tensions/challenges for the team, and the mission of their volunteers.

In this context, interventionist researchers with whom the organisation had contact through a wider research-practice partnership (an EU funded project, COLAB-H2020-MSCA-RISE-2016/734536), suggested an exploration of the views of different stakeholders within the organisation (trustees, staff members, volunteers and beneficiaries) on the organisation as it is and could be in the future. This culminated in a workshop with staff, supporting them to collectively reflect on the current context and contradictions/tensions arising. These reflections would contribute to moving beyond its impasse and develop plans for the future with service redesign.

Conducting a Hybrid Change Lab/Clinic of Activity Intervention

The intervention was inspired by the theoretical and methodological frames of Cultural-Historical Activity Theory (CHAT), especially Clinic of Activity (Clot, 1999; Clot & Kostulski, 2011) and Change Lab (Engeström, 1987; Engeström et al., 1996; Sannino & Engeström, 2017). Common to both these approaches is the use of facilitated and collective meetings between key stakeholders to discuss and design means of organisational change (see Chapter 8 of this volume). This workshop was preceded by an ethnographic phase in which mentors were observed by the first author in their everyday activities, and in which the experiences of different stakeholders, including staff, volunteers and beneficiaries, of working with and for the organisation were explored in interviews. The process was supported through extensive field notes. Observations gave the researcher access to many interactions between staff or volunteer mentors and their mentees in various places: For example, the first author observed first meetings between a mentor and a potential mentee; assessment of mentee needs, in prison and after release; planned regular meetings with mentees in public places; emergency interventions with a mentee; interactions through phone or WhatsApp; reporting of these interactions in the organisation's digital data information system. Additionally, 19 interviews were conducted with mentees ($n = 4$), mentors ($n = 5$), trustees ($n = 3$), staff ($n = 5$), external partners ($n = 2$—police staff and an expert from the mental health hospital). The interviews were based on a narrative format around a few leading questions (beginning with their own experience with the charity). The questions aimed to understand these stakeholders' experience within this VCS organisation, and their understanding of its mission and current challenges. All interviews were audio recorded and transcribed.

All data were thematically analysed based on repeated readings and comparisons of the transcripts. The analysis was discussed as field-work dialogues (Lassiter, 2005) in the research team. The VCR (Voice, Centred, Relational) method of data analysis (Brown & Gilligan, 1991, 1992) was also used for highlighting the perspective of the mentees. The analysis assumed each "person's voice" to be "polyphonic and complex" (Brown & Gilligan, 1992, p. 15), which means that an individual might experience multiple, sometimes contradictory ways of thinking about and understanding situations (Brown & Gilligan, 1992). How a person speaks (and indeed, does not speak) of their experiences, themselves, others and relationships, provides insight into their perceptions and experiences (Brown & Gilligan, 1991, 1992; Doucet & Mauthner, 2008). Early presentations of the work-in-progress with some members of the organisation's team, in a research seminar at the University of Neuchâtel, as well as ongoing informal conversations with team members and academic colleagues, helped us explore and develop these contradictory interpretations.

The whole process was guided by an interventionist perspective aiming at supporting learning, dialogue and collective reflection within the organisation. The analysis simultaneously contributed to our academic knowledge of the role of the mentor in the VCS and to this transformative purpose.

Ultimately, some data were selected to stimulate discussion between staff members, that could eventually lead to organisational learning and innovation. The forum for this discussion was a developmental workshop, designed to offer conditions for authentic and truthful dialogue within the team.

Research Findings from the Analytic Phase: Mentoring in Practice

Based on data collected from interviews and observation, we, as researchers, analysed mentoring as an *activity*, in which the interplay of practical help and human sustained contact is critical. Our analysis highlights five dimensions of mentoring within this organisation from the experiences of mentors and mentees. Mentors' experience shows the challenges of working independently, in an uncertain world, whilst having to manage their emotions and establish boundaries between their personal and mentee's lives. Mentors describe mentoring as a "firefighting exercise" addressing the basic needs of sometimes desperate people—or people in desperate situations. Additionally, the analysis of the experience of the mentees highlights the benefits of this activity; mentoring is seen as a friendly presence, which helps meet basic needs with a human touch and serves as a bridging activity to navigate the complex ecology of services and institutions. These findings echo the challenges and benefits identified by Gosling and Buck (2015), stating that "mentoring may offer a safe space for mentees to practically 'try on' desistance for size, alongside a supportive other".

The Need for Mentors to Work Independently

Some mentors expressed doubts, lacking self-confidence regarding their mentoring. These doubts and feelings seem to be linked to limited training as well as to the need to work on their own, in relative isolation. For most volunteers, the criminal justice services have been a "black box" until they began mentoring their clients. They don't know much about the way criminal justice services are working, and have to discover and learn a lot. The need to meet and discuss with more experienced peers is reinforced by the concrete and emotional complexities of the situations of the mentees, and the ambiguity of the object of their work (Table 7.1).

Table 7.1 Illustrative quotes regarding: *working independently*

	Representative comments
Uncertainty, lack of self-confidence, lack of feedback	"Most difficult I think it's really being isolated being a volunteer, because you don't really have any feedback on what you're doing and as I say you're just not really sure what you're supposed to be doing"
Lack of interactions with peers	"I would like to have more interaction with other volunteers. I think I would have found it useful for other volunteer's view of how they handle strategically the, the relationship with their... with their clients"
Need to learn about the criminal justice system	"I didn't know how prisons ran, I didn't know anything at all, and it's quite an eye-opener. (...) They would really open up to me and tell me, you don't realise just how some people have to live, do you, until you work with them?"

The Emotional Labour of the Mentor and Their Need to Maintain Boundaries

Mentoring in this context means working with people, whose life trajectories have usually been extremely harsh. Mentors reported being emotionally affected by mentees life stories and current circumstances which demand, paradoxically, both regular engagement and personal distance as well as acceptance of one's own limited power to act. Getting this personal distance right is one goal in the training of professional social workers, as well as recurrent difficulty in their professional life. Although it is one main focus of training VCS mentors in this context, it is challenging to get it right in the short training time and limited supervision possibilities of volunteers. Establishing and maintaining correct boundaries is one major difficulty raised both by volunteers and by staff supervising them. The need to "create distance with warmth, empathy and respect" is systemically talked about by staff members. They speak of the difficulty of understanding and establishing boundaries, whilst creating a "therapeutic alliance", which allows mentee and mentor to work together.

Interview data described a need to establish clearly mentors' expectations versus outcomes. Mentors talk of "learning to redefine success", a need to pursue mentoring despite frequent reoffending. Desistance was not seen as a linear path, but one paved with breaks and failures. Becoming aware of the extreme psychological and material difficulties of their mentees, helped mentors cope with the uncertain outcome of their efforts (Table 7.2).

Mentees Need Practical Help and Social Recognition

Mentoring was seen by both mentors and mentees first and foremost as an activity to meet the basic needs of people who are in a desperate situation. Basic needs include food, clothes, a roof or sleeping bag if no roof is available, engaging with health services and probation officers. Mentors also helped beneficiaries meet their legal and medical appointments and get access to welfare payments, identity documents, addiction or health services. The mentor also helped with emotional need such as a beneficiary's need for feeling socially acceptable, and having someone who cares, someone to talk to:

"Support, practical support, can help with lots of things from forms, phone calls, all the way down to just an ear to listen, and this is good for some people. People who don't really have family, I think sometimes just want someone separate to their life to offload, does that make sense? I think you've got probation but like again, sometimes you have this barrier with probation, you're scared to tell them everything, you know, but with them, you're not, because you can trust them" (mentee).

Helping with emergencies and providing social recognition and support go together. This is new for some of the mentees and helps in improving their self-esteem:

"Over the years, with getting in trouble and conviction, things like that, I've kind of alienated myself from my family a bit and all my friends are addicts so I haven't really got a lot of good friends that I can trust so it's nice to have (mentor's name) as somebody that I can call or meet up

Table 7.2 Illustrative quotes: *emotional labour and maintaining boundaries*

	Representative comments
Establish and maintain boundaries	"It's very easy to overstep boundaries (...) One of the things I used to find difficult is that they would say, 'you're my friend' and I'd say, 'no, I'm not your friend, I'm here to support you but I'm not your friend', and that's a difficult one and a lot of people overstep. You've got to help people as much as you can without getting too involved, and without misleading them, because that's too easy too, they do become very clingy" "They would maybe say that I probably overstep my responsibility. In other words the theory of it is, I guess, meet somebody, get to know them, help them on the path and then disengage. Well, I've never been very good at the disengage..."
Work on one's own emotions and expectations	"The challenges are always different because you're dealing with human beings... I enjoy helping people, making a difference. Of course you don't always do that, if you are sensitive to failure then this is not a role for you. On the other hand you need...you learn to redefine success. I mean, success can be keeping somebody, helping somebody stay out of trouble for a month. Or it can be helping them stay out of trouble permanently..." (mentor) "There was a little bit of an adjustment period where I had to reassure myself that I was doing the right thing and that it's not on me if it goes wrong. I think of Am I doing the right thing, yes I'm doing the right thing. You can lead a horse to water but you can't make it drink, all of that stuff it's that constant kind of checking myself, checking my preconceptions and things" (mentor)

with to have a social chat, a coffee. (…) I have a really good relationship with my mother now and (mentor's name) sort of egged me on to do that as well, so he's a good guy. He motivates me, makes me feel good about myself" (mentee).

Mentors are described as providing sound advice in delicate human situations, a valuable resource for people who have no family nor reliable friends.

"Some of what we do as mentors, if you like, is provide conventional solutions to people for whom conventional solutions are not necessarily their first port of call" (mentor).

Keeping away from prison requires (at least partially) the acceptance of dominant social norms. We hypothesise that the personal, trusting relation patiently established between mentor and mentee through their practical engagement with multiple everyday emergencies, makes this (re)connection with the dominant norms possible. In this regard the dominant norm is not only the oppressive norm of the authority, but can be partly appropriated by the mentee because it is expressed and enacted by someone they trust (i.e., the mentor). "Providing conventional solutions", as stated above, the interactions between mentee and mentor implicitly initiated a re-normalisation process based on trust and not fear.

The Importance of the Mentor in Assisting in and Navigating Complex Systems

Mentees have multiple needs which are dealt with by a variety of diverse organisations including commercial companies, public services, charities, churches (soup kitchen, homeless shelters, laundry, meetings of Narcotics Anonymous, hotlines, etc.). The mentors utilise their own knowledge and social skills as well as the VCS' connections to identify these diverse resources and then navigate and liaise with these complex services with the support of the mentor. Mentor help is especially appreciated in interactions with public services, where the VCS reputation and status allow them to advocate for the mentees. In the complex ecosystem of social support for vulnerable people and criminal justice services, mentors play an important role because they are close to the service users and able to navigate this ecosystem efficiently. Their action aims at overcoming the silos of these services and fill in or supplement any shortcomings in their current service offer. One staff member defines their action as "helping an individual to engage with all of the services that they do need" (Table 7.3).

The importance of mentoring lies precisely in the capacity of the mentors to take the side of their mentees, meet them on their terms, whilst navigating the complex official system of institutions and programmes. Another staff member defines their action as "*not providing the services, but providing the glue to the different services they need*". They liaise in a way that considers the psychological fragility of their mentees.

Mentoring is well-recognised and appreciated by the mentees, as well as by partner organisations. Knowledge of local systems and advocacy skills, especially with public agencies, go hand-in-hand with a sound understanding of the delicate psychological condition of mentees. This liaison, orientation and navigation work begins from the prison gate and continues for as long as the mentees are not able to handle these tasks independently.

Conclusion on Mentoring in Practice

Overall, the researchers' analysis of data showed the benefits of mentoring to be multi-layered. The mentor was important for:

(a) meeting clients' basic needs (food, accommodation, health and medication, clothes, communication…)
(b) helping them with administrative procedures (Universal Credit, Identity documents, registration with a General Practitioner, bank accounts, housing, etc.) and advocating for public services
(c) helping with job searches, using computers, budgeting, etc.
(d) helping clients with keeping track of their life, especially keeping important appointments (probation and health appointments) and getting organised
(e) socialising, getting out regularly, meeting people in a positive manner

Table 7.3 Illustrative quotes: *liaising and navigating complex systems*

	Representative comments
Connecting the user with different services, advocating, filling the gaps	"What we are doing essentially is helping an individual to engage with all of the services that they do need. (…) So the key ones that our service users need are going to be substance misuse, mental health services, all those services have been cut, those services also for years are target led, as is probation target led. So what does that mean? That means that they will cherry-pick, do you know what I mean when I say that? They will only go for people that they think that they'll have positive outcomes for, so the people that most need those services are going to be the really hard people, they're not interested in them." (staff member) "They struggle so much to get to appointments and in fact, that's one thing that we help people to do is to get to places and then start engaging with the people that they do need to engage with. So we're not providing the therapy, we're providing the glue to the different services that they need (…)" (staff member)

	Representative comments
Building the capacity of the clients to navigate these complex systems	"You come across stone walls from the NHS, stone walls, you know, it's a hard and it's a harrowing time and without their help I'd have probably topped myself, I'd have probably committed suicide. (My mentor) helped me make appointments and ring people, and she helped me get things in place and organise myself…" (mentee) "A lot of services say, okay come along to my office at ten o'clock on this day, and our clients struggle to do it. For lots of different reasons yes, sometimes it's money, sometimes it's psychology, sometimes it's they don't know how to get there, sometimes it's because they're just terrified to go out the door, they can't get up in the mornings, has been one, so that's essentially what we do" (staff member) "People start to build up their own confidence and then they will not start thinking they're walking around with a tattoo saying 'I'm a criminal' on their heads, which is what most people do feel like when they come out of custody" (staff member)

(f) listening to clients, offering social recognition and contact when friends and family are missing, reducing stress of life after prison, helping to see things clearer, helping to form judgement and to act according to the dominant norms of behaviour.

Our analysis demonstrates that the practical help (points a, b, c, d) and the social benefits (points e and f) happen simultaneously and not independently, through the mentor providing the client with regular everyday support, with respect and human warmth.

Rebuilding Dialogue Around Mentees' Stories

Users' Stories as Dialogical Artefacts

The data collected not only served to build our understanding of the role of mentors in the criminal justice system, but also served as a trigger for dialogue in a service development workshop involving organisational staff. The key question for the researchers as interventionists was then to decide which aspects of the analysis would best support the collective reflection of the staff. The challenge was to identify, in the empirical data collected, some "elements" around which a special kind of professional dialogue—precise, documented, authentic, possibly controversial but respectful—could happen. The first phase of the research had demonstrated the strength of personal engagement of the mentors (volunteers and staff) with the former prisoners. Although different members of the organisation could hold sometimes divergent ideas on what the organisation should be doing in the future, their commitment to the mentees, the *raison d'être* of the organisation, was unquestionable. In informal exchanges and interviews, they expressed recurrent questionings like: *why do some mentees engage with us in the long term, and why do some mentees give up so quickly? Are our services appropriate for mentees and how?* Therefore, when we had to select some materials to trigger collective dialogue and reflection, the first author decided to build short mentees' stories based on excerpts from the interviews.

These stories were built by selecting in the interviews all parts dealing directly with mentees/mentors relationship. In theoretical terms, these stories are dialogical artefacts (Kloetzer, 2018), i.e. edited research data turned into polyphonic materials, which crystallise the multiple voices and reflections of interviewees, and capture some of the dialogues previously held in the course of the research. In our case, the mentees' stories present the own voice of the client, but also reflect indirectly the voices of the others, whom the client has been interacting with—voice of the mentor, of the doctor, of the probation officer, of the judge sometimes. All pieces of data telling about interviewees' relationship to the VCS organisation were included, so that the researcher did not attempt to write a coherent story. Four mentee's stories were constructed for intervention purposes.

Six staff members of the organisation attended the research workshop. The workshop was structured in the following way: first, we shared homemade sandwiches and a cup of tea, then the first author framed the purpose of the workshop, and gave an introduction to some CHAT core theoretical concepts, including the concepts of "activity systems" and "contradictions within the activity system and between activity systems" (see Chapters 2, 3, 5, 6 and 8 of this volume for further detail). Introducing this theoretical model provides a "second stimulus" to help the team take some distance with its own situation and analyse it, using this theoretical lens. The first author also explained how these concepts related to the practice of the organisation, studied in empirical work. Secondly, the researcher briefly presented the empirical work. Thirdly, she introduced the method chosen for the discussion, which was to first read and then discuss each of the mentees' stories. The Clinic of Activity approach uses data (sometimes videos, sometimes narratives, sometimes excerpts of reports) to support the analysis by the workers (here, VCS staff and volunteers) of their own activity in a polyphonic way. We explained how the content of the mentees' stories had been selected; i.e. by extracting in the interviews with the clients all comments which directly referred to their interaction or experience with the organisation under study. We then gave these mentees' stories in paper form to each participant. The stories were discussed one by one and gave rise to vivid exchanges between the workshop participants.

Anchoring Dialogue in Micro-Dramas

Table 7.4 illustrates one of the stories brought to the workshop, extracted directly from an interview with a client/mentee in contact with the organisation.

During the workshop, the mentees' stories play a specific role: each of the participants pick up these stories according to their own ***perezhivanie*** of the situation, in Vygotskian term (Vygotsky, 1994)—which means, through the prism of their own cognitive and emotional experience of the situation (Veresov, 2016, 2017) (Table 7.5).

This excerpt is the beginning of the discussion of the first mentee's story. In this section, we analyse the dialogical dynamics of this excerpt. This analysis of the architecture and dynamics of the conversation is based on an analysis with interlocutory logic, which is described elsewhere (Kostulski, 2004). The discussion on the first story opens with a question from the researcher. The whole sequence selected is then driven by this initial questioning, which relates to "what is important in the service" according to the first mentee (Adrian). Interestingly, all participants contribute to the following discussion, although they pick up very different elements of the story. The story carries indeed potential for open interpretation, as it is very dense, rich, emotional and open to possible and ambiguous meanings. The first staff participant selects a sentence from the written text, which highlights his own priority in mentoring: talking to the people. He doesn't add any comment at this point. The second staff participant selects a different verbatim, "probation has a different agenda", reverts it and attributes it to the mentee in a propositional way: "he thinks that we've got a different agenda from probation"—through this inversion, probation becomes the reference and the organisation represents a deviation to this reference. The third intervention supports this second comment in an indirect way: "really interesting, isn't it?", which remains enigmatic at this point. The fourth staff participant adds her own answer to the initial question, with two quotes, "not being let down", "not having a family", which also refer, in our observation, to her own views on the mentees as having a hard and lonely life. At this point, this juxtaposition of quotes triggers a meta-comment on what is happening in the meeting, i.e., that different people

Table 7.4 Client Adrian—selected quotes from our interview

I met (staff member) actually while I was in prison because he goes into the prison to talk. So I filled in the leaflet and he came and saw me because I had no family, I was homeless before I went to prison, and I needed support. Funnily enough, I found the leaflet because they don't really clean the cells when people move in, and someone else in my cell had obviously had one, so that's how I found it. But I suppose if I'd have asked for one, I'd have got one, but I didn't know about it, so that was lucky. Well, it was all geared up for when I got out. I mean, I met him, I'd actually seen him meeting someone else about seven months before my release, so I spoke to him and he said, well I'll come and see you nearer the date. And then they had an open day in the education block where there were lots of different agencies, people from work and probation, and (staff member) was there. He had a bowl of sweets so I was eating the sweets [laughs], but and then when he did come for the appointment he said this is what I can help you with; life, work, help you get, lots of different things, support, and since I've been out I think it's been great. I had a period of time where I relapsed on the drugs and I wasn't really seeing him (...) because when you come out of prison you don't have much money, I had no clothes, (another staff member) bought me some clothes and a cheap phone with credit, and then after that, because there's Universal Credit benefit but it takes a long time. (...) Nine weeks to get my money so that's a long time, you know. So, in that time, they would get me a food bank voucher, I don't know if they still do it, they used to get an Asda voucher so you could get some food, little things like this. But also, in support, (staff member), he's just support... I just phoned him today because I was going to meet him after you but he's a bit busy so he's going to meet me tomorrow, but he could tell straight away because I'm bit upset today, having to move back and that. Because I have no family, see, no family whatsoever. The family I did have are dead and I've been on my own for many years in addiction, so it's nice to have... okay, probation is cool, but probation more have a set job, don't they? They have to lower the risk of me reoffending which is good, but someone like (staff members) maybe yourself, you're more support, practical support, can help with lots of things from forms, phone calls, all the way down to just an ear to listen, and this is good for some people. People who don't really have family, I think sometimes just want someone separate to their life to offload, does that make sense? (...)
I think you've got probation but like again, sometimes you have this barrier with probation, you're scared to tell them everything, you know, but with them, you're not, because you can trust them. Obviously, there's boundaries but you know they're there, but yeah, a lot of people that come out of prison are just left, a lot of people come out of prison in this country and are homeless straight away and there's no one there to help them. And a lot of people who've been in prison feel a barrier between authority. (...) I always did. I always felt like I can't talk to this person, can't talk to that person. I think I'm doing alright at the minute with (Charity name). I think I'm so glad they didn't close my case, because they could have, because I went missing for a while, but instead they just picked the support straight up, and it's nice isn't it? Because not looking for sympathy but in my life, you're used to people letting you down, but they don't let you down

Table 7.5 Discussion in the workshop between staff following the individual reading of Adrian's story (excerpt)

1. R: So according to Adrian, what's important in (VCS name) service?
2. P1: "Having someone to talk to"
3. P2: He thinks we've got "a different agenda from probation" on the issues of offending
4. P3: This is really interesting, isn't it?
5. P4: "Not being let down, not having any family", that's what really jumped out at me. So it's interesting that we've all got different things that jump out at us isn't it? (nervous laughs)
6. P5: (Staff member) uses sweets to get people to do things
7. P6: That's a standard! (big laughs)
8. P4: Well I like the first sentence actually. "I met (staff member) while I was in prison because he goes into the prison to talk"
9. P1: I think this is a perfect scenario of a (Charity name) client from the beginning when we reach someone in jail
10. P6: I don't think so. I'd probably buy about one or two mobile phones a year and I've never, ever, bought anyone clothes, so that's definitely not
11. P3: Yes it's really interesting, it is really interesting about the difference between what he says. It's really, really interesting
12. R: What do you think is interesting P3?
13. P3: For me, I would almost cry that he didn't think we were interested in helping him stop offending, that to me—to me—is the core of what it is about, it's helping people progress away from the criminal lifestyle. But here for him he thinks that doesn't matter to us...
14. P1: Why do you think so?
15. P3: Because he said that we have a different agenda from probation, the whole agenda
16. P1: Ha...
17. R: It's interesting because you also picked this one, P2, different agenda from probation?
18. P2: I did make a joke, but yeah, even if I go back in offending, I'll have people there who will still work with me so...
19. P3: Yes, which is a good tip. I think we do want people to feel we don't give up and that they can be honest
20. P4: Well personally I think we need to be different from probation because if we're going to be the same as probation then what are we doing?"

pick up different aspects of the situation. A nervous laugh shows some discomfort with this situation. The two following comments from two other members are jokes, probably aiming consciously or not at relieving the atmosphere.

The opening of this workshop, from speech turns 1 to 7, frames rather well the whole problem space, organised in tension between two agendas of rehabilitation: one focused on desistance from crime, the other one on step-by-step re-socialisation. The dynamics of nervous laughs/joke/laughs again is a pattern regularly met in Clinic of Activity interventions, which, in our experience, frequently sets the ground for a second round of deeper dialogue between the participants.

Indeed, in speech turn 8, P1 comes back with a subjective appreciation of the situation as being "a perfect case", which is immediately contradicted (also at the level of appreciation) by P6, who bases their disagreement on the action to "buy" things for the mentee (a phone, or clothes in that case). P3 once again supports indirectly P6's position by stating that this is really interesting. As an explicit disagreement, brutally faced by all participants, threatens the expansion and deepening of dialogue, the researcher makes another intervention, with a direct question at P3, aiming not at closing nor smoothening the disagreement, but at explaining the position of P3. P3's answer is very rich, because it conveys both an emotional reaction ("I would almost cry…") and a well-articulated statement on the positioning of the charity. Speech turns from 12 to 16 serve to make the perspective of P3 explicit, for the benefits in particular of P1, which non-verbally marks in 16 that they now understand what was meant and visibly engage in thinking about this quote "not the same agenda" with a new perspective.

In speech turns 17 to 20, the researcher directly addresses another participant to make their perspective more explicit, opening a new small space of discussion of P2, P3 and P4. P4's perspective is more clearly expressed on this topic on "not the same agenda" at the end of this sequence: "personally I think we need to be different from probation because if we're going to be the same as probation then what are we doing?" This speech turn is also interesting because it joins a subjective positioning and a well-articulated argument.

In the follow-up of this dialogue, not presented here, P1 will reflect aloud on the interpretation we should have of this quote "not the same agenda" for this participant, coming back to the written text and his own knowledge of the case. This shows that in this dialogical space, P3's perspective becomes part of the internal dialogue of P1, and that conversely, P1's internal dialogue becomes, through externalisation, part of the shared reflections of the team.

This sequence is an interesting example of how collective reflection may progress step-by-step with passionate participants, in a well-structured dialogical space around well-designed dialogical artefacts (here, the mentee's edited stories). Disagreements are not ignored but turned, if possible, into motors of development. The sequence opens with the framing of the problem space, showing immediately how different perspectives on rehabilitation, closer or more distant from what how the agenda of probation is perceived, reflect the personal experience and priorities of the different participants. Thanks to the shared reference of mentees' stories which constitute micro-dramas and micro-crises "that we can define as 'micro social situations of development'" (Veresov, 2016, p. 133), in the sense of Vygotsky, it expands into a deeper reflection on this topic.

Analysing Data Collaboratively: An Analytical Mismatch for Potential Development

As mentioned earlier, the data collected all along the research process had a dual purpose: a research logic and an intervention logic. In this chapter, on one hand, we have presented the findings on mentoring in practice coming from an analytical approach of our interviews. On the other hand, some of these research data, selected by one of the researchers, have been simultaneously used by this researcher in a developmental workshop to support the main goal of the intervention: to help the staff collectively reflect and discuss the past, present and future of the organisation and of their mentoring activity.

We argue here that although the analysis of the researcher and of the organisation participants was different, these parts relate, and in fact there are mutual benefits of combining both the analytic approach (the researcher-driven analysis) and the interventionist approach (the participant-driven analysis).

After the analysis of the data from the researcher's perspective, the value and sense of the organisation's service to its clients was clear for the researcher. The analysis of the activity performed by the first author through observations and interviews highlighted (a) benefits, as well as challenges, of the mentoring activity for this population on multiple dimensions (practical, social, emotional, etc.) as well as (b) the interplay between practical, emergency help and the higher-level social, emotional and cognitive benefits for the client, and finally, (c) the important role of the organisation in the ecology of CJS, helping its clients get access to highly specialised and compartmentalised public, private or third sector services (housing, work, health and mental health, etc.)—i.e., the organisation played a boundary crossing role in the field of post-prison rehabilitation.

In a classical research, at that point, the researcher could wish to feedback these important findings to the participants in a final workshop. However, in the first author's experience, sharing the findings of a research with the participants does not help them much in actively engaging in collective reflection, organisational learning and organisational transformation. If the research is sufficiently good, these findings are rarely contested and usually accepted with benevolent attention and without follow-up. In fact, the reaction to the presentation of research findings (of sufficient quality) should be expected to reflect the kind of relations that the researcher has built with participants—trustful relations might allow for more discussions than would distrust or conflict. Here, the quality of relations that the researcher had tried to build with the participants was put into balance with the sometimes tensed and quite emotional disagreements within the team. Following Vygotsky's call for the use of indirect methodologies (Vygotski, 1997), the interventionist-researcher then decided to appeal to the common passion of staff for their clients to try and create a safe space for collective dialogue. To do so, the first author created dialogical artefacts, made of selected parts of the interviews with the mentees, in order to ground and nourish the discussion. From the researcher's perspective, these vignettes or user stories had made concrete or materialised the most relevant aspects of the mentor–mentee relationship, and beautifully displayed the core benefits of mentoring and the core aspects of the organisation's service that should be preserved and expanded in the future. The researcher expected to rebuild this shared understanding of the mission of the organisation with the staff during the workshop, based on close shared analysis of these multi-faceted stories.

Surprisingly then for the researcher, when these user stories were shared in the workshop, that these were instead read by the participants in an unexpected way. It seemed at that time that all participants were cherry-picking very different elements, expressions or sentences, from these stories, and that none of them focused on the three main dimensions identified by the researcher in her own analysis (i.e., multi-dimensional support, interplay of technical help and higher-level support and boundary crossing role of the organisation in the complex local ecology of CJS and support services). Interventions are full of surprises like this. Our point is not that participants should follow researchers' understanding, but that they are supported in taking steps in their own collective (and individual) trajectories. Researchers gain new understanding with these reactions (Engeström & Sannino, 2010; Seppänen et al., Chapter 9 of this book). By attempting to understanding the mismatch between the researcher's and the organisation's perspectives/analyses deepens both the participants' and researchers' understanding of the situation.

The analysis of the dialogical dynamics in the first minutes of the discussion of the first user story presented here shows that this cherry-picking did not happen randomly, but echoed—refracted—the emotional experiences of the participants within the organisation. The dialogue, framed and sometimes made explicit by the interventionist-researcher, constructed stepwise a problem space which was very relevant for the organisation, and helped us jointly understand the contradiction between "being like or not being like" the probation services. The interplay of past experience, personal knowledge and values, affective elements and focused dialogue, allowed for the opening up of a collective space for thinking and reflection—not without tensions, of course. This intervention and the subsequent analysis therefore highlights the discrepancy between the "desk analysis" performed by the researcher on academic bases, informed by her own *perezhivanie* of the intervention process, and the analysis performed during the workshop, informed by the *perezhivanie*, lived experience, of the staff participants. Our analysis of these tensions contributes to highlighting why collaboration between researchers and practitioners, although extremely important, is also rather difficult. It highlights that in this research context, both development and analysis are non-linear, iterative, processes, dynamically integrating varying perspectives from all participants to the research.

If compared to a Change Laboratory or the related Change/Boundary crossing Workshop (Ala-Laurinaho et al., 2017; Seppänen & Koli, 2010) methodologies, the hybrid method applied in this case has emphasised a radical shift towards polyphony or multi-voicedness about the intervention. There does not have to be any final, monolithic/coherent story to be told about the outcome: what is more valuable is what all participants can do with the collective and personal lived experience of dialogue—researchers as well as practitioners.

References

Ala-Laurinaho, A., Kurki, A.-L., & Simonsen Abildgaard, J. (2017). Supporting sensemaking to promote a systemic view of organizational changes—Contributions from activity theory. *Journal of Change Management*, Published online 5 April 2017.

Brown, L. M., & Gilligan, C. (1991). Listening for voice in narratives of relationship. *New Directions for Child Development, 54*, 43–62.

Brown, L. M., & Gilligan, C. (1992). *Meeting at the crossroads: Women's psychology and girls' development*. Cambridge, MA: Harvard University Press.

Bryans, S., Martin, C., & Walker, R. (2002). *Prisons and the voluntary sector: A bridge into the community*. Waterside Press.

Clot, Y. (1999). *La fonction psychologique du travail*. Paris: Presses Universitaires de France-PUF.

Clot, Y., & Kostulski, K. (2011). Intervening for transforming: The horizon of action in the clinic of activity. *Theory & Psychology, 21*(5), 681–696.

Doucet, A., & Mauthner, N. S. (2008). What can be known and how? Narrated subjects and the listening guide. *Qualitative Research, 8*(3), 399–409. https://doi.org/10.1177/1468794106093636.

Dronfield. (1979) *Outside chance: The story of the Newham alternatives project*. Radical Alternatives to Prison.

Engeström, Y. (1987/2015). *Learning by expanding*. Cambridge University Press.

Engeström, Y., & Sannino, A. (2010). Studies of expansive learning: Foundations, findings and future challenges. *Educational Research Review, 5*(1), 1–24.

Engeström, Y., Virkkunen, J., Helle, M., Pihlaja, J., & Poikela, R. (1996). The Change Laboratory as a tool for transforming work. *Lifelong Learning in Europe, 1*(2), 10–17.

Epstein, R. (2009). *The voluntary sector in UK prisons.* Butterworth Tolley Publishing.

Gojkovic, D., Mills, A., & Meek, R. (2011). *Scoping the involvement of third sector organisations in the seven resettlement pathways for offenders* (Third Sector Research Centre, Working Paper 57).

Gosling, H. J., & Buck, G. (2015). Mentoring: Crossing boundaries with care? Helena Gosling and Gill Buck consider mentoring within a criminal justice context. *Criminal Justice Matters, 99*(1), 22–23. ISSN 0962-7251.

Hinde, K., & White, R. (2019). Peer support, desistance and the role of the third sector. *The Howard Journal of Crime and Justice, 58*(3), 329–348.

HM Government. (2019). *Guidance: Mentoring services for people in prison and on probation.*

Hucklesby, A., & Wincup, E. (2014). Assistance, support and monitoring? The paradoxes of mentoring adults in the criminal justice system. *Journal of Social Policy, 43*(2), 373–390.

Hughes, E. (2016). Non-profit and voluntary sector programs in prisons and jails: Perspectives from England and the USA. In *Voluntary sector in prisons* (pp. 21–51). New York: Palgrave Macmillan.

Kloetzer, L. (2018). VET as transformative, collaborative research: Cross self-confrontation, dialogical artefacts, and the development of organizational dialogue in a Swiss factory. *Nordic Journal of Vocational Education and Training, 7*(2), 63–83.

Kostulski, K. (2004). Développement de la pensée et du rapport à l'autre dans une interlocution: «est-ce que c'est un endroit pour poser un paquet de contre-rails?». *Cahiers de Linguistique Française, 26,* 113–131.

Lassiter, L. E. (2005). *The Chicago guide to collaborative ethnography*. University of Chicago Press.

McNeill, F. (2019). *Pervasive punishment: Making sense of mass supervision.* Emerald: Bingley.

Ministry of Justice. (2013). *Transforming rehabilitation: A revolution in the way we manage offenders* (Vol. 8517). The Stationery Office.

Newburn, T., & Shiner, M. (2006). Young people, mentoring and social inclusion. *Youth Justice, 6*(1), 23–41.

Penuel, W. R. (2014). Emerging forms of formative intervention research in education. *Mind, Culture, and Activity, 21*(2), 97–117.
Robinson, G., & McNeill, F. (2013). Purposes matter: Examining the 'ends' of probation. In *What matters in probation* (pp. 292–319). Willan.
Sannino, A., & Engeström, Y. (2017). Co-generation of societally impactful knowledge in Change Laboratories. *Management Learning, 48*(1), 80–96.
Sannino, A., Engeström, Y., & Lemos, M. (2016). Formative interventions for expansive learning and transformative agency. *Journal of the Learning Sciences, 25*(4), 599–633.
Seppänen, L., & Koli, A. (2010, February 10–12). *Exploring work: Employee stories as tools for promoting workplace well-being*. Paper presented at the Towards Better Work and Well-being. Proceedings: 98–104, Helsinki, Finland.
Tomczak, P. (2016). *The penal voluntary sector*. Taylor & Francis.
Veresov, N. (2016). Perezhivanie as a phenomenon and a concept: Questions on clarification and methodological meditations. *Cultural-Historical Psychology, 12*(3), 129–148.
Veresov, N. (2017). The concept of perezhivanie in cultural-historical theory: Content and contexts. In *Perezhivanie, emotions and subjectivity* (pp. 47–70). Singapore: Springer.
Vygotski, L. (1997). *Pensée et langage* (1934). Paris: La Dispute.
Vygotsky, L. S. (1994). The problem of the environment. *The Vygotsky Reader,* 338–354.
Whitehead, P. (2011). *Evaluation report of research at six community chaplaincy projects*. Teesside University.

Websites

www.communitychaplaincy.org.uk.
www.clinks.org.

Part III

Strategies and Methods to Promote Collaboration, Management and Innovation

Researchers in the field of penology have traditionally been objective bystanders, observing and describing current practices in the criminal justice and associated systems. This activity is useful in building the academic and disciplinary understanding of these systems. This knowledge may in turn assist professionals in practice, articulate and reflect on their work activity, potentially disrupting and challenging current assumptions of how things do and should work in these environments. However, researchers have a greater responsibility to practice than this. They have a role as facilitators and agents of change. Part II presents and critically evaluates some of the methods available to researchers to take on this more proactive responsibility within the criminal justice field. Whilst Part I presented some of the current challenges to collaboration, Part II explores methods through which this can be improved. Chapters in this section will focus on the application and transferability of these methods to the criminal justice context and the task of improving collaboration/innovation, rather than the methodological complexities of each approach.

8

A COLAB Model of Workplace Transformation in the Criminal Justice Context

Sarah Hean, Marie Aakjær, Laure Kloetzer, Laura Seppänen, Anu Kajamaa, Päivikki Lahtinen, and Tine Murphy

Introduction

The interface between health/welfare (WS) and criminal justice services (CJS) is a complex adaptive environment. It is a meeting of different "interests, identities, values, and assumptions....embedded within prevailing institutional logics (Thornton & Ocasio, 2008, p. 103). These

This chapter was developed from Hean, S., Aakjær, M., Kloetzer, L., Seppänen, L., Kajamaa, A., Lahtinen, P., & Murphy, T. (2020). *Combining Resources: A Participatory Intervention Promoting Organisational Learning, Social Innovation and Interorganisational Collaborations In Criminal Justice*. Stavanger: UIS Scholarly publications. https://doi.org/10.31265/usps.37.

S. Hean (✉)
Social Work Department, University of Stavanger, Stavanger, Norway
e-mail: sarah.c.hean@uis.no

M. Aakjær · T. Murphy
Centre for Management and Experience Design, University College Absalon, Sorø, Denmark
e-mail: maaa@pha.dk

S. Hean et al. (eds.), *Improving Interagency Collaboration, Innovation and Learning in Criminal Justice Systems*,
https://doi.org/10.1007/978-3-030-70661-6_8

logics are differentiated by different emphases being placed on issues of security/control and care that can challenge interagency relationships. It is however a rich environment for researchers to build knowledge about interagency collaboration, innovation, organisational learning using standard research methods such as observation, interview, surveys, etc. It is also an opportunity for them to take a more active role and develop methods on how to change practice rather than only observe it. It is possible for researchers to do both: develop knowledge whilst changing practice simultaneously (Vygotsky, 1997). Researchers in the prison environment have been criticised for not supporting the implementation of their own research recommendations (Kerrison et al., 2019). In response to this, we present in this chapter a model of organisational transformation in which researchers may offer this support in the criminal justice context and facilitate innovation and organisational transformation. The chapter presents the efforts of a consortium of European researchers and practitioners (COLAB-H2020-MSCA-RISE-2016/734536) working together to merge their combined knowledge of methods of organisational change in other fields and apply these to the CJS. A more detailed description of these individual constituent methods, and how our model was developed, can be found elsewhere (Hean et al., 2020a).

Sannino and Sutter (2011) describe interventions that promote organisational change as a toolkit. The COLAB consortium aimed to develop such a tool kit that has relevance specifically for the CJS context. The key items in the toolkit, and the learning processes it elicits, were created through a cross comparison of methods in which the COLAB members

T. Murphy
e-mail: timu@pha.dk

L. Kloetzer
Institute of Psychology and Education, University of Neuchâtel, Neuchâtel, Switzerland
e-mail: laure.kloetzer@unine.ch

L. Seppänen
Finnish Institute of Occupational Health, Helsinki, Finland
e-mail: laura.seppanen@ttl.fi

had particular expertise. These were adapted to the CJS context. The tool kit took the Change Laboratory as its baseline model but combined this with the strengths of three other methods: Boundary Crossing Workshops (e.g., Kerosuo & Engeström, 2003; Virkkunen & Newnham, 2013; Teräs, 2016), Activity Clinics (Clot et al., 2000; Clot, 1999) and Codesign (Aakjær, 2014, 2018). The chapter does not delve into the theoretical complexity of each method. This detail is well covered in these latter references. It aims instead to describe the key components of this hybrid toolkit (hitherto the COLAB model) in an accessible manner that has relevance for the criminal justice context.

All of the methods that contribute to the COLAB model in some way stimulate innovation in the workplace. These manage joint activity, encouraging participants to engage in a process of cocreation. This is a more creative process than mere cooperation or coordination of work activity. It is a relational process that allows a cross fertilisation of ideas and collective learning to take place.

This learning within the model occurs at many levels. Aakjær's application of codesign (2014, 2018), recognises the individual level learning process taking place during the sessions when participants are exposed to the unfamiliar perspectives of other participants. They assimilate these external perspectives of the heterogenous groups participating in the intervention and adapt their own views accordingly. Individual reflection is central to this learning process.

The workshops, through which the interventions are delivered, also provide an opportunity for the participants to reframe a particular situation or problem collectively (Brandi & Elkjaer, 2011; Elkjaer, 2003). From the Activity Clinic perspective, this collective learning is the product first of the collaboration interactions between the researcher

A. Kajamaa · P. Lahtinen
University of Helsinki, Helsinki, Finland
e-mail: anu.kajamaa@helsinki.fi

P. Lahtinen
e-mail: paivikki.lahtinen@uia.no

facilitating the intervention and the participating professionals. Professionals then appropriate the dialogical frameworks introduced by researchers to facilitate the examination of current and historical working practices. The learning hence moves to a space situated between participant workers, as they learn of each other's resources and perspectives (Kloetzer et al., 2015). Change Laboratories and Boundary Crossing Workshops refer to this space as a zone of proximal development or "the distance between the present everyday actions of the individuals and the historically new form of the societal activity that can be collectively generated as a solution" (Engeström, 1987, p. 174).

All the constituent interventions that fed into the COLAB model describe this collective/collaborative learning and the formation of innovations as an iterative and experimental process that takes place over multiple cycles and with the help of the facilitating researcher (Engeström, 1999; Kajamaa, 2015). The iterative cycles represent a means for rehearsal of new roles and relations between workers and agencies (Halse et al., 2010), which forms the basis for social innovation in practice (Aakjær & Darsø, 2014). Change Laboratory interventionists spell out the dimensions of these cycles in most detail in the description of the so-called expansive learning cycle (Engeström, 1999; Kajamaa, 2015). This forms the underpinning of the potential model intervention being developed through COLAB, a model aimed at facilitating the collective learning process within the CJS context (Fig. 8.2).

The expansive learning cycle is a series of epistemic actions, that lead participants collectively to define, redefine and restructure the object of their activity (Vygotsky, 1997; Engeström, 1987; Leont'ev, 1978). We explore each of the actions within the cycle below and as applied to the CJS context. Overall researchers anticipate that innovations and workplace transformations generated through this cycle will, in codesign terms, allow participants to discover *what is* (framing current problems), imagine new solutions (*what could be—reframing problems*) and explore the viability of new solutions (*what will be*) (Aakjær, 2018) (Fig. 8.1).

Fig. 8.1 Expansive learning cycle capturing collaborative learning within the Change Laboratories model (adapted from Engeström, 1987, 1999, 2004)

The Structure Within Which Collective Learning Is Located

As with the expansive learning cycle process, the description of the structure of the Change Laboratory, that is put in place to manage this collective learning, served as the "baseline" structure for the development of the COLAB model also. We chose this method because of its international application and success as a means of workplace transformation in a variety of workplace contexts including paper mills, factories, entrepreneurial contexts, elderly care, hospitals, schools and newsrooms (see e.g. Engeström et al., 1996; Kerosuo et al., 2010; Virkkunen & Newnham, 2013; Sannino & Engeström, 2017).

The central tenet of the Change Laboratory structure is that researchers facilitate a series of workshops attended by key stakeholders (prison officers, prisoners, health professionals for example). Before these begin, researchers will have conducted a traditional ethnographic research phase at the prison site, collecting observations, interviews and artefacts that reflect the everyday work activity of the prison site. Chapters 2–7 of this volume are typical of this phase. When this phase is complete, researchers and the practice organisation may choose to take an active stance, and transform this data into a cycle of organisational change. The COLAB model describes this cycle.

During the workshops, participants reflect on their working practices at multiple levels (Fig. 8.2). In the vertical plane, the researcher encourages them to explore their working practice in the past, present and future. In the horizontal plane, they do this along a spectrum of abstraction (concrete to abstract). At the most concrete, they work with an item that mirrors their working practice and illustrates the problems within it. Researchers will use the materials they have collected in the ethnographic phase of the intervention as this *mirror*.

At the other end of the abstraction spectrum, participants use theoretical *models* to help them reconceptualise their work activity. This

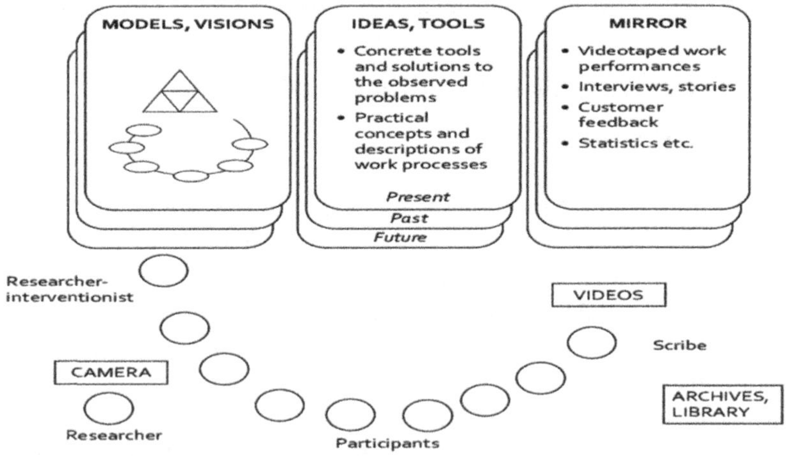

Fig. 8.2 Prototypical layout of the Change Laboratory (Engeström et al., 1996)

helps them make sense theoretically of the built-in contradictions generating the troubles and disturbances depicted in the mirror. Although, theoretical models can be chosen that best make sense to participants, cultural-historical activity systems theory (CHAT) (Sannino & Sutter, 2011) is often used as a tool. Here workplace activity becomes the unit of analysis that drives discussion between workshop participants. This perspective sees the person engaged in the work activity (the subject) as not separate from the social world they inhabit. They are part of the social world and in turn the social world is part of them. Human activity is therefore a social/collective, mediated by cultural artefacts (Leont'ev, 1978; Vygotsky, 1997). Work activity is articulated in terms of a dynamic and multidimensional system and the motivation for doing this work. Prisoner rehabilitation may be one such overarching motive; prison security and control of the prisoner another.

The staff or service users who are engaged in the workshops have a defined purpose within the prison's overall activity and are representative of a wider professional body or community. Their purpose (the *object* of activity), is some entity that meets a human need (Leont'ev, 1978). A prison officer mapping the needs of the newly admitted prisoner would be an example of such a purpose or object.

The way in which this purpose (or object) is performed is mediated by artefacts (e.g. a paper or electronic assessment proforma), rules (e.g., patient confidentiality) and agreed divisions of labour (e.g., the roles and responsibilities assigned to each worker) within an activity system. Every organisation forms such an activity system, a system that exists in relation to neighbouring activity systems and their different objects of activity (Engeström, 2000) (see the model of vision depicted in Fig. 8.2) (further detail of this framework can be read in Chapters 2, 3, 5 and 6 of this volume). Health/welfare and CJS services are two such adjacent activity systems.

Workshop participants, through discussing their work activity along these vertical and horizontal planes, aim to cocreate a third and middle plane representing *ideas* on how things might be changed in current practice. These ideas surface during discussions between participants as a response to the contradictions they have uncovered in the mirror material. They then explore these in a cyclical and iterative manner with regard to their potential capabilities in transforming current working practices. A stepwise implementation of their new vision is planned and monitored by the participants (Engeström et al., 1996; Virkkunen & Newnham, 2013). This cycle is a form of organisational learning or expansive learning.

Although innovation of this kind may occur spontaneously during any interagency meeting between the prison and health/welfare services (see Chapter 2 of this volume), this is often serendipitous as the collaborative process is not made explicit and only understood tacitly. The Change Laboratory, on the other hand, codifies this tacit knowledge. It focuses on how information is shared, the manner in which knowledge can be understood across disciplinary boundaries and combined in such a way that new concepts are cocreated. The Change Laboratory recognises that innovation happens at the boundaries between disciplines and that working across boundaries is a key ingredient of competitive advantage (Engeström et al., 1996; Virkkunen & Newnham, 2013). In traditional models of collaboration, such as the interagency meeting, practice problems are often identified by service leaders and policy makers and at a generic or national level. In Change Laboratories, however, problems are identified by frontline professionals, and the researcher/facilitator helps them reconceptualise these. The problems, and solutions created, are therefore context specific. The Change Laboratory allows bottom-up innovations to be developed where frontline professionals are encouraged to develop their own solutions to the challenges they face.

However, the Change Laboratory had not previously been applied to the challenging and security-driven prison context and the interface with health and welfare services. It was anticipated that the method would need adaptation to this new context, particularly if prisoners are to be included in these events as key stakeholders in service transformation.

Although the COLAB consortium had the Change Laboratory as a focal point, it drew on COLAB expertise in Activity Clinics, Boundary Crossing Workshops and Codesign to explore how a "prison ready toolkit" of organisational transformation/innovation could be developed. All three of these methods had or were being trialled by COLAB members in the CJS context at the time of writing and were hence seen as informative to the current context. In this chapter, we present the final product of this analysis. The product has two main dimensions: An adaptation of the expansive learning cycle describing the organisational learning that could take place within a participating prison (see Fig. 8.1) and the expanded structure of the researcher facilitated and structured workshops (see Fig. 8.3) that built on the base line workshop outlined in Fig. 8.2 (Engeström et al., 1996). The boxes A-H in Fig. 8.3 illustrate how the original Change Laboratory structure has been supplemented with materials/strategies from Boundary Crossing Workshops, Activity Clinics and Codesign approaches.

The authors, utilising their personal experience of each method, extracted the key characteristics of the Change Laboratory and the other constituent models on a 11 dimension framework. This was built on the comparative framework developed by Vilela et al. (2014) to compare participatory methods. The detail of the comparison between methods and the synthesis of the approaches is detailed elsewhere (Hean et al., 2020a).

Dimension 1: Establishing the Need for an Intervention (Fig. 8.1A)

The first stage of the intervention, and the learning cycle, is a practice-driven need of some kind (Kajamaa & Lahtinen, 2016; Engeström et al., 2015; Virkkunen, 2006; Victor & Boynton, 1998). This need may lead organisations to actively seek researcher support (solicited help). The researcher approaching the practice organisation with the offer of unsolicited help is less successful. This is a challenge for consortia such as COLAB whose goal was to explore the utility of a model of innovation in the new criminal justice-related context.

Commitment to the intervention from both prison management and workers is essential. Lack of commitment leads to participants derailing or redirecting interventions. There are several reasons why prisons may lack this commitment:

- Innovation or service development is not the prison's top priority.

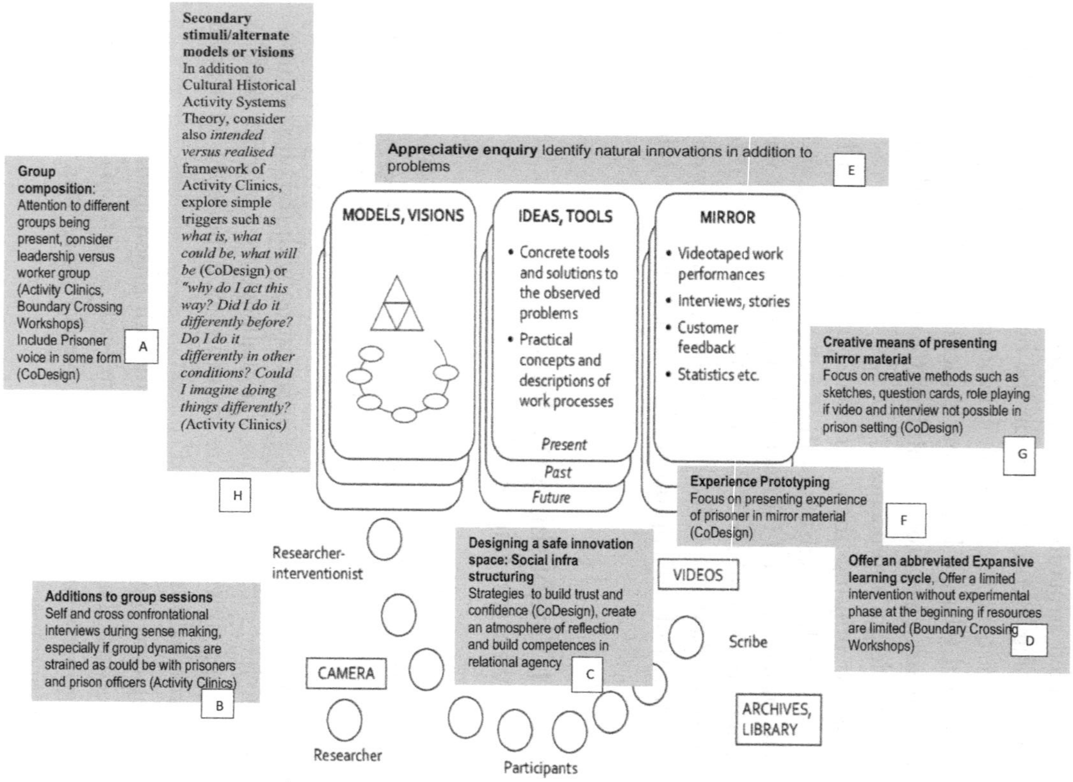

Fig. 8.3 An intervention model with potential utility in CJS/WS context (based on Engeström et al., 1996)

- Culturally and historically the prison is not ready for an extensive change process (Lahtinen et al., 2019; Hean et al., 2017).
- Time and financial resource constraints in the prison limit their drive to innovate and collaborate.
- Prison sites may be willing to host the initial ethnographic study but the intervention itself is more resource intensive. Prison officers must be freed from their responsibilities and getting all stakeholders in one physical location is difficult to orchestrate. There may also be ethical dilemmas if staff are removed from duty to participate. Here, prisoners' rights are violated if they then have a reduced service or must be locked in cells.
- The outputs of bottom-up interventions cannot be predefined making these less appealing to organisational leaders.

The intervention must be seen as meaningful to all parties and an internal champion/sponsor of the intervention within the prison will improve the chances of the intervention being introduced. Contextual adaptations to the intervention method must be made so that goals and methods employed are appropriate to the prison's current needs. Researchers need to discover the priorities and needs of the prison by asking do the organisation want to innovate? who is driving the innovation (leaders or workers, for example) and for what reasons? Are these reasons resource, outcomes or value driven, or for political reasons? Researchers should introduce the broad objective of the intervention but allow the specific outcomes to be generated later through the cocreation process. Aakjær (2014) for example, using a codesign intervention, began with the broad focus of improving the prison environment for both prisoners and officers by decreasing episodes of threats and violence. However, the solutions to achieving this were cocreated during the interventions that followed. Setting these initial broader aims, requires common goal setting exercises, or what Downing-Wilson et al. (2011) calls mutual appropriation strategies. This moves professionals from a *their* to an *our* intervention perspective.

Researchers and the prison leaders should discuss and plan together the need for an intervention phase after the initial data collection has been completed and explore the human resources required. This negotiation process will take many meetings between researchers, prison/welfare leaders and key frontline professionals. Constructing a shared understanding of the intervention process is highly necessary for the local ownership and sustainability of the process. Time is required to build this, paying attention to each others' language, skills and logistical parameters. This will decide when the time is right for the organisation and if an intervention is feasible. Trust and reputation are key here and are often the product of years of relationship building between researchers and their local surrounding practice partners.

Dimension 2: Designing the Structure of the Innovation Space (see Fig. 8.3A, B, D)

After the mandate for the intervention is agreed, an innovation space (Darsø, 2012) in which multiple perspectives are brought together, is created. There is no rule as to the optimal conditions of the innovation space. These vary depending on the resources available and constraints of the prison and participating organisations.

Researchers clarify with prison leaders the resources required to develop an innovation space, and decide together the number, duration and frequency of sessions required. In the Change Laboratory it is usual for 6–10 sessions (2–3 hours each) held with a working group of 15–20 participants. In Codesign, interventions are described in terms of the length of involvement in the prison (8 months to 2 years) with 4–11 participants taking part. These can included prisoners and ex-prisoners (Aakjær, 2014) There may be some instability in group membership and the composition of the participants may vary between sessions. This can threaten the process as the continuity of learning actions gets compromised.

Attention should be given to who attends the workshops in terms of the professions, department or organisations represented (see Fig. 8.3A, C) and the power dynamics these create; whether prisoners, decision-makers (directors, managers and experts) or frontline workers or a mixture of these be included. All of the constituent interventions adhere to the idea that transforming the working environment occurs through the unification of multiple voices. Participants each bring to the workshop different and only partial perspectives of this object of the activity and their own life histories, experiences and institutional contexts. Boundary Crossing Workshops emphasise that actors be of different groups (e.g. different organisations), each crossing professional and organisational boundaries. Activity Clinics focus on the distinction between workers and leadership and codesign approaches focus on including the voices and knowledge of users/citizens.

Rather than a series of uniform workshop sessions, researchers may alternate between facilitating workshops with larger participant numbers (as seen in Change Laboratories, Boundary Crossing Workshops and Codesign) or combine these with interviews between the researcher and one or two workers as used in Activity Clinics (Clot et al., 2000) (Fig. 8.3B). The latter has potential in the CJS/WS context where conducting workshops in secure environments and managing the power differentials between participants are difficult to manage if larger groups are employed. Larger groups may also be more difficult to convene as getting all actors from all organisations in one physical setting at any one given time proves difficult.

The role of the researcher and participant should be made clear for all engaged in the intervention. The researcher has, for example, the role of collecting ethnographic data before the intervention, although workers/participants in the intervention should be consulted on the research design. Change Laboratories emphasise the importance of researchers as more than observers of practice. They are human agents of innovation, supporting practitioner colleagues by facilitating the innovation process (Virkkunen & Newnham, 2013). The researcher and the organisational management have joint responsibility for negotiating whether to do an intervention that follows the ethnographic phase or not. The distribution of tasks between participants during the intervention should be clarified (e.g. record keeping, facilitation) and participants expected to be active in promoting their own learning.

The developmental process is a lengthy and energy consuming process, that may not sit well with the highly pressurised prison environment. The Boundary crossing Workshop has utility here. The Boundary crossing Workshop shares much of the Change Laboratory methods but is a shorter process consisting of only 1–3 meeting sessions making them more feasible politically and logistically (see Fig. 8.3D). Being a shorter process, with no experimental phase included (see Fig. 8.1G), these can serve as a "taster" to motivate practitioners for larger-scale developmental efforts at a later stage (Seppänen & Toiviainen, 2017).

Dimension 3: Managing the Affective or Relational Aspects of the Innovation Space (Fig. 8.3C)

Codesign approaches emphasise the contextual aspects of social innovation, including relational aspects. Good relations within a safe innovation space are important in the high security and potentially volatile prison environment. This environment lends itself to power differentials between different professional groups as well as between officers and prisoners. It is the researchers' ethical responsibility to protect the wellbeing of all participants.

There are challenges to the development of a safe space. Negotiating interagency boundaries during an intervention may cause tensions and silo ways of working. Workshops can raise issues in the workplace that are emotionally difficult to confront and prison norms and rules can threaten the safety of the space. Formal prison rules limit the freedom of inmates to participate in workshops re-enforcing their lower status. Informal rules imposed by fellow prisoners demand that prisoners keep a distance from officers (the us and them) that limits their ability to participate. External work and peer-pressure amongst employees can do the same. These challenges may lead to strong resistance amongst participants to the intervention sessions and the innovation process (Engeström, 2000; Kerosuo, 2006).

Codesign approaches are particularly focussed on providing the structures for a safe innovation space through building explicitly levels of trust and confidence between participants in a process of social infra structuring (Fig. 8.3C) (Aakjær & Brandt, 2012). This is achieved by:

- creating a "relational safety net that opens up for curiosity and inquiry in an inclusive and encompassing community" (Darsø, 2012, p. 118).
- allowing for dialogue, co-creation and learning opportunities, with the aim of improving and innovating practice (Aakjær & Darsø, 2014).
- managing power differentials: power differentials are managed through including professionals from all relevant agencies in similar numbers, recruiting larger numbers of prisoners than officers and making participation voluntary (Aakjær & Brandt, 2012).
- protecting participant anonymity and confidentiality of issues raised during the workshops or the research that preceded these. Although this may be easily controlled externally (what is said in the group remains in the group), internal anonymity during the intervention itself is less easily secured. Prisoners may present feedback to the sessions of their experience of the service. This can leave both workers and prisoners feeling exposed. Getting prisoners, professionals and researchers to cocreate and agree ground rules for interaction during sessions helps minimise this (Aakjær & Brandt, 2012).
- building respect, trust and positive, constructive relations both between participants and between the participants and the researcher. Trust promotes understanding of the individual expertise of each participant. This may be easier to establish during interviews used in Activity Clinics where only one or two people in the interview are involved (Fig. 8.3D).
- maintaining the group's confidence in the process and that solutions will be forthcoming.
- Using reflective theoretical tools, such as the cultural-historical activity systems theory (see Chapters 2, 3, 5 and 6 for further explanation of these models), is believed to help participants distance themselves from the emotion of the situation and to reflect on the situation intellectually (Virkkunen & Newnham, 2013; Schulz et al., 2015).

The development of appropriate social infrastructures to generate innovation in a prison context can only be built slowly over time and should be an ongoing process, dependent on the competence of the researcher-facilitator. Researchers need to be skilled in managing the social infrastructuring process, protecting the workers from potential harm whilst still allowing the participants to guide the direction of discussion. This reflects the concept of relational agency defined as a participant's "capacity to align one's thoughts and actions with those of others to interpret aspects of one's world and to act on and respond to those interpretations" (Edwards, 2009, p. 4). This is managed by encouraging participants to reflect on what they have in common or shared aims in their activity. It is often the client that is this shared focus, but there may be other common needs or shared problems (Seppänen et al., 2015).

Emotions are not always to be avoided in workshops. For Change Laboratories, Boundary Crossing Workshops and Activity Clinics, emotional reactions are also viewed as a trigger for learning rather than a relational factor that may close innovation down. Participants' motivation to take part in sessions and their emotional involvement holds significant power in enhancing organisational learning and change as long as it can be dealt with sensitively and reflected upon collectively (Virkkunen & Newnham, 2013).

Dimension 4: Critically Analysing Current Practices in the Organisation(s) Through Uniting Multiple Perspectives (Fig. 8.1B)

The workshops bring together people from participating organisations who cross individual, social and organisational boundaries during their discussions. Researchers facilitate the examination of cultural and historical dimensions of work activity from these multiple perspectives (Engeström, 1987). This process destabilises each participant's perceptions of current practice (Aakjær, 2018). They encounter new, unfamiliar perspectives that disturb their view of hitherto unexamined organisational norms and "make the familiar strange" (Halse et al., 2010).

Dimension 5: The Identification of Areas Where Organisational Change Is Required (Fig. 8.1C)

After a dialogue between participants has been established, participants explore discontinuities in their overlapping work activity and reach a consensus as to where a transformation of practice is required (Akkerman & Bakker, 2011). The problematisation of the work activity is the responsibility of participants and not the researcher. The researcher may typically create the initial and tentative hypothesis of the current problem areas from the initial research data collected, but this is tested and reformed when presenting the mirror material to the participants. The researchers role is not to impose their hypotheses upon participants. They participate in the process but do not constrain this in any specific direction. Instead shared questions and interests emerge in the course of the intervention.

Traditional ethnographers collect data through empirical observations of the workplace, and perform a qualitative analysis of this material. In contrast, the analysis process in the COLAB model described here is instead conducted by participants themselves, although the researcher may participate in the process. This promotes ownership and credibility of the analysis but faces the traditional researcher critique of reduced dependability and transferability.

The nature of the problem is most carefully theorised in Change Laboratories and Boundary Crossing Workshops interventions. The Boundary Crossing Workshops and Change Laboratories interventions propose that disturbances and contradictions emerge within and between activity systems and drive innovation knowledge and learning (Virkkunen & Newnham, 2013; Kerosuo et al., 2010). In terms of where these lie, contradictions are found within and between activity systems (primary, secondary, tertiary and quaternary contradictions) (see detail Engeström, 1987). They manifest as tensions, disturbances, latent dilemmas, conflicts or "double binds" in local work activities (Engeström & Sannino, 2010).

In exploring contradictions, there is a danger in focusing on what does not work rather than what does. Workshop participants may focus on the contradictions in collaborative practices when there is evidence that workplace activity is already being conducted mutually with flexibility and feelings of autonomy. Professionals from different organisations, whilst working together in a hybrid configuration of actors, with different, potentially competing institutional logics, have often already engaged in learning processes leading to actors being able to oscillate between the institutionalised logic of their own profession and a shared logic centred on the needs of the prisoner (see Chapter 4 of this volume). The problematisation process could therefore be balanced with an appreciative inquiry approach successful in other prison-related research, (e.g. the work by Liebling et al., 1999, 2010) (see Fig. 8.3E).

Dimension 6: Making Collective Sense of Knowledge Presented by Other Relevant Actors of Current and Past Practices (Fig. 8.1D)

Meaning making happens through collaboration between actors and is key to generating innovation in all the interventions. The boundaries between participants from the different CJS and WS organisations are where collective sense making and interorganisational learning take place. Researchers employ a range of strategies to facilitate how CJS and WS workers collectively attempt to make sense of their own (and potentially shared) goals in their daily work. They together explore what each participant does when working with prisoners, why they do it or the benefit from doing this. Change laboratories focus on the historical dimension of these: how it was done in the past, why it is done like it is currently and then how it might best look like in future reconstructions. For codesign approaches, participants make sense of practice through some of re-enactment of their everyday practices (Aakjær, 2014). Boundary Crossing Workshop emphasises the potentially shared objects of activity of different groups, agencies or organisations participating. An Activity Clinic slant offers a careful examination of what was originally intended by service developers and how this compares with the reality of the service delivered. Work tasks are simultaneously something given (a real phenomenon), something participants project onto the other group participating in the intervention, and eventually something that becomes co constructed by the researchers and workers discussing together how this observed workplace activity takes place in the future.

A key strategy in sense making is the use of the concept of double stimulation (Vygotsky, 1978). This is employed explicitly in Change

Laboratories and Boundary Crossing Workshops and implicitly in Codesign and Activity Clinics. Participants are presented with a primary stimulus that triggers the examination of current and historical practices. This is described metaphorically as "a mirror" of the present problems. This mirror data is collected by researchers prior to the sessions, by using ethnographic methods, or may be cocreated in the workshops themselves (e.g. Aakjær, 2014). It is often a videotape made by the researcher during the ethnographic phase preceding the intervention and one they have identified as showing a possible disturbance in the participants' work activity (Hammersley & Atkinson, 1995). Seeking permissions to use video recordings may be problematic in some sensitive or secure environments such as prisons. The mirror material (Fig. 8.3G) could therefore also include audio or written clips of interviews, photographs or sketches of problematic situations, scenarios, drama, role playing, storytelling and story boards (Aakjær, 2014, 2018) (Fig. 8.3G).

A secondary stimulus is a conceptual model that helps participants make sense of the observed primary stimulus. Group discussions and analysis might be triggered, for example, by applying the activity system framework (Engeström, 1987) to describe what the participants are observing. Other theoretical models may also be appropriate. Clot (1999) for example, applies a framework in which the task set (or what is expected from the worker—the normative activity) and the realised activity (what really gets done) are compared. This helps participants examine the demands of the work tasks and the physical, psychological characteristic of the worker performing it. In the codesign approach this distinction is also described but in terms of the difference between canonical and non-canonical work (Brown & Duguid, 1991). Researchers from an Activity Clinic tradition, in their personal self and cross confrontational interviews, use targeted questions such as "*why do you act this way? Did you do it differently before? Do you do it differently in other conditions? Could I imagine doing things differently?*" to stimulate reflection and dialogue and codesign interventionists use reflective statements such as "*what if…?*" (Aakjær, 2018). The simplicity of these statements has an appeal for those participants for whom the activity systems framework is perceived as less accessible. Secondary stimuli developed by the Change Laboratories/Boundary Crossing Workshops participants themselves may also be applied if more meaningful to some participants (see Virkkunen & Newnham, 2013; Sannino, 2015) (Fig. 8.3H).

Dimension 7: Solution Formation, Examination, Experimentation and Evaluation in Situ (Fig. 8.1E, F, G, H)

The next step in the learning cycle involves modelling (Boundary Crossing Workshops, Change Laboratories, Activity Clinics) or prototyping (Codesign) (Fig. 8.1E). Hereby, participants construct an explicit model of a new idea that offers a solution for the identified problem. These could be new products, infrastructure, forms of interaction, constellations of people, services models or organisational practices (Aakjær, 2018; Slappendal, 1996). These are social innovations that are socially driven with an eye on added public value (Mulgan et al., 2007; Alford, 2009).

The solution created by participants is then carefully examined (Fig. 8.1F), before running, operating and experimenting on it in practice in order to fully grasp its dynamics, potentials and limitations in situ (Fig. 8.1G). The implementation experience is then reflected upon in future sessions and evaluated (Fig. 8.1H). From the codesign perspective, the involvement of prisoners (the service user) as evaluators of the new model of activity or innovation, is essential at this point. The group then enter a second cycle of this learning process if required. If the new model is deemed successful, participants consolidate its outcomes into a new stable form of practice (see Engeström, 1987).

At the level of the organisation, learning within the intervention is manifest in its outcomes: the development and transformation of working practices. The object of workplace activity is reshaped by participants in the intervention leading to qualitative transformations of these objects or the activity model as a whole (Engeström, 1987; Engeström & Sannino, 2010). The transformation process is understood through Davydov's (1990) dialectical method of ascending from the abstract to the concrete. The assumption is that all practices have internal contradictions and can undergo transformation. Participants strip away the surrounding detail from the key issue at hand (abstraction) to make sense of a particular element of practice. They then renegotiate and reorganise their practices and trial the alternative by introducing the new proposed way of working back into the complex in situ environment. The workshops, where this process is planned and managed, not only transform practice but also transform social relations between the participants and empower workers and their leaders to act and transform their own work activities now and in the future in a way that is bottom-up and user driven in nature (Clot, 2008).

The scale of transformation that takes place varies. The intervention may be a lengthy process involving multiple iterative cycles, negotiation and hybridisation of alternative perspectives (Virkkunen & Newnham, 2013). Change Laboratories often aim for these larger-scale transformations in activity systems, that may take several years to carry out. Boundary Crossing Workshops interventions are less ambitious, run over only a few weeks with the experimental phase often removed. These are a first light touch and explorative initiative that, if successful, may be taken forward later, resources allowing (Ruotsala, 2014). A balance, between experimentation with the new model of working and the time and energy resource of the organisation, must be found.

Because of the iterative and practice-driven nature of the solution development process, the new models of working practices are often unpredictable. Effective learning and service development is not always guaranteed and it should be accepted that, at times, some interventions only produce micro-cycles of expansive learning (Engeström, 1999) and do not necessarily lead to a cocreation process, profound, expansive learning or workplace transformation (Engeström et al., 2014).

Dimension 8: Reporting (Fig. 8.1H)

Interventions have a political dimension, meaning reporting back to the participant organisations on the outcomes of the sessions, and especially to the leadership, is vital. Activity Clinics detail useful strategies here. They describe an important phase of the intervention being where researchers and workers jointly select video clips of their activity and interviews featuring debates about important aspects and conflicts of their work. These videos are arranged in a final form, a film-based multi-voiced report. This is then presented and discussed with a group of directors, managers and experts. In doing so, the researchers articulate the controversies on the work activity so that they can be reflected upon in order to transform the work organisation. These may be presented as part of the work transformation process to engage leadership or policy makers in the transformational process or at the beginning of an upscaling process (Fig. 8.1I).

Dimension 9: Sustainability and Long-Term Implementation of Agreed Service Changes

Attention should be paid to sustainability in interventions. This relates first to sustaining the network of participants created by the intervention. This is so that this network can go forward together with the concrete changes. Secondly, the method of the intervention can be sustained. Researchers could explore training organisations to run future interventions themselves and for there to be a hand over of the facilitation role to the organisations themselves when researchers withdraw. This could help sustain or adapt the outcomes of these interventions in the long term. This requires willingness on the behalf of researchers to relinquish their ownership of the method. The theoretical complexities of the methods may work against this. Alternatively researchers may consider longer involvement in the practice organisation so as to support the implementation of the new models of working in the long term (Kerrison et al., 2019).

Lastly, sustainability relates to the outcomes of the intervention. Organisational change can be a lengthy process, and efforts are required to anchor and diffuse innovations that arise from the interventions at all system levels. The significance and sustainability of new service prototypes (e.g. new routines, in codesign speak) or new systems of activity (in Change Laboratories and Boundary Crossing Workshops speak) is largely determined by the subsequent commitment to nurturing these by the management and employees (Engeström et al., 2007; Kajamaa, 2011). Boundary Crossing Workshops talk of the importance of including HR departments in this process and Activity Clinics engage all organisational levels in decision-making to achieve the same.

Through the iterative design of the interventions, participants are able to explore and reconsider existing practices and simultaneously rehearse and experiment with the potential of new ways of doing things in practice. This ability to trial and test the developing innovations may contribute to the sustainability of these. Overall, the long-term success of interventions is seen to be dependent on the buy-in and commitment of the organisation itself and the manner in which the organisational leadership and researcher can support and grow this commitment. The processes of implementation, experimentation and transformation, are not well theorised in any of the interventions, perhaps because researchers tend to withdraw at this phase of the learning cycle (Kerrison et al., 2019).

Including the Voice of the Service User in the Intervention (Fig. 8.3F)

The inclusion of frontline workers and service users voice in interventions is another means of assuring sustainability. Policies imposed upon services and workers "top-down" to affect organisational change often do not correspond to the specific client or work situation they encounter. In response, frontline workers develop coping mechanisms whereby they adapt or ignore the policy structures imposed upon them (Fuglsang, 2010). Service users, including prisoners, engage in a similar process, adapting or ignoring the interventions introduced to help them, if these do not fit with what extrinsically or intrinsically motivates them. The interventions, especially codesign, all focus on giving workers and service users voice. This improves the likelihood that innovations have a better chance of being implemented and sustained by workers and service users. Introducing the user perspective potentially reveals the strengths and weaknesses of the organisation more clearly (Junginger, 2007) acting as a lever for participants to reflect, learn and develop their practices. (Meroni & Sangiorgi, 2011).

Interventions often lack service user engagement for a variety of reasons: in Change Laboratories terms, the object of the joined activity (e.g. the prisoner) may be viewed as passive recipient of the service, and hence do not actively get involved in service development. This may be because they are not actively invited to the intervention by researchers. In Activity Clinics, clients do not usually directly participate in the process of analysis and cocreation and hence their perspective cannot be explicitly elaborated. Engeström et al. (2014) suggest that this lack of service user involvement originates from Change Laboratories being so well applied to schools and similar education establishments, where students are not traditionally invited in as vehicles of organisational change, although the potential is there. Similarly, in the CJS environment, prisoners may be excluded politically either because they are not traditionally seen as service users and perhaps not deserving of citizenship and a role in the development of a service designed to control and punish them (see Chapter 12 for an elaboration of this topic). Resources may limit participation also, with not enough officers being available to retain the level of security that is needed to allow the attendance of the prisoner at the workshops (or in fact the researcher into the prison in the first place). Prisoners may also exclude themselves or be unable to participate directly. They may perceive services as something simply given to them in a readymade form rather than produced together between a service provider and client. The client may also feel disempowered in the company of professionals, especially in prisoner settings, and have concerns that they will be seen by other inmates as cooperating with the prison authorities. Other vulnerabilities prevalent in prisoners (e.g. a mental illness, learning disability) may further make them unable to participate in the cocreation process required. Finally, recruitment and continuity of service user engagement may be limited. For example, in Norway, on average, a prisoner stays imprisoned for 6 months. During this imprisonment, a prisoner may be moved to other units and prisons several times. In a lengthy innovative process, therefore, engaging a prisoner is unpredictable. Thought needs to be given on how to give voice to this type of client (Kajamaa & Hilli, 2014; Kajamaa & Lahtinen, 2016).

Prisoners might be involved only at certain phases of the intervention, for example, to manage resource limitations as well as the strain put upon them in the intervention process. They may act as evaluators, for example, of any new model of activity or innovation developed.

An exploration, of *experience prototyping* (Fig. 8.3F) offers further operational insight here. Experience prototyping is a method employed in codesign approaches to find ways in which intervention participants can capture what it personally feels like to experience everyday life in prison, either as a prisoner or employee/officer (Halse et al., 2010; Bate & Robert, 2007; Buchenau & Suri, 2000). By getting as close to the lived experience of the service user as possible, participants explore both where the needs for development lie and then the possible solutions to these service challenges. An experience prototype is a complex sensory exploration of a service or routine (Bate & Robert, 2007). It can be used to better understand how a goal can best be achieved (Meroni & Sangiorgi, 2011). It could involve physically acting out a scene or ways of performing a routine, as a means to explore and develop services through the embodiment of an existing service routine. In the prison system, for example, the enactment of an induction tour for new prisoners through storytelling provided a tangible way in which the prototype of this service change could be experienced by participants (Aakjær, 2014, 2018).

If prisoners cannot be included at all in the intervention, their experience may be at least partially represented in videos of the activities around them (Engeström, 2004; Hasu & Engeström, 2000). These edited videos of work practices (including work with the prisoner) are shown by the researcher to participants and should strongly represent the prisoner's voice and how they perceive the service provided. The challenge is to make video material in a secure environment, and ensuring the confidentiality of information represented within it.

Concluding Comments

We have presented in this chapter the COLAB model of workplace transformation in the prison system. The model consists of an expansive learning cycle adapted for the prison environment describing the learning process (Fig. 8.1) and then the structures that could be put in place to manage this (Fig. 8.3).

The COLAB model is predominantly driven by the theoretically sophisticated and well tested Change Laboratory model. The latter is not without critique and additions from other intervention approaches may address these. The Change Laboratories model does not preclude these new elements and can accommodate and be enriched by these additions (Sannino, 2015). For example, it is suggested that the Change Laboratory lacks attention to power differentials and the emotional labour of its participants (Hean et al., 2020a, 2020b). The prison is an already emotionally charged environment and participants may be less comfortable with an intervention that explicitly unpicks tensions and contradictions within services. So, for example, in the COLAB model, social infrastructuring, the development of a safe innovation space and the use of confrontational interviews used by codesign and activity clinics provides a useful addition. Further, interventions can be resource intensive and difficult to orchestrate so that all stakeholders meet in one physical location at one time. Offering an abbreviated Boundary Crossing Workshop or interviews as used in Activity Clinics may be useful alternatives. Alternatively piggy backing on already existing interagency meetings is a possibility. Lastly, the representation of the prisoners voice in the workshops and the presentation of mirror data that heavily rely on video or audio clips of interviews with prisoners in a secure environment may be problematic and be denied by the prison authorities. Novel and creative means of doing this, as used in codesign approaches, should be explored.

The COLAB model for the CJS context presented is by no means a finished product, and will not be without its challenges when implemented. What now required is the careful evaluation of the model in situ. Particular attention should be paid to expanding on the significance and sustainability dimensions. There is scope for greater theorisation of the implementation, experimentation, evaluation, upscaling and sustainability dimensions of the learning cycle and the ongoing role of the researcher in these processes.

This chapter had at its starting point the view that researchers have a responsibility to facilitate change as well as observe it. This raises issues about researchers' competence and safety when taking this more active role as well as how they care for that of others when they are working in the practice field. Both may be compromised if researchers enter the potentially volatile prison environment with which they may not be familiar. We call for greater training for researchers to manage, facilitate these interventions and especially how they protect themselves and others in unfamiliar environments. There needs to be more in place than the standard risk assessment forms that can be paid lip service in university and national research committees assessing new research projects.

Choosing the Change Laboratory as baseline had held appeal because of the level and consistency of theorisation, international application, context specificity and bottom-up approach to social innovation that gave it a distinctive advantage. However, comparison of this with the other models showed these all to essentially share common values related to multi-voiced, bottom-up approaches to workplace transformation in which problems and solutions are driven by practice. The four models examined vary in their emphasis on one or other dimension and the practical means through which this is achieved. If considered together, however, these create a toolkit of strategies a researcher might mix and match to suit the organisational and national contexts in which they find themselves and its needs. There is little in the COLAB model presented here that will not be recognisable to experts in any of the four constituent models. Our contribution is the merger of strategies in an accessible format and as applied to the criminal justice context.

Acknowledgments The authors contributed equally to the production of this chapter.

References

Aakjær, M. (2014). *Reconfiguring boundaries in social innovation: Co-creating new meaning and practice in a prison context*. Ph.D. dissertation, Aarhus University, Copenhagen.

Aakjær, M. (2018). Co-design in the prison service—A learning perspective on employee-driven innovation. *International Journal of Entrepreneurship and Innovation Management (IJEIM), 22*(4–5), 381–396.
Aakjær, M., & Brandt, E. (2012). Social innovation within prison service. In *Proceedings of the 12th Participatory Design Conference: Exploratory Papers,* Workshop Descriptions, Industry Cases-Volume 2.
Aakjær, M., & Darsø, L. (2014). Innovative læringsrum: At krydse grænserne for det (u)mulige. In H. Adriansen, P. Bramming, N. C. Nickelsen, S. Høyrup, D. Staunæs, & K. D. Søndergaard (Eds.), *Læringslaboratorier og -eksperimenter*. Copenhagen: Aarhus Universitets forlag.
Akkerman, S., & Bakker, A. (2011). Boundary crossing and boundary objects. *Review of Educational Research, 81*(2), 132–169.
Alford, J. (2009). *Engaging public sector clients.* Baingstoke: Palgrave.
Bate, P., & Robert, G. (2007). *Bringing user experience to healthcare improvement: The concepts, methods and practices of experience-based design.* Radcliffe Publishing.
Brandi, U., & Elkjaer, B. (2011). Organizational learning viewed from a social learning perspective. In *Handbook of organizational learning and knowledge management* (pp. 23–41).
Brown, J. S., & Duguid, P. (1991). Organizational learning and communities-of-practice: Towards a unified view of working, learning and innovation. *Organizational Science, 2*(1), 40–57.
Buchenau, M., & Suri, J. F. (2000, August). Experience prototyping. In *Proceedings of the 3rd Conference on Designing Interactive Systems: Processes, Practices, Methods, and Techniques* (pp. 424–433). ACM.
Clot, Y. (1999). *La fonction psychologique du travail.* Paris: PUF.
Clot, Y. (2008). *Travail et pouvoir d'agir*. Paris: PUF.
Clot, Y., Faïta, D., Fernandez, G., & Scheller, L. (2000). Entretiens en autoconfrontation croisée: une méthode en clinique de l'activité. *Perspectives interdisciplinaires sur le travail et la santé* (2–1).
Darsø, L. (2012). Innovation competency—An essential organizational asset. In S. Høyrup, M. Bonnafous-Boucher, C. Hasse, M. Lotz, & K. Møller (Eds.), *Employee-driven innovation—A new Approach.* Hamshire, New York: Palgrave Macmillan.
Davydov, V. V. (1990). *Types of generalization in instruction: Logical and psychological problems in the structuring of school curricula.* Reston, VA: National Council of Teachers of Mathematics.
Downing-Wilson, D., Lecusay, R., & Cole, M. (2011). Design experimentation and mutual appropriation: Two strategies for university/community

collaborative after-school interventions. *Theory and Psychology, 21*(5), 656–680.

Edwards, A. (2009). From the systemic to relational: Relational agency and activity theory. In A. Sannino, H. Daniels, & K. D. Gutierrez (Eds.), *Learning and expanding with activity theory*. Cambridge, UK: Cambridge University Press.

Elkjaer, B. (2003). Social learning theory: Learning as participation in social processes. In *The Blackwell handbook of organizational learning and knowledge management* (pp. 38–53).

Engeström, Y. (1987). *Learning by expanding: An activity-theoretical approach to developmental research*. Helsinki: Orienta-Konsultit.

Engeström, Y. (1999). Innovative learning in work teams: Analyzing cycles of knowledge creation in practice. In Y. Engeström, R. Miettinen, & R.-L. Punamäki (Eds.), *Perspectives on activity theory*. Cambridge: Cambridge University Press.

Engeström, Y. (2000). From individual action to collective activity and back: Developmental work research as an interventionist methodology. In P. Luff, J. Hindmarsh, & C. Heath (Eds.), *Workplace studies*. Cambridge: Cambridge University Press.

Engeström, Y. (2004). New forms of learning in co-configuration work. *Journal of Workplace Learning, 16*, 11–21.

Engeström, Y., & Sannino, A. (2010). Studies of expansive learning: Foundations, findings and future challenges. *Educational Research Review, 5*, 1–24.

Engeström, Y., Kerosuo, H., & Kajamaa, A. (2007). Beyond discontinuity: Expansive organizational learning remembered. *Management Learning, 38*(3), 319–336.

Engeström, Y., Kajamaa, A., Lahtinen, P., & Sannino, A. (2015). Toward a grammar of collaboration. *Mind, Culture, and Activity, 22*(2), 92–111.

Engeström, Y., Sannino, A., & Virkkunen, J. (2014). On the methodological demands of formative interventions. *Mind, Culture, and Activity, 21*(2), 118–128.

Engeström, Y., Virkkunen, J., Helle, M., Pihlaja, J., & Poikela, R. (1996). The change laboratory as a tool for transforming work. *Lifelong Learning in Europe, 1*(2), 10–17.

Fuglsang, L. (2010). Bricolage and invisible innovation in public service innovation. *Journal of Innovation Economics, 5*, 67–87.

Halse, J., Brandt, E., Clark, B., & Binder, T. (2010). *Rehearsing the future*. Danish Design School Press.

Hammersley, M., & Atkinson, P. (1995). *Ethnography: Principles in practice.* New York: Routledge.

Hasu, M., & Engeström, Y. (2000). Measurement in action: An activity-theoretical perspective on producer-user interaction. *International Journal of Human-Computer Studies, 53,* 61–89.

Hean, S., Odegard, A., & Willumsen, E. (2017). Improving collaboration between professionals supporting mentally ill offenders. *International Journal of Prisoner Health, 13*(2), 91–104.

Hean, S., Aakjær, M., Kloetzer, L., Seppänen, L., Kajamaa, A., Lahtinen, P., & Murphy, T. (2020a) *Combining resources: A participatory intervention promoting organisational learning, social innovation and interorganisational collaborations in criminal justice.* Stavanger: UIS Scholarly Publications.

Hean, S., Lahtinen, P., Dugdale, W., Larsen, B. K., & Kajamaa, A. (2020b). The Change Laboratory as a tool for collaboration and social innovation In E. Willumsen & A. Ødegård (Eds.), *Tverrprofesjonelt samarbeid, innovasjon og samskaping.* Oslo: Universitetsforlaget.

Junginger, S. (2007). *Change in the making|Organizational change through human-centered product development.* Carnegie Mellon University.

Kajamaa, A. (2011). *Unraveling the helix of change: An activity-theoretical study of health care change efforts and their consequences* (p. 241). Studies in Educational Sciences. Helsinki: University of Helsinki, Institute of Behavioural Sciences.

Kajamaa, A. (2015). Collaborative work development as a resource for innovation and quality improvement in health care: An example from a hospital surgery. In S. Gurtner & K. Soyez (Eds.), *Challenges in health care management—Are we ready for what comes next?* Cham: Springer International Publishing.

Kajamaa, A., & Hilli, A. (2014). Clients' initiatives and caregivers' responses in the organizational dynamics of care delivery. *Qualitative Health Research, 24*(1), 18–32.

Kajamaa, A., & Lahtinen, P. (2016). Carnivalization as a new mode of collaboration. *Journal of Workplace Learning, 28*(4), 188–205.

Kerosuo, H. (2006). Boundaries in action: An activity-theoretical study of development, learning and change. In *Health care for patients with multiple and chronic illnesses.* Helsinki: University Press.

Kerosuo, H., & Engeström, Y. (2003). Boundary crossing and learning in creation of new work practice. *Journal of Workplace Learning, 15*(7/8), 345–351.

Kerosuo, H., Kajamaa, A., & Engeström, Y. (2010). Promoting innovation and learning through Change Laboratory: An example from Finnish Health Care. *Central European Journal of Public Policy, 4*(1), 110–131.

Kerrison, E. M., et al. (2019). On creating ethical, productive, and durable research partnerships with police officers and their departments: A case study of the National Justice Database. *Police Practice and Research. Routledge, 20*(6), 567–584.

Kloetzer, L., Clot, Y., & Quillerou-Grivot, E. (2015). Stimulating dialogue at work: The activity clinic approach to learning and development. In L. Filliettaz, & S. Billett (Eds.), *Francophone perspectives of learning through work: Professional and practice-based learning* (Vol. 12). Cham: Springer.

Lahtinen, P., Esko, T., Kajamaa, A., Seppänen, L., Johnsen, B., & Hean, S. (2019). *Addressing reoffending through addressing offender mental health Exploring the viability of the Change Laboratory method as means of promoting social innovation in the delivery of integrated mental health care offenders in prison services.* Stavanger: UIS Scholarly Publishing.

Leont'ev, A. N. (1978). *Activity, consciousness, and personality.* Englewood Cliffs: Prentice-Hall.

Liebling, A., Elliot, C., & Price, D. (1999). Appreciative inquiry and relationships in prison. *Punishment and Society, 1*(1), 71–98.

Liebling, A., Price, D., & Shefer, G. (2010). *The prison officer.* London and New York: Routledge, Taylor and Francis Group.

Meroni, A., & Sangiorgi, D. (2011). *Design for services.* Gower Publishing, Ltd.

Mulgan, G., Tucker, S., Ali, R., & Sanders, B. (2007). *Social innovation: What it is, why it matters and how it can be accelerated* (Working paper). Oxford: Skill Centre for Social Entrepreneurship, Said Business School.

Ruotsala, R. (2014). Developing a tool for cross-functional collaboration: The trajectory of an annual clock. *Outlines. Critical Practice Studies, 15*(2), 31–53.

Sannino, A. (2015). The emergence of transformative agency and double stimulation: Activity-based studies in the Vygotskian tradition. *Learning, Culture and Social Interaction, 4,* 1–3.

Sannino, A., & Sutter, B. (2011). Cultural-historical activity theory and interventionist methodology: Classical legacy and contemporary developments. *Theory and Psychology, 21,* 557–570.

Sannino, A., & Engeström, Y. (2017). Co-generation of societally impactful knowledge in Change Laboratories. *Management Learning, 48*(1), 80–96.

Schultz, K.-P., Kajamaa, A., & Kerosuo, H. (2015). Creating innovative work practices through reflexive interventions. *International Journal of Work Innovation, 1*(2), 143–160.

Seppänen, L., Ala-Laurinaho, A., & Piispanen, P. (2015). Logics of fluency in the transformation of the Finnish rail traffic control network. *Production, 25*(2), 278–288.

Seppänen, L., & Toiviainen, H. (2017). Relational agency and the development of tools in service networks. In A. Edwards (Ed.), *Working relationally in and across practices: A cultural-historical approach to collaboration* (pp. 153–171). Cambridge: Cambridge University Press.

Slappendal, C. (1996). Perspectives on innovation in organizations. *Organization Studies, 17*(1), 107–129.

Teräs, M. (2016). Inter-professional working and learning: Instructional actions and boundary crossing and boundary making in oral healthcare. *Journal of Education and Work, 29*(5), 614–636.

Thornton, P. H., & Ocasio, W. (2008). Institutional logics. In R. Greenwood, C. Oliver, K. Sahlin-Andersson, & R. Suddaby (Eds.), *Handbook of organizational institutionalism.* Thousand Oaks, CA: Sage.

Victor, B., & Boynton, A. C. (1998). *Invented here: Maximizing your organization's internal growth and profitability.* Boston: Harvard Business School Press.

Vilela, A. G. R., Pereira Querol, M., Antunes Lima, F., Gomes Lopes, M., Almeida, I., & Jackson Filho, J. (2014, July 19–23). Work ergonomic analysis and change laboratory: Similarities and complementarities between interventionist methods. In T. Ahram, W. K., & T. M. (Ed.), *Proceedings of the 5th International Conference on Applied Human Factors and Ergonomics AHFE 2014*. Krakóvia, Poland: The Printing House.

Virkkunen, J. (2006). Hybrid agency in co-configuration work. *Outlines, 8*(1), 61–75.

Virkkunen, J., & Newnham, D. S. (2013). *The Change Laboratory—A tool for collaborative development of work and education.* Rotterdam: Sense Publishers.

Vygotsky, L. S. (1978). *Mind in society: The development of higher psychological processes.* Cambridge, MA: Harvard University Press.

Vygotsky, L. S. (1997). The history of the development of higher mental functions. In R. W. Rieber (Ed.), *The collected works of L. S. Vygotsky. Vol. 4: The history of the development of higher mental functions.* New York: Plenum.

9

Facilitation of Developmental Tasks in Prisons: Applying the Method of Human-Centred Co-evaluation

Laura Seppänen, Heli Heikkilä, Anu Kajamaa, Päivikki Lahtinen, and Hilkka Ylisassi

Introduction

The changes and transformations of work call for a culture of collaboration, innovation and learning in prisons and elsewhere. To promote

L. Seppänen (✉) · H. Heikkilä · H. Ylisassi
Finnish Institute of Occupational Health, Helsinki, Finland
e-mail: laura.seppanen@ttl.fi

H. Heikkilä
e-mail: Heli.Heikkila@ttl.fi

H. Ylisassi
e-mail: Hilkka.Ylisassi@ttl.fi

A. Kajamaa · P. Lahtinen
Faculty of Educational Sciences, University of Helsinki, Helsinki, Finland
e-mail: anu.kajamaa@helsinki.fi

P. Lahtinen
e-mail: paivikki.lahtinen@uia.no

S. Hean et al. (eds.), *Improving Interagency Collaboration, Innovation and Learning in Criminal Justice Systems*,
https://doi.org/10.1007/978-3-030-70661-6_9

such a culture and the prison staff's capacity to take a proactive stance in developing their collective work, a new facilitation method of *human-centred co-evaluation* (Hyytinen et al., 2019; hereafter HCCE) was applied in a low-security closed prison in Finland. The basic idea of the method is to support employees in their collective efforts to develop work practices by designing and implementing developmental tasks simultaneously with setting goals and finding ways to evaluate and learn from them. In addition to practices, the aim is also to develop the proactiveness of the prison personnel. Proactiveness means that employees take anticipatory actions to create change in how jobs, roles and tasks are executed (Grant & Parker, 2009). Professionals' proactiveness also contributes to their well-being (Honkaniemi et al., 2015; Mäkitalo, 2005). Along with other formative interventions (see Chapter 8), the HCCE method can be seen as a design to stimulate proactivity by enhancing participants' capacity for innovation and reflection about the future. "Formative" here means that facilitators offer participants resources to engage in practical experimentation that can lead to generative, novel outcomes (Sannino et al., 2016). Simultaneously, HCCE helps staff "learn by evaluating" both outcomes and the collaborative processes of experimentation.

In a research project,[1] employees, managers and researchers worked together on the so-called "Developmental tasks" or the development of innovations or experiments that are designed, implemented and evaluated collaboratively with the intention of transforming current working practices in the prison. These tasks were used to enhance two strategic aims of the Criminal Sanctions Agency (CSA) in Finnish prisons: the improvement of prisons' digital services and that activating rehabilitative work be included in the everyday duties of prison officers with inmates to reduce the risk of reoffending. By activating, reciprocal, rehabilitative work we mean the activities that prison officers do with inmates that are designed to change the prisoners' behaviours and prepare them for a crime-free life on the outside. The activities are aimed to

[1] Research project: 'Developing prison practices and enhancing transformational agency of employees by co-evaluating experiments' (2018–2020) (Kokeilujen osallistavalla arvioinnilla käytäntöjen uudistamista ja toimijuutta). Funding: Ministry of Justice, Finland (CSA) and the Finnish Institute of Occupational Health.

motivate/activate the prisoner to engage proactively with their own transformation. This process must be a reciprocal process with both the prisoner and the officer working together with each other towards this common goal.

Historically, the latter has been a task of welfare staff employed in the prison—e.g. social workers, psychologists and educators—while prison officers have mainly been responsible for control and security. Involving prison officers in rehabilitative work can be viewed as a long-term sea change in the orientation, tasks and division of labour in Finnish prison services.

Our aim in this chapter is to describe how developmental tasks with rehabilitative work were co-designed, implemented and co-evaluated between the prison staff, management and researchers. This is the first time the HCCE method has been applied in prisons, and the main focus of the paper is the process of putting the method into practice.

The HCCE method, being part of a broad field of developmental evaluation (Patton, 2011), is about using evaluation for learning and development. Engeström and Sannino (2012) argue that all process theories of learning carry with them instructional assumptions of which facilitators need to be aware. Learners, in our case prison personnel, always proceed differently from what researchers or facilitators had planned. In formative developmental efforts, neither the outcome nor process is a universal given, and researchers do not have a monopoly over them (Engeström & Sannino, 2010). The HCCE offers an expanded view for exploring development efforts and their consequences by viewing 'impact' as a qualitative learning challenge, rather than an accountable target to be achieved (Saari & Kallio, 2011). Evaluation studies drawing from activity theory are not typically interested in causal connections but collect evidence of historically formed relationships, social processes and cyclical nature of change (Kajamaa, 2011).

We pay attention to the "gaps" in current prison activity that was uncovered by the developmental intervention and the HCCE method. However, we also explore the challenges/gaps that the HCCE method itself faces when implemented in prison culture. Following Engeström and Sannino (2012), we have taken these gaps between participants' activities and developmental interventions as potential resources with which to promote learning processes. At the end of the chapter, we discuss the gaps observed in the project, how they inform our understanding of the change taking place, and how researchers have considered the gaps in shaping the HCCE process.

The chapter proceeds as follows. The next section is an introduction to the HCCE method. Second, we will familiarise the reader with the main features of the Finnish prison system, including Prison A where the study took place. This leads on to presenting the developmental process as a narrative, examining first how developmental tasks were designed, implemented and co-evaluated at Prison A. At the end, we discuss the challenges or gaps found during the process, and conclude by highlighting the value of the HCCE method in systematic long-term developmental efforts.

The Method of Human-Centred Co-evaluation (HCCE)

The method of human-centred co-evaluation was recently developed by Eveliina Saari, Kirsi Hyytinen and their colleagues (Saari & Kallio, 2011; Saari et al., 2018; Hyytinen et al., 2019) to support innovation in the digitalisation of services (developmental tasks), and embedding, disseminating and upgrading these in practice. A core device of the method is a multi-criteria evaluation framework through which the impact of an innovation (a local developmental task) can be considered (Fig. 9.1). The framework is a modification of the work by Djellal and Gallouj (2013) of pragmatist origin, although the conceptualisation of learning and development of the HCCE method is based on cultural historical activity theory (Hyytinen et al., 2019).[2] The HCCE method instructs participants to consider the proposed innovation they have co-created together.

[2] A manual of the method is freely available in Finnish (Saari et al., 2018). It has spread into a nationally applied developmental evaluation method in citizens' digital help services, in school experiments and elsewhere. See https://www.ttl.fi/wp-content/uploads/2017/12/kokeilut-kaytantoon-tyokirja.pdf.

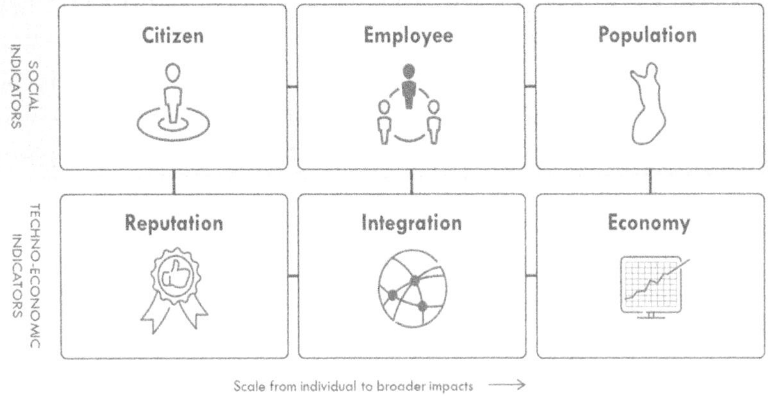

Fig. 9.1 Impact dimensions of multi-value evaluation framework (Hyytinen et al., 2019)

In the social indicators dimension on the *citizen* or *service user* (see Fig. 9.1, first quadrant), participants analyse the value of the product of the developmental task they have produced together from the viewpoint of an individual inmate. The emphasis is on client orientation and the significance of service for him or her. The second quadrant on *employee* directs the discussion to changes the innovation may bring about, changes in the content of work, including work roles, relationships, knowledge and tasks. The impact on clients/service users and employees captures value from the perspective of an individual or a small group of individuals, whereas the impact on *population* helps participants to elaborate on value from a wider perspective, such as of a specific geographical region or its population. In the techno-economic dimension, the focus is on the effects on brand image and on the *reputation* and visibility of actors involved in service development. The value of the developmental task in relation to many interlinked services and to the technology is evaluated in the *integration* dimension. With the last dimension, *economy*, the economic effects of the developmental task can be discussed by considering them from the perspectives of both a single actor or a group of actors and broader society.

The HCCE process is supported by three facilitated workshops. In the first workshop, the participating employees and their supervisors brainstorm and choose one or a few ideas (or developmental tasks) that could respond to clients', employees' or the organisation's needs, after which they carefully design and prepare these. In the second middle-way workshop, the participants consider the impacts of developmental tasks from the user and the worker perspectives. In this phase, it is still possible to modify the developmental task and its criteria if necessary. The third co-evaluation workshop takes place after the experimentation has been put into practice to evaluate its impacts according to the six dimensions presented in Fig. 9.1 (Saari et al., 2018). In this workshop, the work developers, employees, service users and decision-makers are brought together to learn what has been achieved, and what should be accomplished and done in near future. In our study, only the first and third workshops were implemented.

The structure of HCCE is based on the aquarium technique (Aalto-Kallio & Hakulinen, 2009) common in developmental efforts. Here participants alternate between discussing and listening as members either of an "inner circle" or "outer circle". In the third co-evaluation workshop this means that, first, the developmental task is co-evaluated with the framework (Fig. 9.1) by members of "the inner circle" consisting of those who had designed, implemented and used the proposed innovation. Participants then evaluate how the developmental task has succeeded in each of the six dimensions. The aim here is to create new meanings for the developmental task and see new opportunities to develop it (Hyytinen et al., 2019). We will come back to the HCCE method after taking a look at the Finnish prison system, Prison A and the prison officers' rehabilitative work with prisoners.

Features of Finnish Prison Services and "Prison A"

In Finnish prisons, *prison officers* are the ones who most often see inmates while taking care of many practical and control tasks in prison wings. They may advise inmates to attend prison activities and make contact with social workers, psychologists, priests or instructors when needed. Health care professionals, while present in prisons, operate outside the prison system in a national unit responsible for prisoner health care. Other rehabilitative staff are officials of the Correctional Sanctions Agency (CSA) in Finland. *Senior officials*[3] are responsible for working with inmates in their progress with sentence plans and partly act as prison officers' supervisors. Sentence plans are made outside prison in a regional assessment centre of CSA. Besides a director, a prison has two assistant directors, one of which is responsible for security, and the other for rehabilitative programmes for inmates. We can see how the divide of welfare and control is built into the division of labour.

Prison A is a closed low-security prison with approximately 120 male inmates and staff about 80 people. It is known for its culture of good and fluent interaction between inmates and staff. The assistant directors meet twice a week with senior officials. Senior officials meet prison officers occasionally in wings, during coffee breaks and in annual development work discussions, but they do not have the formal right to make supervisory decisions. The prison officers do not have meetings with each other or with other professionals, apart from annual training programmes.

Inmates may voluntarily work or participate in a wide range of educational or rehabilitative activities. Remand prisoners stay for several weeks up to a maximum of a few months in the prison which makes long-term rehabilitation work difficult. Since 2018, the prisons have been collecting written feedback from inmates when they leave the prison of their overall experience of the prison. At Prison A, inmates' responses so far have been positive, although there were negative reports of the first phase of entrance to prison.

To enhance rehabilitative work, the CSA started a long-term transformation of occupational roles in prisons. In 2019, a new form of education was launched for officers to become "responsibility workers" who in the future would do most of the rehabilitative work with a particular inmate, including sentence plan work. Senior officials, in turn, would guide and supervise these responsible workers in their work with

[3] The formal title is senior criminal sanctions official.

inmates. Some officers would continue to work without being responsible workers. This future planned structure, while aimed at supporting rehabilitative work, is now causing uncertainty and feelings of injustice, not least because the salary categories will be renewed accordingly. In this situation, it was necessary for Prison A to make clear that rehabilitative work concerns everyone in the prison, regardless of their occupational status.

Rehabilitative Work with Prisoners

This study originates from a long-term R&D collaboration between the Correctional Sanctions Agency in Finland and the Finnish Institute of Occupational Health. Previously, the ombudsman of the Finnish Parliament had remarked that in Finnish closed prisons, inmates remain too passive and isolated in their cells, and that the CSA needed to pay attention to this problem. This corresponded with the CSA's strategic aim of enhancing more dialogic and innovation creation/activating elements in prison activities for inmates. The way to do this was to develop prison officers' *rehabilitative work* (in Finnish, the word is *lähityö* literally meaning "near work") with prisoners, by promoting local and national developmental tasks that were partly designed and implemented by prison staff.

Supporting inmates rehabilitation and capacity to desist from future criminal activity are central to a prison's aim (Ylisassi et al., 2016, p. 74). For officers' rehabilitation work is about making contact with the prisoner and hereby building trust, and guiding inmates to other health and welfare staff for further support. Combining a rehabilitative approach while maintaining control is not easy and requires prison staff sensitivity, knowing prisoners (dynamic security) and situational awareness. The staff's descriptions of turning difficult situations into successes by using an activating approach explain the opportunities of rehabilitative work (Ylisassi et al., 2016).

Next is an illustration of how a developmental task was co-designed, implemented and co-evaluated with the HCCE method at Prison A.

The HCCE Facilitation of the Developmental Task Process at Prison A

Preparation

The HCCE project at Prison A proceeded on three levels: (1) the national Advisory Board of the project, which decided on a suitable prison and Prison A agreed to participate in the project, (2) the local collaboration between researchers and prison employees (an assistant director and a social worker) responsible for the HCCE project in the prison and (3) the HCCE workshops.

A lot of preparation was needed. First, the researchers (the three authors from FIOH of the chapter) presented the project idea to a group of managers, senior officials and officers at Prison A. It became clear that there was a good culture of rehabilitative work, but they had not yet experimented with new practices nor systematically developed their structures for supporting rehabilitative work. The project thus needed to start with designing the developmental tasks. The practices of "the incoming phase", after the inmate enters the prison until they settle in an allocated wing, was chosen as a prison activity with which staff could experiment.

The developmental tasks were designed in two workshops, after which they were subjected to pilot testing for three months by several officers. The core workshop participants were chosen from among prison officers who were mainly responsible for the security and control of the prison and were increasingly supposed to do rehabilitative work.

Second, individual and group interviews with the personnel of Prison A were carried out so that researchers could become familiar with people in the prison, get to know their work and their views about ongoing changes, especially concerning rehabilitative work, and to collect suitable material (mirror data-see Chapter 8) for the design workshop.

The Design Workshop

Third, the design workshop was planned. The researchers collected excerpts from the aforementioned interviews that depicted the current situation and what was aspired to in the future. These were presented in the form of brief sentences or concepts (Virkkunen, 2007) that were aimed at illustrating the core purpose of prison officers' work activity. This work activity included excerpts that illustrated "relaying information between different professionals and between professionals and the inmate", "getting to know the inmate" "prisoners and professionals getting along with each other". The material presented aimed to demonstrate the way in which prison officers currently attempt to activate inmates to engage in the rehabilitation process, influence their thinking and generally prepare them for reintegration back into society. The materials aimed to demonstrate where there were areas for development and an expansion of current work activity.

The former with its aim was articulated as "relaying information and learning to know the inmates – getting along during prison time" and the latter as "Activating inmates to talk, influencing the thoughts - > getting along in society". They indicate not only a difference or gap between different aims or purposes, but also a temporal gap between now and the future.

The interview excerpts and the model concepts were then shown to participants in the design workshop to prompt discussion about ideas (or tasks) required to address some of the challenges illustrated within the excerpts and model concepts. In addition to the researchers, the participants of the design workshop were prison officers, senior officials, social workers and assistant directors. Service users such as prisoners could be asked to join the HCCE workshops in theory, but in this study, it was not possible for reasons related to research ethics.

In the design workshop, discussion around the current and future model concepts suggests that the transformation of prison work is more complex than merely improving separate processes—rather, it is more likely to be a systemic change that transforms not only individual officers' practices and work orientation, but also the roles and division of labour of the prison. The discussion within the workshop raised new perspectives, such as: control is not separate from activating rehabilitative work: rather, the latter builds *dynamic security* in the prison. It was argued that a functioning security culture of a prison is a precondition for rehabilitative work to be successful. The discussions included many critical expressions as well: e.g. members of organised crime can strengthen the criminal culture and thus hamper rehabilitative work in prison departments.

An illustration of a prisoner's path at the incoming phase when the prisoner is admitted to prison was also used to help design developmental tasks in the workshop. The discussion was facilitated by asking participants to explain how and wherein the pathway information exchange took place, how participants got to know the inmates and got them to talk. When workshop participants reflected on the inmates' path, the researchers emphasised the need for participants to specify in the pathway where service actions took place. This prompted participants to begin looking at improving communication among prison functionaries. They explored in particular how information gained during different steps could better reach relevant functionaries in the prison wings at the point that prisoners are moved from custody to their respective wings. The researchers' aim was to help participants discuss "what we can do", rather than "what those outside prison should do".

As an outcome of the design workshops, two new local developmental task ideas came out. The first was that participants decided officers could begin recording inmates' behaviour in a new digital sentence plan. Here, the officers saw an opportunity to make their rehabilitative work more *visible* both at prison, region and national levels of prison services. Recordings could give more weight to prison officers' perspectives in decisions concerning the inmates. The second developmental task was to redevelop the induction programme that introduced inmates to their permanent cell/wing when they left the custody suites after first entry into the prison. This addresses an issue identified as problematic by inmates and thus indirectly gives voice to the inmates. In the recording task, officers wrote down both positive and negative things about inmates' behaviour and initiatives for their sentence plans. While the aim of both developmental tasks is to improve communication between inmates and staff and within and between occupational groups, we here have concentrated on recording developmental task for simplicity.

The collaboration between the prison staff and researchers was crucial for the success of the project. They jointly have at least two or three encounters per month, either at Prison A or online, for planning the sequence of each step. The key contact points in the prison responsible for liaising with the researchers (a social worker and an assistant director) usefully commented on the researchers' plans, made suggestions, motivated people in the prison to participate and were responsible for organisation of and communication about the workshops and the developmental tasks.

Implementation of the Developmental Tasks

After a pilot project involving some officers, the implementation of the developmental tasks started by introducing them in the official annual training programme of all officers at Prison A. The important transition of leadership from external researchers to prison happened in this phase. Researchers still supported the training with a PowerPoint presentation about the developmental tasks, and they observed this part of the training online but participated with only minor comments at the end about the forthcoming co-evaluation workshops.

The training consisted of useful dialogues about the developmental tasks and critical voices were also heard. For example, a representative of the regional assessment centre participated by giving a talk about the importance of recording, i.e., that the assessment centre needs to make important decisions about an inmate's move from high security to an open (half-way) prison. Good decisions require that there are grounds and evidence for those decisions. A record of the behaviour and needs of the prisoner, recorded digitally of everyday life of the prisoner on the prison wings, as witnessed by officers, is an important source of facts for decision making that can be shared between services.

During the training, the prison assistant manager was expecting everybody to participate by putting the developmental tasks into practice. This is a hierarchical top-down mandate through which an employer has a "direction right" to tell employees what they need to do. This is in opposition to the principles of the HCCE and many other developmental methods in which participation is voluntary and an employee's autonomy is respected, even encouraged. This cultural gap between employees' autonomy and hierarchy exists in developmental efforts in all salaried work but seems to be particularly strong in hierarchic organisations such as prison services. We will come back to this in the discussion.

After the training, the researchers devised paper forms for prison staff to record their experiences of using the new recording system, and the prison managers formulated the necessary documents for the task of recording. Most officers implemented the developmental task and recorded their feedback about them on the paper forms. Some refused to do so "before this extra task is considered in their salary". During the implementation, a social worker interviewed inmates about the developmental tasks. Researchers condensed all the experiences collected for use in the co-evaluation workshop to come. They also developed prompts or assisting questions to unpick each of the dimensions of the evaluation framework (Fig. 9.1) for the co-evaluation workshop.

Co-evaluation Workshop

The workshop started with brief presentations about the developmental task (the digital sentence plan), and the prison staff's and inmates' feedback about it. After that, the inner circle, consisting of five prison officers together evaluated it in the light of each evaluation framework dimension (Fig. 9.1). They were asked to consider how the developmental task would generate value from the perspective of each dimension. Participants were guided to consider both positive and negative changes as well as anticipated and unanticipated effects. The questions were tailored to this developmental task at Prison A.

In the first *client/prisoner* dimension, the questions for the inner circle of the workshop included: What are the benefits and harms of recording for the inmates? How useful are officers' recordings for inmates in reaching the aims of their sentence plans? What changes do inmates see in their relationship and communication with prison staff? Does the recording affect relations between inmates, and how?

The impact on *employee* focuses on changes in the content of work, including work roles, relations, knowledge and tasks. The guiding questions were: How has the developmental task affected the prison officer's role? What are the outcomes of recording on trust-building and activation with inmates? How has the developmental task affected officers' sense of personal safety? Does the recording fulfil its promise of making the officers' rehabilitative work with inmates more visible to others?

With the dimension of *population* the aim is to steer the discussion to evaluate the recording task from the perspective of a specific geographical region with its population. How can the recording affect an inmate's risk of returning to prison? The *reputation* was enquired about by asking: how could the developmental task influence the public image of Prison A and national prison services?

The aim of the *integration* dimension is to provide understanding on how the developmental task aligns with other prison services as well as with data systems. In our case, the main questions were: To what extent has the recording improved the information flow from an officer to other prison staff? To what extent can recording support inmates' path to a crimeless life and reintegration into society? We need to consider here that digital services will be implemented in all Finnish prisons within the next five years or so. How does the task of recording inform the development of digital services in prisons?

Evaluation of *economy* focuses on new potential resources and savings, for example. How do officers' recordings impact the economy and cost-effectiveness of Prison A? How does it affect the allocation of resources such as space, time use and workforce?

After the inner circle had evaluated the developmental task according to the six quadrants in Fig. 9.1, and the questions sketched above, the outer circle came to the fore. It consisted of people who could promote the developmental task by improving or spreading it into wider use. It included actors from the regional office and the evaluation centre of CSA. Collaborators from other services could also be invited. Now the inner circle only listened. The outer circle discussed what they had heard and what they could conclude from the inner circle's evaluation.

They summed up their discussion by writing down their suggestions and presenting: what lessons have been learnt? what should be done next? and how could participants in the outer circle contribute by embedding, spreading or improving the task?

Finally, the inner circle discussed, complemented and decided on suitable future actions, based on the outer circle's proposals. They could also remove some of the suggestions and add their own. The co-evaluation workshop ended by suggesting the ways forward. In this workshop, training and preparing a common set of simple guidelines for recording were the next steps.

Discussion and Conclusion

In our HCCE research project, there was a national strategy to develop rehabilitative work in prison services. This need drove forward the collaboration between the prison authorities and researchers that would become HCCE. Without this need, the HCCE project at Prison A and the developmental tasks that arose from it, would not be there. However, the alignment of developmental, participatory research with this political strategy also increases the complexity of the researchers' role: besides being a facilitator, they need to find a balance between strategic top-down-driven change and employee-driven innovation. Here, we have discussed the HCCE process in terms of gaps observed during the process. These are gaps both in the current prison activity but also in applying the HCCE method itself. The HCCE process has helped us focus on the following gaps:

The Gap Between Control and Rehabilitation in Prison Officers' Work

This reflects the general fundamental and historical contradiction of prison services between security (punishment) and well-being (care) (Laine, 2011). This gap is visible in the division of labour in the prison between those who have security versus rehabilitative responsibility.

However, our study revealed how rehabilitative work is not contrary to security and control, but rather builds on it. Security is not set aside when there is a greater emphasis on care. The notion of dynamic security is an important mediator between control and rehabilitation. For officers, rehabilitative work may find its justification precisely through dynamic security. The developmental task process suggests that we are not only dealing with a transition from control to rehabilitative work emphasising rehabilitation and welfare. Both control and enhancing security for individual inmates and staff members should be integrated into the design, implementation and evaluation of rehabilitative work. There is a need to find solutions through which both security and rehabilitative work can simultaneously be enhanced.

The Gap Between Hierarchic and Participatory Cultures of Development

The HCCE method carries with it an assumption of a participatory, developmental culture that nurtures employees' proactiveness and learning. The traditional hierarchic culture of prison services is poor in encouraging employees' initiatives and innovation. It is hard for employees to activate and empower their clients (such as inmates) if they work in strongly hierarchical cultures (Ylisassi et al., 2016). Researchers and facilitators need to be aware of how different cultures may create pressures for local workers. In the HCCE project, this gap was considered by trying to create dialogues between the needs experienced by prison officers (invisibility of their work; lack of influencing possibilities) and the Criminal Sanction Agency's official rehabilitative work strategy.

The Gap Between the Novel Recording Task and Prison Officers' Traditional Tasks

The recording task nudges officers towards writing down things about the inmates. However, they are being asked to do so at a time when they feel they lack time, motivation and legitimacy to do this. In addition, the HCCE method with its aim of systemic evaluation also requires recording—without making visible the pros and cons of the developmental task as participants see it, the evaluation remains superficial. The recording of the developmental task process thus poses a double challenge of recording for participants (see section on implementation of the developmental tasks earlier). This gap was tackled with the very idea of encouraging people to try out the new model of working. In the training session, prison officers were motivated by hearing how important their recordings were for the regional assessment centre. The promise of having a voice in the co-evaluation workshop gave prison officers motivation to write down their experiences about the developmental tasks.

Cerf (2011) describes participatory research as a joint production of an "artefact" between a researcher and the practical partners in the research-action process. The developmental tasks in our case are such artefacts. They evolve along with the interactions, and the change proceeds as different actors adopt or modify tasks and make them exist for themselves. In action research type of developmental projects, researchers need to pay attention to the different qualities of knowledge produced in the process (Cerf, 2011). It remains to be seen if the officers' developmental tasks will finally exist "for themselves", and if so, in what way they are redefined, made meaningful and evaluated. Even "failed" developmental tasks can be generative for collective learning (De Keyser et al., 2019).

The developmental tasks are not about rehabilitative work only: they also enhance and require multi-professional collaboration between prison staff. Recording observations supports all communication and possibly collaboration within prison and other services (see Chapter 2).

We may see recording and communication as parts of the increasing trend of datafication (Thompson, 2017) and digital technology in prison services (Johnson & Hail-Jares, 2016). Digitalisation enables enhanced information collection and knowledge production for better awareness of work practices. This means better decision-making for managers but also prison staff may access information that is useful for their own work. In prison services, digital information through recording can be used for producing public value for society.

The outcomes of the HCCE project in terms of new practices and employees' proactiveness remain to be studied. The HCCE method provides a welcome theory-based practical complement to implementation and evaluation in formative interventions and it is also a contribution to the wider literature on developmental research. We see that the HCCE process benefits from identifying developmental gaps in and between research and prison services and learns from them. The six-dimension framework (Fig. 9.1) can be used to give voice to differing interests and influence the future actions to be taken in prisons and elsewhere. Some work is still required to structure the argument of what the HCCE method adds to the field.

References

Aalto-Kallio, M., & Hakulinen, H. (2009). Arviointiakvaario-osallistuva menetelmä kaikkien hyödyksi [Evaluation aquarium—A participatory method for the benefit of all. In Finnish]. *Terveyden edistämisen lehti Promo, 59,* 36.

Cerf, M. (2011). Is participatory research a scientific practice? *Journal of Rural Studies, 27*(2011), 414–418.

De Keyser, B., Guiette, A., & Vandenbemt, K. (2019). On the dynamics of failure in organizational change: A dialectical perspective. *Human Relations,* 2019 online first.

Djellal, F., & Gallouj, F. (2013). The productivity in services: Measurement and strategic perspectives. *The Service Industries Journal, 33*(3–4), 282–299.

Engeström, Y., & Sannino, A. (2010). Studies of expansive learning: Foundations, findings and future challenges. *Educational Research Review, 5,* 1–24.

Engeström, Y., & Sannino, A. (2012). Whatever happened to process theories of learning? *Learning, Culture and Social Interaction, 1*(2012), 45–56.

Grant, A. M., & Parker, S. K. (2009). Redesigning work design theories: The rise of relational and proactive perspectives. *The Academy of Management Annals, 3*(1), 317–375.

Honkaniemi, L., Lehtonen, M. H., & Hasu, M. (2015). Wellbeing and innovativeness: Motivational trigger points for mutual enhancement. *European Journal of Training and Development, 39*(5), 393–408.

Hyytinen, K., Saari, E., & Elg, M. (2019). Human-centered co-evaluation method as a means for sustainable service innovations. In M. Toivonen

& E. Saari (Eds.), *Human-centererd digitalization and services* (pp. 57–75). Singapore: Springer Nature.

Johnson, R., & Hail-Jares, K. (2016). Prisons and technology: General lessons from the American context. In Y. Jewkes, B. Crewe, & J. Bennet (Eds.), *Handbook on prisons* (pp. 284–305). New York: Routledge.

Kajamaa, A. (2011). *Unraveling the helix of change: An activity-theoretical study of health care change efforts and their consequences*. Helsinki: Unigrafia.

Laine, M. (2011). Rankaisu ja kuntoutus [Punishment and rehabilitation. In Finnish]. In R. Lavikkala & H. Linderborg (Eds.), *Rikosseuraamustyön kehittämisen kysymyksiä*. Tampere: Rikosseuraamusalan koulutuskeskus 2/2011.

Mäkitalo, J. (2005). *Work-related well-being in the transformation of nursing home work*. Acta Universitatis Ouluensis D Medica 837, Oulu University Press, Oulu.

Patton, M. Q. (2011). *Developmental evaluation: Applying complexity concepts to enhance innovations and use*. New York: The Guilford Press.

Saari, E., & Kallio, K. (2011). Developmental impact evaluation for facilitating learning in innovation networks. *American Journal of Evaluation, 32*(2), 227–245.

Saari, E., Hyytinen, K., Hasu, M., Hyypiä, M., Korvela, P., Käpykangas, S., Leväsluoto, J., Melkas, H., Nordlund, A., Pekkarinen, S., & Toivonen, M. (2018). *Kokeilut käytäntöön -työkirja* [Experiments into practice. Manual. In Finnish]. https://www.ttl.fi/wp-content/uploads/2017/12/kokeilut-kaytantoon-tyokirja.pdf.

Sannino, A., Engeström, Y., & Lemos, M. (2016). Formative interventions for expansive learning and transformative agency. *Journal of the Learning Sciences, 25*(4), 599–633.

Thompson, T. L. (2017). *Datafication of professional practices: A posthuman exploration of new accountabilities and fluencies*. Paper presented at the 10th Conference on Researching Work and Learning, Grahamstown, South Africa.

Virkkunen, J. (2007). Collaborative development of a new concept for an activity. *@ctivités revue éléctronique, 4*(2), 158–164.

Ylisassi, H., Seppänen, L., Uusitalo, H., Kalavainen, S., & Piispanen, P. (2016). *Aktivoiva lähityö. Vankiloiden valvonta-ja ohjaushenkilöstö vuorovaikutuksellista lähityötä kehittämässä*. [Activating interactive work. Prison personnel developing rehabilitative interactive work with prisoners. In Finnish, with English and Swedish summaries]. http://www.rikosseuraamus.fi/material/attachments/rise/julkaisut-risenjulkaisusarja/qmR5zNYVd/RISE_2_2016_Aktivoiva_lahityo_WEB.pdf. Rikosseuraamuslaitoksen julkaisuja 2/2016.

10

Interprofessional Collaboration Concerning Offenders in Transition Between Mental Health and Criminal Justice Services. PINCOM Used as a Framework for HCR-20^{V3} Assessment

Atle Ødegård and Stål Bjørkly

Introduction

Service demands, when offenders make the transition from prison back into society, are complex and challenging. Offenders often need support and help from a range of professionals representing different services (WHO, 2010), as offenders often have multiple problems, including mental health problems. In Norway, for example, studies clearly describe a higher incidence of mental disorders among inmates than among the general population (Cramer, 2014). Among offenders, only 8% have no mental illness, whereas the rest have extensive diagnoses (personality

A. Ødegård (✉) · S. Bjørkly
Molde University College, Molde, Norway
e-mail: atle.odegard@hiMolde.no

S. Bjørkly
e-mail: stal.k.bjorkly@himolde.no

A. Ødegård
Nordland Research Institute, Bodø, Norway

S. Hean et al. (eds.), *Improving Interagency Collaboration, Innovation and Learning in Criminal Justice Systems*,
https://doi.org/10.1007/978-3-030-70661-6_10

disorders, 73%; drug abuse, 51.3%; anxiety, 42%; alcohol abuse, 28.7%; mood disorders, 23%; ADHD, 18%; risk of suicide, 12%; and psychosis, 3.3%) (Cramer, 2014). This calls for the development of new interagency collaboration arrangements (Hean et al., 2015). A major challenge is that services, prison and mental health services for instance, are often fragmented with different responsibilities, laws and regulations.

The main scope of this chapter is to introduce and discuss the feasibility of two tools that may enhance collaboration among service providers. First, we describe the HCR-20^{V3} (Douglas et al., 2013) and suggest how parts of it can be jointly used as a tool for concrete collaboration in the practice field. Next, we present the PINCOM tool, containing a conceptual model (PINCOM) and a research methodology (PINCOM-Q) (Ødegård, 2006). This tool was developed to (a) assist in organising collaboration processes in multilevel interprofessional challenges and (b) increase knowledge about collaboration through a new research methodology (PINCOM-Q). Finally, we present and discuss some relevant issues for professionals engaged in collaboration processes involving offenders' trajectories from prison back into society. It is suggested that the PINCOM can be used within a larger social innovation framework and as a reflective tool during or after structured professional assessment, such as the HCR-20^{V3}.

The Need for Interprofessional Collaboration

Authorities and health promotion organisations, such as WHO, have promoted integration of health and prison services for decades (Wolff, 2002). Still, we do not have much research that illuminates collaboration processes in the trajectory from prison into society. According to Hean et al. (2017a) and a literature review conducted by Brooker et al. (2009), collaboration between the criminal justice system and the mental health field is underinvestigated.

Interprofessional collaboration is often described as a complex phenomenon that needs conceptual models that capture different aspects of the collaboration processes (Reeves et al., 2010). This is evident as there are many definitions of collaboration and related concepts—all of which attempt to capture the complexity of professional interaction

(Barr et al., 2005; Leathard, 2003). When professionals from different services and/or "systems" collaborate, it is not a given that they will have the same conception of what "to do" when collaborating and what they should collaborate about. For example, an offender leaving prison will most probably need several services to be able to cope with life outside the prison. Central needs will often be housing, work, a network, and medical and social services. Professionals working in the prison and professionals working in the community and in special services will need to meet and discuss with the prisoner a plan for life outside the prison. In a qualitative study, Hean et al. (2017a) found that leaders in the field were especially concerned about the distribution of responsibility for the offender across systems. If leaders (and professionals in different systems) only try to demarcate their own responsibility rather than look for joint solutions, collaboration may fail before it begins. In one of the few studies from the Norwegian context, Hean et al. (2017b) explored prison officers' perceptions of collaboration between different systems and professions. It was no surprise that findings showed that prison officers significantly perceived less collaboration with mental health specialists than with nurses and social workers in the prison. The same respondents requested "much greater contact with mental health specialists when dealing with the mentally ill offender" (Hean et al., 2017b, p. 91). In sum, there are clear indications of the need for the development of new approaches to collaboration in the trajectory from prison into society.

However, collaboration is not a goal in itself; actors need to collaborate about something that is useful and has positive and constructive outcomes for the offender. As presented in the beginning of this chapter, we will introduce and discuss the feasibility of two tools that may enhance such collaboration. The last few decades have seen the development of numerous instruments for risk assessment of violence. The HCR-20^{V3} (Douglas et al., 2013, 2014) is the most widely used instrument in risk assessment of violence worldwide. Douglas et al. (2013) claim that professionals should collaborate across disciplines when using the HCR-20^{V3}. Assessment of risk of violence must take into consideration that violence is a context-dependent phenomenon. Thus, when different persons from different services collaborate on using the HCR-20^{V3}, a more nuanced risk assessment results due to the sharing of knowledge. Still, in the practice of collaboration, it is often taken for granted that professionals know how to collaborate. This is not necessarily true. As indicated above, it is not at all clear what professionals (prison officers and mental health professionals) perceive collaboration to be. To arrive at a common understanding of collaboration, the professionals involved need to explore each other's individual understanding. Doing so could even produce new insights about the phenomenon at hand (for example, risk management issues), but also contribute to a broader and deeper understanding of what collaboration is about. New insights could even be understood as an epistemological change. Collaboration among professionals has the potential of moving from simple linear to contextual and reflexive communication (Ødegård & Bjørkly, 2012). As Hoffman (1985) described, the emphasis shifts from a concern with the etiology of a problem to a concern with the meanings that are attached to it. This shift has been described as a principal difference between the understanding of change in first- and second-order perspectives, from a perception of reality as absolute to one that is individually and differentially perceived. In this chapter, we present two tools through which individual perceptions may be aligned during collaboration: the first is the HCR-20^{V3} as a tool for generating contextual and shared understanding of violence risk. The second is PINCOM-Q as a method for identification and development of contextual and shared understanding of interdisciplinary collaboration between professionals involved in the trajectory between prison and society.

The HCR-20^{V3}

As noted above, the HCR-20^{V3} (Douglas et al., 2013) is the most commonly used structured professional judgement tool for violence risk assessment. It comprises 10 historical risk factors, five dynamic risk factors, and a risk management scale with five items about adjustment to future risk-related circumstances. A conventional use of the tool means that personnel in charge of a patient or an inmate at the initial phase of transfer do the assessment and present the results to personnel in the services that will engage with the inmate later on. This sequential, one-by-one approach runs the risk of supporting separate positioning, interprofessional misinterpretations, disagreements, and complications in the transition process.

The first version of the HCR-20^{V3} appeared in 1995, and it belongs to the Structured Professional Judgement (SPJ) tradition (Singh et al., 2016). This approach uses a structured practice based on the "state of the discipline" concerning scientific knowledge and professional practice. *Structured* means that risk assessment is evidence-based and that the tool is a stepwise guideline on how to assess the 20 items. However, the coding of the items is only two (Steps 2 and 3) out of the following seven steps:

1. Gather information.
2. Determine presence of risk factors.
3. Assess the relevance of the risk factors.
4. Develop a violence risk formulation.
5. Develop risk scenarios of violence.
6. Develop risk management strategies.
7. Final opinions and conclusion.

The first step is similar to the starting point for most approaches in clinical assessment. Step 2 is to identify which risk factors are or have been associated with violence for the individual in question. This person may have a history of problems with substance abuse (Item H5) and major mental disorder (H6), recent problems with insight (C1), and symptoms of a major mental disorder (C3) that precipitated the violence that sent him to prison. His treatment or supervision response has been negative (R4) after previous transitions from prison to mandatory community treatment. The assessment of how relevant (Step 3) each item is for current and future violence provides important information for developing risk formulation (Step 4), risk scenarios (Step 5), and risk management strategies (Step 6). The risk formulation is intended to explain *why* violence may reoccur: For example, in cases of decompensation (a decline into ideas of delusional persecution), the individual's emotional distress increases to a level that he cannot cope with, and the risk of paranoid violence "in self-defence" becomes high. The motivation for turning to violence is a means of "acting out" that generates a transient relief and diversion from intolerable internal psychosis-triggered pain. This is termed *negative reinforcement* in behaviour therapy. Based on this interpretation, two different types of risk scenarios are created. One *best-case scenario* may be that he is transferred to mandatory treatment in a community residence with 24/7 follow-up by mental health personnel (R1. Professional Services and Plans). He is put on forced medication and he resumes the work he had before the violent crime. Personnel are trained to identify and intervene if certain warning signs of psychotic decompensation appear (R5. Stress and Coping). A *worst-case scenario* would be that he is moved to different housing and a new workplace where he does not want to stay. His only follow-up by mental health personnel is one session per week in an outpatient clinic (R1. Professional Services and Plans). He ceases medication and starts up again with substance abuse (H5). Even if these examples are somewhat exaggerated for clarity, they illustrate the significance of context (R2. Living Situation) and risk management strategies in theassessment of violence risk for prevention of violence recidivism.

Risk Assessment with the HCR-20^{V3}: The Paramount Role of Context Factors

We will illustrate and discuss now the potential meeting points for collaboration that lie in interdisciplinary discussions and knowledge sharing of information related to relevance, risk formulation (why the violence may occur), risk scenario, and risk management strategies. To meet the criteria for being a *relevant* risk factor, a factor must be (1) functionally related to past violence, (2) likely to influence the person's decision to act in a violent manner in the future, (3) plausible to impair the individual's capacity to employ non-violent problem-solving, and (4) of contextual nature. The latter contextual factors are important in order to understand *why* and to what extent a person will be violent. For example, a *risk formulation,* for an individual acting on violent persecutory delusions as the core risk factor, will be different in a stable and predictable context if compared to when the person is experiencing unstable living conditions. One difference is that in a secure and calm milieu, a person will be helped in response to her emotional distress instead of having her anxiety ignored until it turns into the last resort—violence.

Risk scenarios depict operationalised risk situations or contexts for violence. The difference between a worst-case scenario and a best-case scenario may in fact lie in the different contexts the person finds themselves. There is a huge difference between the scenario of a drug-addict being transitioned from prison to the drug abuse milieu he came from, compared to his entering a structured treatment programme for drug abusers. A context-free risk assessment is therefore not meaningful, and, since professionals from different services are making observations in these different contexts, sharing these observations and interprofessional cooperation between services may inform the assessment of violence risk in an individual case.

Similarly, risk management strategies will be different depending on the context into which these are introduced. We must also consider how the implementation of these strategies in turn changes the context. There are three important steps that must be followed in this process: first, a structured risk assessment of violence that provides information about a person's risk situations is made; second, the likelihood of how often an individual may be exposed to these situations is assessed. Finally, the proper risk management strategy is developed and implemented.[1] If prison and mental health services acknowledge the impact of contextual factors on violence risk, then their sharing of observations and knowledge becomes easier and more valuable in each case. Prison officers are experts on the here-and-now risk in the forensic context and, based on risk scenarios, may suggest risk management strategies to the mental health services. The latter service has expertise on the treatment of psychosis. They also know what kind of living context and follow-up procedure they can offer once the prisoner is released. This allows for a collaborative rather than competing communication whereby the expertise of each is acknowledged. Still, this is not enough to guarantee success.

To help parties grasp the possibility of positive interprofessional collaboration, a bird's eye view of the collaboration landscape needs to be

[1] User involvement is, of course, also a must to succeed in this process. However, since interprofessional collaboration is our main focus here, we do not elaborate more on the role of users in the transfer between services.

developed. In cases where individuals are making a transition from one service to another, a common perspective and understanding of this process needs to be developed. This is where other tools such as the PINCOM fits in.

The Perception of Interprofessional Collaboration Model (Pincom)

The Development of PINCOM and PINCOM-Q

Kelly (1955) claimed that "a person's processes are psychologically channelized by the ways in which he anticipates events" (p. 46). Consequently, professionals from different services will, when engaged in collaboration processes, have their own (idiosyncratic) perceptions of what is going on and how the process should come about. In one study, Ødegård (2005) found indications that perceptions of interprofessional collaboration could be understood at an individual, a group, and an organisational level. The Perception of Interprofessional Collaboration Model (PINCOM) describes 12 facets that make up these perceptions of the collaboration process at these three levels.

PINCOM was developed through a combination of a literature search, theoretical influences from organisational and social psychology, and clinical experience. The result is the following conceptual model—PINCOM (Ødegard, 2006).

Each of the 12 constructs included in the PINCOM was operationalised by four items, producing a 48-item questionnaire, PINCOM-Q.[2]

[2] The PINCOM-Q may be accessed on the webpage NEXUS, which is a national center in USA: "The National Center for Interprofessional Practice and Education was formed in October 2012 through a cooperative agreement with the United States Department of Health and Human Services, Health Resources and Services Administration". Its mission: "The National Center offers and supports evaluation, research, data and evidence that ignites the field of interprofessional practice and education and leads to better care, added value and healthier communities" (https://nexusipe.org). https://nexusipe.org/informing/resource-center/pincom-q-perception-interprofessional-collaboration-model-questionnaire.

PINCOM as an Analytical Tool in the Collaboration Process

In addition to being a quantitative research instrument, the conceptual framework of the PINCOM model may be used in collaboration processes, for example, as starting points for conversations about the meaning of interprofessional collaboration. How this may unfold is depicted in the following brief case illustration about Peter (age 23) who is leaving prison:

> *Peter has served his third sentence in four years in a Norwegian prison. He has been convicted for different drug-related crimes, such as the use of drugs (amphetamine), dealing drugs, and violence towards people in the "community" of drug abusers. Peter grew up in a foster home because his mother could not cope with his behaviour when he started using drugs at the age of thirteen. Presently Peter has decided to try to live a life without drugs, and, upon his release, a meeting has been arranged where the main purpose is the use of the HCR-20^{V3} assessment. Several professionals, from the criminal justice system and health and social services, participate in the meeting together with Peter and his older brother, who works as a carpenter.*

The Norwegian Directorate of Health recommends that violence risk assessments be carried out in an interdisciplinary collaboration context where there is the necessary expertise. Interdisciplinary collaboration in this regard means that different occupational groups of health professionals with expertise in the topic of violence risk work together to do the HCR-20^{V3} assessment. The final assessment should be done by a physician or psychologist who has expertise in risk assessment of violence (Helsedirektoratet, 2020).

How would a meeting around the HCR-20^{V3} assessment unfold in the case illustrated above? Most likely, the discussions would deal with the following topics: resources, adaptation, and feasibility. High-quality collaboration processes are a prerequisite for goal attainment in interdisciplinary work across services (Hean et al., 2017a). As we mentioned earlier in this chapter, prison officers are experts within the forensic context, whereas professionals from mental health services have expertise on treatment of psychosis. Although acknowledging each other's expertise is a prerequisite, this is not enough to guarantee success as *collaboration* is a fuzzy concept (Biggs, 1997). This means that each professional present in the meeting may perceive the process around HCR-20^{V3} differently, including how each understands Peter's problems and strengths, as in, for example, Steps 2–4 in the HCR-20 assessment.

PINCOM Individual level dimensions C1–C4: With regard to collaboration while working within the different steps in the HCR-20^{V3} assessment, it is suggested in PINCOM that professionals will tend to construct different aspects of collaboration during the HCR-20^{V3}assessment in their own way. Some professionals will tend to focus basically on individual aspects of the collaboration process (see Fig. 10.1), such as motivation (C1), role expectancy (C2), personal style (C3), and

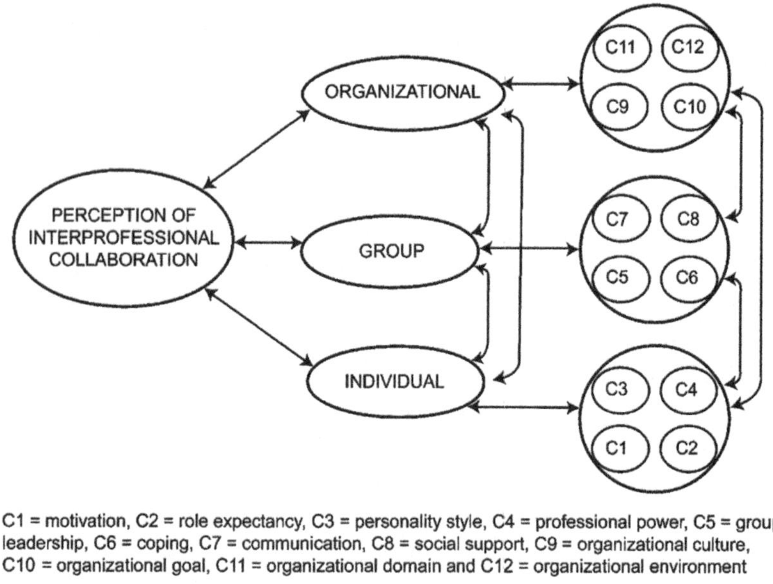

Fig. 10.1 Perception of Interprofessional Collaboration Model (PINCOM) (Ødegård, 2006)

professional power (C4), whereas others tend to focus on group or organisational aspects. Are the professionals present engaged (C1) in helping Peter in his rehabilitation process, for example, showing interest in taking responsibility during his return to society? Or do they see collaboration with other services as unnecessary or futile hereby lacking the motivation to engage? Furthermore, what role expectations (C2) do the participants have for each other while collaborating? For example, what do prison staff expect from mental health professionals, and vice versa? Next, some professionals with expertise in risk management strategies may want to focus on risk specifically in the meeting. If no special attention is given to this professional's individual expertise in the meeting, some participants may feel that others are exerting their professional power (C4) over them. This would most likely disrupt communication in the meeting. It is important to acknowledge each other's competence regarding information and knowledge concerning Peter in both the present and future contexts. Finally, professionals are all different, and some may have a personality style (C3)—for example being very extroverted and talkative. Such a style, of course, might affect interactions among participants, limiting sound dialogue during the HCR-20^{V3} assessment. As a result important information might not come to light during discussions if some of the participants do not describe their perceptions of Peter and his challenges due to tensions among the meeting participants.

PINCOM Group Dimensions C5–C8: Collaboration processes are deeply dependent on the quality of the interaction between the participants. Before Peter's transfer back into the community from prison, there is a need to discuss and plan the collaboration process. A good way to start is to establish a joint transfer group comprising professionals from the prison service and community mental health care. Interactions and interrelations in this group will depend on individual characteristics, as suggested above, but, as well, there will be specific aspects of how groups or teams function that are equally important. PINCOM has included some elements that are considered especially central during collaboration processes: leadership (C5), coping (C6), communication (C7), and social support (C8).

It is difficult to obtain a well-functioning HCR-20^{V3} assessment without some kind of leadership (C5). Who leads during the assessment and what kind of leadership style contributes best to a valid HCR-20^{V3} assessment? The dynamics between a moderator and the rest of the group are very important. The moderator should pay close attention to how different contexts are considered during HCR-20^{V3} assessment and by whom. If important information about Peter's behaviour in certain contexts is supressed, it might have potentially serious consequences. The moderator, therefore, has an important role in planning the collaboration process before transfer starts. Second, groups that function well tend to "experience" or learn coping strategies (C6) and thereby have a greater likelihood of performing even better the next time they collaborate. Communication (C7) is a broad and complex phenomenon and trying to develop good communication processes is complex. Therefore, participants in interprofessional groups, and especially the moderator of the group meeting, should strive hard to accomplish sound communication processes. It is not a given that the professionals in Peter's meeting are able to communicate clearly and mutually about his risk behaviour or other themes in his life. So how should communication unfold to gain the best possible outcome for the HCR-20^{V3} assessment in an interdisciplinary context? This, we believe, is a question that participants in a given meeting probably need to discuss. Finally, a fourth aspect at the group level is social support (C8). To what degree will professionals engaged in interdisciplinary meetings support each other, while working together very often on highly complex cases? For example, are they able to support each other, even though they sometimes disagree or differ on certain aspects during the HCR-20^{V3} assessment?

PINCOM Organisational level Dimensions C9–C12: The third level in PINCOM focuses on organisational aspects of collaboration. To a certain degree, participants will perceive organisational aspects involved in interprofessional collaboration processes differently. For example, organisational cultures (C9) may facilitate or hamper collaboration processes. Some organisations may value collaboration, as this may produce good outcomes for service users and service providers. However, other organisational cultures may rely strongly on what professional "domain" the organisation covers. In the HCR-20^{V3} assessment process concerning Peter, some professionals may become passive if they believe (or argue) that the assessment lies outside their organisational domain

(C11). Likewise, some may claim that the organisation they represent have aims (C10) that do not correspond to issues raised in this particular meeting. Finally, other aspects, such as the organisational environment (C12) may influence collaboration processes between professionals. In the case of Peter, this could be professionals in the justice system, such as lawyers, or health and social services, or professionals from the Norwegian NAV (Norwegian Labour and Welfare Organisation) not being represented in the meeting. Furthermore, the community personnel may have known Peter from three years back before he went to prison and need an update about his progress over his time in prison and his current circumstances. They also have expertise in what kind of follow-up they and other services can provide in terms of living conditions, work options, etc.

Discussion

Risk assessment with the HCR-20^{V3}: An interface for interprofessional collaboration?

As pointed out above, the common denominator for risk relevance, formulation, scenario, and management is the significant role and impact of contextual factors. Professionals from different services have observed a person in different contexts, and this may add synergy to a more multifaceted contextual understanding of an individual and his or her violent behaviour. The structure and predictability when serving time in prison is very different from the open follow-up when individuals are back in the community. The main question is what kind of knowledge and preventive measures are generated by comparing observations of and interactions with a person in different contexts? The answer depends on who participates in the assessment process, their will to collaborate, and the quality of their collaboration in any given case.

Prisoners may be transitioning to criminal justice services in the community or to community mental health services, each of which involves different agencies. In dysfuntional attempts of these agencies to collaborate across disciplines and services, their differences may be invoked as reasons not to be involved in the process. For example, an agency may communicate, "We have different expertise and our expertise is not relevant for rehabilitation of this person" or "We don't have the resources the offender needs to get better". Such positioning, by these professionals, blocks constructive communication and problem solving and serves to maintain the status quo.

In contrast, a constructive approach would emphasise that different expertise and experience of different services, taken together, is a strength. This requires not looking at each other's strengths as a threat but, rather, as contributing to a joint understanding of that professional group and their contribution. For example, professionals from the prison where the person has been for a long time, and who may be involved in a transfer, may have the following to contribute:

- Detailed knowledge about the person.
- Solid understanding of risk relevance and risk scenarios.
- Expertise on risk management strategies that have functioned in the prison context.

Professionals in the receiving context (e.g. the community) may have

- Detailed knowledge about the new context.
- Some understanding of risk relevance and risk scenarios in the new context.
- Knowhow regarding the feasibility of the suggested risk management strategies in the new context.

The implications of this "collaboration complexity" will most likely cause confusion and frustration during collaboration processes, if "the meaning" of collaboration is taken for granted—for example, during the HCR-20^{V3} assessment. It is suggested that PINCOM may help professionals reflect on their understanding of collaboration through, for example, meta-communication processes in order to gain a better common understanding of what they might achieve together. However, presently there is need for further exploration and research on interprofessional and interdisciplinary collaboration during HCR-20^{V3} assessment.

A main message in our chapter has been to emphasise a greater focus on the dynamics between the collaborating parties during HCR-20^{V3} assessment. This corresponds with the Norwegian Directorate of Health's recommendation that violence risk assessments should be carried out in an interprofessional collaboration context. And this is in contrast to the more conventional approach where only personnel in charge of a prisoner do the assessment. It is suggested that the inclusion of contextual factors during HCR-20^{V3} assessment, as provided by the participation of a range of service professionals, may be enhanced by using a differentiated perception of collaboration in line with the core content of PINCOM to enhance this joint assessment.

Employing the two tools, HCR-20 and PINCOM, in combination, as we illustrated in the case of Peter, can be considered a service delivery innovation (e.g., social innovation). "Social innovations are new solutions (products, services, models, markets, processes, etc.) that simultaneously meet a social need (more effectively than existing solutions) and lead to new or improved capabilities and relationships and better use of assets and resources. In other words, social innovations are both good for society and enhance society's capacity to act" (Murray et al., 2010, p. 18). In this regard, the combination of HCR-20 and PINCOM is a social innovative means of conducting risk assessment that may promote higher quality in the rehabilitation process, for both the offender and the professionals involved in the process.

References

Barr, H., Koppel, I., Reeves, S., Hammick, M., & Freeth, D. (2005). *Effective interprofessional education. Argument, assumption and evidence.* Oxford: Blackwell.

Biggs S. (1997). Interprofessional collaboration: Problems and prospects. In J. Øvretveit, P. Mathias, & T. Thompson (Eds.), *Interprofessional working for health and social care. Houndsmills* (pp. 186–200). London, UK: Palgrave Macmillan.

Brooker, C., Repper, J., Sirdifield, C., & Gojkovic, D. (2009). Review of service delivery and organisational research focused on prisoners with mental disorders. *Journal of Forensic Psychiatry & Psychology, 20*(1), 102–123.

Cramer, V. (2014). *Forekomst av psykiske lidelser hos domfelte i norske fengsler/Prevalence of mental disorders among convicted persons in Norwegian prisons*. Oslo: Centre for Health Care South East.

Douglas, K. S., Hart, S. D., Webster, C. D., & Belfrage, H. (2013). *HCR-20^{V3} assessing risk for violence*. Vancouver, BC: Mental Health, Law, and Polocu Institute, Simon Fraser University.

Douglas, K. S., Hart, S. D., Webster, C. D., Belfrage, H., Guy, L. S., & Wilson, C. M. (2014). Historical-Clinical-Risk Management-20, Version 3 (HCR-20V3): Development and overview. *International Journal of Forensic Mental Health, 13*(2), 93–108. https://doi.org/10.1080/14999013.2014.906519.

Hean, S., Willumsen, E., & Ødegård, A. (2015). Using social innovation as a theoretical framework to guide future thinking on facilitating collaboration between mental health and criminal justice services. *International Journal of Forensic Mental Health, 14*(4), 280–289.

Hean, S., Willumsen, E., & Ødegård, A. (2017a). Collaborative practices between correctional and mental health services in Norway: Expanding the roles and responsibility competence domain. *Journal of Interprofessional Care, 31*(1), 18–27.

Hean, S., Willumsen, E. & Ødegård, A. (2017b). Improving collaboration between professionals supporting mentally ill offenders. *International Journal of Prisoner Health, 13*(2), 91–104.

Helsedirektoratet. (2020). https://www.helsedirektoratet.no/faglige-rad/voldsrisikoutredning-ved-alvorlig-psykisk-lidelse.

Hoffman, L. (1985). Beyond power and control: Toward a "second order" family systems therapy. *Family Systems Medicine, 3*(4), 381–396.

Kelly, G. A. (1955). *The psychology of personal constructs, vol I & II*. New York: Norton.

Leathard, A. (Ed.). (2003). *Interprofessional collaboration: From policy to practice in health and social care*. Hove, New York: Brunner-Routledge.

Murray, R., Caulier-Grice, J., & Mulgan, J. (2010). *The open book of social innovation*. London: The Young Foundation. Available at https://youngfoundation.org/wp-content/uploads/2012/10/The-Open-Book-of-Social-Innovationg.pdf. Accessed 1 July 2020.

NEXUS. (2020). https://nexusipe.org/informing/resource-center/pincom-q-perception-interprofessional-collaboration-model-questionnaire.

Ødegård, A. (2005). Perceptions of interprofessional collaboration in relation to children with mental health problems. A pilot study. *Journal of Interprofessional Care, 19*(4), 347–357.
Ødegård, A. (2006). Exploring perceptions of interprofessional collaboration in child mental health care. *International Journal of Integrated Care, 6*(18 December). http://www.ijic.org/.
Ødegård, A., & Bjørkly, S. (2012). The family as partner in child mental health care—Problem perceptions and Challenges to collaboration. *Journal of the Canadian Academy of Child and Adolescent Psychiatry, 21*(2), 98–104.
Reeves, S., Lewin, S., Espin, S. og Zwarenstein, M. (2010). *Interprofessional teamwork for health and social care*. Oxford: Wiley-Blackwell.
Singh, J. P., Bjørkly, S., & Fazel, S. (2016). *International perspectives on violence risk assessment*. New York: Oxford Press.
Wolff, N. (2002). New' public management of mentally disordered offenders: part I. A cautionary tale. *International Journal of Law and Psychiatry, 25*(1), 15–28.
World Health Organization. (2010). *Framework for action on interprofessional education & collaborative practice*. Geneva, Switzerland: WHO.

11

Early Recognition Method: 'Opening Doors' in Risk Management Dialogue Between Mental Health and Prison Services

Frans Fluttert, Gunnar Eidhammer, and Karl Yngvar Dale

Introduction

Working in a closed secure facility requires a lot of employees to keep the work environment safe. Various studies show that prison employees are confronted with a high degree of stress, which can lead to burnout (Andersen et al., 2017; Bezerra & De Mahalhães, 2016; Finney et al., 2013; Gadon et al., 2006). The most important risk factors in burnout

The content is based on the article:
Fluttert, F.A.J. & G. Eidhammer (2018). ERM-Vroegsignalering opent de deur naar risicomanagement observaties en de dialoog met gedetineerden. Proces, 97–1, 25–39.

G. Eidhammer
Oslo University Hospital, Oslo, Norway

F. Fluttert (✉) · K. Y. Dale
Molde University College (MUC), Molde, Norway
e-mail: f.fluttert@pcvanmesdag.nl

K. Y. Dale
e-mail: karl.y.dale@himolde.no

S. Hean et al. (eds.), *Improving Interagency Collaboration, Innovation and Learning in Criminal Justice Systems*,
https://doi.org/10.1007/978-3-030-70661-6_11

are high work pressure, interaction problems with colleagues, supervisors or prisoners, the emotional burden of work and organisational problems. The work pressure is seriously increased in cases of violence against employees; a constant feeling of 'a malaise is in the air' is stressful (Bezerra & De Mahalhães 2016). Despite this observation, Andersen et al. (2017) found no direct relation between burnout among prison employees and violence of prisoners in a study of more than 3000 penitentiary workers. Research in other secure institutions, however, has shown violence from clients towards employees to have a major impact, eliciting feelings of anger, fear and gloom (Finney et al., 2013; van Leeuwen and Harte, 2016).

In order to explain this violence, the emphasis is often on the personal characteristics of clients. However, it appears that situational, relational and environmental factors also make an important contribution to the explanation of the origin of violence (Bjørkly et al., 2019). For example, overcrowding and insufficient limiting of undesirable behaviour are associated with an increased risk of violence. Decisions about the risk of violence tend to be based on studies with a large number of subjects (clients) (Bezerra & De Mahalhães, 2016; Carlsson et al., 2006; Newbill, 2010; Nijman et al., 1997). But it is as important in everyday practice that violence be understood and influenced at an individual level through exploring the behaviour of the potentially violent patient as an individual.

In secured institutions in psychiatry, such as Forensic Psychiatric Clinics [FPC], risk management strategies are well developed and applied to manage and control violence in individual patients. The two most applied risk management models explaining the vision behind risk management strategies are: (1) the Good Lives Model [GLM] and (2) the Risk-Needs-Responsivity [RNR] model. The GLM explains that the focus of risk management should be on assisting the client to develop meaningful life plans for rehabilitation, whereas in the RNR model it is argued that the focus in treatment should be on a structured professional judgement of criminogenic factors matching the patient's risk profile, the needs for treatment and the patient's abilities to comply (Andrew, 2012; Ward, 2002). In the literature and research addressing risk management approaches, the debate about the efficacy of GLM compared to RNR continues (Looman & Abracen, 2013). Some researchers argue that, apart from the focus of risk management, there is much overlap between the models both addressing patient's social factors that contribute to a 'good life' without offending. Most research studying the effectiveness of risk management has focused on the RNR model, showing it to contribute significantly to relapse prevention and reduced reoffending (Looman & Abracen, 2013; Taxman et al., 2013). It is argued that the RNR model facilitates the patients' interaction with care providers, i.e. the professionals learn, in a structured way, to understand how violence can occur, what the consequences may be and especially, how they can control aggressive feelings and behaviours in patients (Douglas et al., 2013). The ERM Early Recognition Method (ERM; Fluttert et al., 2008) is a risk management strategy fitting, in its origins, within the RNR model. The uniqueness of ERM lies, however, as a risk management strategy that emphasises the importance of having the patient involved in the risk assessment, identifying and managing, in structured way, specifically the early warning signs of violence. The ERM strategy focuses on describing early warning signs of behavioural escalation in ERM-plans. The focus is not on unravelling and describing the crisis but on avoiding it and the development of behavioural stability by means of managing early warning signs. ERM research shows that its application in the FPC context contributes to less frequent and less serious violence (Fluttert et al., 2010b).

In the prison context, prisoners also benefit from (treatment) programmes that can provide insight into their behavioural problems and how they can manage these. Here too, the RNR principle is an important starting point. That this is an internationally recognised principle is evident from the fact that the Handbook on the Management of high-risk prisoners UNODC (United Nations Office on Drugs and Crime, 2016), advocates the development and application of risk management programmes according to the RNR principles. The importance of this is also illustrated by Campbell et al. (2010) in a study of 22 prisoners: that showed that offender treatment programmes' using RNR principles contributed to reduced recidivism among prisoners. These prisoners reported that they wanted to improve their lives but did not know how to achieve this. Prison programmes can help with this. These programmes are mostly aimed at the prisoners′ return to society, where their problems become manageable and social integration is promoted. Lesser attention is paid to the application of risk management strategies that prison employees can apply in the day-to-day management of prisoners when they are in the prison itself. The ERM has the potential to address this offering a tool with which to identifying and discussing with prisoners the early warning signs of violence.

Inpatient violence in forensic institutions and violence in prisons evoke fear and stress among employers working in these facilities (Finney et al., 2013; Leeuwen & Harte, 2016). The nature of violence from prisoners towards staff is comparable to the violence from forensic patients towards staff. In both contexts staff are confronted with verbally and physically threatening behaviours (Andersen et al., 2017; van Leeuwen et al., 2016). Despite this, there are hardly any risk management strategies assisting care-givers or prison staff within the prison to understand and manage violence, and reduce violent incidents before they begin. Moreover, there are hardly any risk management strategies in which the prisoner is actively involved in this risk management (Eidhammer et al., 2014; Ray & Simpson, 2019).

Aims

The aims of this chapter are to first explore the complexity and multifactorial nature of violence and its development. It then explains why a structured strategy based on a risk management model is necessary to adequately assess and manage violence. Finally, it addresses how the knowledge and research of the ERM-application in forensic psychiatry services could be transferred and be successfully applied as a violence reduction strategy in prison services. We also explore how risk assessment is an interagency issue and how the ERM can form a means of establishing a dialogue between services and actors. We view this aim as a form of social innovation: 'the development and implementation of new ideas (products, services and models) to meet social needs .... They are innovations that are not only good for society but enhance individuals' capacity to act' (European Commission, 2013, p. 6). These can take the form of new ways of working altogether but can take also the form of the transfer of effective models from one discipline to another. The transfer of the ERM model of risk management into the prison environment represents, therefore, a form of service social innovation. In order to explain this bridge being constructed between risk management between forensic- and prison services, we draw on studies in Norway and the Netherlands where the ERM has contributed to the better management of early warning signs of behavioural escalation and prevention of violence (Eidhammer et al., 2014).

Multifactorial nature of violence and its development

In order to comprehend the complexity of violence, multifactor models explain which factors influence the process towards aggression. We address three angles, from which to understand clients getting aggressive or violent. First, we will explain, by means of the General Aggression Model, how knowledge structures are related to the development of aggression. Next, we will reflect on how criminal attitudes and thinking styles could be understood and effected in treatment. Finally, we will, by means of the Hiday model (Hiday, 1997, 2006), connect the broad spectrum of influential factors and possible violence.

The General Aggression Model (GAM) is framework explaining two main aspects of aggression: the individual's present state, and the individual episodes of aggression. The development and occurrence of aggression is influenced by knowledge structures such as beliefs, perceptual schemata (e.g. perceiving events as hostile), expectation schemata and behavioural scripts (e.g. problems have to be solved with aggression). These knowledge structures affect the following social-cognitive phenomena: the perception of a situation, the interpretation of what is happening, the decision on how to act and the resulting behaviours, e.g. aggression. The knowledge structures are the results of an individual's experiences and perception of social events. Hence, each episode of aggression could serve as a learning trail through which repetitive aggression can be predicted.

A second perspective on violence is offered by Bulten et al. (2009) who conducted research into dimensions in criminal thinking styles among prisoners. Three dimensions of thinking styles can be distinguished, namely: (1) pro-active, anti-social and narcissistic, (2) emotional, reactive and impulsive and, (3) positive, open-minded and pro-social. These thinking styles are not per se separately inhibited in individuals, but each of these are mostly present in a dominant way. Bulten et al. suggested that prisoners with emotional, reactive and impulsive thinking styles could benefit especially from interventions aimed at learning to recognise thoughts that cause them problems.

Compared to the General Aggression Model and Bulten's study, Hiday (2006) developed a more comprehensive model emphasising primarily the main factors related to violence and how they are connected. These factors can interact and influence each other, leading to violence. The Hiday model highlights the importance of identifying personal and contextual factors proposing that there is no single pathway between a mental disorder and violence. Rather, there are many factors that mediate the relationship. For example, the mental illness in psychotic clients (who exhibit violence) cannot be the 'only' explanatory factor. It is also brought on by tense situations, suspiciousness, use of alcohol/drugs and so on.

The models explained above strengthen our understanding of why the identification of early warning signs of aggression and violence are valuable for risk management. For example, in the General Aggression Model and illustrated by Bulten et al. (2009) it is illustrated that the person's cognitive processes such as affect, arousal and thinking style benefit from a systematic approach, an approach that guides the 'decision process' at play when the individual decides whether to engage in aggression behaviours and how they do this. Hiday (2006) added to understanding of this process through explaining the interaction between violence inducing factors and how violence develops from these. Drawing on these principles the core idea of the ERM is that clients in psychiatric institutions, and probably also prisoners, within this process can learn to recognise and manage specifically their early warning signs of violence in order to avoid escalation. By means of this ERM client's awareness of their pathway into violence, they are able to appraise and articulate their own thoughts & behaviours through reflecting on their early warning signs as drawn up in the ERM tool. The aim of the tool is for the users to describe client-specific warning signs, an imminent violent episode, preferably in relation to the client himself. Important in this process is that the client is involved in order to get a 'customised plan' (Fluttert et al., 2008). Prisoners with more pro-active, anti-social and narcissistic thinking styles will hardly profit from strategies aimed at gaining insight in their behaviours because they do not perceive themselves as a problem. In cases of psychopaths these strategies should be avoided, unequivocally, because insight could serve as 'ammunition' to manipulate others, even more.

Both for the symptoms of a disorder and for its expression, there are almost always early warning signs (Fluttert et al., 2008). Tension and risk behaviours accumulate over time and are almost always preceded by the same early warning signs, called 'signature risk'signs or 'the signature of the behaviour' (Birchwood, 2000; Fluttert et al., 2008). These are signs that are very personal to the individual and often 'repetitive' when repeated stress build up occurs. The problem is that such warning signs are not always observable in the environment, because they often only play out in the client's head. That is why a methodical risk management approach, such as ERM, is needed to identify and describe both observable and non-observable signs.

The ERM and the Multivoiced Self

Apart from identifying personalised early warning signs, ERM is useful because it offers a framework to systematically manage both internal and external dialogues with the client about the onset and proceedings of the process of deterioration. By means of the ERM, attention is given to interactions with and about client's perception and behaviours in a so-called 'multivoicedness' sense. This means that the ERM helps prisoners reflect on the dialogue between self and the voice of internal and external others as a means of managing their risk of violent behaviour. The prisoners voice and that of the differing professionals supporting them are captured and expressed when articulating their early warning signs of aggression and how to control these. Moreover, by means of ERM the prisoner is encouraged to engage in a process of self-reflection; the voices in himself are explored and articulated related to aggression. This will be explained by the following theory of the Self.

Within a person, the individualistic 'Self', the awareness of one own perception, is always infused with and responding to voices of others, referred to as 'inner Others'. The Self alters depending on whom the person interacts (Kohut, 1984; Aveling et al., 2015). For example, a client could articulate that he got angry because he thought that the staff disliked and were harassing him. His awareness of anger represents his Self, his I-position. However his conviction about staff represents his 'inner Others'. When evaluating a client's ERM-early warning signs, it is important to explore both what he experiences within himself (internal dialogue) but also the way he then relates to his environment (external dialogue), as we have seen in the General Aggression Model and Hiday model (see above). The relation between the Self and Inner Others is the carrier where aggression could begin with early warning signs. More on the 'Self' and the 'Self Theory' (Kohut, 1984) and how this has been used to analyse ERM interactions and the impact on clients aggressive behaviours can be found elsewhere (Fluttert et al., submitted 2020).

Recognising Deteriorating Behaviours

The ERM assessment tool is approached from the perspective of deteriorating behaviour, in line with the Hiday model. Special attention is paid to the social and interpersonal factors related to the individual behaving violently. From this perspective, the thoughts, feelings and behaviour of the patient can indicate the onset of aggression, and early recognition of these warning signs can help thwart such deterioration. The ERM hence draws further upon theory of social competence. Bartels (2001) developed a model of how patients in forensic care can react with violence when thoughts, feelings and behaviours associated with specific events interfere with their life skills and tasks. Stated simply, individual perceptions and reactions to events are influenced by personality characteristics, life experiences and interpersonal skills. So-called core beliefs (or personal convictions) seem to play a profound role in the shaping of reactions to events. Furthermore, the chain linking the perceptions of events and core beliefs to expressed behaviour can be referred to as a scenario. For patients with a personality disorder, a scenario can be grounded in certain core beliefs and related feelings of anger and thereby elicit accusations, threats or teasing. A profound insight into a patient's ability/competence to cope with stressful situations (e.g., due to delusions), and into the developmental process of aggression, is essential in the dynamic interactional understanding of violence (Bjørkly, 2006).

The central vision behind ERM is that disruptive behaviour, including aggression, develops gradually and that, especially, in the first phase of behavioural disruption, there are opportunities for intervening and stabilising the client's behaviour (see Fig. 11.1 Process of deterioration). Early warning signs of aggression can be defined as changes in individual, thoughts, perceptions, feelings and behaviours of the patient that fall along a spectrum ending at the crisis point that precipitates aggressive

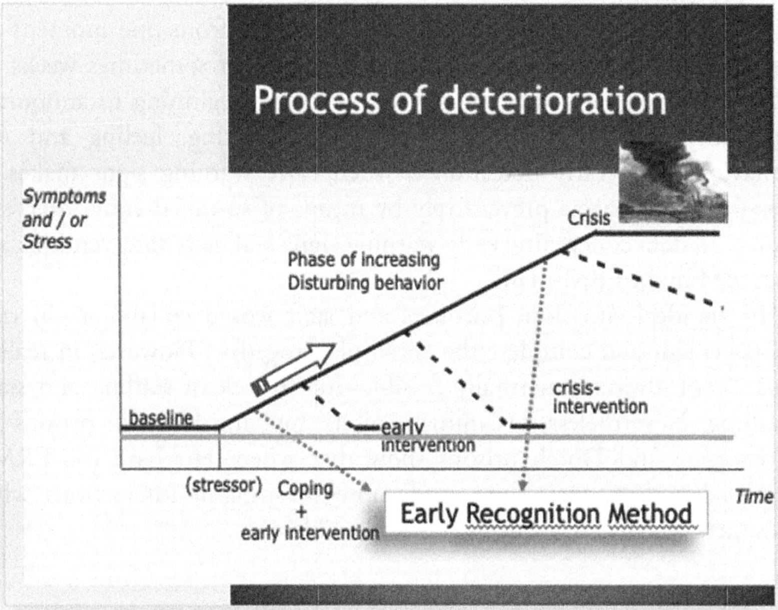

Fig. 11.1 Process of deterioration

behaviour (Fluttert et al., 2008). In addition to the detection of early warning signs it is important to describe the context in which the early warning signs mainly occur. For example, the early warning signal of violence: ‘irritation and anger’ could occur especially when too many people surround the patient.

The baseline in the figure shows the behaviour as we encounter it in stable normal situations. The sloping line symbolises an increasing deterioration of behaviour. Normally we are able to restore ourselves to functioning on the baseline. However, when the stress and/or symptoms of a disorder increase, the behaviour can deteriorate further to a point where no adjustment/de-escalation is possible and a crisis is likely to occur. When applying ERM-plans, we focus on the functional area in the middle of the ascending line. In this area the behaviour is out of balance, but not completely deteriorated. This is the area where the first signs, the so-called early warning signs, occur. This is also the area in which there, pre-eminently, are opportunities for influencing behaviour and prevention.

Behavioural disruption usually does not arise from one moment to the next. Usually there are already a few days, or sometimes weeks in advance, when early warning signs are already beginning to announce instability. This may involve changes in thinking, feeling and /or behaviour. The early detection of such early warning signs makes it possible to intervene preventively by means of so-called early interventions. All data concerning early warning signs and early interventions are recorded in an ERM-plan.

In an ideal situation, prisoners and staff would collaborate in risk management and complete the ERM plan together. However, in reality this is not always structurally feasible due to lack of staffing and staff training. Nevertheless, preliminary pilots applying ERM in prisons in Norwegian and Dutch prisons show that when staff have the ERM-knowledge they start more, and more meaningful interactions with prisoners who are showing aggression problems.

Models of ERM-Plans

Working with ERM-plans has its origins in the treatment of patients with schizophrenia. Birchwood (2000) described how early warning signs in an ERM-plan could be described so that patients themselves learn to recognise these signs and thus prevent psychoses.

In the Netherlands there was increasing attention in the nineties for ERM-plans based on early warning signs. To date four models of ERM-plans can be distinguished:

1. The Basic model. The early warning signs are listed on a checklist. The role of the patient is passive.
2. The Phase model. The different phases of a psychosis or behavioural disorder are described, as well as the corresponding actions for the patient.
3. The Comprehensive model. The early warning signs are described, but also the factors that influence their recognition. These are patient-own factors and factors in the social network. The patient and his social network are actively involved in applying the ERM-plan.
4. The Dynamic model. A further development of the comprehensive model is that, in addition to the early warning signs and factors in the patient and the social network, the factor 'context' is also highlighted. These are descriptions of specific circumstances in which early warning signs could occur. For example, a patient may notice that his increasing desire for alcohol occurs mainly when he feels more lonely and when he has less contact with family. These contexts are usually related to offence-related factors and thus fit with the criminogenic needs detailed in the RNR model (Fluttert & Eidhammer, 2018).

Based on the work of Birchwood, and on the comprehensive model and its associated protocol, Van Meijel et al. (2006) developed the 'Early Signs and Early Intervention Method' for general psychiatry. Fluttert et al. (2008) used this as the basis for the forensic variant and the dynamic model, the Early Recognition Method. ERM has not only been used and studied in mental health care since then, but also was studied in relation to how ERM risk management could be applied to prisoners and what this yields (Fluttert & Eidhammer, 2018).

Generations of Risk Assessment

Thus far, we have described how violence and aggression could be understood in terms of knowledge structures, thinking styles and multiple factors in the context of the individual. We have also explored some of the theoretical underpinnings of the ERM. Next, we will bridge this knowledge to risk management strategies, and in particular, the ERM. Risk assessment in forensic psychiatry is an activity to assess and describe the extent and nature of offending. This is followed by risk management, the activity of enabling clients to manage and control disruptions in their behaviours. In the ideal scenario, risk assessment and risk management activities are carried out together.

Risk management strategies have undergone enormous development over the past decades. A distinction is made between three generations of risk management strategies:

1. The *Unstructured Clinical Judgement*: clinical judgement whereby the worker, from his perspective on the client, gives an opinion about the expected danger.
2. *The Actuarial application:* the application of risk assessment instruments whereby fixed items of behaviour are scored and the final score gives an indication of the expected risk.
3. *Structured Professional Judgement (SPJ)*: whereby agreement is reached between two independent assessors. This is done in a structured manner on the expected recurrence of relapse of violence. The latter is developed on the basis of scored items from risk assessment instruments merged with clinical judgement (Douglas et al., 2013). The aim is to formulate the risk in the most accurate way explaining the client's personalised risk. This so-called 'risk formulation' is a description of possible scenarios of relapse (best case-, worst case-, relapse- and twist scenarios) and risk interventions that help prevent relapse. A twist scenario is an unexpected change of the development of the risk,

e.g. a client who was initially convicted for pedophilia could 'twist' towards more fantasies of sexual abuse with the possible outcome of killing children. The SPJ is the most dynamic and recent approach to risk management. The use of risk assessment instruments is linked in a structured way to risk management strategies. The application of ERM fits well with SPJ in that it determines the early warning signs in relation to risk scenarios. For example, if a client has described a risk scenario in which the use of alcohol is related to violent behaviour, then, while determining the early warning signs, the client will discuss which signs precede the search for or use of alcohol. The HCR-20-V3 (see also Chapter 10 of this volume) is the world's most used risk assessment instrument fitting in the 3rd generation risk assessment (Douglas et al., 2013). This risk assessment instrument enables clinicians in a structured systematic way to assess and rate the most important items related to violence risk on the levels of low, moderate and high risk. A 7 step decision process is articulated within the HCR-20-V3, describing how the instrument should be applied in order to maximise the accuracy of the violence risk assessment.

The ERM is referred to within these 7 steps in the HCR-20V3 manual, referring to it as a promising method to apply the risk management part of the process. The value of ERM is seen as a follow up to the risk assessment conducted in the HCR-20-V3, and recognises the importance of the involvement of the client in assessing and formulating the risk (Ray & Simpson, 2019). This makes it an instrument with potential to stimulate collaboration, interaction and multivoicedness as is very much stressed in the ERM protocol and training session.

The Application of the Early Recognition Method [ERM]

So far, ERM-plans have been described as has how ERM is ideally applied. But how is this applicable for prison staff and prisoners? To highlight this, we first consider the principles of ERM (henceforth, the terms supervisor and client are used). Then we can focus more specifically on ERM for prisoners.

An important aspect of risk management strategies such as ERM is that the supervisor is aware of his or her own basic attitude towards clients. Clients in a closed institution who show resistance or hostility benefit from supervisors who do not immediately judge their behaviour but encourage the client to discuss what is bothering him or her (Meehan et al., 2006). Obviously, structure must be provided to inhibit, for example, scolding, shouting or threatening. At the same time, a client does not have to be motivated externally to be able to cooperate with ERM-plans. Internal motivation is also a form of motivation, e.g. that motivation can increase as a function of the client noticing that working with ERM-plans is not as complex or threatening as he initially thought.

The two most important factors in the process of working with ERM-plans are: (1) the client learns to accept that risk management conversations such as with ERM are not punitive or threatening, and (2) the client learns how to work with ERM-plans, which support him. The enduring benefit of ERM is about 'understanding', and that takes time. ERM-research (Fluttert et al., 2010a) shows that the discussion between client and staff regarding early warning signs is contributing to gain a better, and shared, understanding of the client's perceptions and behaviours. Even when they disagree about the occurrence of the early warning signs, pondering about 'rights' and 'wrongs' (of which there are none), these discussions enlighten client's behaviours in stability and less stable conditions.

The 'ERM- protocol' describes the strategy for guiding the client in the right way when drafting and implementing an ERM-plan. Such a protocol is necessary for supervisors in order to apply the method in a systematic manner, with the right steps and at the right time (Fluttert et al., 2016). The ERM protocol is based on sound scientific intervention research (Meijel et al., 2003; Fluttert et al., 2010b, 2013). Because the ERM focuses on the interaction in relation to early warning signs, this is pre-eminently a dialogue-based strategy. Several studies show that the interaction between care provider and client is the most important factor in influencing aggression during admission. The research into the application of the ERM also showed that weekly discussions between supervisors and clients had a meaningful contribution to reducing the number and severity of aggression incidents (Fluttert et al., 2010a).

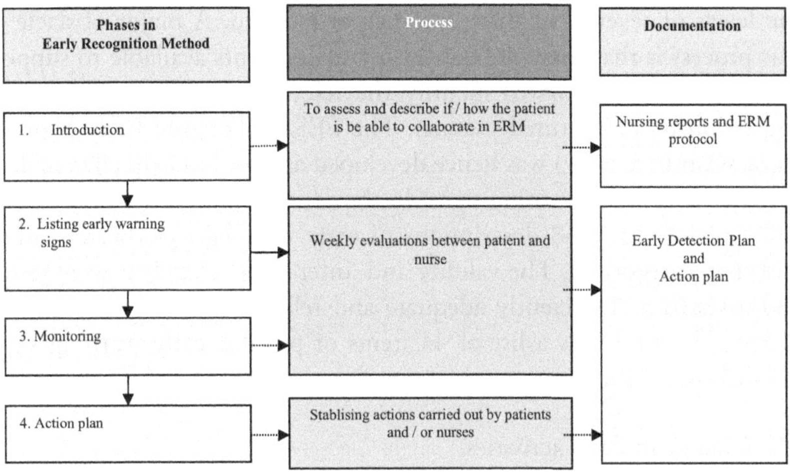

Fig. 11.2 ERM framework

The work protocol (see Fig. 11.2 ERM framework) associated with the ERM consists of four phases, i.e. the steps in which the method is applied: (1) introduction phase, (2) identification phase, (3) monitoring phase and (4) action phase.

Phases of the Protocol

Introduction/preparation phase

The professional explains to the client/prisoner the purpose of the ERM, the ERM-plan and what is expected of him. At the same time, it is assessed at this stage whether and how the client will be able to work with the ERM-plan. The strategy, the way in which ERM is applied, is then decided. If necessary, an ERM-plan can be drawn up without the client's cooperation.

Identification phase

In this phase, early warning signs are listed and described in the ERM-plan. Each early warning sign is described at three levels of severity, (1. stable, 2. disrupted and 3. more disrupted). The means by which the client can learn to recognise their own relevant early warning signal and the levels of severity of these are then articulated. A major obstacle to this process is that there are hardly any instruments available to support clients and supervisors to identify the relevant early warning signs of aggression in a structured manner. The FESAI (Forensic Early Signs or Aggression Inventory) was hence developed as a tool to help clients identify their own early warning signs. In the construction of the FESAI, 167 ERM-plans and 3768 descriptions of early warning signs were studied and then categorised. The validity and 'inter-rater reliability' were tested and assessed as sufficiently adequate and reliable (Fluttert et al., 2011, 2013). The FESAI is a list of 44 items of possible early warning signs divided over 14 main categories, namely:

1. Change in daily activities.
2. Social isolation/decreased social contact.
3. Change of self-management.
4. Physical changes.
5. Changed substance needs (alcohol, drugs, medication).
6. Cognitive changes.
7. Dejection and anxiety.
8. Tension, agitation, anger.
9. Non Violent anti-social behaviour.
10. Disinhibition and impulsivity.
11. More (extreme) sexual fantasies /needs /behaviours.
12. Criminal behaviour.
13. Irrational ideas/perceptions.
14. Very specific changes of behaviours.

Specific warning signs are described within these categories.

Monitoring phase

The monitoring phase involves scanning of the prisoners' behaviour with the aim of recognising the occurrence of early warning signs. The dialogue between the client and the supervisor about the occurrence of early warning signs takes place here. In this phase, discussions often take place between client and supervisor, often from a disagreement about the assessment of the occurrence of the early warning signal. The trained and professional supervisor remains neutral, and tries to explore together with the client how he interprets his behaviour and creates a dialogue about the differences of perception of the same behaviour.

Action phase.

Finally, if possible, an action plan is drawn up together with the client that is part of the ERM-plan. It describes which actions can contribute to stabilisation of behaviour.

The competences required to apply ERM can be trained in a customised ERM-training programme developed for nurses working in (forensic) psychiatry or prison officers in prisons. In these training sessions the staff learns the basic theory behind aggression and violence (as explained earlier) and how to identify and manage early warning signs by means of the ERM protocol.

The ERM as a Tool for Client Involvement and Shared Decision-Making in Risk Management

In recent years there has been more recognition of the client's voice and involvement in treatment planning (Gudde et al., 2015). This is a development that makes clients more assertive with respect to privacy and the right of access to, for example, treatment plans. In addition, current internet use contributes to better access for clients in terms of knowledge about, for example, disorders and treatment options. Social media platforms like Google and Wikipedia are examples of such sources that are often consulted. But also from an ethical perspective, and through a more effective use of care, care providers are more aware of the active role of clients in their guidance and treatment. This also applies to prisoners who, similarly, are aware of privacy rights and the possibilities of media platforms.

'Shared decision-making' [SDM] is an approach based on the principle that there are two experts in care and treatment: (1) the client and (2) the care provider (Legare et al., 2011). We will first explain the SDM model (thus use the term 'care provider'), and next, reflect how this could be valuable when applying ERM in prisons by prison-officers who are involved in taking care of the security in prisons.

The care providers have expertise in the process of diagnosis, risk assessment and risk management. Clients are the experts when it comes to experiences with their problems, i.e. what helps them and what gives meaning to the quality of their lives. Ideally, care providers and clients agree on the nature and purpose of the treatment and risk management. Through an active participation of the client in the treatment programme, the chances are increased that choices are made that suit the client better, to which he or she can connect better, so that the effectiveness increases. There is now enough research in mental health care that show that clients benefit from a process of SDM (Patel et al., 2008). For example, in a systematic review Patel et al. found that in an RCT-study among psychiatric patients, SDM resulted in a trend towards reduced rehospitalisation rates and improvement of self-efficacy of symptom management of mental illness. Also in forensic services, the collaboration between the forensic worker and the client is intended to eventually teach the client to independently control his risk (Kroner, 2012). However, in contrast to the principles of SDM, Eidhammer et al., 2014 showed that patient involvement is scarce in evidence-based risk management strategies. In this review, only the following three risk management strategies were found where the client had an active role in its application: (1) ProLad, a step-wise forward systematic rehabilitation programme (2) ERM, and (3) Anger Management programmes. The ERM, in collaboration with forensic patients, identifies early warning signs whereby the patient gets a better understanding of his deteriorating behaviours.

SDM is a relevant in prison services also, the basic assumption being again that the prisoner is an expert of his own needs or symptoms. In prisons often the prison officers 'know' by intuition when and how prisoners become aggressive. When this 'tacit knowledge' is articulated by describing early warning signs, then prisoners' behaviours could be more accurately described and monitored. This intuition should be harnessed and 'translated' into observable behaviours and recognised in a timely fashion. The ERM can be used as a SDM strategy that 'opens doors' and starts a systematic collaboration between prison staff and prisoners exploring jointly how stability could potentially deteriorate towards aggression. Training for all prison staff is advised before applying risk management strategies such as ERM. In a pilot study in the Netherlands and Norway ERM was taught to prison staff, and in some cases, they were also taught how to collaborate with prisoners in these endeavours. Preliminary results show that prison officers value working with ERM positively because their 'gut feelings' about the prisoners are made concrete and thereby they were better able to cooperate effectively with the prisoner. The ultimate goal would be to train prison officers systematically to gain knowledge in practice of how to apply risk management, such as ERM, resulting in a better management and prevention of aggression in those institutions.

Transfer of ERM-Knowledge Between Forensic and Prison Services

In Norway and the Netherlands there has been interest in the use of ERM among prisoners for several years. The reasons for this transfer of knowledge from the Forensic Psychiatry to Prison context is a need to reduce the occurrence of crisis situations in the prison as well as a tool for professionalisation of prison staff who have an increasingly need for higher competence in risk management as a methodical approach.

Initially the Early Signs and Early Intervention Method was developed for patients with Schizophrenia in general psychiatry (Birchwood, 2000; van Meijel et al., 2006). Elaborating on this concept Fluttert et al. (2008) developed the Forensic ERM version, applied this and studied this renewed ERM intensively. The prison services then showed interest and a process of studying, revising and transfer started in order to develop an ERM Prison version. The main steps are described below. A pilot was done in order to gain knowledge whether the multivoicedness resulted in a ERM version which fits to prison services. The final ERM version appeared to contribute to the collaboration between prison staff but also between prison staff and prisoners. Although the prison is often seen as a non-specialist service, the ERM enabled prison staff to enlarge their knowledge about aggression and how to manage it. Prison staff became prison specialists in ERM. The ERM also acknowledges that all contributing to its completion are experts in their own area whether they be forensic mental health nurses, researchers, prison staff and as such have a contribution to make to the assessment and management of risk.

In Norway, two pilot projects were launched between 2014 and 2016 in prisons in Hustad and Oslo Bredtveit Prison (the latter being a women's prison for long-term prisoners). In these projects, the ERM protocol, as developed for forensic psychiatric clinics, was revised so that an application for the context of penitentiary work became available. This revision process was undertaken as follows:

1. The first step was to formulate with the prison leaders a first draft of a project plan in which the aims, available project resources and research were agreed. At the Oslo-SIFER-Expertise Centre, Norway and at Molde University College, Norway, ERM-project groups were established that worked on revising the 'Forensic ERM-protocol' into a 'Prison ERM protocol' and assisting the prison services in implementing and applying ERM. In each prison a 'key-person' was assigned to be in contact between the prison staff and the expert group.
2. Regional ethical committees' permissions were obtained to run the study.
3. ERM training seminars for the prisons staff served as 'kick-off' meetings; prison staff got familiar with the basis assumption of ERM and how it could be valuable for their work with prisoners.
4. In collaboration between the ERM-project group and the prison, staff discussed revisions to the ERM protocol for prisoners. Apart from the local context, the risk assessment conducted with the model combined the criteria of the RNR model with the conceptual assumptions of ERM (see above) This lead to the first draft of the 'ERM-protocol-Prison version NO'.
5. The first ERM prison protocol was in both prisons applied during 1 year. During this year there were interview-meetings between project group members and prison staff exploring their perceptions of the potential of using the ERM. These discussions lead to adjustments in the protocol mostly concerning the use of terminology and more emphasis being placed on observing behaviours by means of the FESAI.

One year after the start of the pilots a concluding meeting was held between the project group and prison delegates. The project was evaluated and followup actions formulated how ERM to embed in prison practice. Details of these evaluations are reported elsewhere (Eidhammer et al., 2013) but overall interviews with prison staff showed they had found the use ERM a beneficial learning experience. This had been the first project they had experienced in which a particular risk management strategy (ERM) had been systematically discussed with them and through which knowledge and experiences between the forensic and prison fields had been exchanged.

In applying the ERM, and comparing this to the application of the ERM in the FPC, the Prison version of ERM focused more on identifying and observing early warning signs and less on the therapeutic relationship between supervisor and prisoner. Despite the staff being encouraged to discuss early warning signs with prisoners, observations and recordings of signs were more central. The ERM had provided them with a 'tool' to get a grip of risk signs in a structured way. Their daily 'usual' observations and impressions of the offender could now be articulated as early warning signs. The Prison version of the ERM working protocol, transformed into a kind of 'light version', meaning that the therapeutic interactions were re-formulated into directives and instructions and thereby better fitting to the context of prison staff.

Risk management skills are pivotal to the application of risk management strategies such as ERM. Prison staff were well prepared in this regard as they are already trained in monitoring and promoting safety in the organisation and the secured environment. They also expect today to have a greater contribution to make to the rehabilitation of prisoners (Osment 2018). This requires interaction and observation skills, not only to motivate the prisoner to cooperate, but also to be able to observe and manage possible behavioural disruptions in a timely manner. When using ERM in forensic psychiatry, the emphasis is on the interaction between therapist and patient. When applying it in prison institutions, the emphasis is more on making explicit intuitive actions on the basis of experience with prisoners, due to a lack of systematic risk management strategies. If possible, this will be discussed with the prisoner, but such risk management discussions between prison staff and prisoners are not yet customary. The experience so far is that ERM contributes to prison staff being able to systematically make their intuitive observations explicit by describing early warning signs and registering them in the ERM-plan.

Of similar importance is the observation that ERM contributes to the interaction between prison staff and prisoner. When prison staff are able to build up interactions with prisoners in a structured methodical way, this contributes to better cooperation and also a more positive image of prison staff among prisoners (Crewe et al., 2011). Thus, prison staff are not solely providing safety and security, but can also be instrumental in prisoners developing more sustainable and stable behaviours. Ultimately, enabling the prisoners′ rehabilitation back into society. Despite the difference between prison staff and mental health workers, with prison staff having to cover also social work issues, there are also similarities. Both disciplines are at the front line in their institutions. They are both in the position to observe, intervene and collaborate with the clients in case of deteriorating behaviours. For patients and prisoners, the 'frontline' workers are those who care for them 24/7 and thereby have the best opportunity to start systematic risk formulation interactions based on daily observations and experiences. This makes prison officers ideal resources when mental health professionals seek input for identifying and managing ERM-early warning signs.

Preliminary Findings on the Application of ERM Among Prisoners

The first results of the Norwegian ERM-pilot studies are encouraging. After a very short instruction session (lasting a few hours) it appeared that the prison staff could use the ERM-plan to describe early warning signs, including describing, at three severity levels, how the signal can be recognised. Furthermore, the FESAI appeared to provide good insight and guidance to determine the person-specific early warning signs per prisoner. In addition to the prison staff describing the signs in their own words, the FESAI immediately added a code corresponding to the category and the item in question in the FESAI. This provides opportunities for more systematic investigations into the ranking and classification of early warning signs in prisoners. It also appears that the format/layout of the ERM-plan provides sufficient guidance for adequately scoring the occurrence of warning signs over time, i.e. the so-called monitoring of behaviour.

A first rank-order analysis showed that the most common early warning signs had a strikingly similar ranking compared to forensic psychiatry (Fluttert, 2015). In other words, like in forensic psychiatry, the most prevalent early warning signs registered with prisoners were: (1) Tense, agitation and anger, (2) withdrawal from contact and fewer contacts and (3) change in daily activities. In the pilot study in Norway, the prison staff (Eidhammer et al., 2013) indicated that since the implementation of ERM they had gained much more insight into the significance and meaning of prisoners withdrawing. Previously, this behaviour was often seen as 'he is quiet, more in the background'. Now, this is acknowledged as a possible early warning sign in the sense that 'he feels less at ease and tolerates others less well'. The 'withdrawal behaviour' now has a different meaning within the framework of ERM and practice has shifted towards making contact with this prisoner early on in order to determine what is on his mind. Undoubtedly, this is a good starting point to engage in risk management.

In an evaluation in 2017 of the application of ERM observations in the Norwegian women's prison it emerged that staff had started to discuss the ERM-plan with the prisoners, as a natural next step. Although there is no question of a therapeutic interaction, the practical application of discussing the ERM-plan with the prisoner leads to better cooperation between prisoners and staff. An example of this is a prisoner who, for a long time, avoided contact with both prison staff within the institution and with the contact person in the rehabilitation programmes. This prisoner said that through the ERM talks, she gradually began to see that this form of risk management could support her in an existence 'outside' the institution. This insight led to her taking the initiative to discuss her ERM-plan with the contact person 'outside'. However, on the basis of such examples, we do not yet know anything about the effect of ERM on improving the stability of prisoners in the longer term. But, insofar the use of risk management strategies is meaningful for prisoners, and the interaction therein is important (Crewe et al., 2011), it is not unlikely that the ERM is a hope-inducing approach that can facilitate social rehabilitation.

Summary and Conclusions

Working in closed institutions requires a lot of commitment and professionalism from employees when dealing with stress. The likelihood of burnout is present in both prisons and institutions of forensic psychiatry. Actors in both environments have experiences of aggression or feeling 'something is about to happen' with respect to violence.

Aggression and violence (risk) appear regardless of where the person (patient or prisoner) is admitted. The application of risk management strategies contributes to the timely recognition of behavioural deterioration and the ability to manage them. The ERM is a risk management strategy that enables staff to recognise and manage early warning signs of deterioration in a timely manner. In forensic psychiatry, there are ample experiences of ERM in relation to its clinical relevance (Fluttert et al., 2010b, 2013) efficiency in terms of better incident management (Ray & Simpson, 2019).

In this chapter, we suggest the ERM has innovative potential to be transferred as a model into prison environment. Pilots of the ERM in Norway have shown that the ERM contributes to better understanding and control among prison staff of behavioural deterioration in prisoners. Prison staff have learned how to use a structured risk management interaction through ERM. Central to this risk management is the awareness of the occurrence of early warning signs and then the possible application of stabilising early interventions as a response to the onset of behavioural disturbance. We believe that this approach may potentially have utility to prisons across Europe, and might, ultimately, contribute to both safety within the prisons and the rehabilitation of prisoners.

The core element of the ERM-methodology is to identify and adapt new behavioural strategies through direct involvement of the service user. Thus, "multivoiced" collaboration is extensively explored and highlighted in this chapter. The prisoner explores the Self in their hetero and auto dialogues with multiple voices in their environment (Avedeling et al., 2015). Some of these dialogues may trigger violent episodes and need to be addressed before these take hold. The ERM is a means of shared decision-making that can involve specialists (mental health professionals), non-specialists (e.g. prison officers) and the prisoner themselves. It acts as a boundary object through which these stakeholders can cooperate in the interest and safety of all involved.

The ERM is a new model of risk management being applied to the prison context and although preliminary pilots are favourable, more intensive research is required to explore its effectiveness in the prison environment. Doing so, in this new context, will contribute to an even more comprehensive conceptualisation of aggression and violence, and the management and prevention of these. The main challenges to these future endeavours may be a 'paradigm issue' however, i.e. how are prison staff able to put aside their focus on safety and security and switch to a more interactional or caring approach to working with inmates. Training will be required to prepare them for working in a coordinated and systematic manner that enables them to assess and manage instruments, such as the ERM, innovations borrowed from the mental health field.

References

Andersen, D. R., Andersen, L. P., Gadegaard, C. A., Høgh, A., Prieur, A., & Lund, T. (2017). Burnout among Danish prison personnel: A question of quantitative and emotional demands. *Scandinavian Journal of. Public Health., 45*(8), 824–830.

Andrews, D. A. (2012). The risk-need-responsivity (RNR) model of correctional assessment and treatment. In J. A. Dvoskin, J. L. Skeem, R. W. Novaco, & K. S. Douglas (Eds.), *Using social science to reduce violent offending* (pp. 127–156). New York, NY: Oxford University Press.

Aveling, E. L., Gillespie, A., & Cornish, F. (2015) A qualitative method for analysing multivoicedness. *Qualitative Research, 15*(6), 670–687.

Bartels, A. A. J. (2001). The model of social competence in the treatment of forensic youth psychiatry, an in-depth study. In *Antisocial behaviour of youngsters. Determinants and interventions* (ch. 6, pp. 95–124). (Het sociale-competentiemodel in forensische jeugdpsychiatrische behandeling; verdieping en verbreding. In: Antisociaal gedrag bij jeugdigen. Determinanten en interventies). Lisse: Swet & Zeitlinger.

Bezerra, C., & De Mahalhães. (2016). Psychological distress and work stress in correctional officers: A literature review. *Ciência & Saúde Coletiva, 21*(7). https://doi.org/10.1590/1413-7.00502016.

Birchwood, M. (2000). The critical period for early intervention. In M. Birchwood, D. Fowler, & C. Jackson (Eds.), *Early intervention in psychosis*. Chichester: Wiley.

Bjørkly, S. (2006). Empirical evidence of a relationship between insight and risk of violence in the mentally ill; A review of the literature. *Aggression and Violent Behavior, 11*, 414–423.

Bjørkly, S., Wærstad, J. M., Selmer, L. E., Wærp, J., Bjørnstad, M., Leinslie, J. V., et al. (2019). Violence after discharge from forensic units in the safe pilot study: A prospective study with matched pair design. *Psychology Research and Behaviour Management., 12*, 755–766.

Bulten, E., Nijman, H., & Van der Staak, C. (2009). Measuring criminal thinking styles; The construct validity and utility of the PICTS in a Dutch prison sample. *Legal and Criminological Psychology, 14*, 35–49.

Campbell, J., Sellen, J. L., & Macmurran, M. (2010). Personal Aspirations and Concerns Inventory for Offenders: Developements in the measurement of offenders' motivation. *Criminal Behaviour and Mental Health, 20*, 144–157.

Carlsson, G., Dahlberg, K., Ekebergh, M., & Dahlberg, H. (2006). Patients longing for authentic personal care: A phenomenological study of violent encounters in psychiatric settings. *Issues in Mental Health Nursing, 27*, 287–305.

Crewe, B., Liebling, A., & Hulley, S. (2011). Staff Culture, use of authority and prisoner quality of life in pubic and private sector prisons. *Australian & New Zealand Journal of Criminology, 44*(1), 94–115.

Douglas, K. S., Hart, S., Webster, Ch., Belfrage, H., Guy, L., & Wilson, C. (2013). Historical-Clinical_Risk Management-20, Version 3 (HCR-20V3): Development and overview. *International Journal of Forensic Mental Health, 13*, 93–108.

Eidhammer, G., Fluttert, F., & Bjørkly, S. (2014). User involvement in structured violence risk management within forensic mental health facilities—A systematic literature review. *Journal of Clinical Nursing, 23*, 2716–2724.

Eidhammer, G., Fluttert, F., Knutzen, M., & Bjørkly, S. (2013). Report: Early recognition method ERM, Pilotfase 2—2009–2013. Kompetansesenter for Sikkerhets-fengels og Rettspsykiatri for Helseregion Sør-Øst.

European Commission. (2013). *Guide to social innovation.* Brussels: EU commission. Available at https://ec.europa.eu/eip/ageing/library/guide-social-innovation_en. Accessed 1 August 2020.

Finney, C., Stergiopoulos, E., Hensel, J., Bonato, S., & Dewa, C. (2013). Organizational stressors associated with job stress and burnout in correctional officers: A systematic review. *BMC Public Health, 13,* 82.

Fluttert, F., Van Meijel, B., Bjørkly, S., Van Leeuwen, M., Nijman, H., & Grypdonck, M. (2013). Early signs of inpatient aggression in forensic psychiatry: An empirical investigation with the Forensic Early Signs of Aggression Inventory [FESAI]. *Journal of Clinical Nursing, 22*(11–12), 1550–1558.

Fluttert, F., Van Meijel, B., Van Leeuwen, M., Bjørkly, S., Nijman, H., Grypdonck, M. (2011). The development of the Forensic Early warning Signs of Aggression Inventory [FESAI]: Preliminary findings. Towards a better management of inpatient aggression. *Archives of Psychiatric Nursing, 25*(2), 129–137.

Fluttert, F., Van Meijel, B., Nijman, H., Bjørkly, S., & Grypdonck, M. (2010a). Detached concern of Forensic Mental Health Nurses to patients with regard to the Early Recognition Method. *Archives of Psychiatric Nursing, 24*(4), 266–274.

Fluttert, F., Van Meijel, B., Nijman, H., Bjørkly, S., & Grypdonck, M. (2010b). Effect of The Early Recognition Method on the number of aggressive incidents and episodes of seclusions in forensic care. *Journal Clinical Nursing, 19,* 1529–1537.

Fluttert, F., Van Meijel, B., Nijman, H., Webster, C., & Grypdonck, M. (2008). Risk management by early recognition of warning signs in forensic psychiatric patients. *Archives of Psychiatric Nursing, 22*(4), 208–216.

Fluttert, F. A. J. (2015). Early Recognition Method in prison services. Presentation at the Conference of the International Association Forensic Mental Health Services, Manchester, UK.

Fluttert, F. A. J., Bjørkly, S., & Dale, K. Y. (2020). The impact of a discarded diagnosis and focus on early warning signs of aggression on relations between user and municipal service providers—A narrative of a complex case. *Current Psychology.*https://doi.org/10.1007/s12144-020-01055-x.

Fluttert, F. A. J., & Eidhammer, G. (2018). ERM-Vroegsignalering opent de deur naar risicomanagement observaties en de dialoog met gedetineerden. *Proces, 97–1,* 25–39.

Gadon, L., Johnstone, L., & Cooke, D. (2006). Situational variables and institutional violence: A systematic review of the literature. *Clinical Psychological. Review., 26*(5), 515–534.

Gudde, C. B., Oslø, T. M., Whittington, R., & Vatne, S. (2015). Services users' experiences and views of aggressive situations in mental health care: A systematic review and thematic synthesis of qualitative studies. *Journal of Multidisciplinary Healthcare, 8,* 449–462.

Hiday, V. A. (1997). Understanding the connection between mental illness and violence. *International Journal of Law and Psychiatry, 20,* 399–417.

Hiday, V. A. (2006). Putting community risk in perspective: A look at correlations, causes and controls. *International Journal of Law Psychiatry, 29*(4), 316–331.

Kohut, H. (1984). *How does analysis cure?* Chicago: University of Chicago Press.

Kroner, D. G. (2012). Service user involvement in risk assessment and management: The transition inventory. *Criminal Behavior and Mental Health, 22,* 136–147.

Legare, F., Stacey, D., Pouliot, S., Gauvin, F. P., Desroches, S. et al. (2011). Interprofessionalism and shared decisionmaking in primary care: A stepwise approach towards a new model. *Journal of Interprofessional Care, 25*, 18–25.

Looman, J., & Abracen, J. (2013) The risk need responsivity model of offender rehabilitation: Is there really a need for a paradigm shift? *International Journal of Behavioural Consultation and Therapy, 8*(3–4), 30–36.

van Leeuwen, M. E., & Harte, J. (2016). Violence against mental health care professionals: Prevalence, nature and consequence. *The Journal of Forensic Psychiatry and Psychology., 28,* 581–598.

Meehan, T., McIntosh, W., & Bergen, H. (2006). Aggressive behaviour in the high secure forensic setting: The perceptions of patients. *Journal of Psychiatric and Mental Health Nursing, 13,* 19–25.

van Meijel, B., Kruitwagen, C., van der Gaag, M., Kahn, R., & Grypdonck, M. (2006). An intervention study to prevent relapse in patients With Schizophrenia. *Journal Nursing Scholarship, 38*(1), 42–49.

van Meijel, B., van der Gaag, M., Kahn, R. S., & Grypdonck, M. (2003). Relapse prevention in patients with schizophrenia. *Archives of Psychiatric Nursing, 17*, 117–25.

Newbill, W. A., Marth, D., Coleman, J. C., Menditto, A. A., Carson, S. J., & Beck, N. C. (2010). Direct observational coding of staff who are the victims of assault. *Psychological Services, 7*(3), 177–189.
Nijman, H., Allertz, W. F. F., Merckelbach, H. L. G. J., Campo, J. L. M. G., & Ravelli, D. P. (1997). Aggressive behaviour on an acute psychiatric admission ward. *European Journal of Psychiatry, 11*(2), 106–114.
Osment. L. (2018). *The complexity of rehabilitation in open and closed prison settings.* Master Thesis, Lund University, Sociology of Law Department.
Patel, S. R., Bakken, S., & Ruland, C. (2008). Recent advances in shared decision making for mental health. *Current Opinion Psychiatry, 21,* 606–612.
Ray, I., & Simpson, A. (2019). Shared risk formulation in forensic psychiatry. *Journal American Academic Psychiatry Law, 47*(1), 22–28.
Taxman, F., A. Pattavina, M. Caudy & Joseph Durso (2013). The empirical basis for the RNR model and updated RNR conceptual framework. In F. S. Taxman & A. Pattavina (Eds.), *Simulation Strategies to Reduce Recidivism.* New York: Springer Publishers.
United Nations Office of Drugs and Crime. (2016). *Handbook on the crime of high risk prisoners.* New York: United Nations Publications.
Ward, T. (2002). The management of risk and the design of good lives. *Australian Psychologist, 37*, 172–179.

12

People in Contact with Criminal Justice Systems Participating in Service Redesign: Vulnerable Citizens or Democratic Partners?

Jonathan Parker, Vanessa Heaslip, Sara Ashencaen Crabtree, Berit Johnsen, and Sarah Hean

Introduction

In this chapter, we explore the contested concept of vulnerabilities in the context of criminal justice and mental health, 'vulnerable' being a category into which people in contact with criminal justice system (CJS) are usually placed without critique. Normative positions suggest

J. Parker (✉) · V. Heaslip · S. Ashencaen Crabtree
Bournemouth University, Poole, UK
e-mail: parkerj@bournemouth.ac.uk

V. Heaslip
e-mail: vanessa.heaslip@uis.no

S. Ashencaen Crabtree
e-mail: scrabtree@bournemouth.ac.uk

B. Johnsen
University College of the Norwegian Correctional Service (KRUS), Lillestrom, Norway
e-mail: Berit.Johnsen@krus.no

S. Hean et al. (eds.), *Improving Interagency Collaboration, Innovation and Learning in Criminal Justice Systems*,
https://doi.org/10.1007/978-3-030-70661-6_12

vulnerability is possessed by 'offenders' themselves owing to certain characteristics they hold. This will be critiqued as limited and indicative of structural power relations. An alternative consideration is presented of vulnerability as a social construction. Drawing on an 'etemic' understanding of vulnerability (Heaslip et al., 2016), allowing integration of agentic and structural factors, we call for the inclusion of offenders in the design and conduct of services and models of organisational learning, innovation and collaboration that transform these practices.

We take a reflexive approach in our writing that requires us to be open about the positions we hold in personal, professional, disciplinary and theoretical terms underpinning the critical stances adopted. We comprise two British women, one Norwegian woman, one South African woman and one British male. Collectively we bear social work, nursing, inter professional practice and penology backgrounds and are versed in critical social science perspectives. This influences the standpoints taken here in our understandings of penal policy, ethnographic approaches and voice.

To commence, we will summarise some of the developments in service provision that includes the voice of those connected with services.

The Centrality of Voice and Inclusion

There is an ongoing debate concerning terminology used in referring to those who have contact with professional services. Within health and social care, terms such as 'patient', 'service user' or 'client' are common; however, these have been contested owing to the discourses underpinning them. We would choose to use the term 'citizens' when referring to individuals who are in contact with any professional service and this is subsequently used here in reference to people in contact with criminal justice and health services (including the incarcerated and subjected citizen together with the professional).

V. Heaslip · S. Hean
University of Stavanger, Stavanger, Norway
e-mail: sarah.c.hean@uis.no

Our professional backgrounds mean we favour a UK social work perspective but it is not just in social work that citizen involvement is increasing (Tew et al., 2012; Bowers et al., 2016; Austin & Isokuortti, 2016); and not just in the UK (Duygulu & Abaan, 2013). However, the evidence in UK social work provides a grounding from which to develop wider practices and to understand the ways in which greater inclusion can be developed in authentic ways across countries and cultures.

The perspective of citizens who use social work services has been a feature of social work in the UK since the development of generic education under the Central Council for Education and Training in Social Work (CCETSW), exemplified by Mayer and Timms' seminal work in 1970—*The Client Speaks*. The involvement of citizens in education and training has also been a requirement of social work qualifying courses in the UK following the introduction of minimum degree-level qualification in 2003. Within healthcare, the movement of involving citizens has grown across Europe over the last few decades (Dent & Pahor, 2015). Within the UK, it is an expectation that citizens will be involved in nursing courses since 2010 (Nursing Midwifery Council [NMC], 2010) and allied health professionals since 2018 (Health Care Professions Council, 2018) healthcare courses since 2010. The history of involvement in education and training is well-rehearsed in Molyneux and Irvine (2004), Beresford and Boxall (2012), and Irvine et al. (2015). Two recent works offer a more comprehensive overview of the history of citizen involvement in health and social care (see the editorials to special editions by McLaughlin et al., 2016; Duffy et al., 2017). Involving citizens in the education of future health and social care professionals, some of whom will work in the CJS, offers authentic insights into the lived experience of a service or experience (Scammell et al., 2015; Parker, 2021; Heaslip et al., 2018) providing a contrasting perspective to the professional discourse.

There are barriers to involving service users that include training and support needs (Moss et al., 2007), power issues (Anka & Taylor, 2016) and the need for meaningfulness in any inclusion that belies its mandatory status. What is clear is that there has been a growth in research undertaken and knowledge gained through the practice of inclusion (Gupta & Blewett, 2008; Hughes, 2017). We are still somewhat unclear of the ways inclusion of citizens in health and social care assists the process or, if it does, how it then creates better practice. However, evidence from practice is growing.

Citizen experiences are fundamental in the development and review of health and social care services. Within England, there is a commitment towards strengthening 'patient and public involvement' in health (NHS England, 2017) and in Norway 'patients' are referred to as radical agents of change with the right to work alongside professionals in design and development of good healthcare services (Erlandsen, 2018). Despite the power- and discourse-laden language of 'patients' in health care, it is apparent there is a growing political and public acceptance of the importance of engaging with citizens using services in the design and redevelopment of health and social care services and research into them.

In this chapter we consider how the voice of those in contact with CJS might influence service development and ask why it might be important to include the voice of people who have those connections. The rise of populism and punitive methods in CJS are exemplified well by recent UK politicians (Gayle, 2019) and these views promote and fortify populist perspectives amongst the general public. So, we may ask why to include the voice of these people who are unpopular, excluded and subject to punishment (something which may include professionals working in these areas as well). In response we return to our codes of ethics and professional value bases that we as authors originate from, acknowledging the politically left-leaning aspects of most human service professions. But there are also pragmatic as well as moral and political justifications. These concern the economic costs of mental ill-health and the incarceration of those transgressing national laws. Regardless of penal systems and their philosophies—whether punitively inspired, paternalistically welfare based or rehabilitative in thrust—reducing future offending and integrating citizens into society in social and economically productive ways represents positive gains for those communities and for the mental health of those citizens. Thus finding ways of reducing recidivism that are acceptable and appropriate to those who have had contact with CJS and amplifying their voice is fundamental to future service development.

The Contested Concept of Vulnerabilities

Citizen involvement is predicated on a number of things including power relations but also on the basis that those citizens connected with services are inherently vulnerable. As human beings, we are all vulnerable to some extent and the term remains loaded and contested, in terms of associated power implications and who may apply to such, to whom and to what end (Penhale & Parker, 2008; Parker et al., 2012; Heaslip, 2013). For instance, those citizens who are subject to CJS interventions in the UK may be considered vulnerable because of the removal of freedoms and rights. When in contact with the CJS they may be exposed to 'criminals', drug use, violence and other brutalising behaviours often associated with CJS contexts to a lesser or greater degree. However, it may also be assumed that those subject to CJS interventions make the professionals dealing with them or, indeed, the general public, vulnerable because of their perceived 'dangerousness'—a discourse developed through interventions and the power of common-sense assumptions that Foucault (1979) and Bourdieu (1977) expose so clearly—or through association with those people (Parker, 2007).

Thus, we must hold that vulnerability is an elusive as well as a contested concept. If we were to pursue definitions rigidly we run the risk of excluding subjectively or culturally legitimated understandings. Our working definition of vulnerability, for use in respect of citizen involvement, is *connotative*, associated with the underlying feelings and meanings of diverse professional and citizen group cultures; rather than being *denotative*, which, in its precision, may exclude or delegitimise others; recognising that, at times for research purposes, we may need to denote specifics, whilst acknowledging difference and breadth. We suggest that any person can be vulnerable but some are more susceptible than others because of contexts, positionings and responses to that person by others rather than because of their innate characteristics.

Examining anthropological features of vulnerability identifies that human beings are poorly equipped physically and are dependent on sociality; herein lies both their potential flourishing, but also their potential vulnerability (Kottow, 2004). Thus, vulnerability is a 'condition humana' which affects us all (Kottow, 2003, p. 461). Within this perspective it recognises that some groups may be more than vulnerable as a central feature of the human condition owing to external factors and sociopolitical norms, whilst acknowledging the individualistic nature of vulnerability. Such approaches carry advantages in avoiding assumptions that vulnerability is an inevitable consequence of gender, age and socio-economic status. Vulnerability, therefore, exists as a lived experience of the individual's perception of self and their resources to withstand such challenges. Vulnerability is contextual; based on the experience of exposure to harm through challenges to one's integrity. Kottow (2003, 2004) argues that a distinction needs to be made to identify individuals who are more than ordinarily vulnerable, which he refers to as 'vulnerated' or susceptible. In that these individuals suffer from double jeopardy; as they suffer from both an elevated risk of vulnerability as a greater likelihood of harm resulting from these problems. Kottow (2003, 2004) argues that this should be separated from vulnerability and should be referred to as susceptibility, as vulnerability is an essential attribute of humanity, whereas susceptibility is a specific accidental condition to be diagnosed and treated. Kottow's approach is contextual and can be applied to people in contact with the CJS.

Approaches to vulnerability within health and social care (HSC) settings have tended to focus on susceptibility and risk of disease, ill-health, disadvantage and misfortune and so on. This thinking is rooted in the power of the professional to subject the 'vulnerable person' to the gaze of concern and control. In the CJS the gaze may, on the other hand, also reflect the vulnerability to danger experienced by the gazer. These understandings are often considered to be denotative but we would argue for a fluid approach allowing for individual responses to context and a relational approach to vulnerability that sees it in interactions, socio-political, cultural and historical contexts. This allows multidisciplinary relationships to flourish in situ rather than being mandated by impersonal policy directives.

These emphases highlight the 'wounding' dimension of vulnerability which links to the etymological derivation of the term: from the Latin root *vuln*—and verb *vulnare* meaning 'to wound'. However, there is a stage prior to actual wounding—physical or emotional—which takes place in the shadowy state of potentiality for 'wounding', 'harm' and 'danger'. This preliminary state seems to underlie the susceptibility/risk hypothesis and links also to the concept of *liminality*. The risk of, or susceptibility to, wounding makes the person vulnerable but they are in a state between actual physical or psycho-social experience and the non-wounded state; they are betwixt and between, neither one nor the other (Parker et al., 2012). In this liminal world, professionals in CJS, HSC and those experiencing interventions from these services become vulnerable. People who have experienced incarceration or other interventions from CJS move from citizens to diminished persons. Those working in these systems who experience such liminal transitions oscillate between a degree of socially beneficial functioning and/or challenging personally diminishing policies and state practices that control and create vulnerability. In these ways professionals and those experiencing professional gaze and intervention become liable to risks, dangers, liabilities—vulnerability.

As we noted earlier, everyone is potentially vulnerable depending on the ways in which we define 'the concept. Labelling theory helps us to problematise the concept further. To refer to someone as vulnerable is often taken automatically to assign them a label that would usually be seen in a negative light—it is assumed to be a pejorative term (Penhale & Parker, 2008). Labelling theory focuses not on acts in themselves but on the labelling of certain acts as being deviant, states of being or minority groups that do not represent cultural or majority norms (Becker, 1963). In itself, this exposes the taken-for-granted discourses that reflect socio-cultural power relations (Foucault, 1979; Gaventa, 2002). Being labelled as deviant creates a stigmatic role, and, taking Goffmann's (1959, 1963) dramaturgical approach, is then performed socially by both the labeller and labelled and other social actors involved.

'Vulnerability' is a label. People subject to CJS interventions may be expected to assume the characteristics associated with this label (and almost performing a 'sick role', Parsons, 1975), and act accordingly' (Becker, 1963; Lemert, 1951). It is easy to see how our actors within the CJS become stigmatised through their vulnerability, considered weakened and necessarily subject to certain disciplinary practices (Parker, 2007; Parker et al., 2012). The term 'vulnerable people' refers to people who, by virtue of their circumstances, by the way professional services are organised/operated, and by the way that wider society treats adults with different needs, are then placed in a position that creates further need. For example, the mentally ill criminal is placed in prison and becomes more ill as a result. A moral imperative therefore arises in ensuring that the voice of these people is heard in planning and developing services that act as resistance against this stigmatisation and reduces current power imbalances.

Service Development Interventions and the Dialectic of Agent and Structure

We turn now to how citizens with vulnerabilities can be included in service development and innovation in practice. There a range of models of organisational learning, change and innovation that facilitate change but we choose by way of illustration one such model, the Change Laboratory (CLM) (see Chapter 8 of this volume). The detail of this model and its many applications, are detailed comprehensively elsewhere (Virkkunen & Newnham, 2013; Kerosuo et al., 2010; Engeström et al., 1996, 2014; Sannino et al., 2016b; Sannino & Engeström, 2017). Our intention is not to critique this model per se, or describe its application, but use it as an example of a well-tested model of service transformation that has application in the CJS context but which faces the challenges of including the voice of the vulnerable service user (see Chapter 8 and Engeström et al., 2014).

Briefly the model is a bottom-up and participatory model of organisational transformation with its theoretical origins in Cultural-Historical Activity Theory (CHAT) and the theory of expansive learning. The latter is an iterative and collective transformation process led by key stakeholders involved in service innovation and facilitated by researchers (Virkkunen & Newnham, 2013; Sannino et al., 2016a). There is growing evidence of the use of CLM within many professional sectors (e.g., Engeström et al., 1996; Kerosuo et al., 2010; Virkkunen & Newnham, 2013; Morselli et al., 2014; Englund & Price, 2018; Sannino et al., 2016b; Sannino & Engeström, 2017).

However, the use of CLM within the CJS has to date been largely non-existent. In this case, the focus would be on development of the prison service, questioning the purpose of the service and whom it primarily serves. Exploring the potential for a CL application in the field requires an examination of possible challenges it faces in this new context, before implementing it uncritically in the field for the first time. This is the task of COLAB, an EU-funded project (COLAB-H2020-MSCA-RISE-2016/734536) that aimed to promote innovation and interorganisational learning and interagency collaboration within the CJS (see Chapters 1 and 8 of this volume). The inclusion of the voice of the prisoner in the CLM was a particular focus of this consortium.

Before we explore in this chapter the possibilities and potential limitations of including the prisoner voice in CLM in this CJS context, we need to remind ourselves of the foundational principles of expansive learning (Guzmán, 2018; Engeström, 2015).

On face value these principles appear straightforward; however examining these principles with regards to CLM within the CJS, and the involvement of vulnerable prisoners leads to potential challenges, which we will explore before identifying potential solutions to these. The first principle regarding the unit of analysis can be easily undertaken within the CJS process, comparing the degree to which different agencies work within the service. It is in the second founding principle of collection dimensions of capturing multiple voices and worldviews that we begin to see the potential challenges. Wilson et al. (2018) define worldviews as culturally based points of reference that individuals use to experience and think about the world. They help us to interpret and understand our existing context and experiences, which in turn inform our ways of working and thinking. Inherent to CLM method is a willingness to see, hear and understand the worldviews of others and to contrast your perceptions of the activity in moving forwards as part of the action cycle. However, the degree to which individuals are willing to be open to understand the worldview of others has to be considered within the context of wider societal discourses and values regarding crime and punishment. Comparing two different approaches towards crime and offenders in Norway and the UK, Scandinavian approaches focus upon prisons as places of rehabilitation (Kriminalomsorgen, 2019; Pratt, 2008a, 2008b; Pratt & Eriksson, 2013) where citizens who are imprisoned receive support and rehabilitation to enable them integrate themselves back into society following their release. Imprisonment itself is the punishment in Norway, whereas this is compounded in the UK by the removal of other amenities. In comparison, UK society sees prisons as having three roles: to protect the public, retribution and punishment and finally, rehabilitation (Gauke, 2018). The UK prides itself as having a tough approach to criminal justice, creating potential barriers for criminal justice staff to value or appreciate the worldview of offenders. Whilst the third founding principle (Table 12.1) identifies the importance of focusing upon a historical dimension, we argue that in the CJS context, the broader socio-political or structural dimensions that this may encompasses, will be particularly important when understanding and appreciating the world views of agents in the CLM process.

Taking aside values regarding worldviews there are also challenges with regards to capturing the voices of the offender. A critical aspect of the CLM process is the mirroring process in which data collected from a variety of sources (e.g. the daily interactions of professionals with each other and with the offenders) is shared with another (e.g. workers and offender representatives) in order to stimulate thought and reflection. Questions need to be asked regarding how this data would be collected: common approaches use experiential videos, yet few CJS organisations allow the use of video recording within their service due to concerns regarding confidentiality. Additionally, there are logistic issues as shown in a British study by Hughes et al. (2017) of 93 young people

Table 12.1 Principles of expansive learning (Guzmán, 2018)

1. There is a minimum unit of analysis: this is a collective, artefact-mediated, object-orientated activity system in its interaction with at least one other activity system that is itself collective, artefact-mediated, object-orientated
2. There is a collective dimension: Participants are involved in learning and represent multiple voices with differing thoughts, world views and forms of expression
3. There is a historical dimension—there is an acknowledgement that there are transformations of the activity over time
4. Contradictions play an essential role as triggers for change and development—contradictions are the historical accumulation of structural tensions within and between activity systems
5. There is the possibility of expansive transformations in activity systems, accomplished when the object and the motives of activity are reconceptualised and there are new possibilities

serving custodial sentences (mean age 16.9). They identified that 47% of the sample demonstrated 'overall language skills' significantly below average for their age range, this included 20% (n = 19) meeting the threshold for consideration of impairment noting significant difficulties. Communication is a fundamental aspect of the CLM process, and often theoretical conceptual models are presented in complex language which may not be readily accessible to individuals with lower educational attainment, common in offenders (Taylor et al., 2018). There is also another obstacle concerning language. In a multinational and multicultural context, which many prisons and prison research are becoming and the language of communication may not be the mother tongue of several of the participants (and a number of the researchers). Because of insecurity and a lack of language skills, participants may be reluctant, or even unable, to articulate and share their thoughts and opinions adequately. This increases the risk of important information and nuances concerning expressing worldviews, contradictions and tensions (Table 12.1) becoming lost in the process.

Another key aspect in expansive learning is the transformative process (Table 12.1). During a CLM, participants rather than researchers take a leading role in designing their future by engaging in joint analysis of their activity (Engeström, 2015). This promotes a sense of agency and empowerment that is beneficial in ensuring their commitment to organisational changes. However, this is challenging within the CJS context when individual inmates are involved who do not have the same control of their future as other participants (prison staff for instance). Herein lays the challenges with regards to unequal power base.

A normative positioning of people experiencing CJS interventions (e.g. the prisoner in prison) and those who intervene (e.g. the prison officer) is one of unbalanced power relations because of assumed differentiated moral worth. This allows interventions to be enforced from positions of supposed moral integrity and socially accepted and legitimated power. However, models such as the CLM engage with these debates in a different way starting from the fundamental human rights of individuals to participate and to fair treatment. This reflects not a deontological Kantian position, whereby these rights are lost as a result of proscribed behaviours, but instead a situation ethics model that recognises, despite the transgression of overtly and covertly agreed behavioural norms, the right to participation and fair treatment remain. This presents a contradiction (also noted in Chapter 9 of this book) that may require the original CLM to evolve to address these.

Critical Ethnography—the Moral Enterprise of Ethnography

A key dimension of the CLM, as mentioned earlier, is the collection of mirror data from everyday working practices within the prison, to stimulate discussion within the organisational development process. These represent a diversity of perspectives constituting multi-agency, cross-cultural participants and made up of both practitioners and researchers. It is the role of the researcher (see Chapter 8 of this volume) to collect this mirror data in the first instance and ethnography has been viewed as a dominant data-gathering approach. It is not difficult to comprehend why ethnography would be a popular methodological choice for this large, complex, interwoven enterprise. At a basic level, ethnography is fluid rather than prescriptive; it pursues fruitful avenues rather than being constrained by set variables; it avoids hypotheses normally, although is guided by theoretical positions and empirical ontologies such as demographic data (Scheper-Hughes, 2009). Fundamentally qualitative in nature, it can also accommodate quantitative and statistical data. Furthermore, although focusing on social interactions in the fieldwork encounter via different interviewing strategies, ethnography can happily accommodate reports and documentary evidence as data (Ashencaen Crabtree, 2012). Data is not gathered in staged laboratory settings but in naturalistic settings, where real people actually function and do the things they tend to do in their lives: for example, the hospital ward, the classroom, the indigenous village as well as the 'total institution' (Goffman, 1961): the asylum and the prison. An ignored perspective in doing prison ethnography is recognising the challenge of this experience in this environment. A prison constitutes an emotionally demanding context, and the researcher may occasionally find themselves in potentially dangerous situations. Besides, novice researchers may enter the field with a high level of anxiety and struggling to cope with their emotions (Jewkes, 2012; Sloan & Wright, 2015). It is from this perspective that we can view the researcher as vulnerable within the service development processes, such as the CL, rather than the prisoner, as discussed earlier. However, emotions may constitute epistemological significance worth exploring (see e.g. Sparks, 2002; Fransson & Johnsen, 2015).

A very important contribution of feminist epistemologies is that of self-reflexivity, where the researcher is transparently written into the ethnographic account (Ramazanoglu & Holland, 2002), in a 'warts and all' approach, as being the lens through which all data is gathered and processed—or textualised' to employ van Maanen's (1988) useful term. To summarise, ethnography offers itself as the 'Swiss penknife' of methodologies, adaptable, flexibly multi-tooled. A particularly efficacious aspect of ethnography within models such as the CLM are observation techniques, which can supplement interview or even, at times, be substituted for them. Much can be learned through this technique, but the essential quality of such observation lies in its criticality. There can be no mere casual watching by the researcher but rather a conscious, deliberate, engaged scrutiny in order to understand what is being seen and what it could mean. A high level of criticality characterises ethnographic observation, in which the attempt to connect the minute or local instance to a larger, structural phenomenon, which Atkinson (2015) describes as identifying the ethnographic detail as an instance of a bigger example. This position tends to challenge the idea that generally qualitative data cannot be used to generalise to a bigger picture. However, whilst this may be true in terms of details and specifics—and that caution and caveats need to be acknowledged—the critical ethnographer can legitimately seek to draw connections from the specific to the structural where data appears to warrants this (Ashencaen Crabtree et al., 2016). Thus, critical observations of prison officers undertaking their routine morning tasks, as is central to the CLM model, might offer illumination into the operational ubiquities of daily practices by officers in that institution, which in turn may lead to a deeper insight of the underlying philosophies or raison d'être of prison services in that region or context. This is the case whether those observations are undertaken by members of the CJS as a means of enhancing critical reflexivity, as part of the role, or by external observers, practitioners or researchers working to improve services through applying and facilitating organisational change using models such as the CL.

Self-reflexivity and critical engagement begins to mark out the territory of what one could refer to as 'moral ethnography' (Ashencaen Crabtree, 2013), which in any collaborative activity such as the CLM we believe should be central if comprehensive inclusion and participation is to be achieved and voices heard. More, however, is needed to truly occupy this contestable terrain. Moral ethnography requires that the little heard and muted voice is amplified, whether that is the voice of the rough sleeper, the patient with dementia, or the incarcerated citizen—and that the moral ethnographer seeks to create the space whereby that which is rarely heard can be uttered and those whom are silenced can speak (Ashencaen Crabtree, 2012). The obvious critique to this idealised notion is that what is said and recorded, what has been learned through the process of ethnographic analysis, in which data is effectively decoded and reformed for public digestion, all of this of course is selected by no other than the ethnographer themselves. There is no objective positionality, no hygienic neutrality, no appeal to the legitimacy of uncontaminated laboratory conditions (all highly dubious claims in themselves), but rather that all are subject to the subjective and that the integrity of ethnography lies in the validity of a paper trail of evidence and the plausibility of the account (Hammersley & Atkinson, 2007).

Ethnography with the incarcerated citizen participant, needs, perforce, to be moral in its outlook, engagement (De Laine, 2000) and dissemination given that the power differentials between researcher and subject are normally wide. Even more so between subjects/participants of the CLM when the status of one is that of the free person and the other that of the imprisoned (Ashencaen Crabtree, 2012). What may these muted voices tell us of their material conditions, their emotional and psychological inner drama, their yearnings, loves, animosities and indifferences? Useful comparisons can here be drawn between the stigmatised labelling of the offender and the insane in reference to the historically 'mad' in Britain (a term employed deliberately here and in opposition to the sanitised medicalism 'mental illness'). Porter (2006) tells us that being viewed as irrational ravings emanating from seemingly incorrigible 'Bedlamites', such utterances were not thought to merit recording. By the nineteenth and twentieth century, and emerging from the brutalities of North American institutional care, we begin to find the written, and often eloquent, accounts of suffering from usually freed patients (Geller et al., 2011). Separated by the long distance of time and a comforting belief in social progress, such account is variably poignant, bewildering and bizarre but not immediately startling in that we are inured to the notion that the past is often inexplicable viewed through contemporary frames, which will shortly themselves be similarly anachronistic to others. We may also be aware that the prison and asylum guards of yesterday would no doubt have had a very different tale to tell had their voices also been recorded—being an interesting example of how even the apparent oppressor can be silenced until invited to speak (Ashencaen Crabtree, 2012); and that association with the stigmatised merely creates shared stigma by association (Parker, 2007, 2021). What then can we learn from moral ethnography with the incarcerated citizen, if we assume for one heady moment that we or anyone else are actually interested in hearing these words from the unattractive peripheries of society? Indeed the dilemma continues for once words are spoken, what then do we do with these accounts, particularly if they are controversial, troubling, offensive or even risky to the speaker and maybe to the listener as well? These are moot questions the moral ethnographer must perpetually address, particularly as ethnography has been charged with being an exploitative and one-sided relationship from which participants often gain little in comparison with the kudos and career and financial advantages open to the 'successful' researcher (Stacey, 1991). To engage in moral ethnography of itself invests significance and importance to the words of participants; however, marginalised or ostracised they may be in society, the exercise of which suggests that the speaker is also equally invested with the social stature that makes peripheral voices worth listening to.

Ethnography throws up troublesome data at times and in turn creates ethical dilemmas. The new British Home Secretary, Priti Patel, has been reported in the media as robustly asserting that the UK Government's approach to law and order will be concerned with ensuring that offenders 'literally feel terror' (Gayle, 2019). An ethnography comparing the penal approach in Britain to that of Norway, for example, might reasonably focus on the apparent polarities in correction ethos, tentative portrayed earlier in this chapter as punitive versus rehabilitative. Yet, this dualism may be less stark than is suggested if we adopt a somewhat mischievous Foucaldian (1967) interpretation. For this we must consider eighteenth-century institutional care of the insane in England. Foucault considers the *prima facie* humanity of the Quaker approach, exemplified by William Tuke's small, private institution, 'The Retreat' (Ashencaen Crabtree, 2012). Here, and in sharp contrast to less edifying forms of containment elsewhere, Tuke adopted an approach which came to known as 'moral treatment' in order to pacify and cajole the patient into modifying their behaviour towards conformity with expected norms of conduct, for example partaking of afternoon tea with propriety and properly attired (Ashencaen Crabtree, 2012). Moral treatment would be recognisable today in some of its essential elements as promoting a normalising and rehabilitative approach. Foucault (1967) however, argues that moral treatment imposed a heavy yoke of burdensome consciousness and conscience on patients forcing obedience upon them to adopt normative modes of conduct. The existential and anarchic freedom of the lunatic is denied where sanity (and therefore physical freedom) is contingent upon demonstrated outward respect for conventions, which Foucault (1967) offers as possibly more humane than chains and bars but is nonetheless a system of oppression.

If we apply this argument to penal systems cross-culturally and consider the apparent contrast between contemporary British and Norwegian correctional forms, then the view suddenly alters. Conceivably the incarcerated citizen in Britain endures the overcrowding, peer violence, squalor and misery of overcrowded and apparently rat-infested cells (Perraudin, 2017) but may experience internal freedoms unknown to those where rehabilitated compliance is demanded by officials, which Foucault's analysis reveals as outwardly as merely a more civilised and far less brutal form of age-old paternalistic oppression (Foucault, 1979).

DiMaggio and Powell (1983) set out a neo-Weberian approach to understanding organisations. This approach suggested a tendency towards conformity or convergence of forms and behaviours through coercion (policies, legislation and so forth), mimicry and adopting the practices of those perceived to be successful or valued, and normativity when practices become embedded and tacitly accepted as the way one does things. At face value there may be an element of determinism that prevents the possibilities of change. However, this need not be the case as the subsystems of organisations are the individual agents who, when exposing underlying discourses underpinning organisational behaviour subject them to scrutiny, evaluation and potential change. Thus the CJS and health services (HS) are bound to act in specific contextual ways according to socio-political and professional regulation, success is copied (often uncritically), and certain approaches become mainstream and unquestioned. Including the voice of citizens involved, as those subject to such or as professionals within these services, challenges this isomorphic convergence in provision and raises the possibility of change. Furthermore, understanding the position of individuals in contact with these services as somewhat liminal—neither as free citizen nor as someone outside the law (since they have been subject to the law)—we see a process of losing one's status and becoming reclothed in a different social cloth through interaction with these systems. The process is dialectic and works through the thesis of professional on the one hand, the antithesis of the citizen voice on the other hand, and eventually moving towards a novel synthetic, and hopefully constructive, way of being. Without this reflective dialectic we run the risk of perpetuating normative practice behaviours and whilst it may be argued that voice can be represented through video and audio clips, these run the risk of being subject to the hidden discourses of individual professionals and professions. Thus we argue for an upset in the power balance and the synchronous involvement of all those within CJS not just the professionals.

Ways Forward for Including Offenders in Service Redesign

We have explored the contested and fluid nature of 'vulnerability', which in itself has profound implications for service design, delivery and evaluation. To ensure that power imbalances are addressed, and that services develop according to the gamut of human need, citizen participation is central to service evaluation. Our contention throughout this chapter has been that models that aim to encourage organisational learning, innovation and collaboration in the CJS (such as the CLM) could be adapted to better include the voice of the citizen in contact with the CJS. The impact of constructed vulnerabilities may be countered by engagement of citizens and is essential to break down labelling and stigmitatisation often found in service development. Researchers providing mirror data for models of service development need to be aware that they hold their own biases when collecting and presenting this data to participants and need to be critical of their own ethnographic practices

Models of service redesign such as the CLM seeks to make a positive impact on the CJS, and collaborating services, to assist those involved with CJS into pro-social, participatory ways of living. These seek ways of improving CJS and health and welfare service provision which has three immediate strands to it: the enhancement of professional achievement and outcome; the reduction of service and social cost; the reduction of individual harm and susceptibility to personal wounding and enhancement of social position of those in contact with CJS. We contend that a central plank in this is the inclusion of the voice of those who are excluded and marginalised by their contact with CJS.

Ways of amplifying that voice are varied. If we can enter the world of the other through participatory methodologies such as the CLM and its employment through ethnographic techniques, we create the conditions in which dialectics may occur. The normative thesis of the CJS is challenged by citizen voice as an antithesis. If we remain open to the possibilities created by synthesising the conflicting theses we may present novel understandings and ways of developing services that meet our objectives. By exploring filmic, dialogic, drawn, fictive and poetic modes of communication across the activity systems involved in CJS we offer those with reduced or marginalised power and voice the means to resist and state their case or position. So, enhancing the voice of people in contact with CJS can be achieved through different communicative methodologies and an overarching ethnographic approach, and increases the possibilities for reducing power imbalances. However, we must also add a caveat. These approaches can only work if structural conditions allow the development of such democratised approaches to service development. Cultural perspectives also exert a powerful impact at local, organisation and structural levels and need to be taken into account when determining ways forward. If a top-down perspective drives service development then all participants within the activity systems remain excluded and changes are rendered less possible. As academics, practitioners and those in contact with CJS a commitment is required to illuminating service provision and impact through our ethnographic approaches, which must be critical. We use our illuminations to develop micro and meso-level practices, and disseminate our work to challenge macro-level assumption and normative practice.

References

Anka, A., & Taylor, I. (2016). Assessment as the site of power: A Bourdieusian interrogation of service user and carer involvement in the assessments of social work students. *Social Work Education, 35*(2), 172–185. https://doi.org/10.1080/02615479.2015.1129397.

Ashencaen Crabtree, S. (2012). *A Rainforest Asylum: The enduring legacy of colonial psychiatric care in Malaysia*. London: Whiting & Birch.

Ashencaen Crabtree, S. (2013). Research ethics approval processes and the moral enterprise of ethnography. *Ethics & Social Welfare*. Advance Access https://doi.org/10.1080/17496535.2012.703683.

Ashencaen Crabtree, S. (2018). Reclaiming romance: The moral quest to excavate the hidden voice of the oppressed. In K. Egay, S. Sophia, & C. S. Hew (Eds.), *Beyond romance: Reflections on research in Sarawak*. Sarawak: UNIMAS Press.

Ashencaen Crabtree, S., Parker, J., Crabtree Parker, I., & Crabtree Parker, M. (2016). *Death of the Dragon God Lake: Voices from Tasik Chini, Malaysia.* Kuala Lumpur: SIRD.

Atkinson, P. (2015). *For ethnography.* Los Angeles and London: Sage.

Austin, M. J., & Isokuortti, N. (2016). A framework for teaching practice-based research with a focus on service users. *Journal of Teaching in Social Work, 36*(1), 11–32.

Becker, H. S. (1963). *Outsiders: Studies in the sociology of deviance.* Free Press Glencoe.

Beresford, P., & Boxhall, K. (2012). Service users, social work education and knowledge for social work practice. *Social Work Education, 31*(2), 155–167.

Bourdieu, P. (1977). *Towards a theory of practice.* Cambridge: Polity Press.

Bowers, L., James, K., Quirk, A., Simpson, A., Sugar, Stewart, D., & Hodsoll, J. (2016). Reducing conflict and containment rates on acute psychiatric wards: The safewards cluster randomised controlled trial. *International Journal of Nursing Studies, 58*(102), (epub). https://doi.org/10.1016/j.ijnurstu.2015.12.006.

Duygulu, S., & Abaan, S. (2013). Turkish nursing students' views on practice assessments and service user involvement. *Contemporary Nurse, 43*(2), 201–212.

De Laine, M. (2000). *Fieldwork, participation and practice: Ethics and dilemmas in qualitative research.* London: Sage.

Dent, M., & Pahor, M. (2015). Patient involvement in Europe—A comparative framework. *Journal of Health Organization and Management, 29*(5), 546–555.

DiMaggio, P., & Powell, W. (1983). The iron cage revisited: Institutional isomorphism and collective rationality in organizational fields. *American Sociological Review, 48*(2), 147–160.

Duffy, J., McKeever, B., Laughlin, H., & Sadd, J. (2017). Service user and carer involvement in social work education—Where are we now?—Part 2. *Social Work Education, 36*(2), 125–127.

Engeström, Y. (2015). *Learning by expanding: An activity-theoretical approach to developmental research* (2nd ed.). Cambridge: Cambridge University Press.

Engeström, Y., Sannino, A., & Virkkunen, J. (2014). On the methodological demands of formative interventions. *Mind, Culture, and Activity, 21*(2), 118–128.

Engeström, Y., Virkkunen, J., Helle, M., Pihlaja, J., & Poikela, R. (1996). The Change Laboratory as a tool for transforming work. *Lifelong Learning in Europe, 1*(2), 10–17.

Englund, C., & Price, L. (2018). Facilitating agency: The Change Laboratory as an intervention for collaborative sustainable development in higher education. *International Journal for Academic Development, 23*(3), 192–205.

Erlandsen, A. E. (2018). *A vision for a high performing and sustainable health care system.* Available from https://www.regjeringen.no/en/aktuelt/a-vision-for-a-high-performing-and-sustainable-health-care-system/id2619759/. Accessed 10 Aug 2018.

Foucault, M. (1967). *Madness and civilization: A history of insanity in the age of reason.* London: Tavistock.

Foucault, M. (1979). *Discipline and punish.* London: Penguin.

Fransson, E., & Johnsen, B. (2015). The perfume of sweat: Prison research through Deleuzian Lenses. In D. H. Drake, R. Earle, & J. Sloan (Eds.), *The Palgrave handbook of prison ethnography* (pp. 187–198). Basingstoke: Palgrave Macmillan.

Gauke, D. (2018). *Prison reforms speech.* Available from https://www.gov.uk/government/speeches/prisons-reform-speech. Accessed 10 Aug 2018.

Gayle, D. (2019, August 3). Home Secretary Priti Patel criticised over wish for criminals to 'feel terror'. *Guardian.* Available at https://www.theguardian.com/politics/2019/aug/03/priti-patel-home-secretary-wants-criminals-to-literally-feel-terror. Accessed 18 Aug 2019.

Gaventa, J. (2002). *Power after Lukes: A review of the literature.* Brighton: Institute of Development Studies.

Geller, A., Garfinkel, I., & Western, B. (2011). Paternal incarceration and support for children in fragile families. *Demography, 48*(1), 25–47. https://doi.org/10.1007/s13524-010-0009-9.

Goffman, E. (1959). *The presentation of self in everyday life.* New York: AnchorBoks.

Goffman, E. (1963). *Stigma: Notes on the management of spoiled identity.* Englewood Cliffs, NJ: Prentice-Hall.

Guzmán, W. C. (2018). A Change Laboratory professional development intervention to motivate university teachers to identify and overcome barriers to the integration of ICT. *Outlines-Critical Practice Studies, 19*(1), 26–90.

Gupta, A., & Blewett, J. (2008). Involving service users in social work training on the reality of family poverty: A case study of a collaborative project. *Social Work Education, 27*(5), 459–473.

Hammersley, M., & Atkinson, P. (2007). *Ethnography: Principles in practice* (3rd ed.). London: Taylor Francis.

Health and Care Professions Council. (2018). *Service user and carer involvement*. Available from https://www.hcpc-uk.org/education/resources/education-standards/service-user-and-carer-involvement/. Accessed 1 Oct 2019.

Heaslip, V. (2013). Understanding vulnerability. In V. Heaslip & J. Ryden (Eds.), *Understanding vulnerability: A nursing and healthcare approach*. Oxford: Wiley Blackwell.

Heaslip, V., Hean, S., & Parker, J. (2016). The etemic model of Gypsy Roma Traveller community vulnerability: Is it time to rethink our understanding of vulnerability? *Journal of Clinical Nursing, 27*(17/18), 3426–3435.

Heaslip, V., Scammell, J., Mills, A., Spriggs, A., Addis, A., Bond, M., Latchford, C., Warren, A., Borwell, J., & Tee, S. (2018). Service user engagement in healthcare education as a mechanism for value based recruitment: An evaluation study. *Nurse Education Today, 60*(1), 107–113.

Hughes, M. (2017). What difference does it make? Findings of an impact study of service user and carer involvement on social work students subsequent practice. *Social Work Education, 36*(2), 203–216.

Hughes, K., Bellis, M. A., Hardcastle, K. A., Sethi, D., Butchart, A., Mikton, C., et al. (2017). The impact of multiple adverse childhood experiences on health: A systematic review and meta-analysis. *The Lancet Public Health, 2*(8), e356–366. https://doi.org/10.1016/s2468-2667(17)30118-4.

Irvine, J., Molyneux, J., & Gillman, M. (2015). 'Providing a link with the real world': Learning from the student experience of service user and carer involvement in social work education. *Social Work Education, 34*(2), 138–150.

Jewkes, Y. (2012). Autoethnography and emotions as intellectual recourses: Doing prison research differently. *Qualitative Inquiry, 18*(1), 63–75.

Kerosuo, H., Kajamaa, A., & Engeström, Y. (2010). Promoting innovation and learning through Change Laboratory: An example from Finnish Health care. *Central European Journal of Public Policy, 4*(1), 110–131.

Kottow, M. (2003). The vulnerable and the susceptible. *Bioethics, 17*(5–6), 460–471.

Kottow, M. (2004). Vulnerability: What kind of principle is it? *Medicine, Healthcare and Philosophy, 7*(3), 281–287.

Kriminalomsorgen. (2019). *About the Norwegian Correctional Service*. Available from https://www.kriminalomsorgen.no/information-in-english.265199.no.html. Accessed 12 Aug 2019.

Lemert, E. M. (1951). *Social pathology: A systematic approach to the theory or sociopathic behavior*. New York: McGraw-Hill.

McLaughlin, H., Sadd, J., McKeever, B., & Duffy, J. (2016). Service user and carer involvement in social work education—Where are we now?—Part 1. *Social Work Education, 35*(8), 863–865.

Molyneux, J., & Irvine, J. (2004). Service user and carer involvement in social work training: a long and winding road? *Social Work Education, 23*(3), 293–308.

Morselli, D., Costa, M., & Margiotta, U. (2014). Entrepreneurship education based on the Change Laboratory. *The International Journal of Management Education, 12*(3), 333–348.

Moss, B. R., Dunkerly, M., Price, B., Sullivan, W., Reynolds, M., & Yates, B. (2007). Skills laboratories and the new social work degree: One small step towards best practice? Service users' and carers' perspectives. *Social Work Education, 26*(7), 708–722.

NHS England. (2017). *Patient and public participation policy.* Available from https://www.england.nhs.uk/wp-content/uploads/2017/04/ppp-policy.pdf. Accessed 10 Aug 2018.

Nursing Midwifery Council. (2010). *Standards for pre-registration nursing education.* London: NMC.

Parker, J. (2007). Disadvantage, stigma and anti-oppressive practice. In P. Burke & J. Parker (Eds.), *Social work and disadvantage: addressing the roots of stigma through association* (pp. 146–157). London: Jessica Kingsley.

Parker, J. (2021). *Social work practice* (6th ed.). London: SAGE.

Parker, J., Ashencaen Crabtree, S., Chui, W. H., Kumagai, T., Baba, I., Azman, A., et al. (2012). WAVE: Working with adults who are vulnerable—A comparison of curricula, policies and constructions. *Revista de Asistenţă Socială, 11(3),* 1–18.

Parsons, T. (1975). The sick role and the role of the physician reconsidered. *The Milbank Memorial Fund Quarterly: Health and Society, 53*(3), 257–278.

Penhale, B., & Parker, J. (2008). *Working with vulnerable adults.* London: Routledge.

Perraudin, F. (2017, December 19). Conditions at Liverpool prison the worst ever inspected, says report. *Guardian.* https://www.theguardian.com/uk-news/2017/dec/19/hmp-liverpool-prison-conditions-inspectors-report.

Porter, R. (2006). *Madmen.* Stroud, Glos: Tempus Publishing Limited.

Pratt, J. (2008a). Scandinavian exceptionalism in an era of penal excess, part I: The nature and roots of Scandinavian exceptionalism. *British Journal of Criminology, 48*(2), 119–137.

Pratt, J. (2008b). Scandinavian exceptionalism in an era of penal excess, part II: Does Scandinavian exceptionalism have a future? *British Journal of Criminology, 48*(3), 275–292.
Pratt, J., & Eriksson, A. (2013). *Contrasts in punishment: An explanation of anglophone excess and Nordic exceptionalism.* Abingdon: Routledge.
Ramazanoglu, C., & Holland, J. (2002). *Feminist methodology: Challenges and choices.* London: Sage.
Sannino, A., & Engeström, Y. (2017). Co-generation of societally impactful knowledge in change laboratories. *Management Learning, 48*(1), 80–96.
Sannino, A., Engeström, Y., & Lahikainen, J. (2016a). The dialectics of authoring expansive learning: Tracing the long tail of a Change Laboratory. *Journal of Workplace Learning, 28*(4), 245–262.
Sannino, A., Engeström, Y., & Lemos, M. (2016b). Formative interventions for expansive learning and transformative agency. *Journal of the Learning Sciences, 25*(4), 599–633.
Scammell, J., Heaslip, V., & Crowley, E. (2015). Service user involvement in pre-registration general nurse education: A systematic review. *Journal of Clinical Nursing, 25*(1), 53–69.
Scheper-Hughes, N. (2009). The ethics of engaged ethnography: Applying a militant anthropology in organs-trafficking research. *Anthropology News, 50*(6), 13–14.
Sloan, J., & Wright, S. (2015). Going in green: Reflections on the challenges of 'getting in, getting on, and getting out' for doctoral prison researchers. In D. H. Drake, R. Earle, & J. Sloan (Eds.), *The Palgrave handbook of prison ethnography* (pp. 143–163). Basingstoke: Palgrave Macmillan.
Sparks, R. (2002). Out of the "digger": The warrior's honour and the guilty observer. *Ethnography, 3*(4), 556–581.
Stacey, J. (1991). Can there be a feminist ethnography? In S. B. Gluck & D. Patai (Eds.), *Women's words: The feminist practice of oral history.* London and New York: Routledge.
Taylor, R., Miller, R., Mouzon, D., Bloustein, E., Keith, V., & Chatters, L. (2018). Everyday discrimination among African American men: The impact of criminal justice contact. *Race Justice, 8*(2), 154–177.
Tew, J., Ramon, S., Slade, M., Bird, V., Melton, J., & Le Boutillier, C. (2012). Social factors and recovery from mental health difficulties: A review of the evidence. *British Journal of Social Work, 42*(3), 443–460. https://doi.org/10.1093/bjsw/bcr076.
Van Maanen, J. (1988). *Tales of the field*. Chicago: University of Chicago Press.

Virkkunen, J., & Newnham, D. S. (2013). *The Change Laboratory: A tool for collaborative development of work and education*. Rotterdam: Sense Publishers.

Wilson, D., Heaslip, V., & Jackson, D. (2018). Improving equity and cultural responsiveness with marginalised communities. *Journal of Clinical Nursing, 27*(19–20), 3810–3819.

[illegible]

13

Avenues of Opportunity: Journeys of Activities Through Third Sector Organisations

Angela Turner-Wilson, Stuart Dearborn, and Catherine Bullen

Introduction: Beyond Prisons

The use of prison as a means of 'punishing' and 'correcting' those who have allegedly committed a crime against society is open to debate. Indeed, the benefits and problems of giving people a custodial sentence continue to rage in socio-economic and political domains across the globe. Retributive incarceration does remain popular in liberal democracies as well as totalitarian regimes, despite questions as to whether this

A. Turner-Wilson (✉)
Department of Medical Science and Public Health, Bournemouth University, Bournemouth, UK
e-mail: aturnerwilson@bournemouth.ac.uk

S. Dearborn
The Footprints Project, Poole, UK
e-mail: stuart@footprintsproject.co.uk

C. Bullen
Wiltshire Health and Care, Salisbury, UK

S. Hean et al. (eds.), *Improving Interagency Collaboration, Innovation and Learning in Criminal Justice Systems*,
https://doi.org/10.1007/978-3-030-70661-6_13

is the right approach (Jordan, 2003; Scott, 2013). One field of interest that has tried to move beyond this lies in restorative justice, which has, over the last few decades, become popular, especially in Europe and Scandinavia. It has been defined as a "process whereby parties with a stake in a specific offence collectively resolve how to deal with the aftermath of the offence, and its implications for the future" (Marshall, 1996, p. 37). It places emphasis on conflict resolution and societal responsibilities (Cunneen & Goldson, 2015). In Norway, for example, it can be related to practices that prioritise the importance of the welfare system for those in prison and during resettlement. As such third sector organisations (TSOs) play a part. These not-for-profit, voluntary agencies (sometimes referred to as non-governmental organisations or NGOs) are neither public nor private (National Audit Office, 2019) and are part of the world of rehabilitation, change and decriminalisation. In many countries, they are crucial in the complex world of the 'afterwards', the time when someone who has been released from prison is working towards reintegrating back into society. However, this period has no clear end date and restorative justice is, as Crawford (2015) has argued, 'Janus-faced' as it asks those involved to be simultaneously looking backwards and forwards across time.

Third Sector Organisations and the Criminal Justice Service

A number of authors have discussed the role of TSOs in relation to ex-prisoners. Some have considered how TSOs support those released from prison who have immediate needs such as housing (Mills et al., 2013; Ellison et al., 2013) or require help with physical and psychological issues such as self-harming behaviours (National Institute for Health Research UK, 2020). Others have explored how TSOs are involved in assisting older or younger individuals, or those with learning difficulties (Forsyth et al., 2017; Acar & Tekin, 2011; Kelly et al., 2012). In respect to restorative justice, there are discussions about the role of TSOs in the provision of support for victim and offender mediation, such as Lo's (2019) dissertation thesis concerning this work in Hong Kong.

Wider more general insight into TSOs is slightly less common, although papers such as Kaufman (2015) delve into the importance of these institutions as places that deepen citizenship for ex-prisoners. This chapter contributes to this corpus of material by considering TSOs from a very specific person-centred lens. It asks what TSOs might offer, what are their benefits, their challenges and can they really contribute to change and opportunities for ex-prisoners after they are released?

We gain some answers to these questions through insights from work undertaken by an individual called Roger (not his real name), who had joined a team of researchers on a European funded grant whose mission was to optimise collaboration and integration between criminal justice and health and welfare services across the European Union (EU). Roger had been in contact with the criminal justice system, but was now employed in a not-for-profit organisation in the UK. One of his contributions to the study, along with colleagues, was to travel through different regions of Norway to explore and document interagency practices. This work offers insights based on this journey.

Social Anthropology and Ethnography

Given the focus of this work, an anthropological approach offered a sound theoretical fit. Social anthropology considers areas such as laws, social control, kinship and symbolism to name but a few (e.g. see Hendry, 2016). It is a philosophy that can provide a "direct immersion in a culture" with, "field experiences (that are) focused not so much by formal research methods, as by the unique talents and interests of the anthropologists..." (Haines, 2017, p. 3) and one might add this can include all who utilise ethnographic frameworks. The use of ethnography in seeking to understand prisoners is not new, see for example Drake et al's. (2015) edited book. One contributor to this text, Hammersley (2015, p. 27) has argued that ethnography is about, "producing 'close-ups' of social phenomena". To achieve this, postmodernist perspectives can be useful.

Context and Place

Traditionally anthropology concerned itself with undertaking detailed studies of culture within single sites (e.g. see Van Maanan, 2011). This approach was sometimes based on the search for 'universal truths', an idea rejected by postmodernist factions. Lyotard (1984, p. xxiv), for instance, famously stated that he had an "incredulity toward metanarratives". Unlike the empirical generalist perspectives, postmodernism is about deconstructing world views. Within anthropology, it offered approaches that included working on multilocal projects which included interdisciplinary (Marcus, 1995) or even interpersonal insights. It could create a "translocal network of relationships" (Hannerz, 2003, p. 209). Bearing this latter point in mind, the field visits for this study involved different locations, but they were all part of one country, in this case, Norway. The team went to the City of Oslo, Stavanger in Rogaland, Molde in Møre og Romsdal, Bergen in Vestland, and Tromsø in Troms og Finmark. These are all towns and were selected as 80% of people live in the major cities in Norway (World Population Review, 2020). However, they did offer different regional perspectives, and importantly several TSOs are based in these areas.

TSOs usually act as formal and, or informal community groups that seek to meet their users' needs, but they are not immune to criticism. It has been suggested, for instance, that they should be more evidenced based (e.g. see Jardine & Whyte, 2013). Whilst this is a debate beyond the scope of this work, one area that TSO might look to in order to address these concerns lies in organisational learning. This is a concept by which organisations drive knowledge creation, which can, in turn, lead to innovation and new ways of thinking (Wang & Ahmed, 2003). It is an approach that can contribute to effective practice. Organisational learning has an underpinning philosophy of shared visions and team working (Retna, 2006), especially important when thinking about how networks, relationships and common goals come together (Teeters & Jurow, 2018). Organisational learning is about context and place, but it also speaks to people who are inside and, or outside specific communities.

Self and Other

So, it was not just the concept of place that matters in this work, for as McGarry and Mannik (2017, p. 76) note, "for anthropologists, the focus is on dialogic anthropology. In other words, anthropologists view the production of knowledge as always taking place within an interaction, so meaning is relational". Ethnography has also been about the etic (outsider) and emic (insider) perspectives, concepts, which have been discussed in this field for many years (Olive, 2014). Roger, the key protagonist in this narrative, slid between the etic and emic. He was for example, a researcher, a professional and, in addition, someone who had experienced prison first-hand. It could be argued that this research was, "part of (a) reality that (co-) generates and (co-) constructs socially" Flick (2014, p. 4), and one that celebrates the standpoint of 'the outsider within' (Adler & Adler, 2008, p. 17).

Working in anthropological studies and travelling to different locations are not without its challenges for the self. Issues such as 'adverse incorporation' (societal mechanisms that seek to keep people in disadvantaged situations) (Khan et al., 2015) may still be present, especially for researchers such as Roger. They may encounter social boundaries defined as "objectified forms of social differences, manifested in unequal access to and unequal distribution of resources (material and non material) and social opportunities" (Lamont & Molnár, 2002, p. 168). Challenges that are not unfamiliar to those who have been incarcerated.

Capturing Insights

As Marcus (1995, p. 97) notes, "strategies of quite literally following connections, associations, and putative relationships are....at the very heart of designing multi-sited ethnographic research". With ethical agreements in place, this is the approach used by Roger and his colleagues. They used 'jottings' which were deemed to be the best option as it allowed everyone to capture their life-world views on the spot (Bernard, 2011). Their notes formed reflective narratives of the self and other within the storytelling of the third sector.

Modes of Analysis

Written narratives provide a means to capture reflections. They can act as a way of finding meaning in the human experience (Lee et al., 2004). Yet there are complexities within narrative analysis and ethnography as Gubrium and Holstein (1999, p. 570) highlight, "what is conveyed" in storytelling is "circumstantially consequential for both the storyteller and his or her audience". There is, they continue, a degree of 'authorial' narratives which bind the informants' accounts into contextual understandings. In relation to this project once the field notes were complete Roger and the team reviewed the narratives seeking patterns of commonality and variation through constant readings and comparison (Silverman, 2000). Coding was undertaken to support this.

Jones and Watt (2010, p. 163) remind us that, "ethnography without a theoretical framework is just description", but they also note that all data has something to say, and it is still the researchers who consciously or unconsciously prioritise and edit the material. Therefore, when we consider this study's findings and discussions they are tied to these principles. For example, Roger used a loose term, 'activities' to describe the many and varied opportunities that ex-offenders can participate in within the third sector.

Insights and Discussion

Five key themes emerged from the analysis. These were:

- Outdoor opportunities
- Community opportunities
- Hidden opportunities
- Social boundary crossing opportunities
- Organisational learning opportunities.

Outdoor Opportunities

It is recognised that contact with the outdoors has positive health benefits. The literature is rich within this field. Barnes et al. (2019), for example, noted that contact with nature enhances mental health, self-esteem and cognitive functioning and that these affects appear to cross different groups and populations. A number of TSOs both in the UK and Norway offer outdoor-related activities for their service users. This is important as long periods of incarceration in a prison setting (such as those held in high security) can create what has been termed nature deficit, and whilst work has been done to try to overcome this, such as the use of Moss-in-Prisons project in the US (prisoners collecting and caring for different types of moss) (Nadkarni, 2017), it does not fully address the need. This is where the TSOs can help.

Roger and his research colleagues noted that the link between person and outside is especially strong in Norway, where the idea of being outdoors for leisure purposes is very much part of their culture. One third sector organisation offered over 50 different activities. Howe (2019) noted that the 'friluftsliv' (a Norwegian term) relates to the self within nature. Its meaning is broad and can be used to describe undertaking outdoor sports like football, mountaineering or just going for a simple walk. Indeed, many towns in Norway have parks, often at their centre, such as those in Bergen, Olso or Stavanger.

Interestingly Roger and the team noticed that 'bad' weather such as rain or snow appeared to have no effect on participation in the outdoor activities offered by TSOs in Norway. The underlying philosophy in this country appears to be that as long as the correct clothing is worn, the weather poses no obstacle to outdoor life ('Det finnes ikke dårlig vær, bare dårlige klær') and in fact, it can even help one feel positive about life generally (Bourrelle, 2018). So, despite the weather, some of the TSOs in Norway noted that there was a waiting list for people to apply to join. A popular walking area for many who wish to engage with nature is a path that leads almost directly from one of the TSOs offices in Bergen up towards Mount Floyen.

Although positive, it is worth noting that there is a cost to providing access to many of these activities. The hire of halls, the price of the 'right' clothing, the fees for pieces of sports kits and so forth are not cheap. This represents the more problematic side for the not-for-profit societies who can often struggle to find funds. Roger and his colleague noted that in some TSOs, service users are asked to pay a fee if they wish to participate in activities. This can, for some, be a challenge. Poverty for those who have been in contact with the CJS is very real. As one former UK prisoner stated, "the prison sentence does not end when the prison gates open" (Foster, 2017). For example, in the UK a person is currently given £46.00 release grant to supposedly see them through until they can obtain government-provided benefits (usually at least 6 weeks) or get a job. However, the benefits system is fraught with difficulties and obtaining paid work can be hard. Therefore, a severe lack of money can constrain not only those released from prison but can also affect those who seek to support them back into society.

Community Opportunities

Apart from promoting activities in the outdoors, TSOs also provide a lot of social support. They offer, for example, regular sessions for people to meet with others, potentially useful for those who have completed a custodial sentence and are looking to find comradeship and re-engagement with society. In addition, many offer signposting to vital services such as places that offer accommodation (although sometimes this is only very short term), healthcare, food banks and access to clothing. Some also provide individual appointments to discuss ways forward such as how to re-enter the job market. This was the case, for example, with the Red Cross in Tromsø. Although not directly in the town centre it was reasonably easy to access for those able to walk. It could be identified by the presence of the Red Cross flag outside.

On his journey, Roger chatted to two colleagues in Norway who acted as peer supporters within a TSO. Roger noted that they stated they were always welcome to go back to the service where they were clients, and some do opt to become volunteers. In a survey of 23 countries, it was found that people were more likely to undertake voluntary work in countries such Norway (67% in their case), Austria and Switzerland, but this figure was much lower in countries such as the UK, Russia, Poland and Bulgaria (Huppert et al., 2009). Whilst not specifically representing ex-prisoner volunteers, this is, nevertheless, interesting. Embedded into the social world in Norway is an understanding that helping and building capacity within your local community matters. Simon and Mobekk (2019, p. 815) note that "the term 'dugnad' (a Norwegian word) refers to a sort of voluntary work done as a community or collective. Traditionally, 'dugnad' is a way of solving local common tasks by means of collective efforts from the community". These authors continue, "voluntary organisations (in Norway) adopted 'dugnad' as they emerged in the nineteenth century". In light of this, it might be suggested that those using TSOs may feel more at ease volunteering and tapping into different steams of social support, compared to those from other countries. This is important as acting in a voluntary capacity can improve a sense of shared social identity and enhances feelings of wellbeing (Gray & Stevenson, 2019) which can be helpful for those who have been in prison.

Special holidays are common in many countries throughout the world. Norway is famous for a festival known as Constitution Day celebrated on 17th May. Whilst the day has a strong focus on children, it also provides the adults with an opportunity to dress in their local national costumes. The festivities are not only confined to Norway, as celebrations also occur in other countries that have immigrant Norwegian people, such as the US, Canada and Russia. The wearing of the 'bunad' in Norway (their national costume) creates a collective identity, although there are many variations of the clothing. Those seeking to link with TSOs at this time will almost inevitably be caught up with these celebrations. So, whilst it is an excellent opportunity to mix with friends and family, it may also, occasionally, highlight difference (though that is not its intension). TSOs can be helpful at these times when, perhaps ex-prisoners may feel a sense of otherness, the outsider, the stranger in the crowd.

Hidden Opportunities

Some not-for-profit associations support individuals with addictions to, for instance, alcohol, gambling and drugs. Those attending may have had a custodial sentence, but this is not always the case. These organisations may offer support meetings and a safe place to talk. Sometimes these meetings are closed to anyone who is not part of the group to ensure anonymity. Roger had been in contact with these services in the UK and was therefore also comfortable in making links through these routes internationally. However, meetings were not open to the rest of the research team. Roger reported that many opportunities existed for ex-prisoners which were highlighted during some of these meetings, but this information was generally only shared amongst the groups. Nevertheless, it is worth noting that members from these associations, such as narcotics anonymous (see Narcotic Anonymous World Services, 2020) provide educational talks and presentations to professionals, academics and others, and by doing so create a bridge between their world and the wider society.

Continuing the theme of hidden opportunities many countries offer 'free' activities. For example, in Oslo, there is a large sculpture park, Vigeland, which is open to all and has over 200 full-size statues of people from all age groups often in active stances. They represent life, and many emotions are captured ranging from happiness to anger, from love to despair.

The importance of art in prisons is well recorded (e.g. see Mayou's [2016] discussion about a collection of objects made by prisoners in countries which have experienced violent times such as Chile, Vietnam, Yugoslavia, Algeria to Afghanistan and Rwanda), but there is sometimes less emphasis placed on third sector inputs and outputs. Rafter (2014, p. 129) offers an interesting insight into the world of visual criminology. He says it is, "the study of ways in which all things visual interact with crime and criminal justice, inventing and shaping one another". One might argue that places such as Vigeland provide this. For example, one statue placed along the bridge that enters the park depicts a man with outstretched arms reaching for the sky that may speak of success. Parks such as Vigeland can be seen as settings that offer those in the 'afterwards' spaces to view, to contemplate, to reposition their ideas and thoughts on humanity within their own life-worlds.

Of course, sculptures can be seen in many urban locations. A life-sized bronze statue of a young girl stands by the door of a Mcdonald's restaurant in Bergen. This is a place which offers reasonably priced hot drinks and meals in a warm comfortable setting. Roger visited this location during this study. It may be proposed that the presence of art at places such as fast-food restaurants addresses the inclusivity for viewing this medium.

In addition, there are many examples of free places to visit in urban and rural settings, such as parks, botanical gardens and outdoor gyms. Local communities also sometimes run free events such as music or art festivals. An interesting example of free art lies in a Banksy-type piece of work found on the wall of an unassuming building in Tromsø. It is a picture of a little girl with a bucket and spade. The sun is shining above, her shadow is clearly visible. However, when viewed in the winter this seaside scene is juxtaposed with the heavy snow on the pavement in front of the art, a regular occurrence in a town that lies within the Arctic Circle. The viewer of this image is invited into summer, even in the darkest of days. The Polar night in Tromsø occurs from November to January when the sun does not rise, and it is recognised that light matters within Norwegian culture. It can be argued that the picture of the little girl on the wall represents hope, especially important for those on the margins of society who cannot travel elsewhere to seek sunlight.

There are then activities and things to see and do in urban settings, but these are not always celebrated for their social and therapeutic benefits, especially for those seeking to re-establish themselves after being in custody. Whilst not all are run by TSOs, they act as TSO opportunities, and can therefore be said to be a little bit more hidden.

Social Boundary Crossing Opportunities

Roger had joined this research team with enthusiasm which never waned, and indeed the importance of community-engaged research is increasingly recognised as beneficial to a research study (Page-Reeves & Regino,

2018). The very act of undertaking this work and engaging with TSOs meant Roger crossed a variety of social boundaries. It is not uncommon for individuals such as Roger to suffer stigmatisation by those in society who think they are not to be trusted and label them with names such as ex-offenders, addicts and criminals. Indeed, those who have been in contact with the CJS are sometimes perceived to have deficiencies in education, knowledge and skills (Pogrebin et al., 2014). Yet Roger was able to overcome this. He was of course already employed, a considerable achievement since many from disadvantaged groups often struggle to even become volunteers within societal groups (for example see Southby & South, 2019). Nevertheless, Roger successfully navigated his way through the complexities of multiple organisations. He was an agile thinker adapting to the different situations that arose as a result of the research study. He became an international representative who was comfortable discussing his work on a more scholarly platform. In a sense, the research project and visits to the third sector hubs acted as a change agent for Roger, and indeed for those who worked alongside him. The life-world experiences encountered by all shifted, altered and changed everyone's realities. In relation to a peer supporter Roger met in the Red Cross in Norway he said,

> I was interested in one of the things one of these guys said, he said he has a new identity, meaning his new way of life has brought him a new identify from his old life of crime and drug use. And part of him staying on the right path for him is helping others join in the activities to help their confidence and help them become part of the activity.

Organisational Learning Opportunities

Roger, along with his research colleagues, shared their own perspectives and insights with the service users, volunteers, paid employees that they met on this journey, and they, in turn, reciprocated. As we have seen, the ideas and cultural insights that emerged were holistic and did not take a single perspective. These diverse, but important pieces of knowledge supported the idea of organisational learning. As an example, Roger had recognised the importance of outdoor and social activities for ex-prisoners, and on his return to the UK from Norway he looked for opportunities to further incorporate this within the TSO. One of Roger's proposals involved improving in-house training for volunteers in whatever activity they were interested in (within reason). This would expand choice for service users and provide further knowledge, skills and deeper social engagement for everyone involved. The approach had the added benefit of TSO working more collaboratively with businesses and others (some who may be able to provide additional funding) who may not traditionally link with those who have been in contact with the CJS. Boundary crossing may occur, and all could learn in what Roger called 'building togetherness'. Of course, as Roger highlighted, data collected ethically and sensitively (via, for instance, group discussions, one to one sessions, or even from a family member reporting a positive change in their significant other) could further inform the direction of the activities and whether improvements or changes could or should be made. Feedback on success could be shared with those in the wider community through, for example, presentations, radio advertising, newsletters, magazines and social media. New communities of practice (groups comprised of members from outside the traditional professional or organisational boundaries) adopting a "shared repertoire" (Hughes et al., 2007, p. 4) could develop as a result of such initiatives with each building new cells in an ever increasing honeycomb of collaborative work. This could, in turn, have the potential to influence local policymakers and divert funding streams towards TSOs.

Conclusion

This work highlights the importance of the third sector and their role for ex-prisoners. The narratives embedded within postmodern ethnography discuss and reflect how different activities might contribute to the physical, psychological and social wellbeing of those who have had contact with the CJS. The strands of opportunities are opened-up further with insights from different international perspectives, especially those between Norway and the UK. It is also recognised that the research journey was, itself, a contributing factor to widening opportunities, noted in the text on social boundary crossing. However, and importantly, the smorgasbord of ideas that emerge from this ethnographic work demonstrates that ideas and thoughts can be shared and organisational learning, in all its variants, can take place often naturally and seamlessly. Indeed, this work highlights that different TSOs and those outside this sphere can learn not only from each other, but also from the wider society. Through these glimpses from Roger and his colleagues, it is clear that TSOs deserve much more attention from researchers, academics, professionals, business leaders, politicians, ex-prisoners and their families as these places play such a key role in supporting those who find themselves lost in the 'afterwards'.

References

Acar, Y. B., & Tekin, U. (2011). The roles of non-governmental organizations in German youth justice and assistance system: Cologne model. *Review of International Law & Politics, 7*(25), 205.

Adler, P. A., & Adler, P. (2008). Of rhetoric and representation: The four faces of ethnography. *Sociological Quarterly, 49*(1), 1–30.

Barnes, M. R., Donahue, M. L., Keeler, B. L., Shorb, C. M., Mohtadi, T. Z., & Shelby, L. J. (2019). Characterizing nature and participant experience in studies of nature exposure for positive mental health: An integrative review. *Frontiers in Psychology, 9*. https://doi.org/10.3389/fpsyg.2018.02617.

Bernard, H. R. (2011). *Research methods in anthropology* (5th ed.). London: Rowman & Littlefield.

Bourrelle, J. S. (2018). *The social guidebook to Norway* (3rd ed.). Mondå Forlag.

Crawford, A. (2015). Temporality in restorative justice: On time, timing and time-consciousness. *Theoretical Criminology, 19*(4), 470–490. https://doi.org/10.1177/1362480615575804.

Cunneen, C., & Goldson, B. (2015). Restorative justice? A critical analysis. In B. Goldson & J. Muncie (Eds.), *Youth, Crime and Justice* (2nd ed.) (pp. 137–156). London: Sage.

Drake, D. H., Earle, R., & Sloan, J. (Eds.). (2015). *The Palgrave handbook of prison ethnography*. Basingstoke: Palgrave Macmillan.

Ellison, M., Fox, C., Gains, A., & Pollock, G. (2013). An evaluation of the effect of housing provision on re-offending. *Safer Communities, 12*(1), 27. https://doi.org/10.1108/17578041311293125.

Flick, U. (2014). *The Sage handbook of qualitative data analysis*. London: Sage.

Forsyth, K., Archer-Power, L., Senior, J., Meacock, R., Webb, R., & Emsley, R., et al. (2017). The effectiveness of the older prisoner health and social care assessment and plan (OHSCAP): A randomised controlled trial. *Health Services and Delivery Research, 5*(31). https://doi.org/10.3310/hsdr05310.

Foster, R. (2017, August 10). What happens when you finally get released from jail? One former prisoner explains. *Metro*. https://metro.co.uk/2017/08/10/what-happens-when-you-finally-get-released-from-jail-one-former-prisoner-explains-6831114/. Accessed 27 June 2020.

Gray, D., & Stevenson, C. (2019). How can 'we' help? Exploring the role of shared social identity in the experiences and benefits of volunteering. *Journal of Community and Applied Social Psychology*, 1–13. https://doi.org/10.1002/casp.2448.

Gubrium, J. F., & Holstein, J. A. (1999). At the border of narrative and ethnography. *Journal of Contemporary Ethnography, 28*(5), 561–573.

Haines, D. W. (2017). *An introduction to sociocultural anthropology: Adaptations, structures, meanings* (2nd ed.). Boulder: University Press of Colorado.

Hammersley, M. (2015). Research 'inside' viewed from 'outside': Reflections on prison ethnography. In D. H. Drake, R. Earle, & J. Sloan (Eds.), *The Palgrave handbook of prison ethnography* (pp. 21–39). Basingstoke: Palgrave Macmillan.

Hannerz, U. (2003). Being there ... and there ... and there! Reflections on multi-site ethnography. *Ethnography, 4*(2), 201–216.

Hendry, J. (2016). *An introduction to social anthropology: Sharing our worlds* (3rd ed.). Basingstoke: Palgrave Macmillan.

Howe, L. A. (2019). Not everything is a contest: Sport, nature sport, and friluftsliv. *Journal of the Philosophy of Sport, 46*(3), 437–453. https://doi.org/10.1080/00948705.2019.1622126.

Hughes, J., Jewson, N., & Unwin, L. (2007). Introduction. Communities of practice: A contested concept in flux. In J. Hughes, N. Jewson, & L. Unwin (Eds.), *Communities of practice: Critical perspectives* (pp. 1–16). Abingdon: Routledge.

Huppert, F. A., Marks, N., Clark, A., Siegrist, J., Stutzer, A., & Vittersø, et al. (2009). Measuring well-being across Europe: Description of the ESS well-being module and preliminary findings. *Social Indicators Research, 91*(3), 301–315. https://doi.org/10.1007/s11205-008-9346-0.

Jardine, C., & Whyte, B. (2013). Valuing desistence? A social return on investment case study of a throughcare project for short-term prisoners. *Social and Environmental Accountability Journal, 33*(1), 20. https://doi.org/10.1080/0969160x.2013.768088.

Jones, J. S., & Watt, S. (2010). Making sense of it all. In J. S. Jones & S. Watt (Eds.), *Ethnography in social science practice* (pp. 157–172). Abingdon: Routledge.

Jordan, B. (2003). Criminal justice, social exclusion and the social contract. *Probation Journal, 50*(3), 198–210. doi: 0264-5505(200309)50:3;198–210;035887.

Kaufman, N. (2015). Prisoner incorporation: The work of the state and non-governmental organizations. *Theoretical Criminology, 19*(4), 534–553. https://doi.org/10.1177/1362480614567172.

Kelly, J., Collier, A., & Stringer, J. (2012). Providing a learning disability in-reach service for young adult offenders serving a sentence of Imprisonment for Public Protection. *Journal of Learning Disabilities & Offending Behaviour, 3*(3), 139–149. https://doi.org/10.1108/20420921211305882.

Khan, S., Combaz, E., & McAslan Fraser, E. (2015). *Social exclusion: Topic guide* (Revised Edition). https://gsdrc.org/wp-content/uploads/2015/08/SocialExclusion.pdf. Accessed 27 June 2020.

Lamont, M., & Molnár, V. (2002). The study of boundaries in the social sciences. *Annual Review of Sociology, 28*, 167–195. https://doi.org/10.1146/annurev.soc.28.110601.141107.

Lee, C. D., Rosenfeld, E., Mendenhall, R., Rivers, A., & Tynes, B. (2004). Cultural modelling as a frame for narrative analysis. In C. Daiute & C. Lightfoot (Eds.), *Narrative analysis: Studying the development of individuals in society* (Chapter 1.3, pp. 38–39). London: Sage.

Lo, H.-K. (2019). *Restorative justice and Confucianism in Hong Kong*. http://eprints.mdx.ac.uk/26455/. Accessed 27 June 2020.

Lyotard, J.-F. (1979). *La condition postmoderne: rapport sur le savoir*. Les Editions de Minuit. English edition: Lyotard, J.-F. (1984). *The postmodern condition: A report on knowledge* (G. Bennington & B. Massumi, Trans.). Manchester: Manchester University Press.

Marcus, G. E. (1995). Ethnography in/of the world system: The emergence of multi-sited ethnography. *Annual Review of Anthropology, 24*(1), 95–117.

Marshall, T. (1996). The evolution of restorative justice in Britain. *European Journal on Criminal Policy and Research, 4*(4), 21–43. https://doi.org/10.1007/BF02736712.

Mayou, R. (2016). Prisoners' objects: The collection of the International Red Cross and Red Crescent Museum. *International Review of the Red Cross, 98*(3), 749–760. https://doi.org/10.1017/s1816383117000595.

McGarry, K. A., & Mannik, L. (2017). *Practicing ethnography: A student guide to method and methodology*. Toronto: University of Toronto Press, Higher Education Division.

Mills, A., Gojkovic, D., Meek, R., & Mullins, D. (2013). Housing ex-prisoners: The role of the third sector. *Safer Communities, 12*(1), 38. https://doi.org/10.1108/17578041311293134.

Nadkarni, N. (2017). Branching out. In T. L. Fleischner (Ed.), *Nature, Love Medicine* (pp. 27–40). Torrey, UT: Torrey House Press.

Narcotic Anonymous World Services. (2020). Welcome to www.NA.org. https://na.org/. Accessed 27 June 2020.

National Audit Office. (2019). *What are third sector organisations and their benefits for commissioners?* https://www.nao.org.uk/successful-commissioning/introduction/what-are-civil-society-organisations-and-their-benefits-for-commissioners/. Accessed 27 June 2020.

National Institute for Health Research, U. K. (n.d.). (2020). *Skin camouflage for women prisoners with self-harm scarring (COVER)*. https://clinicaltrials.gov/show/NCT02638974. Accessed 27 June 2020.

Olive, J. L. (2014). Reflecting on the tensions between emic and etic perspectives in life history research: Lessons learned. *Forum: Qualitative Social Research, 15*(2), Art 6.

Page-Reeves, J., & Regino, L. (2018). Community-university health research partnerships: Challenges and concrete, plain language strategies for community engagement in research. *Anthropology in Action, 25*(2), 1–12. https://doi.org/10.3167/aia.2018.250202.

Pogrebin, M., West-Smith, M., Walker, A., & Unnithan, N. P. (2014). Employment isn't enough: Financial obstacles experienced by ex-prisoners during the re-entry process. *Criminal Justice Review, 4,* 394–410. https://doi.org/10.1177/0734016814540303.

Rafter, N. (2014). Introduction to special issue on visual culture and the iconography of crime and punishment. *Theoretical Criminology, 18*(2), 127–133. https://doi.org/10.1177/1362480613510547.

Retna, K. S. (2006). The learning organisation. *International Journal of Learning, 13*(1), 95–101. https://doi.org/10.18848/1447-9494/cgp/v13i01/48178.

Scott, D. (Ed.). (2013). *Why prison?* Cambridge: Cambridge University Press.

Silverman, D. (2000). *Doing qualitative research: A practical handbook*. London: Sage.

Simon, C., & Mobekk, H. (2019). Dugnad: A fact and a narrative of Norwegian prosocial behavior. *Perspectives on Behavior Science, 42*, 815–834. https://doi.org/10.1007/s40614-019-00227-w.

Southby, K., & South, J. (2019). A rapid review of barriers to volunteering for potentially disadvantaged groups and implications for health inequalities. *VOLUNTAS: International Journal of Voluntary and Nonprofit Organizations, 30*(5), 907–920. https://doi.org/10.1007/s11266-019-00119-2.

Teeters, L. A, & Jurow, A. S. (2018). Relationships de Confianza and the organisation of collective social action. *Ethnography & Education, 13*(1), 84–99. https://doi.org/10.1080/17457823.2016.1271992.

Van Maanan, J. (2011). *Tales of the field* (2nd ed.). Chicago: University of Chicago Press.

Wang, C. L., & Ahmed, P. K. (2003). Organisational learning: A critical review. *The Learning Organisation, 10*(1), 1–21. https://doi.org/10.1108/09696470310457469.

World Population Review. (2020). *Norway population 2020*. https://worldpopulationreview.com/countries/norway-population/. Accessed 27 June 2020.

14

Facilitating Understanding of Ex-Prison Service Users' Needs: The Utility of Q Method as a Means of Representing Service User Voices in Service Development

Siv Elin Nord Sæbjørnsen, Sarah Hean, and Atle Ødegård

Introduction

Involvement of service users in practice and in research has been driven primarily by governmental authorities' demands for their involvement. However, professionals may regard involvement of service users in service development as demanding and time consuming (Slettebø et al., 2010).

S. E. N. Sæbjørnsen (✉) · A. Ødegård
Molde University College, Molde, Norway
e-mail: Siv.E.N.Saebjornsen@himolde.no

S. Hean
University of Stavanger, Stavanger, Norway
e-mail: sarah.c.hean@uis.no

A. Ødegård
Nordland Research Institute, Bodø, Norway
e-mail: Atle.Odegard@hiMolde.no

S. Hean et al. (eds.), *Improving Interagency Collaboration, Innovation and Learning in Criminal Justice Systems*,
https://doi.org/10.1007/978-3-030-70661-6_14

This is particularly the case when service users are prisoners or ex-prisoners and power differentials between them and the professionals are great and the prison hierarchy works against the engagement of prisoners. In the latter case, several reasons have been identified: prisoners are not regarded as deserving, peer pressure from fellow inmates and lack of resources required to allow prisoners' participation while retaining secure conditions (Chapter 8, Hean et al. in this volume). Similarly, the voice of the prisoner may be difficult to include because of ethical restrictions—for example, research ethics committees not allowing researchers to engage prisoners in service development projects because of their vulnerability (see Bjørkly & Ødegård, 2017; Chapter 9, Sepannen et al. in this volume). Thus, novel ways that can overcome these obstacles are required to get the voices of prisoners/ex-prisoners included as service users in service development and organisational learning.

In this chapter we introduce Q methodology (Brown, 1991/1992; Stephenson, 1953) and suggest how this research method can be applied in order to reveal the views of service users in contact with the criminal justice system. An empirical research example based on ex-prisoners' experiences of service provisions in an UK mentorship organisation will be presented to illustrate the method and to critique its utility as a means of representing the service user voice during service development interventions and action research type projects.

Exemplar Study

The aim of the study was to explore the experiences of service users of a volunteer organisation in southern England that provided services to people leaving prison to facilitate their societal reintegration after leaving prison. The service provision encompassed meeting clients' various acute needs and mentoring. The study sought to give the client a voice in the further development of the service. The focus was particularly on younger clients, whose age and other vulnerabilities (e.g. literacy) had made representation of their voices in service development challenging in the past. The study was part of a wider project led by a consortium of

European researchers and practitioners (COLAB-H2020-MSCA-RISE-2016/734536) working together to merge their combined knowledge of methods of organisational change in other fields and apply these to the criminal justice system. This project had identified that representing the service user voice in organisational change and innovation interventions (see Chapter 8 of this volume) in this context was problematic, and Q method was proposed as having the potential to address this issue. Twenty-one young people (19 males and 2 females, aged 19–30) were recruited for the study.

Q Method

Q method was developed by William Stephenson in the 1930s, aiming to develop a method for systematic investigation of human subjectivity, such as persons' viewpoints, feelings or preferences. The method and its methodology represented something new and innovative and met scepticism and resistance for many years, particularly from the prevailing objectivist perspective. However, during the last decades, Q method has increasingly been recognised and applied in several new research fields, including social policy (Brown, 1980), psychology (Goldstein & Goldstein, 2005), human geography (Eden et al., 2005), child welfare (Ellingsen, 2011), interprofessional collaboration (Sæbjørnsen, 2017) and ex-prisoners' experience of service provisions (Sjo & Sæbjørnsen, 2018). Q method has contributed to valuable insight into viewpoints, meanings, thoughts and feelings of people in vulnerable situations.

In brief, participants in a Q study are asked to relate to a set of stimuli and to express their perspectives by use of these stimuli. The most frequently used form of stimuli is statements, but other forms of stimuli, such as images, have also been used (Stephenson, 1980; Størksen et al., 2011; Taylor & Delprato, 1994). However, hereafter, such stimuli will be referred to as *statements*. The participants are asked to relate to a set of statements and then to sort the statements according to their subjective meaning, such as in order of subjective importance. The individual participant's sorting procedure is often referred to as a Q sort. The analyses will show how participants share their subjective viewpoints.

Through the analyses, the identification of similarities and differences, as well as attempts to reach a consensus, viewpoints and perspectives will become visible.

The research process of a Q study can be explained in the following four steps (Brown, 1991/1992; van Exel & de Graaf, 2005):

1. Concourse identification
2. Q sampling
3. Q sort administration
4. Analysis and interpretation.

Step 1: Concourse Identification

The *concourse* constitutes a central element in Q methodology, which is the basis of the Q method. The concourse represents everything that is communicable on the topic under investigation (Brown, 1980; Stephenson, 1953) or 'the flow of communicability surrounding any topic' (Brown, 1991/1992, p. 3). In Norway, the concept has been translated to *kommunikasjonsunivers* (Thorsen & Allgood, 2010) meaning communication universe, which refers to the different ways of expressing information about the topic. Different groups will describe the topic in different ways, but the most important outcome being aimed at is the emergence of different subjective statements that together form a picture of the participants' subjective viewpoints or perspectives about the topic.

The purpose of this first step is to identify the concourse around the topic of investigation, which involves identifying all relevant statements pertaining to the topic. A total of 200 statements or more is not unusual at this step. Transcripts from in-depth interviews with participants are often the basis for concourse identification. Often, only a few interviews (3–4) are sufficient for concourse identification (Ellingsen et al., 2010), and a large number of potential statements may be derived from the interviews for Q set development. This is known as a *naturalistic concourse approach* (Ellingsen, 2011; Sæbjørnsen et al., 2016). Each statement is pasted onto a card to form a pile of so called Q sort cards. By using statements derived from interviews with service users, the statements become meaningful and understandable to the service user. Involving them in the development of this tool in this way may contribute to the service users' feeling recognised and being taken seriously by the service providers (Honneth, 2008; Sæbjørnsen, 2017). Such a form of service user involvement may even contribute to the development of a trusting relationship between service provider and service user.

Concourse identification may also take a theoretical approach. Such an approach entails the researcher, in a systematic way, seeking to represent what is likely to be part of a hypothetical communication on a selected topic (Kvalsund & Allgood, 2010). For this purpose, statements are derived from other media, such as newspapers, literature or from daily communication between human beings (Brown, 1991/1992; Corr, 2006). The third approach to concourse identification constitutes a combination of naturalistic and theoretical approaches (Sæbjørnsen et al., 2016).

Step 2: Q Sampling

The identified concourse constitutes the basis for the statements that the participants will be asked to examine. However, handling a very large number of statements will be difficult for the participants; hence, it is important to make a systematic reduction in the number of statements, seeking to ensure that nuances in the identified concourse remain. This selection process is referred to as the Q sampling, in which the Fisher Block Balance Design (Stephenson, 1953) is useful for categorisation and balancing, as well as a reduction of statements. After this process, the number of statements will often have been reduced to 20–50, depending on the study topic and the participants' ability to relate to different statements. The development of the Q cards (and the statements written on them) should be conducted by a researcher who is competent in Q methodology, but service users as well as service providers could be involved in the selection of statements.

In the Q sampling it is important to select statements that allow for self-reflection so that the participant can weigh the subjective significance or how important the statements are to him or her (Brown, 1980; Thorsen, 2006). This is known as *psychological significance* (Kvalsund & Allgood, 2010). When developing the Q sample for the study, it is therefore recommended to avoid statements that would just result in 'agree' or 'not agree'. Whether the statements are formulated negatively or positively does not influence the results of the study because the results only depend on the participants' ranking of the statements. However, it is recommended to formulate most statements positively because it eases the participants' sorting.

Step 3: Q Sort Administration

A Q study can be accomplished even with a relatively limited number of participants, and more than 50 participants would be unusual. Prior to Q sort, the researcher gives sorting instructions, such as 'sort the statements in accordance with the degree to which you agree with it' or 'sort the statements in accordance with the degree to which it is important to you'. Each of the participants will be asked to rank order the statements, by sorting the cards onto a Q sort grid. This grid is a template provided by the researcher upon which the participant can place their cards in order of their perceived relevance to their own personal situation. Most often the participants in a Q study sort the cards once. However, it would also have been possible to ask participants to do several Q sorts, based on different instructions, for the purpose of comparing the different Q sorts. For example, the American psychologist Carl Rogers took advantage of this opportunity when he applied Q method in individual therapy. First, he asked the clients to sort the cards according to their 'ideal self' and then according to their 'real self' (Smith, 2001).

The scale and shape of a Q sort grid may vary from study to study, but the ranking of statements is horizontal and not vertical, which means that the rank order inside one column is always irrelevant. The grid example shown in Fig. 14.1 has a scale from −5 to +5, which means that the participants in that specific study had a choice of 11 different values

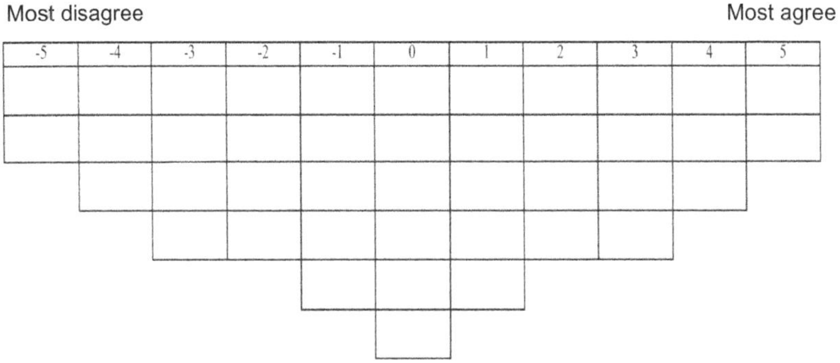

Fig. 14.1 Q sort grid

available for the rank ordering. During a Q sort, the participant will place the statement that he most agrees with on +5 and those of the remaining statements that he agrees with on the +4 columns, and so forth. A corresponding procedure will be used for the statements that the participant agrees with least. The limited spaces available in the +5 row and the −5 row forces the participant to prioritize which statements he will give one of these 'exclusive' values.

In order to ease the sorting of the statements onto the grid, the participant will first be asked to sort the cards into three piles: 'most agree', 'least agree' and 'more neutral/not quite sure'. As shown in Fig. 14.2, the participant then starts with sorting the cards from the 'most agree' pile onto the right (plus) section of the grid before moving on to the cards from the 'least agree' pile onto the left (minus) section of the grid. Finally, the participant sorts the cards from the last pile on to the middle section of the grid.

Prior to Q sorting, and sometimes also during Q sorting, the researcher must explain practicalities and guide the participant on how to sort the cards, but do so without influencing their views. It is important that the researcher enables the participant to feel secure and free to express his subjective views.

After the Q sort, the researcher will normally ask the participant to look over the Q sort, in order to make adjustments, if needed. The sorting procedure often makes the participant more conscious about

Fig. 14.2 A participant performing a Q sort

his viewpoints, which he might not have been aware of prior to the Q sort. In conformity with other research approaches, Q method provides a picture of a participant's view at the time of a Q sort performance. Nevertheless, the perspectives will normally be relatively stable, and a test-retest-reliability (same sorting at two different points in time) from $r = 0.80$ up to 0.90 is anticipated (Brown, 1980).

Step 4: Analysis and Interpretation

The result of each participant's Q sort will be subjected to person-centred factor analysis or a 'by person factor analysis'. This means that it is the individual Q sort or perspective, consisting of each participant's valuation of each of the statements (for example from −5 to +5) that is subjected to factor analysis, not the single statement or item as in traditional, explorative factor analysis. PQMethod (Schmolck, 2002) is the most commonly applied analysis programme in Q studies. The software programme can be downloaded free of charge (http://schmolck.org/qmethod/downpqwin.htm).

All the participants' Q sorts are put into the programme for Q factor analysis, person by person. In Q factor analysis, a factor consists of *persons* who have sorted the statements similarly. This is different from conventional factor analysis, where clusters of variables constitute the factors. Based on the emerging factors, the researcher will make an analytical assessment about how many factors to retain for the final factor solution. Selection of a final factor solution is often based on a factor eigenvalue and the number of significant loadings that the factor is based on (Watts & Stenner, 2012). The factors, which are often referred to as perspectives, represent different perspectives prevailing among the participants, and usually a Q study identifies several different perspectives. This means that persons who have similar, though not identical, subjective viewpoints contribute to define the same factor. The factors show the typical way that the participants who define the perspective have sorted the cards. After the computer-based analysis, the factors or perspectives are further interpreted by abduction. In this abductive interpretation, the researcher seeks to understand the different perspectives the Q analysis has pinpointed and what these represent. Further investigation of the factors, including what the factor expresses, important and unimportant statements in this perspective and the particular properties of the specific factor can convey a good picture of which viewpoints each perspective represents. This means that a statement can have a different meaning depending on which context it is placed in, and should, hence, be interpreted holistically. A procedure using 'crib sheets' as described by Watts and Stenner (2012) may be useful in this systematic factor interpretation. For interpretation of each factor, the 'crib sheet' procedure involves focusing the overall configuration of the statements, identification of statements that were ranked higher and lower than in the other factors, and statements that were ranked in the outer edges of the grid, that is, −5 and +5. The analysis reveals each perspective's characteristics and also what the participants have in common across the different perspectives that have emerged.

Illustrative Example of Using the Q Method With Ex-Prisoners as Service Users

Participants

Twenty-one young ex-prisoners (19 males and 2 females) aged 19–30, with experiences from imprisonments in England, participated in this study. Type of crime as well as number and duration of imprisonments varied among the participants, but the majority had expiated sentences related to substance misuse. The participants were recruited by the third sector charity organisation and their partners in southern England who had the remit of mentoring people in contact with the criminal justice system, especially after their release from prison.

Materials and Procedure

This Q study was carried out in accordance with the steps commonly used in Q studies (Brown, 1991/1992; van Exel & de Graaf, 2005).

- *Identification of the concourse.* Semi-structured interviews with three ex-prisoners and one professional with expert knowledge of the field were conducted. Based on the transcribed interview texts, a total of 199 statements were identified as belonging to the concourse of young ex-prisoners' views about their situation, needs and possibilities.
- *Development of the set of statements (Q set or Q sample).* The statements were selected from interview texts. The selection of statements for the Q set involved development and application of a two-dimensional scheme, inspired by Fisher's balanced block design, as recommended by Stephenson (1953). The purpose of using such a categorisation tool is to strengthen concourse representativeness in the Q set (Sæbjørnsen

et al., 2016). The Q set (consisting of 42 statements) and the Q sort grid (Fig. 14.1) were tested by research colleagues and professional service providers, which resulted in amendment of some of the statements.

- *Administration of the Q sorts.* The Q set was presented to the participants on 42 statement cards, with one statement printed on each card. The participants were asked to relate to the statements and sort them into the grid, in accordance with the degree to which they agreed with the statements. In order to simplify the sorting procedure, the participants first read through the statements or had the statements read aloud and conducted a preliminary sort into three piles (agree, disagree and neutral/uncertain). The participants sorted the cards without interference from the researcher or others. The researcher answered clarifying questions and took notes of participants' comments and deepening expressions.
- *Analysis and interpretation* of the data obtained from Q sorts and participants' comments during the sorting procedures.

Analysis

In Q studies, factor interpretation is based on the understandings that the factors represent (McKeown & Thomas, 1988), and the researcher searches for the best plausible explanations (Stephenson, 1961; Wolf, 2004). As suggested by Watts and Stenner (2012), the interpretation of each factor was based on the overall configuration of the participants' statements, statements that were ranked higher and lower than in the other factors, and statements that were ranked −5 and +5.

The 21 completed Q sorts were entered into the computer programme PQMethod (Schmolck, 2002) for data analysis. The Q sorts were then subjected to factor analysis using a principal component analysis with a Varimax rotation (Shemmings, 2006; Stainton Rogers, 1995). The rotation of factors is used in accordance with the criterion of simple structure, which means that the factors are distinct from each other, and the factor structure can then be meaningfully interpreted by the researcher (Munro, 1997). The emerging factors revealed how the participants' shared viewpoints clustered together and which statements that the participants, on the same factor, typically had rated positively or negatively.

Ethical Considerations

Approvals were obtained from the Norwegian Centre for Research Data (NSD). Initially, the participants were informed both verbally and in writing about the research project. The participants gave their written consent. They were informed that all information, such as how they sorted the cards and their verbal comments, would be treated anonymously.

Findings and Factor Interpretation

A principal component analysis with a Varimax rotation resulted in three factors (Table 14.2). The correlation between the factors was low (Table 14.1), indicating the presence of differing perspectives.

The factor loadings indicate the degree to which each Q sort correlates with each of the three factors, as shown in Table 14.2. An X marks a Q sort loading significantly on one factor. The closer a Q sort is to 1, the more equal it is to the factor:

As shown in Table 14.2, 8 of the 21 participants loaded significantly on Factors 1, 6 on Factors 2 and 7 define Factor 3. A visual inspection of the factors is a common approach in Q. The resulting factor scores (z scores) were converted back to the original values of the scale used in the

Table 14.1 Three factor correlation matrix

	F1	F2	F3
F1	1.0000	0.3397	0.3967
F2	0.3397	1.0000	0.2005
F3	0.3967	0.2005	1.0000

Table 14.2 Factor matrix with an X indicating a defining sort

Q sort	F1		F2		F3	
1	0.1611		0.4216	X	0.0148	
2	0.7024	X	0.3778		0.2349	
3	0.7101	X	0.3946		0.2519	
4	0.1403		0.4075		0.4687	X
5	0.0075		0.8495	X	-0.0151	
6	0.3779		0.5454	X	0.0290	
7	-0.0057		0.0409		0.7263	X
8	-0.0765		0.5840	X	-0.0444	
9	0.6059	X	-0.2663		0.2809	
10	0.8257	X	0.1906		0.1619	
11	0.5644	X	0.2561		-0.0404	
12	0.2674		0.5146	X	0.4254	
13	0.1389		0.4094		0.6154	X
14	0.3720		-0.1375		0.5674	X
15	0.6443	X	-0.2544		-0.0046	
16	0.0133		-0.1267		0.7505	X
17	0.1131		-0.1042		0.5374	X
18	0.1779		0.3871		0.5580	X
19	0.3489	X	0.0571		0.0358	
20	0.1293		0.7915	X	0.0547	
21	0.5267	X	0.2905		0.2036	
Explained variance %	17		17		15	

factor matrix. How each of the statements was typically sorted by each of the three factors is shown in Table 14.3.

Each factor consists of *persons* who have sorted their statements similarly. Therefore the factor analysis showed the following three groups or types of participant.

Factor 1—The Prison Weary Optimist

The participants associated with Factor 1 seem to have had a very difficult time in prison, but were still optimistic about the future. All 8 participants were male, aged 21–30 years. Their age at first time of imprisonment varied from 15 to 22 years, and the number of imprisonments varied from 1 to 12. Seven of these boys had drug/alcohol problems and mental health difficulties, and two of them needed to see

Table 14.3 Factor scores for each statement

No.	Statement	No.	Factor 1	Factor 2	Factor 3
1	When I came out, I was a bit shocked of all the different org. that were there to help	1	– 3	3	– 1
2	In prison, I felt like I was left there with my life crisis and nobody helped me to find out what kind of help that I needed	2	4	– 3	– 1
3	I've lost all ties with my family	3	– 3	– 5	0
4	I really need treatment for my anxiety and/or depression	4	– 1	– 4	5
5	Reading and writing are very difficult to me	5	– 4	– 5	– 4
6	I have somebody who really cares for me, that has taken me under his/her wings	6	0	0	– 1
7	When I came out, I had someone that helped me to look for what help I could get	7	– 1	4	– 2

(continued)

Table 14.3 (continued)

No.	Statement	No.	Factor 1	Factor 2	Factor 3
8	It's easier talking to someone that has been in prison. It's the little things, little stories, we have a crack about it, we have a laugh	8	0	0	–2
9	I was brought up around crime and drugs and things that normal people wouldn't be doing...	9	1	3	4
10	I have someone who really cares about me, that I can call at any time, just help me thinking	10	3	4	1
11	I've got help to become more aware of things that use to get me into trouble	11	1	–1	2
12	I have plenty of skills and knowledge that will be useful in a decent job	12	2	2	2
13	I just keep myself strictly to straight people now	13	–1	1	0

(continued)

Table 14.3 (continued)

No.	Statement	No.	Factor 1	Factor 2	Factor 3
14	My life is actually getting very well, so I'm looking forward to the future now	14	5	5	$\underline{-2}$
15	I am being supported by someone who grew up with the same issues as me and that has managed to change from a criminal way of life	15	−2	−2	−2
16	It's really important to me to get in contact with my family again	16	2	$\underline{-2}$	2
17	My helpers have helped me to believe that I am capable of changing my lifestyle	17	1	2	1
18	If I make a serious decision to make a new life, no drugs and no crime, I am fully capable of doing it	18	3	3	3
19	It's really useful to see probation weekly the first year after release	19	$\underline{-4}$	$\underline{0}$	$\underline{3}$

(continued)

Table 14.3 (continued)

No.	Statement	No.	Factor 1	Factor 2	Factor 3
20	The most important to me is to get my own space, where I can go back and say this is my key, my bed, my things	20	1	4	5
21	To get help in prison, you have to constantly be pushing them, until they start wondering why you are behaving like that	21	4	0	−1
22	I came out and almost everything was prepared for me, also a place to live	22	−3	1	−5
23	If I had the resettlement team from the start, I would start working on myself and on the resettlement in prison	23	−1	−1	0
24	It's frustrating that it takes so long to get to see the mental health services. If it was easier I would have seen them long time ago	24	3	−4	4

(continued)

Table 14.3 (continued)

No.	Statement	No.	Factor 1	Factor 2	Factor 3
25	Prison has helped me too. If I was just out on the street, I wouldn't be able to start my education	25	– 2	1	– 3
26	If it wasn't for XXX or similar org, I wouldn't have the stuff that I needed to start moving on in my life. They helped me get back to normal	26	0	2	3
27	It'd be easier if all my helpers kept in contact and work together. It'd be easier to meet them all in one spot, rather than go to all of them weekly	27	0	1	0
28	I don't get anything out of probation. They just want to know that you are not taking drugs or doing crime	28	2	– 1	– 3
29	The prison officers really care about the prisoners	29	– 5	– 3	– 1

(continued)

Table 14.3 (continued)

No.	Statement	No.	Factor 1	Factor 2	Factor 3
30	Prison life isn't nice. It's similar to outside. People get robbed; people try to beg up for the need for the day and getting as much food as they can	30	4	–2	0
31	Actually, I don't care too much if I have to go to prison again. It's almost like a holiday. I kind of like it there	31	–5	–4	–5
32	In prison I was asked what I was thinking about doing when I got out, like housing and getting a job…	32	–4	3	–3
33	The only reason that I went to the alcohol/drug treatment is that probation sent me there	33	–1	–3	–4
34	I'm thinking completely different now. I just want to live life as a normal person. Crime and drugs are not what I want to do no more	34	5	5	2

(continued)

Table 14.3 (continued)

No.	Statement	No.	Factor 1	Factor 2	Factor 3
35	When I get annoyed or frustrated, I seem to forget all about what I've learnt about how to stay out of trouble	35	– 2	2	0
36	I talk with my mentors/helpers about how I can handle different stressful situations that might occur	36	0	– 1	1
37	If I'm having some sort of crisis in my life, I always ask for help	37	0	0	– 3
38	If I get bad news or something like that, I used to take drugs/drink alcohol which often brings me into trouble	38	1	– 1	4
39	I wanted to move on with my life, but after I got out I've been charged for other offences. I'll have to do my time…[in prison]	39	– 3	– 2	– 4

(continued)

Table 14.3 (continued)

No.	Statement	No.	Factor 1	Factor 2	Factor 3
40	The lack of contact between probation and other services often puts me in stressful situations, such as disturbing other appointments	40	3	–3	1
41	It'd be better if XXX or similar org. could come to see you before release, coming to speak to you so you get to know them and can make some plans	41	2	0	3
42	I am good at controlling my feelings and my temper. I never get carried away by frustrations and things like that	42	–2	1	1
Explained variance			17%	17%	15%

Note Values with underlining represent distinguishing statement values for the specific factor at significance level $p < .0.5$. Distinguishing statements refer to key viewpoints in each factor (Watts & Stenner, 2012) and to their being significantly unique for each specific factor. The distinguishing statements are underlined factor scores in Table 14.3. For example, it is typical and unique for participants associated with Factor 3 to have a statement number 42 on −5. Statements marked * represent consensus statements. Only statements 11, 21 and 25 are marked as consensus statements, which means that they are ranked quite similarly in all the factors (Watts & Stenner, 2012) mental health services. Except for one, all of the boys grew up in their parents' homes. Only one boy reported that he had no contact with his family. The participants' housing arrangements varied: some were in hostels or shared flats, some in 'supported accommodations', and one stayed with his parents. Five boys had some regular day activity, such as work or following a treatment programme.

The Factor 1 participants expressed bad and painful experiences from prison life (#30/+4) including having a life crisis with no help being available (#2/+4), at least in the cases of those who did not constantly and every day, 'beg for help and act weird' (#21/+4). These boys seemed to believe that prison officers did not at all care about the prisoners (#29/−5). When in prison, they did not seem to have been offered any counselling or anyone to talk to in order to prepare for life after release (#32/−4). Avoiding new prison terms seemed really important to these participants (#31/−5). Even after prison release, these boys did not seem impressed by the number of different organisations offering them help (#1/−3). They did not seem to have had anyone ready to help them with such issues as needing a place to live after release (#7/−1). The boys expressed that it was quite frustrating that it was so difficult to get mental health services (#24/+3). They all saw probation services regularly, but they did not seem to find that useful (#19/−4). More than any other factor, these boys expressed that the lack of contact between probation and other services had put them in stressful situations, such as disturbing other appointments (#40/+3).

Despite bad experiences from prison and little useful help in order to resettle after release, these boys seemed positive and very optimistic about the future (#14/+5). Somehow, they were thinking differently at that point. They strongly expressed that they wanted to live life as a normal person, without crime and drugs (#34/+ 5), and they seemed to trust their own ability to succeed with such plan (#18/+ 3). Interestingly, Factor 1 gave the statement 'I have someone who really cares about me, that I can call any time, just help me thinking' quite a high value (#10/+ 3). These relationships may be important recourses for these boys, for their positivism and motivation for change.

Factor 2—The Resilient Optimist

The overall impression is that the 6 male participants, age 20–29, who constituted Factor 2, ignored difficulties and reached for possibilities. Feelings of having someone who care and a sound mental health seemed to reduce the suffering they experienced as a result of a lack of other basic life amenities. Age of first imprisonment varied from 13 to 25, and the number of imprisonments varied from one to four. Only two boys reported drug/alcohol problems. Except for one boy, the participants reported that they did not need any help from mental health services. Four boys grew up in their parents' home, and two grew up in foster homes and/or children's homes. Only one boy reported extensive contact with his family, and one boy had no family contact at all. The boys' housing situations varied from hostel, sleeping on a friend's sofa or just living on the street, and they saw it as very important to get their own space (#20/+ 4). Except for one boy who worked occasionally, these boys had no regular day activity.

The typical Factor 2 participant seemed to think that life was currently getting very good and was optimistic about the future (#14/+5). Crime and drugs seemed to have been a part of their upbringing (#9/+3), but they emphasised that they had completely changed their way of thinking and just wanted to live life without drugs and crime (#34/+5). Unlike the other factors, these boys did not seem to have felt left alone in crisis when in prison (#2/−3). Rather, they expressed having had some help in prison (#25/+1), such as counselling about how to handle life after release (#32/+3). These boys did not seem to have experienced prison life as being as hard as the other factor groupings did (#30/−2), but they did not want to go back to prison again (#31/−4), and they did not agree that prison officers really cared about the prisoners (#29/−3).

Different from the other factors, the Factor 2 participants did not seem to experience any mental health difficulties (#4/−4 and #24/−4). They emphasised that they had someone who really cared about them, whom they could talk to about anything (#10/+4). They also had somebody who helped them when they were released #7/+4), and they had not lost contact with their family (#3/−5). More than the other factors, these boys seemed to have been surprised by the many organisations that were offering to help them resettle after release (#1/+3).

Factor 3—The Lonely, Indigent and Ill

The overall impression of Factor 3 is that the 7 participants associated with it, 2 females and 5 males, suffered from loneliness and lack of care and having several unmet basic needs, particularly due to a lack of mental health treatment and a good place to live.

The participants were from 19 to 30 years old. Their age at their first time in prison varied from 16 to 25 years, and the number of imprisonments varied from 1 to 11. Three participants reported alcohol/drug problems. Five participants reported that they needed mental health services. Three of the participants grew up in foster homes and children's homes, and four in a parent's home. Except for one participant, the Factor 3 participants reported that they had little or no current contact with their family. The housing situation for these participants varied from shared flat, hostel and living on the street. None of them had regular day activities.

The typical Factor 3 participant seemed to emphasise that their two most important needs were a proper place to live (#20/+5) and anxiety treatment (#4/+5). The long wait to see the mental health service caused them frustration (#24/+4). Nothing seemed to have been prepared for them before release (#22/−5). They seemed not to have received any help when in prison (#25/−3), nor did anybody there ask them about plans after release, such as how to get a place to live or a job (#32/−3). They seemed very convinced that they did not want to go back to prison again (#31/−5).

More than the other factors, Factor 3 participants emphasised that they were brought up around crime, drugs and things 'normal people' would not do (#9/+4). If they, for example, got bad news, they used to take drugs and then often got involved in more crime (#38/+4). When experiencing life crises, it was not their habit to ask for help (#37/−3). However, they seemed to appreciate the help they got from the third sector organisation (#26/+3), and they would like it if workers from this organisation had come to see them when in prison (#41/+3). Unlike the other factors, these participants seemed to find it quite useful to see probation (#19/+3 and #28/−3), and those who attended alcohol/drug treatments did not express that they did it just to 'please' probation (#33/−4). Less than the other factors, this grouping of participants had somebody who really cared for them (#6/−1), and they did not have anybody to help them resettle and find a place to live after release (#7/−2).

Discussion

In this chapter we have introduced Q methodology (Brown, 1991/1992; Stephenson, 1953) and shown how this research method can be applied in order to reveal the views of service users in contact with the criminal justice system. We now discuss the utility of this analysis in terms of how it uncovers service users' perspectives and may be employed in service development as well as what its strengths and weaknesses are.

Service Users' Perspectives

The findings reveal that service users' perspectives, although with some overlap, vary considerably, as demonstrated by the three Q factors emerging in the analysis.

The differences in perspectives tell us that service users do not have a single voice and should not be understood as a homogeneous entity. Findings in this study support those of Larsen et al. (2019) that ex-prisoners are as different from each other as are those in any other groups of people. Many ex-prisoners suffer from drug addiction, mental health issues and re-offending, but not all of them do. Differences in situations and needs require flexibility in the service provision system. This should be reflected in, for example, development of a rehabilitation plan by an organisation such as the third sector organisation involved with this particular sample. Some ex-prisoners need help with the basic things in life, such as housing and having enough money to buy food and clothes. Others may have additional or different needs related, for example, to mental health issues. Ex-prisoners may also vary considerably with regard to how they perceive the world. As Factor 1—*Prison weary optimist* showed, these boys had a relatively optimistic view of the future. Optimism also characterised Factor 2—*Resilient optimist*. The participants associated with Factor 3—*Lonely, indigent and ill*, however, seemed to have many unmet basic needs that coloured their hopes for the future.

It has been suggested that the differences in perspectives, as a result from the use of Q method, would not be easily accessible in, for example, research interviews. Sometimes participants in a Q study want to deepen single statements, explain the way that they have sorted the cards or share some reflections after the sorting procedure. This is an opportunity for additional valuable information to be collected on the theme of the Q study. In order to collect such information, if the participant agrees, the Q sorting can be audio recorded and then transcribed. Such information would normally be treated in the same way as interview data (Shemmings & Ellingsen, 2012). However, it is important to emphasise that participants who do not want to elaborate or share their views verbally are not required to do so.

Some people, when in vulnerable positions in life, may appreciate opportunities to elaborate verbally about their difficulties, perhaps as a way of trying to get rid of some frustration. Others, in similar positions, but with a different personality, might try to avoid such elaboration and refuse participation in traditional interview-based studies. The Q sort may prove more comfortable for them, therefore. Both of the two different 'types' of persons may represent significant and different views. In studies aiming to explore views of persons who share a specific and particularly vulnerable position in life, such as persons newly released from prison, views from both of these types should be included. The flexibility in the Q method, which has been appreciated by many researchers in various research fields (Sæbjørnsen & Ellingsen, 2015), offers a means of including both types of participants. Some will only perform the Q sorting, while others will also take the opportunity to comment and deepen what they express through the Q sorting. Hence, Q studies may achieve a greater broadness within the participant group under study, compared to studies that rely on data from surveys or interviews alone (Sæbjørnsen, 2017). However, although participants' comments may imply valuable qualitative data, the Q sorts will always constitute the most important data in a Q study.

In a broader sense, ex-prisoners having new ways to express themselves through the flexibility of the Q methodology may also expand their opportunities for personal growth and development. Bandura's (1994) concept *self-efficacy* is relevant in this context, as it pinpoints central essential aspects of recovery processes and recovery-oriented practices.

Perceived self-efficacy is people's beliefs about their capabilities to produce designated levels of performance that exercise influence over events that affect their lives. Self-efficacy beliefs determine how people feel, think, motivate themselves and behave. Such beliefs produce these diverse effects through four major processes. They include cognitive, motivational, affective and selection processes (p. 1).

According to Bandura, then, a strong sense of efficacy enhances human accomplishment and personal well-being in many different ways, but people who doubt their capabilities will shy away from difficult tasks that they see as personal threats. The most effective way to create a strong sense of efficacy is through mastery experiences. For example, achievement of a new crime- and drug-free life after prison release implies many challenges, yet it is not impossible, as is also documented by Sjo and Sæbjørnsen (2018) and Landheim (2016). However, anything that contributes to strengthening an ex-prisoner's self-efficacy may increase his possibility of achieving a goal of a 'new life' after prison release. By being able to express their subjective world views and present their perspectives in this non-threatening and non-confrontational method, ex-prisoners will feel empowered as well as increase the likelihood that adequate services can be offered to this group of service users. Q methodology may be one step in this direction.

Service User Involvement

The service user perspective must be considered in service development. As already described, Q methodology, which is designed for investigation of human subjectivity (Brown, 1980), is useful for gaining insight into these views in a less confrontational and accessible format. The method can be adapted to different participant groups, ages and cognitive levels, and nuanced information about service users' needs may be easily obtained both in the Q sort and any recording of interviews during this process. This is in contrast to more quantitative tools such as questionnaires where the service users' responses do not take into consideration the 'subjectivity' of the person. On the other hand, the method is also less direct and confrontational in style compared to face-to-face interviews, and Q sorting provides a less stressful, perhaps even playful, way of presenting one's perspective.

Although Q sorting may simply be a tool to evaluate the range of experiences and types of the service users, the Q sort cards can also be used in client-professional interactions more widely. The administration of the Q sort cards may therefore serve as the basis for dialogues and reflections between actors, including the ex-prisoner himself. For example, multiple copies of the set of Q sort cards and Q sort grid may be made and given to each case worker/mentor working with ex-prisoners for them to use as a shared tool for reflection in one-to-one sessions with a service user. By asking the service user to sort the cards and discuss this process, case workers may be able to raise sensitive subjects for further communication and discussions between the service user and themselves, the service provider(s), in a gentle, unaggressive fashion. Service users may develop their insight and understanding, acquire new knowledge and self-reflectivity through the Q sorting (Sæbjørnsen, 2017; Sjo & Sæbjørnsen, 2018). The fact that participants in Q studies are forced to value each statement subjectively and prioritise statements in relation to one another implies reflection on issues mentioned in the statements. As a result of the Q sort process, new personal, subjective opinions and new understanding may evolve.

This new understanding may convey a change in mindset that may be very useful in interventions with ex-prisoners who aim at a new start in life. The Q method may therefore be used to measure a client's progress over time, by asking the service user to sort the statements in his first meeting with the mentor, and then, after some weeks, ask him to make a new sort and compare the results. Every completed Q sort may also be captured in a photo and be used as a point of reference in later meetings. The service user may be given a copy of the photos, as a documentation or reminder of an ongoing change. A Q methodological approach may possibly also be used in combination with other clinical tools presented in this book, such as the HCR-20 and ERM (see Chapters 10 and 11).

Finally, the Q method can also be used to compare views of service users and views of mentors (see Chapter 15). Experienced mentors may feel that they have built up some general knowledge about service users that they can present in service development sessions. However, it is possible that the service user and mentor perspectives might not agree. For example, the mentor could be less optimistic about the potential of the service user to remain crime free. However, such conflicts may be used creatively, as an approach to get deeper insight into the service user's view or feeling and/or an opportunity for the service user's and mentor's joint engagement in addressing differences in views.

Q Methodology—Some Potential Challenges

Although Q method has been used by researchers in this chapter and later in Chapter 15 to understand young ex-prisoners' life situations and experiences of the case study third sector mentorship charity, about its utility as a tool for both individual service user work and utility for service development, some challenges should be mentioned. As already alluded to, development of Q statements is a time-consuming process, but one important advantage is that the process is likely to result in a well-tailored tool for investigation of the subjective views of a group of participants. We illustrated here Q statements developed for use in the third sector mentorship charity. If the aim is to develop a Q set that can be transferred to service users in other contexts, in other services, for example, this advantage may also be seen as a problem. However, it is possible to develop a context-neutral basis for statements, consisting, for example, of 20–30 statements, and, in addition, develop some context-specific statements that can be added to the Q set. Further, as already suggested, Q method may be applied in therapy and as an approach to dialogue between mentor and service user. However, as in all therapeutic dialogues with people in vulnerable situations, it is important to be aware that triggering sensitive issues could cause a service user frustration and despair that will need to be addressed. The use of Q sorting in dialogues between service users and mentors should therefore be used cautiously.

Concluding Remarks

This chapter has exemplified and suggested how Q methodology can be applied to elicit ex-prison service users' views in research, in therapy or in dialogues between service user and mentor, as well as in including service users' voice in service development. The method is undoubtedly flexible and may be used for several purposes. However, it would also have been interesting to test Q method as a means of stimulating dialogue during a Change Laboratory workshop and other service development models (see Chapter 8).

The value of involving people in vulnerable situations in service user involvement should always be weighed against the risk involved with it. Applying Q method as a means of including service users' voices in a service development workshop should thus probably be based on results of Q sorts performed by a representative group of anonymous service users, prior to the workshop. Involving one to two service user representatives in a workshop to comment on their views and discuss with service providers might be an even better way to involve service users in service development worth exploring in further studies.

References

Bandura, A. (1994). Self-efficacy. In V. S. Ramachaudran (Ed.), *Encyclopedia of human behavior* (Vol. 4, pp. 71–81). New York: Academic Press.

Bjørkly, S., & Ødegård, A. (2017). Brukermedvirkning i praksisnær forskning—hva er det, og hva gir det? [Service user involvement in practice research—What is it, and what does it provide?]. In A. M. Willumsen & E. Støkken (Eds.), *Brukerstemmer, praksisforskning og innovasjon* [User voices, practice research and innovation] (pp. 123–135). Kristiansand: Portal Press.

Brown, S. (1980). *Political subjectivity: Applications of Q methodology in political science*. New Haven: Yale University Press.

Brown, S. R. (1991/1992). *A Q methodological Tutorial*. Retrieved from http://facstaff.uww.edu/cottlec/QArchive/Primer1.html.

Corr, S. (2006). Exploring perceptions about services using Q methodology. In G. Kielhofner (Ed.), *Research in occupational therapy: Methods of inquiry for enhancing practice* (pp. 389–400). Philadelphia: E.A. Davis Company.

Eden, S., Donaldson, A., & Walker, G. (2005). Structuring subjectivities? Using Q methodology in human geography. *Area, 37*(4), 413–422.

Ellingsen, I. T. (2011). *Adolescents in foster care and their families: A Q methodological study on family perceptions*. Ph.D. Doctoral thesis, University of Stavanger, Stavanger, Norway.

Ellingsen, I. T., Størksen, I., & Stephens, P. (2010). Q methodology in social work research. *International Journal of Social Research Methodology, 13*(5), 395–409.

Goldstein, D. M., & Goldstein, S. E. (2005). Q methodology study of a person in individual therapy. *Clinical Case Studies, 4,* 40–56.

Honneth, A. (2008). *Kamp om anerkjennelse: Om de sosiale konfliktenes moralske grammatikk* [The struggle for recognition: The moral grammar of social conflicts]. Oslo: Pax.

Kvalsund, R., & Allgood, E. (2010). Kommunikasjon som subjektivitet i en skoleorganisasjon [Communication as subjectivity in a school organization]. In A. A. Thorsen & E. Allgood (Eds.), *Q metodologi: En velegnet måte å utforske subjektivitet* [Q methodology: An appropriate means for exploration of subjectivity] (pp. 47–76). Trondheim: Tapir Academic Press.

Landheim, A. (2016). *Et bedre liv: historier, erfaringer og forskning om recovery ved rusmiddelmisbruk og psykiske problemer* [A better life: Narratives, experiences and research about recovery from substance misuse and mental health problems]. Gyldendal Academic Press.

Larsen, B. K., Hean, S., & Ødegård, A. (2019). A conceptual model on reintegration after prison in Norway. *International Journal of Prisoner Health, 15*(3), 282–292. https://doi.org/10.1108/IJPH-06-2018-0032.

McKeown, B., & Thomas, D. (1988). *Q methodology*. Iowa: Sage University Paper.

Munro, B. H. (1997). *Statistical methods for health care research* (3rd ed.). New York: Lippincott.

Schmolck, P. (2002). *PQMethod download page for Windows users*. Accessed on April 16, 2014, from http://schmolck.userweb.mwn.de/qmethod/downpqwin.htm.

Shemmings, D. (2006). Quantifying qualitative data: An illustrative example of the use of Q methodology in psychological research. *Qualitative Research in Psychology, 3*, 147–165.

Shemmings, D., & Ellingsen, I. T. (2012). Using Q methodology in qualitative interviews. In J. F. Gubrium, J. A. Holstein, A. B. Marvasti, & K. D. McKinney (Eds.), *The SAGE handbook of interview research: The complexity of the craft* (pp. 415–426). Thousand Oaks, CA: Sage.

Sjo, E., & Sæbjørnsen, S. E. N. (2018). *Hva er det som virker? Hva er det som virker på veien fra kriminalitet, rus og dårlig helse mot et liv uten ny kriminalitet og rusavhengighet, bedring i psykisk helse, trivsel og stabilitet?* [What is working? What is working on the way from criminality, drugs and poor health towards a crime and drug free life, improved health, prosperity and stability] (Working Paper 2018:8, accessible from http://hdl.handle.net/11250/2583150). Molde, Norway: Molde University College and Møreforskning Molde.

Slettebø, T., Oterholm, I., & Stavrum, A. (2010). *Brukermedvirkning i det statlige regionale barnevernet* [Service user involvement in the governmental regional child welfare]. RAPPORT 2010/3. Accessible from https://bufdir.no/bibliotek/Dokumentside/?docId=BUF00001076. Oslo, Norway: Diakonhjemmet University College.

Smith, N. (2001). *Current systems in psychology: History, theory, research, and applications*. Belmont, CA: Wadsworth/Thomson Learning.

Stainton Rogers, R. (1995). Q methodology. In J. A. Smith, R. Harré, & L. Van Langenhove (Eds.), *Rethinking methods in psychology* (pp. 178–192). London: Sage.

Stephenson, W. (1953). *The study of behavior: Q—Technique and its methodology*. Chicago: University of Chicago Press.

Stephenson, W. (1961). Scientific creed—1961. *The Psychological Record, 11*, 1–25.

Stephenson, W. (1980). Newton's fifth rule and Q methodology: Application to educational psychology. *American Psychologist, 35*(10), 882–889.

Størksen, I., Thorsen, A. A., Øverland, K., & Brown, S. (2011). Experiences of daycare children of divorce. *Early Child Development and Care, 182*(7), 807–825. https://doi.org/10.1080/03004430.2011.585238.

Sæbjørnsen, S. E. N. (2017). *Exploring adolescent service users' subjective views about participation in "responsible teams"*. Doctoroal thesis, accessible from http://hdl.handle.net/11250/2441908. Molde, Norway: Health & Social Science, Molde University College and Volda University College.

Sæbjørnsen, S. E. N., & Ellingsen, I. T. (2015). Q metode—et praktisk redskap ved innovasjon i kommunene [Q method—A practical tool for innovation in the municipalities, in Norwegian]. In E. Willumsen & A. Ødegård (Eds.), *Sosial innovasjon—fra politikk til tjenesteutvikling* [Social innovation—From politics to service development, in Norwegian] (pp. 249–266). Bergen: Fagbokforlaget A/S.

Sæbjørnsen, S. E. N., Ellingsen, I. T., Good, J. M. M., & Ødegård, A. (2016). Combining a naturalistic and theoretical Q sample approach: An empirical research illustration. *Operant Subjectivity: The International Journal of Q Methodology, 38*(2), 15–32.

Taylor, P., & Delprato, D. J. (1994). Q methodology in the study of child phenomenology. *Psychological Record, 44*(2), 33–53.

Thorsen, A. A. (2006). A pathway to understanding Q methodology. *Journal of Human Subjectivity, 4*(2), 33–53.

Thorsen, A. A., & Allgood, E. (2010). Introduksjon til Q boken og begrepsavklaring [Introduction to the Q book and concepts]. In A. A. Thorsen & E. Allgood (Eds.), *Q metodologi: En velegnet måte å utforske subjektivitet* [Q methodology: An appropriate means for exploration of subjectivity] (pp. 15–22). Trondheim, Norway: Tapir Academic Press.

van Exel, J., & de Graaf, G. (2005). *Q methodology: A sneak preview*. Downloaded 16 April 2014, from http://qmethod.org/articles/vanExel.pdf.

Watts, S., & Stenner, P. (2012). *Doing Q methodological research: Theory, method and interpretation*. London: Sage.

Wolf, A. (2004). Research strategies for policy relevance. *Social Policy Journal of New Zealand, 23*, 65–85.

15

Do We Need the Users' Voice? An Empirical Research Example Comparing Views of Service Providers and Ex-Prisoners: Implications for Practice

Siv Elin Nord Sæbjørnsen, Sarah Hean, Kristin Røvik, Bjørn Kjetil Larsen, and Atle Ødegård

Introduction

Understanding the rehabilitation needs of a person in contact with the criminal justice system is a complex task, especially when it comes to facilitating their reintegration after release from prison. The

S. E. N. Sæbjørnsen (✉) · K. Røvik · B. K. Larsen · A. Ødegård
Molde University College, Molde, Norway
e-mail: siv.e.n.sabjornsen@himolde.no

B. K. Larsen
e-mail: Bjorn.K.Larsen@himolde.no

A. Ødegård
e-mail: Atle.Odegard@hiMolde.no

S. Hean
Social Work Department, University of Stavanger, Stavanger, Norway
e-mail: sarah.c.hean@uis.no

A. Ødegård
Nordland Research Institute, Bodø, Norway

S. Hean et al. (eds.), *Improving Interagency Collaboration, Innovation and Learning in Criminal Justice Systems*,
https://doi.org/10.1007/978-3-030-70661-6_15

effectiveness of rehabilitation processes is dependent on an understanding of the factors that can increase the risk of reoffending. Offenders often face similar challenges, both when entering prison and upon their release. Issues like substance abuse, violence, poor physical and mental health, unemployment and poor housing are common. Prison rehabilitation programmes are fundamental to address these needs and reduce recidivism in the long term. These rehabilitation programmes need to be flexible, in order to respond to the ever changing nature of the challenges and needs faced by prisoners. Hence, the services providing them need to be innovative and engage in constant service development, something often achieved in small steps and incrementally. At other times there are calls for radical changes in service delivery. Both are understood as social innovation (Hean et al., 2015).

User involvement is generally seen as important to the credibility of these social innovation interventions but involving prisoners or ex-prisoners in this process can be problematic because of the vulnerability of this group as well as security issues. Involving service users in service development can be demanding and time consuming (Slettebø et al., 2010). Bjørkly and Ødegård (2017) argue that although the service user voice is often very useful and a prerequisite for high quality research and innovation, user involvement is not always possible—for example due to the mental state of the service user or the fact that newly released ex-prisoners are often in a particularly vulnerable place in life. Involving them in research or service development may be synonymous with exposing them to unnecessary emotional stress.

However, encouraging prisoners/ex-prisoners' to reflect directly on their experience of a service or current life status, may be beneficial by raising their consciousness and motivation for a 'new life' upon or on release. Recovery-oriented practices, for example, focus upon strengthening the service user's recourses, promoting personal responsibility and positive identity and creation of hope. Empowering the service user, supporting development of self-government and gaining insight into issues of offender reintegration from the prisoner's perspective, has proven to be essential to the success of these recovery-oriented practices (Slade, 2013; Sjo & Sæbjørnsen, 2018; Landheim, 2016). This, however, is often absent in practice. Larsen et al. (2019), for example, in a qualitative study of Norwegian re-offenders, found that there was a mismatch between the psycho-social needs expressed by offenders themselves and what the welfare services actually provided in the reintegration process. Similarly, Morse et al. (2014) reported experiences of an 'evil cycle' of relapse and recidivism, a result of what prisoner see their needs as being, being left unaddressed.

Balancing the benefits of prisoner direct engagement in innovation versus the challenges this may cause operationally, leads to questions whether service users should be included in the innovation processes with researchers and practitioners directly or whether the professional perspective of their needs might suffice.

Further, social innovation aside, we query whether an alignment of professional and offender/exoffender perspectives is also important for effective professional-prisoner relationships. Self efficacy may be a mediating factor here. Bandura (1994) describes self-efficacy as follows:

> Perceived self-efficacy is defined as people's beliefs about their capabilities to produce designated levels of performance that exercise influence over events that affect their lives. Self-efficacy beliefs determine how people feel, think, motivate themselves and behave. Such beliefs produce these diverse effects through four major processes. They include cognitive, motivational, affective and selection processes. (Bandura, 1994, p. 1)

According to Bandura (ibid.), a strong sense of efficacy enhances human accomplishment and personal well-being in many different ways, but people who doubt their capabilities will shy away from difficult tasks that they see as personal threats. The most effective way to create a strong sense of efficacy is through mastery experiences. For example, for ex-prisoners developing a skill and securing a job after release will go a long way to boosting their future self-esteem and efficacy. Another way is through the vicarious experiences provided by social models, such as seeing people similar to oneself having succeeded in their efforts. Ex-service users being engaged in service provision could provide such an opportunity. Strengthening people's beliefs in their ability to remain crime free can also be done by key people, such as the mentor, engaging in social/verbal persuasion, which again can influence exoffenders to try hard enough to succeed and promote development of skills and a sense of personal efficacy. Modifying self-beliefs of efficacy may also be done by reducing stress reactions and altering' their negative emotional proclivities and misinterpretations of their physical states' (Bandura, 1994, p. 3). It is anticipated that self-efficacy is enhanced if both mentor and offender share views on the prospect of a positive future.

To reflect on these questions, this chapter will explore and compare the views of professional mentors working in the third sector offender mentorship organisation, with the views of the service users (ex-prisoners) engaged in this service. As in Chapter 14, Q methodology is used as the method for exploring this subjectivity.

Using Q Methodology to Compare Views

Several research approaches and methods could be used to explore different views of the rehabilitation process. The value of Q methodology as one of these (Stephenson, 1953; Brown, 1991/1992) and as a means to explore subjective perspectives (views) is explored elsewhere in this book (see Chapter 14). This chapter adds to this discussion by presenting its value in comparing differing perspectives, specifically of ex-prisoners and mentors. This value has been shown in other contexts by Ellingsen et al. (2012), for example, who applied Q methodology to compare the perceptions of foster children, foster parents and biological birth parents on the concept 'family'.

Following the approach taken by Ellingsen et al. (2012), the point of departure for the comparison described in this chapter was the 42 statements that were already developed and applied to capture the voice of ex-prisoners/service users (see Chapter 14 for ex-prisoner perspectives). The statements were developed through interviews with service users on their situation as ex-prisoners, their needs and available services that supported their reintegration back into society.

Each of these statements was then modified to capture the mentors' perspective of ex-prisoners' understanding of their situation (see Table

14.1, Chapter 14). For example the statement '*I am good at controlling my feelings and temper. I never get carried away by frustrations and things like that*', was changed to '*Most of them are good at controlling their feelings and temper. They don't get carried away by frustrations and things like that*'.

The modified statements (see Table 15.1) were then applied to two men and three women mentors using the Q method (see detail of method in Chapter 14). Hereby, the participants expressed views about the ex-prison service users' situation, needs and service provision, by sorting the 42 statements according to the degree to which they agreed with the statements. The ranking scale from −5 to +5 (see Fig. 14.1), gave the participants a choice of as many as 11 different ranking values for each statement. The results of the service providers/mentors Q sorts are presented in Table 15.1. The mentors were recruited from a volunteer organisation in southern England that provides services to exoffenders in order to facilitate their reintegration after leaving prison. The service provision encompassed meeting service users' various acute needs and mentoring. Two of the mentor participants were employed by the organisation and three performed voluntary work.

The results of the five mentors/service providers' Q sorts and the three Q factors (or average perspectives) presented in Chapter 14 constituted the total of eight 'participants' in a new factor analysis presented in Table 15.2. Due to the small number of mentor participants, an additional qualitative comparison of service providers' and service users' viewpoints was also conducted. While the factor analysis may reveal similar or shared perspectives between mentors and ex-prisoners, the qualitative comparison focused on differences in views. Six statements that seemed to represent the most differing views between the two participant groups, ex-prisoners and mentors, were selected for qualitative comparison and presentation here. The five mentor participants' Q sorts and the three service user average perspectives (factors) presented in Chapter 14 was included in this comparison.

Approvals were obtained from the Norwegian Centre for Research Data (NSD; Project Number 54746) and Bournemouth University Research Ethics Committee. All participants were informed about the research project before they voluntarily agreed to participate.

Table 15.1 Mentors' Q sorts

Mentors' Q sorts (M1–M5)						
Stm.	M1	M2	M3	M4	M5	Statements 1–42
1	1	−1	−2	0	1	When they come out, they are often a bit shocked of all the different organisations that are there to help
2	0	3	4	3	0	In prison, they often feel like being left there with their own life crisis and nobody help to find out what kind of help that they need
3	−4	3	−3	1	1	Most of them have lost all ties with their family
4	5	2	0	4	3	Most of them really need treatment for anxiety and/or depression
5	−1	0	0	−3	2	Reading and writing are very difficult to most of them
6	−4	−4	−4	0	5	Most of them have somebody who really care for them, that has taken them under their wings
7	−3	−2	−3	−3	−3	Most of them, when they come out, have someone to help them to look for what help they can get
8	0	−2	−2	2	0	They find it easier talking to someone that has been in prison. It's the little things, little stories, they have a crack about it, they have a laugh
9	3	2	0	1	0	Most of them are brought up around crime and drugs and things that normal people wouldn't be doing…
10	−3	−3	−3	−3	1	Most of them have someone who really cares about them, that they can call at any time, just to help them thinking
11	1	1	3	5	1	We help them to become more aware of things that use to get them into trouble
12	2	−2	−1	0	−3	Most of them have plenty of skills and knowledge that would be useful in a decent job
13	−2	−3	−2	−4	−4	Many of them keep themselves strictly to straight people after release

Mentors' Q sorts (M1–M5)						
Stm.	M1	M2	M3	M4	M5	Statements 1–42
14	−3	−4	−3	−5	−4	After release, many would say that their life is actually getting very well, and that they are looking forward to the future
15	−4	−5	−5	1	−1	I am one of the service providers who grew up with the same issues as them and I have managed to change from a criminal way of life
16	4	0	0	0	2	It's really important to most of them to get in contact with their family again
17	1	3	2	1	1	We always try to help them to believe that they are capable of changing their lifestyle
18	−1	0	−1	0	0	Most of them think that if they make serious decisions about starting a new life, no drugs and no crime, they are fully capable of doing it
19	−1	−1	−1	3	0	It's really useful to them to see probation weekly the first year after release
20	1	4	5	5	1	The most important to them is to get their own space, where they can go back and say 'this is my key, my bed, my things'
21	−1	−2	5	−1	−2	To get help in prison, you have to constantly be pushing them, until they start wondering why you are behaving like that
22	−5	−3	−5	−4	−4	When they come out, almost everything is normally prepared for them, also a place to live
23	3	1	1	4	5	If they had the resettlement team from the start, they would start working on themselves and on the resettlement in prison
24	0	4	2	−2	5	To many of them, it's frustrating that it takes so long to get to see the mental health services. If it was easier, they would have seen them long time ago
25	−3	2	1	3	−2	Prison does help them too. If they were just out on the street, they might not be able to start an education

(continued)

Table 15.1 (continued)

Mentors' Q sorts (M1–M5)						
Stm.	M1	M2	M3	M4	M5	Statements 1–42
26	2	0	1	4	−2	If it weren't for us (service providers) they wouldn't have the stuff that they needed to start moving on in their lives. We try to help them to get back to normal
27	3	5	4	3	−1	It'd be easier to them if we (service providers) all kept in contact and collaborated. It'd be easier to them to meet all in one spot, rather than to see us all weekly
28	1	2	1	0	−1	They don't get anything out of probation. Probation just want to know that they are not taking drugs or doing crime
29	0	−3	−1	−1	−3	The prison officers really care about the prisoners
30	2	−1	3	1	2	Prison life isn't nice. It's similar to outside. People get robbed; people try to beg up for the need for the day and getting as much food as they can
31	−2	1	0	−1	4	Actually, I don't think they care too much if they have to go back prison again. Its almost like a holiday. Some even seem to like it there
32	0	−1	0	−1	3	In prison, they are asked what they are thinking about doing when they get out, like housing and getting a job…
33	0	0	1	−1	2	The only reason that they go to see EDP is that probation send them there
34	5	1	3	−2	4	Many of them change and start thinking completely different. They just want to live life as a normal person and don't want to do crime and drugs anymore

Mentors' Q sorts (M1–M5)

Stm.	M1	M2	M3	M4	M5	Statements 1–42
35	5	1	3	−2	4	When they get annoyed or frustrated most of them seem to forget all about what they've learnt about how to stay out of trouble
36	3	4	3	2	3	We talk with them about how they can handle different stressful situations that might occur
37	−2	−3	−3	−4	−1	When they are having some sort of crisis in their life, most of them always ask for help
38	4	0	2	2	3	When they get bad news or something like that, most of them use to take drugs/drink alcohol which often brings them into trouble
39	−1	−1	−2	−3	−1	They all want to move on in life, but after release most of them get charged for other, previous offences. Then they have to go back to prison
40	2	3	4	−2	0	The lack of contact between probation and other services often puts them in stressful situations, such as disturbing other appointments
41	4	5	2	2	4	It'd be better if we could come to see them before release, coming to speak to them so they get to know us, and we can make some plans
42	−5	−5	−4	−5	−5	Most of them are good at controlling their feelings and temper. They don't get carried away by frustrations and things like that

Table 15.2 Factor matrix with an X indicating a defining sort

Q sort	Factor 1		Factor 2		Factor 3	
F1	0.8808	X	0.3231		0.1004	
F2	0.1708		0.7953	X	−0.2072	
F3	0.1581		0.5735		0.6331	X
M1	0.2599		−0.2406		0.7853	X
M2	0.1835		−0.0229		0.8275	X
M3	0.4757		−0.2158		0.7332	X
M4	−0.2120		0.1617		0.8249	X
M5	−0.0422		−0.4839		0.7255	X
Explained variance %	**15**		**18**		**44**	

Results

Q methodology represents a middle ground between quantitative and qualitative research techniques, and therefore a qualitative and quantitative analysis of values in a Q study is essential. In this section we will therefore first present the mentors' views, qualitatively including a brief interpretation of the overall configuration of the statements and reflection on some of the most conspicuous statement ratings, specifically. Thereafter, we will present the comparison, which include factor analysis and a qualitative comparison based on visual inspection of six selected statements where mentors and exoffenders disagreed the most.

The Mentors'/Service Providers' Views

Like the ex-prisoners in the service user study (Chapter 14), the five mentors performed a Q sort. The ratings that each mentor (M1–M5) gave the 42 statements are presented in Table 15.1

The Q sort results presented in Table 15.1, for some of the statements, the mentors seem more or less to agree. For example, the mentors seemed particularly to agree that the service users are not good at controlling their feelings and temper when they get frustrated (they gave statement #42 the score −5 or −4). There are some differences on other statements, although there are few examples of differences exceeding six of the 11 possible rating values (from −5 to +5). The greatest differences were in statement #12 (ex-prisoners have skills that would be useful in a job) where mentors have not sorted the statements equally (from −3 to +2). Similarly, on Statement #31 (Actually, I don't think they care too much if they have to go back prison again. Its almost like a holiday. Some even seem to like it there), where values ranged from +4 to −2.

Comparison of Mentors' and Ex-Prisoners' Viewpoints

In the service user study (Chapter 14) all the 21 ex-prisoners' Q sorts were subjected to the computer-based factor analysis, PQ Method (Schmolck, 2002). The analysis resulted in three factors (F1–3) which constitute the average perspective of, respectively 8, 6 and 7 service users. The three resulting factors were interpreted and each group of exoffenders designated the titles of *The prison weary optimist* (F1), *The resilient optimist* (F2) and *The lonely, indigent and ill* (F3). As outlined in Chapter 14, a factor in a Q methodological study consists of 'persons' who have sorted the statements similarly, but not identically. The participants who 'constitute' a Q factor share the same average perspective.

In this study, the five mentors' Q sorts as presented in Table 15.1 and the three average Q sorts/perspectives of the ex-prisoners (F1–3) were subjected to the computer-based factor analysis. The analysis, which based on a total of eight 'participants', resulted in three new factors, presented as Factor 1, Factor 2 and Factor 3 in Table 15.2. In this table, F1, F2 and F3 refer to the three average perspectives of the ex-prisoners and M1−M5 refers to the mentors' Q sorts.

Table 15.2 show that the three original factors from the service user study, F1, F2 and F3 load, respectively, on the new Factor 1, Factor 2 and Factor 3. Strikingly, all the five mentors' Q sorts (M1−M5) load on Factor 3, and share perspectives with F3, which is the average perspective of seven service users, characterised as *The lonely, indigent and ill.* In this study, as in the service user study (Chapter 14) Factor 3 can be described as the most pessimistic perspective. In other words, mentors perspectives are most in tune with the pessimistic perspectives of the lonely, indigent and ill group of exoffenders they work with. They do not share the optimistic views that characterise other groups of offenders in receipt of their service.

In addition to the above factor analysis, a qualitative comparison was conducted, based on visual inspection of a selection of six statements that represented statements where there was the most disagreement between service users and service providers. The selected statements and the corresponding results from the individual mentors' Q sorts (M1–M5) and ex-prisoners' average perspectives (F1–3) in the service user study is presented in Table 15.3. The left column of the table refers to number of the six selected statements (10, 12, 14, 18, 31 and 42). The next five columns marked M1–M5 refers to Mentor 1–5 and their individual score on each of the selected statements. The three right columns of the table, marked F1–F3, refers to Factor 1–3 in the service user study (the three average perspectives), and the score on each of the selected statements. Factors represent a weighted average of Q sorts performed by participants who sort the statements similarly.

Table 15.3 show the mentors' ranking (P1–5) and the ex-prison average rankings (F1–3) of six selected statements where there was clear differences between the mentors' and ex-prisoners' perspectives:

Statement #10: '*Most of them have someone who really cares about them, that they can call at any time, just to help them thinking*'.

This statement was given the negative score −3 by four out of five mentors (i.e. P1, P2, P3 and P4), while one mentor (P5) have given this statement the score +1. In other words, four mentors do not believe that most ex-prisoners have somebody who care for them, that they can call for help and support at any time. As such they are most in agreement with exoffenders from *the lonely, indigent and ill* (F3) group. Although even the F3 group are more optimistic on this statement than are most of their mentors (only one mentor (P5) agreed with F3 on this statement, both scoring +1). The mentor perspective has very little congruence with those of *The prison weary optimist* (F1) and *The resilient optimist* (F2) who were service users that both believe that positive supportive relationships were available to them (scoring, respectively +3 and +4). These differences in views may imply that mentors do not have sufficient insight in service users' network. Alternatively, service users may include

Table 15.3 Comparison of viewpoints: service providers' versus service users' viewpoints, based on, accordingly, single Q sorts and average perspectives on six selected statements

Comparison of viewpoints Service providers/mentors (M1–M5) versus ex-prison service users (F1–F3)									
Mentors 1–5						Statements from the service provider study/service user study	Average perspectives of service users, F1–3		
Statement number	**M1**	**M2**	**M3**	**M4**	**M5**		**F1**	**F2**	**F3**
10	−3	−3	−3	−3	1	Most of them have someone who really cares about them, that they can call at any time, just to help them thinking/I have someone who really cares about me, that I can call at any time, just to help me thinking	3	4	1

(continued)

Table 15.3 (continued)

Comparison of viewpoints Service providers/mentors (M1–M5) versus ex-prison service users (F1–F3)									
12	2	−2	−1	0	−3	Most of them have plenty of skills and knowledge that would be useful in a decent job/I have plenty of skills and knowledge that will be useful in a decent job	2	2	2
14	−3	−4	−3	−5	−4	After release, many would say that their life is actually getting very well, and that they are looking forward to the future/My life is actually getting very well, so I'm looking forward to the future now	5	5	−2

Comparison of viewpoints Service providers/mentors (M1–M5) versus ex-prison service users (F1–F3)										
18	−1	0	−1	0	0	Most of them think that if they make serious decisions about starting a new life, no drugs and no crime, they are fully capable of doing it/If I make a serious decision to start a new life, without crime and drugs, I know that I am fully capable of doing it	3		3	3

(continued)

Table 15.3 (continued)

Comparison of viewpoints
Service providers/mentors (M1–M5) versus ex-prison service users (F1–F3)

31		−2	1	0	−1	4	Actually, I don't think they care too much if they have to go back to prison again. It's almost like a holiday. Some even seem to like it there/Actually, I don't care too much if I have to go to prison again. It's almost like a holiday. I kind of like it there	−5	−4	−5

Comparison of viewpoints
Service providers/mentors (M1–M5) versus ex-prison service users (F1–F3)

42	−5	−5	−4	−5	−5	Most of them are good at controlling their feelings and temper. They don't get carried away by frustrations and things like that/I am good at controlling my feelings and temper. I never get carried away by frustrations and things like that	−2	1	1

the mentor in their reflections here, seeing the mentor as the person that they can call at any time.

Statement #12: *the belief that service users have skills and knowledge that would be useful in a job.*

All three ex-prisoner types seemed confident of their employability in this regard (+2 across F1, F2 and F3). However, with the exception of Mentor 1 (+2), the Q sorts of mentors do not reflect this service user optimism (M2 −2, M3 −1, M4 0 and M5 −3) regarding their future employability.

Statement #14: *Their life is getting better and they look forward to the future.*

The prison weary optimist and *The resilient optimist* seem very confident about a brighter future (statement #14/both +5), while the mentors seem more pessimistic (ranked from −3 to −5).

Statement #18: *They are capable of starting a new life, free from crime and drugs if they make a serious decision about it.*

All three types of ex-prisoners groups felt that they were capable of starting a new life, free from crime and drugs if they made a serious decision about it (+3 across all ex-prisoner types). Mentors are again more pessimistic (ranked from −1 to 0).

Statement #31: *Actually, I don't think they care too much if they have to go back to prison again. It's almost like a holiday. Some even seem to like it there.*

All ex-prisoner types are adamant that they do not want to return to prison and had not found their time there easy (F1/−5, F2/−4, F3/−5). Mentors were less convinced and while generally believing that ex-prisoners were unlikely to want to return (M1/−2, M3/0, P5/+4) some mentors seemed convinced this was a possibility (M2/+1 and M5/+4).

Statement #42: *Most of them are good at controlling their feelings and temper. They don't get carried away by frustrations and things like that/*

According to the mentors', ex-prisoners have very poor abilities in controlling their feelings and that they easily get carried away by frustrations (Score given by M3 was −4 and the remaining mentors scored −5). In contrast, the ex-prisoners, especially The prison weary optimist and The resilient optimist had at least some belief in their own capability of controlling feelings and temper (F1/−2, F2/+1 and F3/+1).

Discussion

Overall this small scale and exploratory study has shown that offenders believe their behaviour is under control, that they have a positive future, that they can stay off drugs, that they have the possibility of finding employment and that they are able to remain outside of prison. Mentors are less positive (less naive or more cynical, perhaps) on the likelihood of all of these being possible. Mentors may have developed these attitudes for a variety of reasons including their own experiences of previous clients and hence knowledge of the challenges facing these people. They may also hold an unconscious bias against offenders, regardless of their experiences, influenced by societal and media representatives of this group.

The impact of a mismatch in mentor-offender perspectives on the mentor service user relationship and self-efficacy.

The comparison of viewpoints presented in Table 15.2 indicates that service providers, with a few exceptions, have a rather poor belief in the service users' abilities, recourses and future hope, in contrast to the views of service users who are more optimistic. Mentors and ex-prison service users view their situation, needs and potential in different ways, and this mismatch is likely to have implications for the mentor-service user relationship and the service provision in the rehabilitation process (Larsen et al., 2019). Whichever group prove to be right, there will be challenges facing the ex-prisoner in their aim to get a new life, free from crime and drugs and they will need several forms of help and support. Difficult but not impossible (Sjo & Sæbjørnsen, 2018; Landheim, 2016) and the mentor may be key to an exoffenders self belief/efficacy that he has got what it takes to do so (Bandura, 1994). The ability of a mentor to act as this key will be severely compromised, if not damaging, if mentors themselves do not believe that such change is doable. All of the above strategies to enhance self-efficacy are likely to be compromised if the mentor is less than positive about an ex-prisoner's ability to succeed in the first place. Poor professional expectations, as demonstrated in this study, may contribute to failures in rehabilitation programmes an eventually higher rates of recidivism (Graunbøl et al., 2010). Diminishing a person's perception of self-efficacy, may reduce his chances for change, by convincing him that he does not have what it takes (ibid.). This mentor's disbelief in the ex-prisoner's possibilities for change will permeate the mentor's attitude towards their work with the exoffender and they risk convincing the ex-prisoner that the targeted change is an unattainable goal. This could occur through the processes of exoffenders experiencing the stigmatisation of the ex-prisoner, that leads to antisocial behaviours entered into through the processes of a self-fulfilling prophesy (Rosenthal, 1994). For F3 ex-prisoners, their beliefs of the futility of their efforts are confirmed, and for F1 and F2 ex-prisoners their self belief may be eroded. If a 'recovery-oriented approach' is to work with these ex-prisoners (Sjo & Sæbjørnsen, 2018; Landheim, 2016), it is crucial that the mentor empower the service user and support their development of self-government (Slade, 2013). The basic in recovery-oriented practices is that the helper seeks to strengthen the service user's recourses, promote his personal responsibility, promote a positive identity and create hope. To achieve this, mentors need continually to examine their own stereotypes held of ex-prisoners, working against introducing bias into their interactions, and actively working towards promoting self-efficacy in their clients. The latter starts with the mentor expecting the best of and for them.

But why do mentors continue to mentor ex-prisoners, if they do not believe change is possible? It is possible that mentors get too occupied with meeting the acute, basic needs of the many service users, such as food and a bed for the night, and that they lack capacity to focus on the more long-term form of help, such as a lifestyle change. It may not only be the self-efficacy of the offender that is under threat here, but that of the mentor as well. Being in a constant fire fighting state, never able to effectively help ex-prisoners change in the long term, can do little to contribute to build mentors' self-efficacy. Whether it is the experiences of offenders failures or their own, if a mentor's belief in ex-prisoners' possibilities for change gradually weakens, mentors will be increasingly less able to help ex-prisoners break free from a trajectory characterised by crime, drugs and re-imprisonment (ibid.). Constantly meeting acute needs, and in return, receiving gratitude from the ex-prisoner in need, may create a view of ex-prisoners as extremely pitiful, wretched and totally dependent on the service providers help. Such understanding will, at least, make it difficult to convince the ex-prisoner that he has got what it takes to stand independently and start a new life.

Fortunately, the situation is not quite as pessimistic as the chain of thoughts above might seem. There are differences in viewpoints also among the mentors in this example study, and there are many examples of ex-prisoners who have successfully changed their lifestyle through support from recovery-oriented helpers (Sjo & Sæbjørnsen, 2018; Landheim, 2016). It may be useful to remind mentors of significant success stories to create hope and belief, in service users as well as in service providers. It may also be useful to use the Q sort cards described here and in Chapter 14 as a tool for mentors to gain insight into the world of the exoffender during consultations. It may also be used as a crossing boundary tool for clients and mentors to work together and compare their own views and the reasons behind them, hence building a path for communication between them.

The impact of a mismatch in mentor-offender perspectives on service user involvement in social innovation.

The second question posed in this chapter was the advisability of service user engagement in social innovation.

Leading on from the concept of multivoicedness discussed in Hean et al. Chapter 1 and Fluttert et al. Chapter 11, professionals participating in developmental interventions such as the Change Laboratory model may be called on to represent the voice of the offender into the developmental workshops and discussions. This may be advocated because the vulnerability of the exoffenders themselves may be an issue if they were to participate in the workshops in person. However, our study suggests that although the professional may represent the ex-prisoners' voice to some extent (see the agreement on many of the Q sort statements), they are also less likely to dwell on the positives of the ex-prisoners' future and their potential, but instead be more realistic/cynical about their prospects. Ideally therefore it would be best for the voice of the ex-prisoner to be heard directly and that allowing the professional to represent the service user is not ideal. If this is not possible, as will be determined by the individual intervention/context the intervention is being implemented in, then other means of presenting the view of the ex-prisoner, that does not solely rely on the interpretation of the service provider. Using the results of the ex-prisoners' Q sort of statements could be one way of achieving this, for example, using the cards and the sort as mirror material (see Hean et al., Chapter 8). Alternatively, interventions should acknowledge the bias being introduced by including the professional perspective alone.

Conclusion

This study is a small scale pilot study, comparing mentor and service user perspectives of ex-prisoner's future and successful reintegration and the tentative findings presented here must be trialed with larger population groups. However, the study suggests that, at least on a tentative basis, mentors have more pessimistic views of ex-prisoners prospects than the ex-prisoners themselves. This mismatch is likely to impact on the self-efficacy of the ex-prisoner. It also suggests that professionals are not best placed to represent the voice of the ex-prisoner in developmental interventions adequately. We recommend mentors examine their own perspectives of the ex-prisoner and work against any potential negative stereotypes they act upon unconsciously in their professional practice. Further, although we acknowledge the vulnerability of the ex-prisoner in the innovation process, we recommend that attempts be made to include the voice of the service user first hand into developmental work, creating a safe space into which this voice can be heard.

References

Bandura, A. (1994). Self-efficacy. In V. S. Ramachaudran (Ed.), *Encyclopedia of human behavior*. New York: Academic Press.

Bjørkly, S., & Ødegård, A. (2017). Brukermedvirkning i praksisnær forskning – hva er det, og hva gir det? I Støkken, Anne Marie og Willumsen, Elisabeth (red.), *Brukerstemmer, praksisforskning og innovasjon* (pp. 123–135). Kristiansand: Portal forlag.

Brown, S. R. (1991/1992). *A Q methodological tutorial*. Retrieved from http://facstaff.uww.edu/cottlec/QArchive/Primer1.html.

Chikadzi, V. (2017). Challenges facing ex-offenders when reintegrating into mainstream society in Gauteng, South Africa. *Social Work, 53*(2), 288–300.

Ellingsen, I. T., Stephens, P., & Størksen, I. (2012). Congruence and incongruence in the perception of 'family' among foster parents, birth parents and their adolescent (foster) children. *Child and Family Social Work, 17*(4), 427–437.

Graunbøl, H. M., Kielstrup, B., Muilvuori, M.-L., Tyni, S., Baldursson, E. S., Gudmundsdottir, H., Kristoffersen, R., Krantz, L., & Lindsten, K. (2010). *Retur- En nordisk undersøgelse af recidiv blandt klienter i kriminalforsorgen, Kriminalomsorgen i Danmark, Finland, Island, Norge og Sverige* [The return—A nordic study of reoffending]. Available at https://kriminalitetsforebygging.no/wp-content/uploads/2016/11/Retur-om-recidiv-i-kriminalforsorgen.pdf.

Hean, S., Willumsen, E., Ødegård, A., & Bjørkly, S. (2015). Using social innovation as a theoretical framework to guide future thinking on facilitating collaboration between mental health and criminal justice services. *International Journal of Forensic Mental Health, 14*(4), 280–289.

Larsen, B. K., Hean, S., & Ødegård, A. (2019). A conceptual model on reintegration after prison in Norway. *International Journal of Prisoner Health*. https://doi.org/10.1108/IJPH-06-2018-0032. Permanent link to this document: https://doi.org/10.1108/IJPH-06-2018-0032.

Landheim, A. (Ed.). (2016). *Et bedre liv: historier, erfaringer og forskning om recovery ved rusmiddelmisbruk og psykiske problemer*. Gyldendal akademisk.

Morse, D. S., Cerulli, C., Bedell, P., Wilson, J. L., Thomas, K., Mittal, M., Lamberti, J. S., Williams, G., Silverstein, J., Mukherjee, A., Walck, D., & Chin, N. (2014). Meeting health and psychological needs of women in drug treatment court. *Journal of Substance Abuse Treatment, 46*(2), 150–157.

Rosenthal, R. (1994). Interpersonal expectancy effects: A 30-year perspective. *Current Directions in Psychological Science, 3*(6), 176–179.

Sjo, E., & Sæbjørnsen, S. E. N. (2018). *Hva er det som virker? Hva er det som virker på veien fra kriminalitet, rus og dårlig helse mot et liv uten ny kriminalitet og rusavhengighet, bedring i psykiskhelse, trivsel og stabilitet?* (Arbeidsnotat 2018:8). Høgskolen i Molde og Møreforskning Molde.

Slade, M. (2013). *100 ways to support recovery* (2nd ed.). London: Rethink Mental Illness.

Slettebø, T., Oterholm, I., & Stavrum, A. (2010). *Brukermedvirkning i det statlige regionale barnevernet*. Service user involvement in the governmental regional child welfare, in Norwegian RAPPORT 2010/3.

Schmolck, P. (2002). *PQMethod download mirror.* Accessed April 2014. Available at http://schmolck.userweb.mwn.de/qmethod/downpqwin.htm.

Stephenson, W. (1953). *The study of behavior: Q-technique and its methodology*. Chicago: University of Chicago Press.

Sæbjørnsen, S. E. N., Hean, S. & Ødegård, A. (2021). Facilitating Understanding of Ex-Prison Service Users' Needs: The Utility of Q Method as a Means of Representing Service User Voices in Service Development. In: S.C. Hean, A. Kajamaa & L. Kloetzer (Eds.) Improving collaboration, innovation and organisational learning in penal systems. S. C. Hean, Improving Interagency Collaboration, Innovation and Learning in Criminal Justice Systems.

16

Reflecting on Researcher/Practice Relationships in Prison Research: A Contact Hypothesis Lens

Sarah Hean, Liv Jorunn Skippervik, Richard Heslop, and Caroline Stevens

Conducting research in the field of criminal justice systems (CJS) often involves cooperative working relationships between researchers from academia and working professionals from prisons and other CJS institutions. This is encouraged by policy makers and research funders insisting on user informed research on the one hand, and research-based practice

S. Hean (✉) · L. J. Skippervik
Social Work Department, University of Stavanger, Stavanger, Norway
e-mail: sarah.c.hean@uis.no

L. J. Skippervik
e-mail: liv.j.skippervik@uis.no

R. Heslop
Bournemouth University, Poole, England, UK
e-mail: rheslop@bournemouth.ac.uk

C. Stevens
The Footprints Project, Poole, UK
e-mail: caroline@footprintsproject.co.uk

S. Hean et al. (eds.), *Improving Interagency Collaboration, Innovation and Learning in Criminal Justice Systems*,
https://doi.org/10.1007/978-3-030-70661-6_16

on the other (e.g. Marie Sklodowska Curie Actions-EU Commission, 2019). The assumption is that positive working relationships between these two sectors are beneficial for both parties. There are many recorded benefits of partnerships, between criminal justice organisations (such as police, probation and prisons) and research/university institutions. For the practice partner, these benefits include access to methodological expertise (e.g. evaluation methods) (Drawbridge et al., 2018; Clodfelter et al., 2014; Nilson et al., 2014; Secret et al., 2011; Cunningham, 2008), extra resource or expertise in areas where there is limited capacity (Clodfelter et al., 2014; Nilson et al., 2014; Cunningham, 2008), information which helps improve services and decision making (Nilson et al., 2014) and intellectual stimulation (Cunningham, 2008). There are noted benefits for the academic partner also. The partnerships provide an opportunity for researchers to apply knowledge to real life problems/testing and refining theories in situ (Drawbridge et al., 2018; Clodfelter et al., 2014; Nilson et al., 2014). A better understanding of practice environment for both researchers and students is developed (Kerrison et al., 2019; Clodfelter et al., 2014) and researchers are able to collect data from the field and new and alternative data sources (Nilson et al., 2014). Researchers can hereby also be more in-tune with the needs of the community and society, making research more relevant and of public value (Clodfelter et al., 2014; Nilson et al., 2014). They can disseminate research findings to a broader audience (Nilson et al., 2014) and build a more diverse professional network (Clodfelter et al., 2014).

However, achieving these benefits is challenging. Logistically, challenges lie in limited human resources available in the CJS partner to support the influx of researchers into the institution (Drawbridge et al., 2018) and incompatibility of researchers and practice partners working schedules (Clodfelter et al., 2014). A high turn over of research students and staff entering CJS institutions can disrupt services interfering with their consistency and routine (Cunningham, 2008). There may be an over reliance on the drive and charisma of key gatekeepers and this may eventually threaten the stability and long-term duration of the relationship (Worden et al., 2014).

Communication can be problematic between partners. There may be a lack of clarity of what the research hopes to achieve, a lack of clarity on roles as to who should do what in the partnership as well as differing expectations about what the research hopes to achieve and time frames in which this can be delivered (Cunningham, 2008; Nilson et al., 2014; Clodfelter et al., 2014; Worden et al., 2014). These communication challenges can be exacerbated by cultural, language and historical differences between the two sectors (Clodfelter et al., 2014; Nilson et al., 2014). Practitioners, for example, report being intimidated by academic knowledge or being put off by dry, complicated, long-winded "academic speak". These differing cultural backgrounds are manifest in differing and competing priorities (Cunningham, 2008; Clodfelter et al., 2014) and different outcomes having different value for each partner (e.g., academic publications have different value in the two sectors—Nilson et al., 2014).

Challenges often come down to a fundamental lack of trust between academic and practice sectors, practice organisations being concerned about the confidentiality of information they provide researchers (Nilson et al., 2014; Kerrison et al., 2019) and fear that researchers won't present the full practice picture (Kerrison et al., 2019). They fear any innovation and departures arising from the research may threaten their local political and historical status quo even costing them their jobs (Drawbridge et al., 2018; Kerrison et al., 2019). At the end of the day, practitioners feel they, and not the researcher, will be held ultimately accountable for any impact of the research on practice both negative and positive (Kerrison et al., 2019). On the other hand, researchers feel frustrated that practice is not always ready to hear the outcome of evaluations and that their research recommendations are not taken up (Drawbridge et al., 2018). A lack of researcher support during the implementation of their own recommendations is often blamed for this (Kerrison et al., 2019).

To overcome these challenges, and promote the many benefits, policy makers and leaders of partnerships require a deeper understanding of the mechanisms underpinning these. Currently, studies of the benefits of partnerships are predominantly in the US context and little is known about the processes in the European context or any theorisation through which these benefits can be managed. Rudes et al. (2014) developed a framework spelling out the five key dimensions with which to manage CJS–academic partnerships effectively. These dimensions comprise means of negotiating access, having written agreements in place, goal setting, continual and iterative feedback and relationship building. This framework offers clear operational conditions for effective partnerships but offers less on the reasoning behind why these dimensions have an impact. Our chapter addresses this shortfall by exploring the use of the theoretical lens of the contact hypothesis to offer some of the required theorisation. The contact hypothesis provides an analytical framework with which partnerships between CJS and academic partnerships can be explored and better understood. Such an understanding provides the route to developing strategies through which these relations can be optimised in the interest of the subject discipline. It also contributes to the eventual care and management of people in contact with the criminal justice system. We apply our reflections to a typical European academic practice partnership (COLAB) in this field to redress the current North American bias.

The Contact Hypothesis

The contact hypothesis has developed from the seminal writings of Allport (1954) that explored the origins of intergroup prejudice. This proposed that the best way to promote positive intergroup encounters, is to bring the groups together. This contact provides an opportunity to learn about the other group and avoid the ignorance that promotes prejudice. Interactions with another social group may mean individuals revaluate their own norms and knowledge. This is a "process of deprovincialisation" in which members of different groups learn there are different ways of seeing the world (Pettigrew, 1997, p. 141). It is hoped that intergroup friendships will form during intergroup contact. These facilitate empathy and a sense of identification with the outgroup. These may later be transferred to all members of the other group more widely (Pettigrew & Tropp, 2006).

The contact hypothesis proposes, however, that contact alone is not enough for positive intergroup relationships. In fact, forcing two social groups together may potentially threaten the social identity of each respectively. This can confirm negative outgroup stereotyping. The contact hypothesis instead proposes that a number of conditions must also be present during this contact period if members of each group are to set aside their negative intergroup attitudes. The conditions, elaborated on since those originally proposed by Allport (1954), include that each group in the contact situation should have equal status, experience a cooperative atmosphere during the time of contact, be working together on common goals, have the support of the authorities of their individual institutions (institutional support), be aware of both participating group similarities and differences, have positive expectations of the contact event and that the members of the groups each perceive the representatives of the other group to be typical members of the group they represent. If these conditions are in place, positive stereotypes of other groups can develop, stereotypes that will foster positive intergroup working (Allport, 1954; Barnes et al., 2006; Paluck et al., 2019).

The contact hypothesis has wide appeal for its simplicity and operationability that makes it useful for policy makers (Paluck et al., 2019). It is well tested and used to explain and develop strategies to improve relations between groups of differing ethnicity, religion, culture, gender, age, disability, working groups and sexuality (e.g. Allen, 1986; Addelston, 1995; Beullens, 1997; Callaghan et al., 1997; Schofield & Sagar, 1977; Connolly & Maginn, 1999; Liebkind et al., 2000; Paolini et al., 2004; Pettigrew & Tropp, 2006). Extensive reviews of the contact hypothesis literature (Pettigrew & Tropp, 2006; Paluck et al., 2019) have shown that contact leads to positive intergroup attitude change. Empirical evidence on the impact of each of the conditions taken individually was difficult to establish and for all population groups (at least in the quantitative studies selected in these reviews). However, the conditions tended to interact and generally work best if taken holistically and conditions combined. The reviews propose that the key process in this structured form of contact is that "familiarity breeds liking" (Pettigrew & Tropp, 2006, p. 766).

In this chapter we propose that the contact hypothesis has relevance in the field of prison research also: professionals from the criminal justice services (CJS) and researchers from academia are two social groups who make close contact during collaborative research projects. Taking this theoretical lens challenges the assumption that contact alone between the two sectors is enough for positive relationships to develop. We examine each of the recommended conditions of contact originally described by Allport (1954) and elaborated by others (Barnes et al., 2006), using one illustrative example of a CJS–academic partnership (COLAB) to do so. This leads us to reflect on potential future strategies through which frameworks supporting CJS–academic partnerships might be manipulated. We explore how consciously managing conditions of contact in researcher/professional interactions may promote the cocreation and innovation required of these intersector academic–practice collaborations and as aspired to by popular rhetoric.

An Example of a Typical Criminal Justice/Academic Partnership

COLAB (Horizon 2020 funded COLAB MSCA-RISE project number 734536) is a partnership of European researchers comprising of 7 Universities and 3 CJS practice organisations from Norway, Finland, UK, the Netherlands, Denmark and Switzerland. COLAB research focuses on building effective models of collaboration between mental health and criminal justice services with the intention of impacting on mental illness in the prisoner population and reducing reoffending rates. Researchers in the partnership identified the Change Laboratory Model (CLM) (Engeström, 2011) of workplace transformation as a more effective means of supporting interagency collaborative practice. They proposed this as a means to optimise the effectiveness of mental healthcare provision to offenders through a model that fosters innovation and collaborative processes. The aim of the consortium was to explore the utility of the Change Laboratory Model in the CJS context and to enrich international research cooperation in this field. The work of the consortium is funded by the European Commission Marie Curie Actions (https://ec.europa.eu/programmes/horizon2020/en/h2020-section/marie-sklodowska-curie-actions). This funding body encourages intersector and international knowledge exchange partnerships that are operationalised through physical reciprocal secondments between academic and practice partner organisations. The refusal of the

EU Commission to allow virtual collaborations during the COVID 19 pandemic, and insistence that physical secondments across sectors and countries continue, is evidence of the importance the EU has placed on the physical contact between these academic and practice groups. The underlying assumption is that putting international researchers and practice professionals in close physical proximity, during these intersector project staff exchanges, will lead to useful knowledge exchange opportunities and enhance research–practice interactions. In the long term, in contact hypothesis speak, a central goal is a breakdown of intergroup stereotyping and negative group interactions. The contact between the different professionals is hoped to alter their respective views of the world in an attempt to seek consistency between participants' old cognitions, and to overcome the cognitive dissonance they encounter when meeting the different perspectives of the partner group members (Festinger, 1997).

The authors of this chapter are four typical COLAB members whose current identity crossed the practice/academic researcher sectorial borders in a variety of different ways. Two of us previously worked in the criminal justice system (social work, law and the police), but now work in researcher roles in the Norwegian and British University environment respectively (Liv and Richard). One is a pure researcher (Sarah) working in the Norwegian and UK university systems concomitantly. Lastly, Caroline, at the time of writing the chapter, was the newly appointed CEO of a participating UK voluntary sector organisation. The organisation is typical of what Abrams and Moreno (2019) define as an organisation predominantly comprising of volunteers that provides non-governmental (or non-profit) services to people in the community in contact with the criminal justice system. She has a Ph.D. in Natural Sciences but draws on her extensive experience in the voluntary sector in the UK in her current position. The authors used the contact hypothesis and the key contact conditions to reflect on the effectiveness of the COLAB partnership/consortium. Table 16.1 lists questions, based on the contact hypothesis, that we used as an aid for our reflection.

We present in this chapter a synthesis of these reflections. We combine the reflections of the four authors with similar reflections in the literature on other CJS–academic partnership working. We applied

Table 16.1 Conditions of contact

• Describe the point of contact between researcher and practice partner? • Do you perceive the researcher and practice partners to be on an equal footing? Explain. On what dimensions are they equal or not? • What does a cooperative atmosphere mean to you? Does this exist between partners and how can this be achieved? • Describe your respective goals? Are any shared? • Do have the support of your leadership during this interaction? How is this manifested? Is there a culture of collaboration with the other sector embedded in institutional policy/culture? Is working with the other sector seen as important by leaders • In terms of competences as well as values, how are you similar to your collaborative partner, how different? • Do you think the partner is typical of people in practice/academia? Explain? • What are the expectations of the other partner? Would you say you had positive or negative expectation of your partners? Explain

a simple analytical framework to the material searching specifically for the perceived *benefits* of the partnership, the *challenges, conditions of contact* between researcher/professional members and lastly *recommendations*. The latter are potential strategies through which the contact conditions proposed in the contact hypothesis might be optimised in this and other researcher/professional partnerships engaging in research and innovation activity in the criminal justice field.

Perceived Benefits of the Colab Academic–Practice Partnership

From the practice perspective, Caroline, as leader of an English voluntary sector professional partner, reflected positively on the utility of COLAB interactions and her experience as a practice partner working with both UK and Norwegian university researchers. These exchanges had contributed to the *personal development/competence of her staff*. One staff member had even registered for a doctoral programme at one of the partner universities. Interactions with university partners offered insight into the research process and specifically research into interagency working. Staff had improved their ability to cross national and professional cultural boundaries in their own practice, and had become more outwardly focused in their everyday practice as a result of their secondment experiences in Norwegian universities. The *professional networks* of her staff had increased, participants from this organisation having previously described the relationships between their organisation and the UK university for which Richard and Sarah work (also one of the COLAB partners) as non-existent. They now engaged with researchers from their regional university as well as the wider number of research and practice organisations represented in the COLAB consortium.

There was some reference to the partnership having provided further *resources* to the organisation: students and researcher staff from the local university had volunteered in this third sector organisation, contributed to tenders/bids being developed by the practice organisation and training events run for volunteers. There was, however, little made explicit about tangible instances where the secondments had made a *significant change in the development of current services.*

There were benefits for academic partners also, with a marked improvement in *the understanding of how practice works for both students and researchers:* through COLAB activity, staff at Caroline's voluntary sector organisation now taught on crime and health-related programmes in Richard and Sarah's university. Her staff were also cowriting with researcher colleagues in funding proposals and publications (as illustrated in the current chapter and others in this volume). This had enriched the *validity and public value* of these publications. Sarah reflected, as COLAB coordinator, how researchers working with the practice organisation, had found the shadowing experiences and research studies conducted in this English voluntary sector context had exposed them to the everyday lives of practice professionals and offenders. This leads them to better understand the language of practice and the service user. By actively working with professionals, researchers had gained insight into the challenges facing this sector internationally. Their growing *cultural competencies* served as a platform with which researchers could build their future careers in which their research could be more tightly affiliated with the needs of practice.

The authors reflected on how benefits did not only accrue through intersector interactions but that *intrasector learning* was also important. Researchers had learnt within their sector and across national lines. They described how they had learnt alternative theoretical and methodological approaches from other international and national researchers. Similarly, professional partners described how they had learnt about strategies in reoffending and offender rehabilitation from other public and third sector organisations in other European contexts.

> *Staff have also enjoyed and benefitted from visiting other researcher and practice related projects. The success of the project now depends on how well we imbed our learning into our practice for the future.* (Caroline)

In describing personal development, additional expertise, resources, research validity and being closer to the field, the benefits that members of this European academic practice consortium describe, mirror those reported by US partnerships elsewhere (Clodfelter et al., 2014; Nilson et al., 2014; Drawbridge et al., 2018; Kerrison et al., 2019). But what does appear unique in this European consortium is the development of cultural competences in our members that relates to the international and intersector exchange requirements imposed on the partnership. It was disappointing, however, that there was a lack of apparent impact on service design that had been reported in some of the US partnerships. We discuss later how the conditions of contact proposed in the contact hypothesis may account for some of these outcomes.

Challenging Intergroup Interactions

COLAB interactions were described as challenging and emotive by both researchers and professionals. For Sarah, as a career researcher, the researcher–professional interactions present in COLAB are exciting, stimulating but frustrating experiences. Liv reflects on the emotional challenge of crossing both sector and disciplinary boundaries. She talks of her first meeting with COLAB members as challenging her disciplinary confidence:

> *Meeting with all involved did not make me more confident. My legal method of research by interpreting the law, court decisions and documents was quite different from sociological method.* (Liv)

For Caroline, and other practice partners, they sometimes felt overrun by researchers during COLAB activity, that their voice was not heard sufficiently within the consortiums activity and that research rather than practice agendas predominated.

> *With a small team .... we have hosted a large number of researchers. Whilst the researchers have been able to undertake their work I do feel that a little more input from us could have been helpful.* (Caroline)

They find that COLAB research and the day job can make competing demands. Caroline for example reflects on coming to grips with the requirements of COLAB at the same time as taking on the new role of CEO in the company, managing the requirements of COLAB as well as making the changes to the structure and shape of future delivery of her organisation.

> *... we fundamentally feel that developing collaborative networks and learning from academia is important for our successful service delivery but are also aware of the demands made upon our resources.* (Caroline)

Sarah as coordinator also commented on the competing commitments of all partners in COLAB and how this threatened the project's deliverables. The different levels of autonomy members had within their own institutions were influential here. The high level of autonomy in researcher institutions meant it is easier to engage them and achieve individual agreement to participate in collaborations. However, these participants then ran the danger of becoming overcommitted as a result of this autonomy and were less likely to be held to account if the goals of the collaborations were not met. Practice institutions in contrast were often governed by more standardised procedures through which workload and permissions to engage in external activity are managed. They tended to be less open to this risk of personal overcommitment but having lesser autonomy, limited their degree of personal involvement depending on the available resource.

Sarah reflected on the relatively short history of the COLAB partnership, three years old at the time of writing, and that members did not know each other previously. She reflects that it takes time for trust to develop between partners, and this is particularly difficult to establish when the partnership is a new one and considering the geographical distances between partners. COLAB met briefly only during short secondment periods (on average a month) and when members met as a full consortium but once a year. She also reflected on issues of perceived accountability of the project. Although, as coordinator she felt this lay with her, she was aware that some of the other COLAB practice members, in facilitating access of researchers to practice sites (such as regional prisons), had mentioned that it was their relationship with these other organisations that was ultimately at stake here. This reflects the experiences of other academic–CJS partnerships where practice professionals believe they will be ultimately held accountable for any intervention recommended or introduced by the university. It is suggested this view can be exacerbated if universities do not stick around for implementation of any recommendation they may have made (Kerrison et al., 2019).

The reflection of COLAB members of the emotional and cultural challenges of crossing both sector and disciplinary boundaries, reflects findings in other studies where the interface of academic CJS cultures proved difficult. Practitioners were reported as intimidated by academic language in these studies for example (Clodfelter et al., 2014; Nilson et al., 2014). However, in our consortium, fellow academics were also intimidated by the language used by other academics, so this is not unique to the academic CJS cultural interface alone.

The logistical challenges mentioned by Drawbridge et al. (2018) and Cunningham (2008) are also relevant in the COLAB situation, the practice organisation feeling overrun by researchers during COLAB activity. Further our experiences in COLAB also reflect what Cunningham (2008) and Clodfelter et al. (2014) find in the US context, where competing demands of the day job impact on both the researcher and practice professionals' ability to focus on the partnership goals. Barriers to building trust are also reflected in other partnerships internationally (Nilson et al., 2014; Kerrison et al., 2019). The lack of voice of the practice organisation seems particularly relevant in the COLAB situation, however, although this may be related to the lack of shared expectations of the research also described by Nilson et al. (2014).

Examining the Conditions of Academic–Practice Contact

We turn now to a discussion of some of the key contact conditions proposed by the contact hypothesis. We explore how these may or may not be present in the consortium, and others like it and if these could possibly account for the benefits and challenges described.

Equality

One of the key conditions proposed by the contact hypothesis is that all participants should be of equal status when contact is made. This could reduce intergroup animosity engaging all parties in the collaborative work uninhibited by status differentials (Hewstone, 2003). The four COLAB members believed that, at a superficial level, professionals from practice and researchers in the consortium did work on a level playing field, particularly at an interpersonal level. The consortium was described as collegial and horizontal rather than hierarchical in nature. However, manifestations of inequities were demonstrated in other ways. The practice partners described a need to have greater say in consortium activity, feeling they were subjects of research rather than co-designers or participants in an exercise of co-enquiry. Researchers in the partnership felt equally frustrated with this. They were unsure how to free up the communication channels that would allow shared goals to develop and the voice of the practitioner to be more effectively presented in the consortium activity. This was despite researchers seeking input during the proposal writing phase, during management group meetings, consortium conferences and in the planning and feedback documentation that accompanied each intersector secondment.

The authors reflected that inequality may also have originated from differences in the numbers of practitioners from practice organisations (7 staff in 3 organisations) compared to researchers (23 research staff in 7 research organisation) in the consortium structure.

Each member spoke of their personal competences they brought to the consortium whether this is as a professional or researcher. They describe the distance or lack of overlap between professional and researcher competences at times, and how privileging one over the other may be problematic in achieving equality. The disparities in number and sizes of participating institutions may have inadvertently privileged researcher over practitioner knowledge in this case.

Sarah talks of her intention that the consortium followed a collaborative leadership model (Vanvactor, 2012), one that promoted actively "*ongoing integration of ideas and interdependency among multiple stakeholders throughout*" (Vanvactor, 2012, p. 561). She was aware that a hierarchy of coordinator/leader and management group structure still remained. The researcher perspective of Sarah, as COLAB leader, may have contributed to the dominance of researcher knowledge in the consortium's activity.

Privileging certain knowledge may also be dependent on the context and the activity in which practitioners and researchers engage. In consortium conferences, for example, disparities in theoretical knowledge between practitioners and researchers were made obvious. Disparities in research experience, not only between practitioners and researchers, but also within researcher–researcher interactions, were evident. This meant that researchers and professionals often put their own expertise aside and moved into the identity of learner rather than expert. They then failed to share their own personal expertise with the rest of the consortium. For example, Liv had expertise as a lawyer and social worker in restorative justice methods and negotiation within the criminal justice system and she was key to informing the development of the collaboration CLM models being explored in COLAB. She reported not initially feeling comfortable sharing this information because she lacked expertise in some of the other theoretical models (Cultural Historical Activity Systems theory—Engeström, 2001, for example) that dominated discussion.

Equality differences were also observed in intraorganisational, as well as interorganisational, interactions: leaders in the organisations often signed up for engagement in COLAB as a prestigious EU grant. Sometimes other staff members were then expected to conduct the detail of work they had not signed up for personally. For example, the research wing of a participating justice ministry was engaged as a professional partner. They then negotiated with individual prisons in the region to open their prisons to researchers. This may mean that, when one person/department in an organisation signs up for a project, this may impact on those who were not engaged in this decision-making. These individuals may hence be less motivated or have less capacity to participate as a result.

Institutional Support

Another key contact condition between CJS professionals and academic research is that the partnership, and its resultant project work, is supported by each institution's leadership. The four COLAB members reflected mostly on the operational level of this intuitional support. They described the permissions given by organisational leaders for participants to go on secondments and engage in research projects. These permissions were granted by trustees and CEOs in the COLAB practice organisations and heads of department, faculty leads and deans in academic institutions. This buy-in signals leaders' confidence and trust in the future of the collaboration and offers it legitimacy as part of staff's everyday working tasks. At a strategic level, Sarah, as coordinator, described achieving institutional support politically by aligning EU, university and practice policy with COLAB objectives when developing the consortium and hereby getting institutions to agree to participate in the original application. She referred specifically to institutional policies promoting researcher–practice partnerships and using the rhetoric of research-led teaching, user-informed research, evidence-based practice and internationalisation agendas to bring institutional leaders on board.

Cooperative Atmosphere

For people in practice such as Caroline, a cooperative atmosphere is tightly linked to institutional support. It was demonstrated through engagement of her organisation's trustees in COLAB processes, agreeing that staff be interviewed and freed from their work commitments to go on secondment visits. For Liv, a cooperative atmosphere is demonstrated by members' willingness to use time on COLAB activity and work with each other. She describes members being open and willing to help out, explain and reach common understandings. Members did so with a culture of hospitality curiosity, non-defensiveness and honesty about the challenges facing COLAB and what can be realistically achieved within individual and organisational constraints.

For Sarah, establishing a cooperative atmosphere in COLAB is about being consciously respectful of different positions, workframes and other work commitments. Instances of poor communications about when secondments would take place and expectations about what the nature of the secondment activity would be, tested this cooperative atmosphere. Secondment planning and feedback forms were designed to improve these channels of communication, although the use of these tools was not always achieved consistently, suggesting these communication tools were poorly understood and/or designed.

She also described a cooperative atmosphere as one that enabled COLAB members to share their disciplinary knowledge (including field experience) and discuss paradigm differences in a safe, creative space and in an atmosphere of reciprocity and shared responsibility. This was essential for building trust between members that would promote collaborations. Some of the institutional reports she had received from all COLAB partners reflected how researchers sometimes had become frustrated when practice institutions had not allowed access to practice sites or did not engage with research or interventions planned by researchers.

This is probably an indication that the needs of these professional participants were not being met (Virkkunen & Newnham, 2013).

Having Common Goals

Common goal setting is key to building positive relations between academics and prison staff (Rudes et al., 2014; Drawbridge et al., 2018). The premise here is that researcher–practice collaborations will be more productive if the personal goals of individuals participating in the consortium align with each other.

All of the authors in this chapter reflected that, at an abstract level, the COLAB consortium members shared a common goal of wanting to address the problem of reoffending and reintegration of prisoners back into society. For Sarah, however, it was the operationalisation of this goal and the more detailed goal setting that was problematic. She describes issues related to a lack of goal and role clarity within the design and delivery of more specific consortium activities. This was both important and challenging at two time points:

At the *design phase*: she reflects that, despite attempts to engage all partners in goal setting, there was a certain passivity and acceptance of the preliminary goals being set in the research/partnership application proposal. Many participants (academic and practice) took a leap of faith when signing up for the partnership. It later transpired that, in operationalising the goals set by the proposal, the actual substance behind each goal, was unsurprisingly often poorly understood. She felt this had threatened the potential for the project to get off the ground and later the commitment to its delivery by both researcher and practice participants.

Sarah describes how seeking funding for this research consortia had been driven predominantly by the academic partners due to the time and financial pressures to deliver the bid by a set deadline. This constrained how much she as coordinator was able to actively engage with the practice organisations during this time. Hence the immediate relevance of the project to current practice demands was not always immediately obvious to participants. This was especially because of the language in which the bid had been written that catered for the EU commission reviewer audience.

As coordinator, Sarah also described the difficulty experienced when writing the bid of finding a balance between allowing members to set their own goals versus setting goals for participants to address the wider objectives of the EU commission and the overall project's deliverables. She struggled to fully engage both practice and research partners in the proposal writing process in ways that were not merely tokenistic, whilst simultaneously communicating the overall vision of the project and meeting the funding application deadlines.

These challenges continued into the *implementation and delivery phase* of the project: each member of COLAB had personal goals whether this be to achieve a doctorate, improve their promotion opportunities or improve practice. Individual organisations had individual goals related to their remit: universities had the goal of contributing to the body of knowledge around collaboration in the criminal justice system. Practice organisations, such as Caroline's third sector organisation, aimed to improve their service delivery models. Caroline described her goals in COLAB as allowing staff to learn and reflect on their current practice and imbed best practice from other countries. She describes her organisation as a small team where it is otherwise easy for staff to become overly focused on current delivery in their small area. They seldom find time to research or reflect on best practice. She hoped that working with a range of researchers from different countries would enable staff to adopt a more reflective and informed approach to their practice, looking upwards and outwards for new approaches. She came to the consortium half way through its delivery period and felt unclear if her needs and goals were being addressed explicitly in the group.

Similarly, Liv came to the project a year into its delivery. As she found the restorative justice approaches not to be reflected or apparently compatible with current group activity, she questioned her motivation to be in the group. However, in beginning to cowrite this chapter, her contribution, in terms of understanding of negotiation theory and practice to COLAB goal setting activity, became clearer.

In Sarah's reflections, creating common and commonly understood goals was successful when practitioners and professionals engaged together during their secondment periods on common projects in which both parties actively participated. Cowriting publication or funding bids, coteaching on training events in practice or university teaching modules and/or disseminating together in various conference venues were typical examples of this. Hereby common goals negotiated by COLAB members became tangible, leading to improved intergroup relations rather than aspired ones. It also worked well when COLAB members were given permission to be flexible in their interpretation and delivery of the original larger project goals, as suited their own personal expertise and interests. Where it did not work well, researchers had come to the practice organisation with preset agendas. Professionals were viewed as gatekeepers to gain access to research data, rather than coparticipants. Although professionals were always highly cooperative in these instances, they often then failed to see the direct benefit of these research projects to their own organisations in the long or short term. It also did not work well if members were frightened to deviate from the original project remit and followed the original protocol regardless of their understanding or expertise. On the other hand, others sometimes found it difficult to adapt their own personal interests to fit within the broader remit of the COLAB project. They continued with these personal goals without linking these directly to the COLAB vision. Sarah describes searching for a mid ground, a balance between motivating the individual and allowing for creativity and exploitation of individual members expertise versus the need for a coherent vision for the partnership.

Identifying Similarities and Appreciating Differences

It is anticipated that the identification of similarities and appreciation of differences between the participating groups fosters both the cohesion within the group required and the dovetailing of key competences for the effective delivery of the project (Hewstone, 2003; Stephan & Stephan, 1984). For COLAB members, common values related to the subject focus area.

> *COLAB participants share the common value of believing rehabilitation of people in contact with the CJS is possible and desirable and that we share a rehabilitation philosophy towards punishment and custody.* (Sarah)

> *I would hope that all partners share core values around supporting individuals in the best way possible and this is certainly my perception of the people I have met to date.* (Caroline)

It was not clear if the consortium had stressed sufficiently the common values related to offender rehabilitation in order for members to feel bonded and have developed feelings of empathy. Cohesion of the group was felt to be strong but many members speculated whether this was due to personal similarities and the development of friendships generated through social informal interactions.

Differences between professional and academic COLAB members lay in their knowledge expertise, although the differences were not always appreciated. Richard talks clearly of the mystification of some of the participants, researchers and professionals alike, when facing some complex researcher theory for the first time. Similarly he talks of many researcher participants who, whilst bringing an outsider perspective, also have little or no professional experience and the resultant limitations this may bring to the field.

> Members…*find themselves out of their comfort zone when trying to make sense of some of the complex research paradigms and theoretical frameworks which the broader COLAB project draws on. Even for some of us with established sociological researcher backgrounds, theoretical frameworks such as 'activity theory' and the 'Change Laboratory model' can be quite challenging, if not downright bewildering!* (Richard)

Richard questioned whether there was an appreciation of knowledge differences between members and a desire to learn from each other or whether differences had led to a group of individuals who, regardless of background, had a pervading fear of being an imposter.

What is described here may demonstrate how a threat to group identity impacts on an individual's intergroup interactions (Branscombe et al., 1999). These threats may relate to a group's underlying characteristics being misrepresented or undervalued (e.g. lawyers being described as not trustworthy or academics not being in touch with the real world). Another threat is to that of group distinctiveness, where group members may feel their distinctiveness from another group(s) is being undermined. Hean et al. (2006), whilst exploring the stereotypical profiles held by university students of health professionals, identified clear perceived similarities and differences between professions: similarities between midwives and nurses for example and the complementary profiles of nurses and doctors on the other. They questioned, however, if the complementary competences of the doctors and nurses were equally valued. In our experiences of the COLAB consortium, there appeared to be an emphasis on difference between members in terms of their knowledge base. These differences were valued but served to make some members feel insecure, focusing on the competences they lacked, rather than an appreciation of the contribution of all the different expertise that each individual brought to the partnership.

Having Positive Expectations of Researcher–Professional Interactions

Having positive expectations of the outgroup may make it more likely, in a process of self fulfilling prophesy (Hewstone, 2003), that interactions between academics and professionals will be a productive one. Some COLAB members expressed having had few prior expectations of the partnership, however, and that, in fact, initial expectations were exceeded. Caroline, for example, had few expectations as she had not been part of the CEO from its inception, "*inheriting it*" from a previous CEO. She describes her only expectations as being that visitors were polite and professional and that her "*staff would be well looked when visiting other partners and this had in reality exceeded her expectations*".

Others had positive expectations that may have been disappointed and/or unrealistic. Liv had expected greater interaction with other COLAB members. Although she met with them during annual COLAB events, she had not had as much contact with them as initially anticipated. Overall, closer and more frequent contact between researchers and practice professionals was often less intense than initially intended as staff from the host often needed to prioritise their primary work commitments during an academic's visit. Geographical distances between partners also meant that contact was restricted to the time of the secondment alone.

Sarah had anticipated great contact between members and that they would demonstrate greater autonomy, self directed activity and ownership of their projects. However, members' commitments outside of the consortium activity limited this. There was instead an initial need for more directed leadership as members of this new partnership got to know each other, each other's skills and ways of working, and familiarised themselves with a complex research design. It suggested her initial expectations had been unrealistic or required the project to mature for a period of time before these were realised. Unfulfilled expectations may have come from initially little understanding on both sides of the constraints facing the other organisation (Kerrison et al., 2019).

Individuals Are Seen as Typical of Their Group

Wider stereotypes of a group are changed if the individual of the outgroup with whom one is interacting is seen as typical of that outgroup and not the exception (Hewstone, 2003). Reviews of the contact hypothesis literature conclude that if contact changes a person's attitude to people of the outgroup with whom direct contact was made, attitudes are transferred to other situations and members of the outgroup that participants have not met (Pettigrew & Tropp, 2006; Paluck et al., 2019).

In COLAB, some members are uncomfortable with stereotyping, preferring to see members as individuals rather than an outgroup. Caroline for example states:

> I *am not sure what a typical research partner would be. Having been a laboratory researcher, a qualitative and quantitative researcher I have met a myriad of different researchers. I think people are people. If we can come*

> *together to look at what works best, learn from each other and from service users this has to be a good thing.*

For others, they felt they didn't know enough about the individual or the group to make a judgement, as Liv states:

> *I don't know, I don't know how they were recruited, and I don't know them well as persons. Some do fulfill my idea of stereotypes.*

It is hoped that the COLAB experience should foster future collaborations between researcher and professional partners in the future, whether it be the continuation of this particular network or indeed in fostering professional researcher relations with partners yet unknown. But it was difficult from current reflections to determine the degree to which this may be the case, and may indeed be something to consider after the project's completion.

Conclusions and Recommendations

We have reflected here on our personal experiences of the conditions of contact within COLAB as a typical CJS–academic partnership in the European context. In retrospect, we now turn to some recommendations through which these conditions may be optimised in the future. We present these recommendations as a combination of the reflections on our own personal experiences, the recommendations shared in the North American literature on CJS–academic partnerships and intersector partnerships in general.

It should be noted at this junction, the limitations of the recommendations provided: this chapter is a theoretical and reflective commentary, using the contact hypothesis as a tool with which we have been able to make sense of our personal experiences. We cannot claim, however, any empirical evidence proving the contact hypothesis in this context as yet. More empirical evidence is required now to explore whether these have been the experiences of all our COLAB members or, indeed, if these have transferability to other consortia of this kind. We have no objective measures of the presence or absence of any one of the necessary conditions and we would recommend that, in the future, the outcomes and conditions explored in these reflections are more formally investigated. These investigations could include the measurement of change in attitudes to the *outgroup*, the presence of the conditions explored here, and the casual relationships between these.

We are not alone in this call for greater empirical evidence. Pettigrew and Tropp (2006) and later Paluck et al. (2019) show that in general contact reduces prejudice between clients but there remains limited empirical evidence supporting the impact of the individual conditions proposed by Allport (1954). Both reviews confine the evidence to randomised control trials, something difficult to orchestrate realistically in monitoring the impact of contact conditions in CJS–academic partnerships. More qualitative work is required to unpick the complexity and interrelated nature of these contact conditions and the analysis of our reflections here is the first step in this direction. With the above limitations in mind, we end the chapter with recommendations to improve CJS–academic partnerships as viewed through the contact hypothesis lens.

Recommendations Related to Equality

Every effort should be made to allow both academics and professionals to express freely their different capabilities and build shared values, mutual respect and insight into each other's perspectives. (Vo & Kelemen, 2017). More attention could be given to designing consortia where organisations of similar size are matched where possible and attempts made to recruit equal numbers of practice and researcher organisations. We concur with Aakjær (2013) who, working in prisoner-prison officer collaborations, recommends that the less powerful group should be overrepresented in group interaction so as to balance out the power differentials that may exist. In CJS–academic partnerships, having larger numbers of practice partners may balance the privileging of researcher knowledge that may occur otherwise.

Both professionals and researchers should take joint leadership of the consortium, with both practice professionals and researchers taking key leadership roles in the implementation and decision-making in the project (Cunningham, 2008; Secret et al., 2011; Worden et al., 2014). Even if leadership is nominally distributed, power differentials may hinder this from being operationalised. Virkkunen and Newnham (2013) suggest that the potential power differentials and inequalities between partners are often tacitly accepted. An awareness of how distribution of knowledge between participants is dependent on both the power differentials between members and the personal tools and theories that the leaders of the consortium employ, is therefore necessary. The potential for this imbalance should be made explicit and early in consortium development. It requires the articulation of the needs of all partners and making clear that these have equal priority within the consortium's activities.

Consortia could also explore the tools for building partnerships that might make better sense to practice partners. This could mean that knowledge exchange should not only follow traditional lines of seminar or conference meetings but include also shadowing of a professional's working days, apprenticeship models and study tours of both the researcher and practice setting. This will only be possible if the research goals cater to the priorities of both professional and research organisations and has institutional/managerial buy in.

Recommendations Related to Institutional Support

Pettigrew and Tropp (2006) suggest this is one of the most impactful contact conditions on intergroup attitude change and collaboration. Getting organisational leaders on side is key to the researcher–professional partnership. Institutional support is assured by the marriage of organisational and consortium strategic directions. Leaders should formally recognise engagement in the consortium, through inclusion of the work formally in staff workplans, and formalised memoranda of understanding between organisations (Nilson et al., 2014; Rudes et al.,

2014; Drawbridge et al., 2018). Staff should be encouraged to actively participate in the research, and be rewarded for doing so.

Clodfelter et al. (2014), and Kerrison et al. (2019) suggest that practice organisation may be more likely to buy in if methods such as action research are used that is more solution orientated. In the COLAB, project the Change Laboratory method is such a method but whilst appealing, the resource required to deliver this method remains an impairment to future collaborations. Further, a formalised COLAB consortium agreement was signed between all participating organisations that acted as a lever to assure resources were committed on all sides to the project work. This had only a partial success as other work commitments often had to take priority.

Recommendations for Building a Cooperative Atmosphere

A cooperative atmosphere may be developed through actively identifying the hurdles that block the attainment of researchers and professional goals. Consortium leaders need to remove these to ensure all partners' needs can be met. In other words, it is important to identify the priorities, constraints and costs of the partnership to both partners (Rudes et al., 2014; Drawbridge et al., 2018) and ensure there is minimum disruption to practice services (Secret et al., 2011).

Effective communications channels are also essential for the development of a cooperative atmosphere. Knowledge sharing is key to this process and could be achieved through the use of tools of communication or boundary objects (Star & Greisemer, 1989). These are artefacts or tools that are understood by all members regardless of group and span the barrier between practice professionals and academics. These are tools have meaning in both camps and mediate and facilitate the planning of effective knowledge exchange opportunities. In COLAB, intersector secondment planning forms and other monitoring forms were such tools. However, individual members of consortia need to understand the purpose of these tools and be trained in using these as boundary objects, preferably completing these forms cooperatively.

Building trust and a sense of co-dependence is essential for a cooperative atmosphere. Bringing in a trusted third party (such as a union or communications officer) as a mediator has been suggested. This individual should be able to maintain an ongoing dialogue, maintaining communication through continuous and iterative feedback on emerging and final findings (Secret et al., 2011; Clodfelter et al., 2014; Nilson et al., 2014; Rudes et al., 2014; Worden et al., 2014; Drawbridge et al., 2018; Kerrison et al., 2019). Communication also involves the researcher providing feedback on the progress of their research in a way that provides evidence on the issues in which the partner had shown interest Similarly academics may need to compromise on the nature of their outputs, investing in analyses that will never appear in the form of a journal publication but has utility for the organisation (Worden et al., 2014).

These suggestions are all in keeping with the conditions for the development of a community of practice: "*a group of people who share a concern or a passion for something they do and learn how to do it better as they interact regularly*" (Wenger, 2006, p. 1). Ideally, CJS–academic partnerships aspire to becoming such a community of practice. A community of practice not only recognises the need for an open dialogue between CJS and academic partners inside the consortium but a dialogue with those outside of the consortium as well (Wenger et al., 2002; Wenger, 2006). In CJS–academic partnerships, these external bodies could include the wider CJS community such as government ministers or other academic institutions. What Rudes et al. (2014) describe as continuous and iterative communication, Wenger (2006) describes as creating a rhythm for the community and the development of a range of different spaces, both public and private, within the partnership in which different levels of participation can be orchestrated (Wenger, 2006; Clodfelter et al., 2014; Worden et al., 2014). There is a need to combine a feeling of both familiarity/safety within the partnership but combined with excitement and a common spirit of discovery (Wenger, 2006; Secret et al., 2011).

Partnerships should consider also the development of strategic plans in which values and operational details to establish a collaborative atmosphere within the partnership can be explicitly articulated. This goes beyond the remit of the formalised memoranda of agreement or consortium agreements that focus on legal obligations rather than values. In the COLAB consortium, for example, grant and consortium agreements between partners and between COLAB and the EU, were supplemented with strategic and operational plans that were explicitly structured on community of practice principles (Wenger et al., 2002).

Recommendations for Goal Setting

The contact hypothesis proposes that CJS–academic partnerships should involve researchers and practice professionals collaborating to set common shared goals. This marries with the community of practice perspective (Wenger et al., 2002) that suggests working together on a common activity or goal will improve social learning and collaborative outcomes. Collaborative goal setting and planning is essential and should be done in such a way that the long-and short-term beneficial advantages to all in the partnership are made visible (Secret et al., 2011; Rudes et al., 2014; Nilson et al., 2014; Drawbridge et al., 2018). This ensures all members of the partnership see the personal value of participation (Wenger et al., 2002). Following on from the setting of common goals, members should clarify project roles, commitments, responsibilities and expectations about the deliverables coming from each goal and their intended use (Clodfelter et al., 2014; Nilson et al., 2014; Worden et al., 2014).

There should be some flexibility in the setting of partnership goals, allowing what Wenger et al. (2002) describe as a design for evolution. In other words, the interests of the partnership should change to accommodate both the changing needs of the offender population, prisons and academic members. The partnership should be flexible enough, and in fact welcome, the opportunity to reset or adapt goals as the partnership progresses.

At all points in the project, there is a need to explore how to maximise the engagement of all members in the goal setting process. The COLAB consortium, for example, was horizontal in leadership style, and consortium leadership has little or no formal or managerial authority over its members. This meant all members had an active role to play in driving the partnership forward. Leaders in each participating institution were engaged at the macro level, setting the broader project vision. Other members were engaged at the level of individual constituent micro projects. Activity at this level was not micro managed by the leaders of the partnership. Individual members cannot, and should not, rely on rigid guidelines from the partnership leadership to guide all their efforts. All members of the consortium have a responsibility to identify and negotiate goals, exploring where individual goals are not aligned with overall partnership ones and realigning these.

Negotiation is defined as "when two or several parties, with partially conflicting interests, try to reach a common decision" (Rognes, 2015, p. 14). Theories that underpin this negotiation process have potential as a useful lens to manage clear common goal setting at the time of proposal writing or when renegotiating project goals (see Table 16.2). The needs of all must be met and their values uncompromised, but negotiation is required around the way of achieving this. For instance, although the research outputs and the enhancement of the service are the respective (and unnegotiable) needs of academic institution and practice organisations, participants may negotiate on the project time lines and working schedules to achieve these (Worden et al., 2014).

Recommendations Related to Appreciation of Similarities and Differences

To appreciate the similarities and differences between groups, the members must first get to know each other's skillsets. Staff in practice could learn to understand and appreciate the basics of research. The consortium leadership could orchestrate some basic training in research methods for them, for example (Clodfelter et al., 2014). Similarly academics could shadow practice professionals and engage in tours of the practice organisation to learn of practice based competences.

Both CJS and academic leaders should emphasise the similarities between the two sectors and the staff within them, especially the common desire to improve the lives of the prison population and staff. This is likely to improve cohesion in the partnership and the cooperative

Table 16.2 Negotiation theory as a means of underpinning goal setting activity

Negotiation theory (Fisher et al., 2012) proposes that different parties need a clear perception of their own goals. They need to be able to see these as wholly or partially different from the goals of others in the consortium, and then to decide whether or not they are willing to negotiate around these. If partners are willing to negotiate goals, then negotiation begins with members of the consortium conducting a preliminary scoping exercise of the needs and goals of potential collaborators. Each individual spells out the dream or ideal goal of their activity on the one hand (the so called best alternative to negotiated alternative) (Fisher et al., 2012). This is contrasted with the bare minimum that they are willing to accept in the negotiation (the worst alternative to negotiated alternative—Vindeløv, 2013). This is a starting point for negotiating a commonly accepted goal and should be done explicitly and early in a consortium's development
After clarification of the stakeholder different goals, a negotiation process can begin to arrive at mutually acceptable common or at least compatible goals. This can be mediated by an objective facilitator (Rognes, 2015). Sarah as COLAB coordinator sometimes took this facilitator/mediator role. Other consortia might consider a third more neutral party to mediate this process. The type of negotiation strategy undertaken depends on the length of time participants have known each other, their knowledge of the other and the complexity of the problems for which solutions are being developed (Rognes, 2015). The longevity of the researcher-practice partnership, and the length which each individual member has been participating, should be taken into account when assessing how researcher-professional negotiations can be managed
When starting out any negotiation, researchers and professionals present their positions or current stand points (what they say is wanted). It is these stand points that are to be negotiated. In order to do this, the interests and needs that underpin these standpoints should be explored (why they want it) (Vindeløv, 2013; Rognes, 2015). Needs (e.g. a need for safety and respect) and interests (having an opportunity and space to be heard) are closely underpinned by values (e.g. democratic values) (Vindeløv, 2013). Values and group identities are hard, and often impossible to negotiate. Negotiations between researcher and practice partners should stress either where commonly held values lie and/or find ways of safeguarding the values of all participants. Promoting offender wellbeing and rehabilitation are in the interest of both researcher and professional partners in COLAB for example but partners may initially disagree on how they can go about achieving this. Researchers for example see building knowledge about prisons, securing future research funding and disseminating this knowledge as the way of achieving this. Practice partners, on the other hand, focus more specifically on their service duties to their vulnerable and complex clients, managing and securing limited resources. Exploring the motives behind these apparently opposing positions may make it more possible to find common ground. The group must question whether it is possible to meet the interests of all parties and/or whether there are alternate ways to satisfy their needs. The desired end point is for the voice of all parties to be heard and the interests of both parties safeguarded

(continued)

Table 16.2 (continued)

The negotiation process has many dimensions and may raise many issues. Conflict is one such dimension. Conflict, however, is an acceptable part of the negotiation process. Nils Christie (1977) in his iconic article "conflict as property" and the use of restorative justice, suggests that conflict should be owned by the people engaged in the conflict and to allow them to use their personal conflicts as a means of growth. This means the consortium leadership should not try to resolve conflicts themselves for the rest of the group but allow individual professionals and researchers working together to explore their different individual project conflicts and find personal solutions. A criteria for using conflicts in that way is that participants are willing to explore what is in the conflict, why it came up and who is involved. Conflicts over different positions, interests and needs will always exist. The question is how we understand them, and then deal with them.

atmosphere required. Whilst commonalities in professional values are important, so too are personal similarities encouraged through informal social events where partnership members get to know each other not only as researchers and professionals but as people.

However, the different competences academics and professionals bring to the table need to be made explicit also and equally valued without any one set of skills outweighing the other in importance. In COLAB for instance, academic knowledge of formative interventions may have been perceived as more valuable than other competences. This may have impeded knowledge exchange opportunities and cocreation. The COLAB strategic document had attempted to redress this balance by making explicit the differences and similarities in COLAB member knowledge. This was done through cross tabulations of skills versus the organisation that provided these. This showed where expertise in each partner was either supplementary or complementary to those provided by others.

Consortium leaders could also promote an appreciation of difference through developing an atmosphere of interdisciplinary learning rather than of competition. At the end of the day, academics and professionals need to feel their individual competences both set them apart from each other but are equally valued at the same time: that professional and academic knowledge are held in similar esteem.

Recommendations Related to Having Positive Expectations

Researcher/professional partnerships should pay attention to the expectations members have of each other. This may be as much about managing expectations, rather than only promoting positive ones. Positive expectations are likely to bear fruit through processes of self fulfilling prophesy, but expectations also need to be realistic to avoid disappointment and the negative reactions that may result from this. Motivation is important here also. Engaging overcommitted staff to engage in a partnership is unlikely to breed positive expectations and partnership leaders should work on voluntary participation driven by the intrinsic motivations of the individual members. Attention should also be given to how the partnership is generated in the first place. Who has approached who? Has practice approached the university or vice versa? Practice organisations may have more positive expectations if they have approached the university for their support rather than the other way around.

Final Thoughts

The use of the contact hypothesis has enabled us to compare our findings with those in the North American context, showing the common benefits and challenges that CJS–academic partnerships share regardless of national context. The cultural context and the national policy context did not feature explicitly in the discussions of either our consortium or in the literature. The only national differences that came up seemed to relate to the structure of the research partnership: in the US partnerships described, the direction of travel is very much the researchers moving into the realm of the practice professional. In the EU partnership explored here, the direction of travel is reciprocal with researchers being seconded to practice but also the reverse. This funding structure, multinational and multisector in character, means that intercultural dimensions both strengthen and challenge EU partnerships in particular if compared to US partnerships. A more thorough examination of national partnerships structures, as guided by funding regulations, and the impact on productivity, would be a useful way forward in the field.

The partnership had been beneficial for both academic and practice partners but, perhaps more so for the researcher whose key priorities had been met (research publications new practice sources of data). Those of practice partners (service design) were less met, although unexpected learning had taken place in terms of cultural competence. Perhaps this disparity came from a lack of equity in the consortium when it came to representation and poor common goal setting conditions.

The attitudes of the academic and practice professionals in COLAB towards each other were positive, an outcome perhaps of a good cooperative atmosphere having been established within the partnership. Expectations of each other had not been negative although not necessarily positive at the beginning either. There was instead a more neutral, *a lets see what happens* approach. Friendships however formed across national and sector lines that further promoted a safe and cooperative interaction.

We find that the conditions highlighted in the contact hypothesis (especially related to dimensions such as goal setting and a cooperative atmosphere) dovetailed with those conditions recommended by literature using other alternative lenses (community of practice literature—Wenger, 2006 and the components of practice researcher partnerships, Rudes et al., 2014).

Our analysis suggests that equity in a partnership is more than being considerate of the fact that the voice of all in the consortium should be heard during project interactions. It is more complex and the initial structure of the partnership (in terms of initial attitudes towards the other group and the composition of the partnership) may mediate how equity plays out in the implementation of the collaborative partnership work.

Whilst common goal setting is listed in the contact conditions (Allport, 1954) and in the CJS–academic partnership literature (Secret et al., 2011; Rudes et al., 2014; Nilson et al., 2014; Drawbridge et al., 2018), concrete strategies/tools with which leaders in the partnership may work together to negotiate these common goals are absent. We raise the relevance of negotiation theory as a potential cognitive tool with which to develop a tangible means of goal setting and recommend that its utility be explored in greater depth in the future.

Paluck et al. (2019) suggest that the contact conditions should be seen as a whole rather than individual conditions to be manipulated in isolation. The building of intersector trust within CJS–academic partnerships is the key and overarching theme that combines the individual conditions together. Partnerships build trust at an interpersonal level through the development of a cooperative atmosphere and at an institutional level through gaining institutional support. Holding positive expectations of future interactions and believing other members have common values and that everyone's voice is heard equally in the partnership also builds this trust. It is this trust that enables the partnership to function and for members to act and be willingly to share their knowledge and time. It is this trust in the individual partnership members that will allow members to participate in CJS–academic partnerships in the future and for the academic–professional partnership to be viewed as a learning opportunity and innovative space (Darsø, 2012).

The analysis suggests that we have a lot still to learn about the optimal individual contact conditions and the configuration of these that are required. More empirical evidence, especially qualitative approaches, is required to explore this, the impact on partnership performance, the degree to which conditions were controlled in the contact and the duration of contact (Paluck et al., 2019). However, our reflections suggest that seeking out this evidence is indeed worthwhile. Articulating our experiences and those of others in terms of the conditions of contact between academics and CJS professionals has helped us propose tangible ways in which the intergroup relationships within these partnerships can be facilitated. The simplicity of the contact hypothesis, and the tangible quality of the conditions of contact, provided a clear way to articulate our experiences and provide explanations and recommendations that made sense to us, and confirmed those elsewhere, on how to improve the intersector relationships within the consortium going forward. Consciously managing conditions of contact in researcher/professional interactions may promote the cocreation and innovation required of these intersector academic–practice collaborations to which we all aspire.

References

Akjær, M. (2013). *Reconfiguring boundaries in social innovation.* Doctoral thesis. Aarhus University, Aarhus.

Abrams, L. S., & Moreno, L. (2019). The voluntary sector role in youth and young adult justice services: A comparative case study of Finland and England/Wales. *Youth Justice, 19*(3), 278–298.

Addelston, J. (1995). *Exploring masculinities: Gender enactments in preparatory high schools.* Unpublished dissertation. New York: CUNY.

Allport, G. W. (1954). *The nature of prejudice.* Cambridge, MA: Perseus Books.

Allen, P. T. (1986). Contact and conflict in industry: Social psychology and society. In M. Hewstone & R. Brown (Eds.), *Contact and conflict in intergroup encounters.* Oxford: Blackwell.

Barnes, D., Carpenter, J., & Dickinson, C. (2006). The outcomes of partnerships with mental health service users in interprofessional education: A case study. *Health and Social Care in the Community, 14*(5), 426–435.

Beullens, J. (1997). Ageism in health care. *Acta Hospitalia, 37*(4), 41–51.

Branscombe, N. R., Ellemers, N., Spears, R., & Doosje, B. (1999). The context and content of social identity threat. In N. Ellemers, R. Spears, & B. Doosje (Eds.), *Social identity: Context, commitment, content* (pp. 35–58). Blackwell Science.

Callaghan, P., Shan, C. S., Yu, L. S., Ching, L. W., & Kwan, T. L. (1997). Attitudes towards mental illness: Testing the contact hypothesis among Chinese student nurses in Hong Kong. *Journal of Advanced Nursing, 26,* 33–40.

Clodfelter, T. A., Alexander, M. A., Holcomb, J. E., Marcum, S. C., & Richards, T. (2014). Improving probation officer effectiveness through agency—University collaboration. *Criminal Justice Studies, 27*(3), 308–322. Routledge.

Connolly, P., & Maginn, P. (1999). *Sectarianism, children and community relations in Northern Ireland.* Ulster: Coleraine: Centre for the Study of Conflict, University of Ulster.

Christie, N. (1977). Conflict as property. *British Journal of Criminology, 17,* 1–26.

Cunningham, W. S. (2008). Voices from the field. *Action Research, 6*(4), 373–390.

Darsø, L. (2012). Innovation competency—An essential organizational asset. In S. Høyrup, M. Bonnafous-Boucher, C. Hasse, M. Lotz, & K. Møller

(Eds.), *Employee-driven innovation—A new approach*. Hampshire and New York: Palgrave Macmillan.

Drawbridge, D. C., Taheri, S. A., & Frost, N. A. (2018). Building and sustaining academic researcher and criminal justice practitioner partnerships: A corrections example. *American Journal of Criminal Justice, 43,* 627–640.

Engeström, Y. (2001). Expansive learning at work: Toward an activity theoretical reconceptualization. *Journal of Education and Work, 14*(1), 133–156.

Engeström, Y. (2011). F. design experiments to formative interventions. *Theory & Psychology, 21*(5), 598–628.

EU Commission. (2019). *Marie Skłodowska-Curie actions*. https://ec.europa.eu/research/mariecurieactions/msca-actions_en. Accessed November 2019.

Festinger, L. (1997). *A theory of cognitive dissonance*. Evanston, IL: Row Peterson.

Fisher, R., Ury, W., & Patton, B. (2012). *Getting to yes*. London: The Random House Business Books.

Hean, S., Macleod Clark, J., Adams, K., & Humphris, D. (2006). Will opposites attract? Similarities and differences in students' perceptions of the stereotype profiles of other health and social care professional groups. *Journal of Interprofessional Care, 20*(2), 162–181.

Hewstone, M. (2003). Intergroup contact: Panacea for prejudice? *The Psychologist, 16,* 352–355.

Kerrison, E. M., et al. (2019). On creating ethical, productive, and durable research partnerships with police officers and their departments: A case study of the National Justice Database. *Police Practice and Research, 20*(6), 567–584. Routledge.

Liebkind, K., Haaramo, J., & Jasinskaja-Lahti, I. (2000). Effects of contact and personality on intergroup attitudes of different professionals. *Journal of Community and Applied Social Psychology, 10,* 171–181.

Nilson, C., et al. (2014). Community-engaged scholarship: The experience of ongoing collaboration between criminal justice professionals and scholars at the University of Saskatchewan. *Criminal Justice Studies, 27*(3), 264–277. Routledge.

Paluck, E. L., Green, S. A., & Green, D. P. (2019). The contact hypothesis re-evaluated. *Behavioural Public Policy, 3*(02), 129–158. https://doi.org/10.1017/bpp.2018.25.

Paolini, S., Hewstone, M., Cairns, E., & Voci, A. (2004). Effects of direct and indirect cross-group friendships on judgments of catholics and protestants in Northern Ireland: The mediating role of an anxiety-reduction mechanism. *Personality and Social Psychology Bulletin, 30,* 770–786.

Pettigrew, T. F. (1997). Generalized intergroup contact effects on prejudice. *Personality and Social Psychology Bulletin, 23,* 173–185.

Pettigrew, T. F., & Tropp, L. R. (2006). A meta-analytic test of intergroup contact theory. *Journal of Personality and Social Psychology, 90*(5), 751–783.

Rognes, J. (2015). *Forhandlinger*. Oslo: Universitetsforlaget.

Rudes, D. S., et al. (2014). Build to sustain: collaborative partnerships between university researchers and criminal justice practitioners. *Criminal Justice Studies, 27*(3), 249–263.

Schofield, J. W., & Sagar, H. A. (1977). Peer interaction patterns in an integrated middle school. *Sociometry, 40,* 130–138.

Secret, M., Abell, M. L., & Berlin, T. (2011). The promise and challenge of practice—Research collaborations: Guiding principles and strategies for initiating, designing, and implementing program evaluation research. *Social Work, 16*(1), 9–20.

Star, S. L., & Greisemer, J. R. (1989). Institutional ecology, 'translations' and boundary objects: Amateurs and professionals in Berkeley's Museum of vertebrate zoology. *Social Studies of Science, 19*(3), 1907–1939.

Stephan, W. G., & Stephan, C. W. (1984). The role of ignorance in intergroup relations. In N. Miller & M. B. Brewer (Eds.), *Groups in contact*. New York: Academic Press.

Vanvactor, J. D. (2012). Collaborative leadership model in the management of health care. *Journal of Business Research, 55*(4), 555–561.

Vindeløv, V. (2013). *Konfliktmægling: en refleksiv model*. København: Jurist-og Økonomforbundets Forlag.

Virkkunen, J., & Newnham, D. S. (2013). *The change laboratory*. Rotterdam: Sense Publishers.

Vo, L., & Kelemen, M. (2017). Collaborating across the researcher-practitioner divide. *Journal of Organizational Change Management, 30*(6), 858–871.

Wenger, E. (2006). *Communities of practice: A brief introduction* (pp. 1–6). Available at https://wenger-trayner.com/introduction-to-communities-of-practice/. Accessed 1 May 2020.

Wenger, E., McDermott, R., & Snyder, W. M. (2002). *Cultivating communities of practice*. Boston: Harvard Business Press.

Worden, R. E., et al. (2014). Research partners in criminal justice: Notes from Syracuse. *Criminal Justice Studies, 27*(3), 278–293.s. Routledge.

17

Developing a Training Programme for Collaborative Practices Between Criminal Justice and Mental Health Services: The Gap Between Intentions and Reality

Atle Ødegård and Elisabeth Willumsen

Introduction

The main intention of the EU funded COLAB project (COLAB-H2020-MSCA-RISE-2016/734,536) was to introduce new ways of collaborating and innovating into the criminal justice system (CJS) context. This would be supported by interprofessional training in the field (Hean et al., 2015a). This need for interprofessional training is supported by The Lancet Commission (Frank et al., 2010) who stated that there is a necessity for a 'global social movement of all stakeholders'

A. Ødegård (✉) · E. Willumsen
Molde University College, Molde, Norway
e-mail: Atle.Odegard@hiMolde.no

A. Ødegård
Nordland Research Institute, Bodø, Norway

E. Willumsen
Faculty of Health Sciences, University of Stavanger, Stavanger, Norway
e-mail: elisabeth.willumsen@uis.no

S. Hean et al. (eds.), *Improving Interagency Collaboration, Innovation and Learning in Criminal Justice Systems*,
https://doi.org/10.1007/978-3-030-70661-6_17

to promote 'transformative professional education' to improve health care (p. 3). To develop such education, academics and researchers need to interact and follow closely the needs of the field of practice. This was highlighted in the *World Declaration on Higher Education for the Twenty-First Century: Vision and Action* (UNESCO, 1998) which recommended higher education and research be available to most people and benefit society. In Norway, a main partner country in the COLAB consortium, authorities explicitly emphasise the strengthening of academic-practice research partnerships, i.e. that representatives from the field need to take part in all phases of a research process (Alstveit et al., 2017; Norwegian Research Council [NRC], 2012; White Paper no. 4 [2018–2019]). Based on this framework, the assumption is that partnership between academia and practice is necessary to improve services in health and welfare and services should be prepared/trained to work in this way. Such a partnership served as a starting point for the COLAB project. One of objectives of the COLAB project was to develop a training programme in collaborative practices. The aim was to improve collaboration competences and awareness and readiness for the innovation interventions described in Chapter 8. The target audience were frontline professionals working in criminal justice (CJS) and mental health services (MHS).

As will be illustrated in this chapter (and also Chapter 16 of this volume), it is not a given that the original plans for a project will work out as intended when implemented in practice. Although academics and frontline professionals may both have good intentions, they may also have very different views of the world. For example, academics may introduce what they regard as interesting collaboration models but these may not necessarily be models that are regarded by frontline professionals and users as relevant to their needs. Hence, there may be a gap between academics/researchers and frontline professionals in their different understandings of what is needed in the field. This gap may be much greater than expected and will be elaborated on in this chapter.

Aim of the Colab Project

The Change Laboratory Model (CLM) is basically an activity where participants from different systems and/or organisations are brought together to reflect on their working practices. The CLM has had great success as an intervention in a range of different contexts (see e.g. Engeström et al., 1996; Virkkunen & Newham, 2013). The CLM has potential in the CJS/MHS field (Hean et al., 2018), for professionals from across different contexts to explore each other's perspectives and consequently reach new solutions for service delivery that is context-specific and user informed. A potential for innovation might arise during this collaboration process (see also Chapter 8 where the CLM is presented and elaborated).

In the COLAB project entitled *Improving Collaborative Working Between Correctional and Mental Health Services* (Hean, 2016), the aim was to validate that the Change Laboratory Model (CLM) was ready for implementation in CJS practice. As Hean (2016) argued in the proposal to the EU:

> *The Change Laboratory, highly successful internationally and in other clinical contexts, is a new idea in prison development, none as yet being applied to the challenges facing the MHS and CS. The wickedness, complexity and unpredictability of challenges facing interagency working in these secure environments means that piloting the CLM is premature and it must first be adapted to the MHS/CS context.* (p. 2)

The COLAB project consists of several work-packages (WPs), and the present chapter focuses on one of these: the process of developing a training programme that would prepare professionals for their participation in interventions such as the CLM. Academics, together with a third-sector mentorship charity (non-academic partner), were responsible for designing a preliminary framework for training key skills in interprofessional collaboration for frontline professionals in the field. Various challenges arose during the collaboration which affected both the intentions of the project as a whole (EU proposal level) as well as the implementation of designing and carrying out the training programme (practice, real world level). Hence, contradictions between these levels occurred that played out in the collaborative efforts that took place and needed to be resolved.

Aim of This Chapter

The aim of this chapter is to contribute to an elaboration of central issues and possibilities involved in developing a training programme to improve collaboration in the intersection between the CJS and MHS. The main theme is to illustrate and discuss the gap between initial plans (proposal descriptions) and designing/planning the training programme in (real time) practice, as well as to reflect on the learning that took place in this process. The chapter provides a perspective on the issue of aligning academics' and frontline professionals' contributions, in terms of views, goals, roles and utility.

Theoretical Anchoring

The COLAB project deals with the partnership between academia and practitioners in the field with the object of improving collaborative dimensions of the work carried out by criminal justice system practitioners and those in mental health services. Two levels of interface are identified: (1) the EU proposal level, consisting of the intentions, objects, plans and deliverables constituting the structural framework of the original project proposal submitted and approved by the EU Commission and (2) the practice, real time level, involving the design and implementation of a training programme designed to improve the awareness and readiness for innovation and interventions among frontline professionals. In order to understand and analyse the two levels and the interplay between them, the concepts of *community of practice* and *boundary practice* (Wenger, 1998) are relevant. Interfaces connect different communities of practice, such as academia and those of CJS and MHS in our case, and the interactions between them may be regarded as a practice in itself, a *boundary practice* where learning takes place. According to Wenger

(1998), such boundary practice may present sources of disagreement, misunderstandings and conflicts, but also opportunities for constructive collaboration and agreement, mutual knowledge development, and innovation and change. Several terms and concepts have been developed to nuance activities relevant to understanding the boundary crossing, such as *boundary object* and *boundary work* (Star & Greisemer, 1989; Wenger, 1998). In relation to the COLAB project, the training programme can be characterised as a *boundary object* connecting academics and frontline professionals, and the collaboration process that took place to design and implement the programme can be characterised as *boundary work*.

Social Innovation (SI), Interprofessional Learning and Collaborative Practice

Research partnerships between academia and the field of practice can also be understood as sites for innovation where new relationships for collaboration, different ways of knowledge production and designing/implementing change to improve services for the benefit of service users are created. The EU has launched social innovation (SI) as a strategy for designing new solutions to societal challenges (Bureau of European Policy Advisers, BEPA, 2011), which is particularly relevant for health and welfare services (Willumsen & Ødegård, 2015). A much-used definition of SI focuses upon how new ideas (products, services and models) meet social needs in the field and create new social relationships or collaborations (Murray et al., 2010; BEPA, 2011).

This means that SI has the potential to create solutions that can meet unmet social needs, within and across different welfare services. There may be innovations in the form of new products or services that help create social interaction, collaboration between people, and between people and organisations, services or businesses. In principle, SI contains the same components as other innovations (Bessant & Tidd, 2016), but the social aspect, creating social added value to deal with a social need, is not necessarily a prerequisite or consequence of all innovation. Hence, SI is regarded as relevant for the COLAB project as well as for the development of the training programme as the concept helps in understanding the complex and unpredictable collaborative interactions between academics and practice taking place to find new solutions to deficits in collaborative competences in frontline professionals working in CJS and MHS.

A literature review on innovation in health, education and welfare (Crepaldi et al., 2012) emphasises the relevance between innovation and collaboration. The authors characterise innovation in three dimensions: (1) the relational, with direct relationship between the user and the service provider, (2) the procedural, where innovation and dissemination is a continuous process and (3) the interactional, where generation and dissemination of innovation takes place within and between complex systems, contexts or areas of implementation. In other words, such innovations are characterised by being process-oriented and can include a variety of actors and their interactions at both macro and micro levels.

In exploring the relationship between SI and collaboration, it is relevant to distinguish between interprofessional learning and collaborative practice, although, in reality, learning and practice will intertwine. According to WHO (2010), 'Interprofessional education occurs when two or more professions learn about, from and with each other to enable effective collaboration and improve health outcomes' (p. 13). It is suggested by Ødegård (2006) that interprofessional collaboration may be perceived as a multilevel and multifaceted phenomenon. The wickedness of collaboration (Brown et al., 2010) may therefore be understood within this complexity. For example, some aspects of collaboration have to do with organisational factors such as 'organisational culture' and 'organisational domain'. Group aspects, such as 'communication between team members' or 'group leadership', are also central in collaboration processes. Finally, everyone participating in collaboration processes will have their individual perceptions of what to expect of themselves and others. For example, some participants may be motivated to collaborate whereas others are not. This implies that when trying to establish collaborative practices, collaboration arrangements between frontline professionals on either side of the MHS/CJS fence have to take into account a range of perspectives that have to be reflected in the training programme.

Iversen and Johannessen (2020) suggest that there is a strong connection between interprofessional collaboration and innovation as interprofessional organisational practice is often an unclear practice where practitioners have to give up some of their usual practices to create a whole new collaborative situation. In this regard, interprofessional organisational practice becomes a new practice that emerges from ordinary and uniprofessional practices. To the extent that this occurs, such a practice will thus bear all the hallmarks of being an innovation practice (Iversen & Johannessen, 2020).

We can, therefore, recognise an innovative potential when professionals take part in collaborative processes creating a new situation, a boundary practice (Wenger, 1989) moving from their uniprofessional background into an interface with their interprofessional organisational practice. The training programme is regarded as a boundary object and boundary work has to be in progress. This includes collaborative and innovative processes, as well as mutual learning, all needed to complete the design and implementation of the training programme.

Co-Creating New Solutions

When designing and developing a training programme of interactions, the concept of co-creation can be applied in order to address the complex elements related to interactions, collaboration and innovation between academics and the people in the field. Co-creation is relatively new to the field, and there is no unified understanding of the concept (Røiseland & Lo, 2019). However, the concept can include relationships between public actors, civil third-sector representatives and the private sector. Collaborative governance, networking and partnership are central issues. Co-creation may function as a fruitful approach when alternatives related to service provision and problem solution are deemed necessary for improving organisational structures and services.

Bason (2010) emphasises two advantages with co-creation. One is diversity, whereby a wide range of ideas may emerge during co-creation processes, providing more opportunities to find good solutions. The other advantage is related to anchoring and execution. Both identification of problems and design of solutions and implementation will be more firmly rooted among individuals who actively participate in the design of proposals for new solutions. Under those circumstances, the opportunity to achieve positive change may become correspondingly greater. As Bason (2010) argues, 'Co-creation can thus lead to radical solutions that overcome the silos, dogmas and groupthink that trap much of our current thinking, and can give us more and better outcomes at lower cost' (p. 9).

According to Torfing et al. (2014), innovation processes are characterised by several phases: first, a problem identification phase, in which a problem is recognised and defined. In this phase and throughout the innovation process, those in the field, including both the users and service providers, can make a major and important contribution by explaining what the problem is and the ideas they have for solutions (Bason, 2010; Voorberg et al., 2015). Second, the development phase, consists of creative processes, where individuals try to think outside the box to find new ideas or possible solutions. During the third phase, the test phase, the best ideas will be tried out in practice and any adjustments can be made. Next is the fourth phase, the implementation phase: This phase identifies and selects the most suitable solution to be used. In this phase, relevant solutions risk not being prioritised. Finally, the selected idea/solution can be shared with others through upscaling and dissemination (the dissemination phase). The innovation process tends to be more circular in practice, which will be illustrated by our experiences.

Designing and Implementing the Training programme—An Illustration

In the COLAB, the training programme was considered an important outreach event of the project and was regarded as social innovation. Beneficiaries were to be professionals in mental health services, prison service professionals, service leaders, policy makers and training commissioners. Initially the training module (named WP3) was intended to raise awareness of the relevance and impact of collaborative and innovative practice, within and between services, and to offer international insights into reducing offender ill health. The content of the training was to be delivered as a workshop, once in Norway and once in the UK to non-academic partners and frontline professionals working in CJS and MHS regionally. The workshop was planned to be held at non-academic sites to promote access to a wider number of frontline staff.

In the development of the programme much of the contact between the academics (who had the lead in the development of the WP3) and frontline professionals had to occur during so-called secondments. Academics had secondments in the UK, with a third-sector mentorship charitable organisation. During the secondments, academics and frontline professionals had meetings to explore each other's contexts, the potential for collaboration and what type of contributions were needed from collaborating partners to design and implement the training programme. For example, academics and professionals from practice discussed needs and opportunities to introduce collaboration/innovation training into the training of prison officers, on the one hand, and mentors on the other. In addition, the non-academic partners went on secondments for research experience in academic partner organisations to deepen their learning of research activities and knowledge development.

From Plans to Real Life—Illustrative Episodes

The COLAB proposal to EU contained several tasks and deliverables that also concerned the training programme. The deliverables, however, were plans that had to be discussed with the participants in the project—and especially the target group, professionals working in and outside the prison—to anchor ideas and discuss utility (cf. Bason, 2010; Torfing et al., 2014; Voorberg et al., 2015). The episodes below illustrate how different views played out in real life, and how 'plans/intentions' and 'the practice reality' became incompatible as contradictions arose during the co-creation process. According to the proposal, central tasks and deliverables for the training programme were the following:

- To pilot the programme with a select group of frontline professionals in two national contexts.
- To develop a framework, describing theory of Change Laboratory and other models of collaboration.
- To organise and arrange training workshops to be delivered in the UK and Norway.
- To evaluate the programme.

However, when operationalising these tasks and deliverables began, some obstacles and contradictions emerged. Some of these became apparent in a relatively quiet way, whereas others emerged abruptly and caused a major shift in the initial plans. Below we present some selected episodes to illustrate aspects of the collaboration and innovation processes taking place and how the differences between the academics and frontline professionals played out. These episodes show why there was a need to change the original plan. Academics appeared to perceive the EU application differently, including having an alternative understanding of 'training' than frontline professionals.

Episode 1: The COLAB Familiarisation Meeting: 'Tell Them Who We Are'

The first meeting in the COLAB project, where all participants met, was hosted by one of the UK university Partners. Several members presented their future plans in the project, and participants discussed different options for realising the project's aims. When a frontline professional from one of the COLAB practice partners was asked what the most important thing about the project was, seen from his point of view, he responded instantly: 'Tell them who we are'. Elaborations on this statement led us to understand that frontline professionals did not necessarily know about each other, especially not the work being done by professionals across services.

Comment: This episode illustrates that frontline professionals do not seem to consider themselves as being part of a larger system of service providers, as other professionals from other services do not know much about them. They felt they were not on the service map. This might have had implications for the development of a training programme about collaboration.

Episode 2: 'They Have Such Basic Needs'

During a meeting when the authors of this chapter were on secondment in the UK, a frontline professional made the following statement (referring to the service users): 'They have such basic needs'. After some questions about this, we came to understand that some of the advanced collaboration ideas proposed in the COLAB application and strategic plan written by academic partners, were far off target when compared to the acute and immediate needs of the practice organisations with whom they were working. We were told that persons leaving prison, often after several years, have a whole range of basic problems that have to be dealt with, that they seldom have any money, lack housing, have no work, are in need for education and so forth. Many also have major health issues, physical and/or mental.

Comment: This episode illustrates the lack of alignment of goals between academics and frontline professionals. It seemed like academics also wanted the basic needs of the offenders to be addressed, but assumed that collaboration, as a process, was the way to achieve this end. Practitioners apparently were more interested in *how* that's done; how offenders can function in daily life—focusing on the end point. The academics reflected on the professionals' views and thought perhaps they weren't so interested in collaboration after all because basic needs must be prioritised. The academics concluded that most of the practitioners were probably interested more in how they could manage risk and reduce reoffending, than in improving the abstract concept of collaboration.

Episode 3: 'Forget Courses—People Do not Have Time'

Some months later, an academic and a frontline professional met while the professional was on secondment at one of the university COLAB partners. The academic asked if the secondee could maybe help with some input into the planned training programme that was going to take place—one workshop in Norway and one in the UK. The secondee looked at the academic for a few seconds and said: 'Forget courses—people do not have time'. The academic was surprised, but also relieved. He was surprised because the secondee was so clear in her statement and relieved as he had been thinking a whole lot about how to design such a course in a realistic and useful manner and wondered about all the obstacles.

Comment: Through the deliverables presented in the EU application, the academics were committed to a 'solution' even before the project started. However, faced with the 'reality' described by the frontline professionals, the solution (training programme) was not an expedient option. In the professionals' work situations, resources are scarce and trying to establish a training programme that almost nobody would be attending becomes irrelevant.

Discussion

The main aim of the present chapter has been to elaborate some issues and possibilities for developing a training programme to improve collaboration in the intersection between the CJS and MHS. As Hean et al. (2015a) argue, there is a lack of interprofessional training in the field of CJS and MHS. This calls for innovation, and particularly social innovation, which concerns new ideas that work to address pressing social needs (Murray et al., 2010; BEPA, 2011). This means that the innovation does not need to be a 'product', but rather new ways of organising services in the transition from prison back into society.

In general, innovation in the public and third sector should create values for the common good and add benefits to the community. Related to the development of the training programme, those aims require extensive dialogue with relevant partners and actors who would be allowed to participate and influence the various phases of the process (cf. Bason, 2010; Torfing et al., 2014; Voorberg et al., 2015). Hence, when developing a training programme, one has to take into consideration the unpredictable nature of such processes, which means that proposed measures might be changed. Based on the experiences during the collaboration and innovation process and in light of the theoretical framework introduced, we present an illustration (Fig. 17.1) that links different aspects of the process. The figure shows how the 'training programme' is connected to practice 'needs' and 'perceived outcomes'.

A main theme of this chapter was to illustrate and discuss the gap between initial plans (proposal descriptions) and designing/planning a training programme in (real time) practice. The episodes above illustrate that the plans for training were challenged from the very start. The first episode (*Tell them who we are*) (see '1' in Fig. 17.1) from the initial COLAB meeting does not explicitly illustrate this, but raises some interesting points on which to reflect:

The episode says something about the need for information exchange between professions and agencies in the CJS and MHS field, and between academics and professionals, about each other's roles and functions. According to the frontline professional who brought this forward, it is not at all given that collaborating partners know about each other organisations and the services available for persons returning to society after imprisonment.

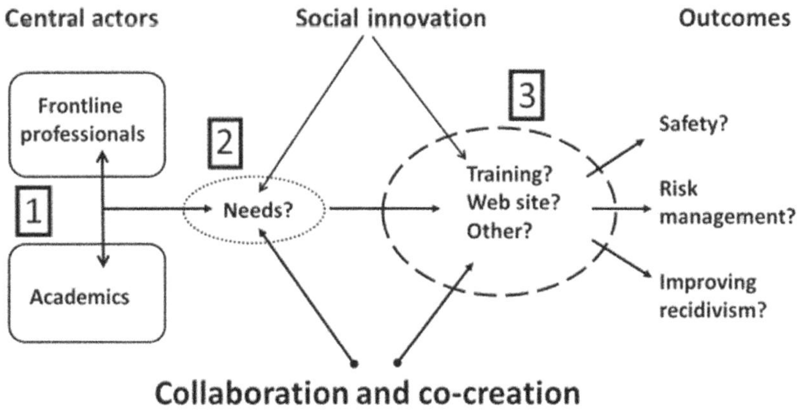

Fig. 17.1 Complexity behind outcomes in the CJS/MHS field

'Tell them who we are'—seems quite easy, but how do we do it? Is mutual training across agencies the right way, as, for example, in workshops? How many frontline professionals do we reach by following the original plan for the training events? Could there be other learning activity options? The authors of this chapter think: Yes!!! The question really is whether generic training is the right approach to the needs in the field. Actually, *training* may be the wrong word completely. Maybe the academics tried to provide a solution to a problem that they knew little about. Retrospectively, should the academics' tasks not have been to offer training programmes or other products, but rather to facilitate an exchange of knowledge and learning defined by the frontline professionals? In other words, the academics' role should rather be to support change and not to provide predefined solutions. Such a change approach (see Chapter 8) would probably have opened up constructive dialogues and co-creation processes.

In Episode 2, *They have such basic needs* (see '2' in Fig. 17.1), academics and frontline professionals may have perceived the needs of the CJS and MHS field very differently. Academics had, in the EU application, identified 'collaboration' as the target issue and wanted to introduce models that could potentially give positive outcomes for the different actors involved. Frontline professionals, on the other hand, were focused foremost on offenders' basic needs, such as housing, food, clothing and getting an identity document. This was also highlighted in the vision of the volunteer organisation participating in COLAB and with the stated aim to build stronger, more integrated local communities by providing person-centred support for offenders or those who are at risk of offending, reducing reoffending and increasing life chances.

Episode 2 illustrates the boundary work that is going on in the mutual boundary practice in which academics and professionals are participating and the importance of them learning from each other (Wenger, 1989). The parties have to engage in dialogues, try to take different perspectives and sort out disagreements in order to create opportunities for development and change. In this regard, Episode 2 also illustrates that the academics' focus had been mistaken. At a research level, academics can explore how collaboration between services will allow the basic needs of the offender to be more effectively addressed. The Voluntary organisation participating in COLAB is in fact a boundary crossing organisation in itself—in its remit and everyday practice. It aims to link offenders with various agencies and to improve collaboration in order to help offenders access services to meet their social needs. But what can we do to enhance this collaborative practice—when resources available to help offenders, at least in the UK, are very scarce? And how could these issues be approached in a training programme?

The third episode (see '3' in Fig. 17.1)—*Forget courses—people do not have time*—is linked to the prior episode. Episode 3 was of major importance and represented a turning point for further development of 'the training programme'. It became clear that an alternative to the suggested training programme had to be developed because frontline professionals unequivocally expressed that people would not have time to participate in a training workshop. Instead, the secondee suggested a 'website of some sort'—as frontline professionals would easily access this when they had some minutes free from other duties. The idea of developing a website gave a more flexible solution and opportunities for all participants to contribute. The academics and frontline professionals had reached a more manageable solution as a result of their boundary work (Wenger, 1989). The first phase of the process of developing a training programme, developing the understanding of the challenges and defining central problems was difficult due to academics' and frontline professionals' different views and experiences. The academics felt obliged to follow the initial intentions set out in the EU proposal and the subsequent deliverables, whereas the practitioners were confident that these intentions would not work very well in practice.

The development of a website as a resolution to these challenges may be regarded as an innovation, a product innovation. Related to the phases of innovation processes and the involvement of users (Bason, 2010; Torfing et al., 2014; Voorberg et al., 2015) the change of direction of the initial 'training programme' is a good example of how participants influence collaborative and innovative processes of co-creating mutual efforts (Iversen & Johannessen, 2020; Willumsen & Ødegård, 2020). Based on this new starting point, the activity of the work package (WP3) moved into a development phase (Torfing et al., 2014), allowing for creative processes to find new ideas or possible solutions regarding design and content for the website. In order to involve most of the participants (project members in the COLAB project), they were all invited to contribute ideas to the website. Experts from one of the University's IT Department were asked to join in the development of the website, and it was decided to construct a portal consisting of a menu including theoretical presentations, learning sections, podcasts (audio and video) and links to other relevant knowledge sources. The website is under construction and will be tested at the university college responsible for WP3. Later, after adjustments, the plan will be upscaled and fall to the permanent management by the host university of the COLAB project.

Social Innovation Through Collaboration and Co-Creation

Collaboration and co-creation are both central in our understanding of SI (see Fig. 17.1). SI simultaneously meets social needs and creates new social relationships or collaboration. In Fig. 17.1 this is illustrated in several ways. The 'needs' should be met, but as we have seen above, it is not a given how 'needs' are understood. Furthermore, SI both embeds and creates collaboration. Potentially, co-creation may take place in all relationships, and Hean et al. (2015a) refer to Bason (2010) and highlight four dimensions required for such development.

Consciousness

As illustrated by the episodes above, there is a need for different practice organisations, working with ex offenders, to inform each other, both as organisations and as professionals, about their various roles and responsibilities. This can be done in face-to-face courses, but there are other options as well. For example, as suggested by a frontline professional in Episode 3, an informative webpage could very well facilitate information exchange. Such creation however, raises many questions: Will each network configuration be different from organisation to organisation? If so, how do we help organisations map and connect with their social networks? How is the need for innovation or proactivity in the workforce encouraged through a webpage? And will a webpage actually provide useful knowledge for frontline professionals?

Capacity

It is suggested that the proposal for the training programme in the COLAB project somewhat overlooked the lack of capacity in some of the systems. Both Episode 2 and 3 demonstrate that it is more or less impossible for frontline professionals to engage in traditional training programmes—such as two two-day workshops. The reason is the serious lack of time practitioners in a clinical context have where there are calls for immediate action to help offenders receive basic services in the transition from prison back into society. There is no time for training, in the formal sense at least. It is possible that 'learning' rather than 'training' should have been the focus described in the original proposal. Learning at the individual and organisational levels is happening all the time. Still, as illustrated above in the Episodes 2 and 3, there is reason to argue that the development of a formal training programme and formal formative interventions is not the way forward because of lack of capacity. If this is the case, in what way can learning be supported? How do we achieve maximum learning with minimum resources as a prerequisite for a training programme?

Co-Creation

Ideally the idea of co-creation is relevant. But again, major lack of time and other resources will most likely limit co-creation processes taking place. It became very clear to us during our work in the COLAB project that some issues cannot be solved without basic discussions between participants to include diversity and obtain anchoring (Bason, 2010). How, for example, do different professionals, organisations and countries perceive 'punishment and rehabilitation'? The answer to questions like this have massive implications for how collaborative practice unfolds and for what kind of knowledge development is needed in the interface between CJS and MHS. Basically, co-creation processes (as with learning) require a certain level of resources at the organisational level before co-creation can take place at the individual/relational level.

Courage

The last point concerns leadership. What is leadership in the field of CJS/MHS, and in contrast to that in academia, and what possibilities do leaders have to develop 'bridges' across sectors and professional domains? What kind of leadership is required to achieve the needed courage to develop these bridges? It seems quite clear that leaders in all systems (academia, CJS and MHS) will need to organise arenas for frontline professionals to meet and connect. Once in the same arena, these professionals could profit from developing a thorough understanding of collaboration as a phenomenon, by focusing on different aspects and levels of collaboration (cf. Ødegård, 2006).

Final Comments

A main idea with the COLAB project was to bring academia and the field of practice closer together, to build networks across 'different worlds'. This is important as it is not a given that academics/researchers understand the needs of those working with offenders in the so-called real world like, as do the frontline professionals. A training programme was suggested (WP3) to bridge the interface and to foster interprofessional education to improve collaborative practice. However, as illustrated above, there appeared to be a divide on several levels, on a proposal level and on practice/real time level, as well as between the levels.

When writing proposals, researchers are required to describe and argue for their goals and deliverables, which means that in order to obtain their funding, they have to design concrete tasks and outcomes that are to be accomplished. The funding competition reinforces the effort to plan and anticipate solutions that give direction to the relevant research activities. Thus, when the researchers obtain funding and are carrying out their research, they feel obliged to comply with the accepted proposal in order to complete deliverables and obtain continuation funding. Such were the start-up conditions that directed what the focus and tasks were for the researchers who were responsible for the training programme (WP3). However, after examining the CJS/MHS interface and talking to different involved parties, the gap between the proposal and reality became obvious. Another aspect of the gap that became apparent is illumined in the theoretical framework of SI, collaboration and co-creation (Bason, 2010; Hean et al., 2015b) which emphasises that there are evolving, dynamic and unpredictable processes that cannot be foreseen. Given that a training programme should facilitate such processes, it is almost impossible to carry one out if you are trying to implement a predefined solution. There has to be opportunities for reconsideration. A third gap between theory and practice arises from the training versus reality of frontline practitioners' preoccupation with offenders' basic needs and access to services. Although the researchers were educated clinicians and were aware of offenders' needs, they were primarily focused on delivering collaborative education and practice focused on how services could improve the practitioners' collaborative work on a system level. They also felt obliged to fullfil the deliverable of a training programme outlined in their proposal.

As illustrated in this chapter, much boundary work took place (Wenger, 1998). Different views, goals and roles played out in dynamic interactions, and project participants arrived at an agreement to change the content of the deliverable. In particular, the question of the utility of the proposed training programme was intensely discussed, provoking a change. In retrospect, we can observe that a great deal of learning took place, such as learning about each other's knowledge and views, about the interface and contexts of CJS/MHS, the various agencies responsible for offenders, learning about challenges regarding research and practice and the collaboration needed to improve services. We conclude that it takes courage and commitment to work out such boundary work, and it is important to be prepared for the challenge of this endeavour.

References

Alstveit, M., Willumsen, E., & Ødegård, A. (2017). Forskningssamarbeid mellom praksisfelt og akademia—en utforskning av dette samspillets rolle i kunnskapsutvikling. [Research collaboration between fields of practice and academia—An exploration of this interaction's role in knowledge development]. In A. M. Støkken & E. Wilumsen (Eds.), *Brukerstemmer, praksisforskning og innovasjon* [User voices, practice research and innovation] (pp.149–167). Kristiansand: Portal Akademisk Forlag.

Bason, C. (2010). *Leading public sector innovation: Co-creating for a better society*. Policy Press.

Bessant, J., & Tidd, J. (2016). *Innovation and entrepreneurship*. Wiley.

Brown, V. A., Harris, J. A., & Russell, J. Y. (2010). *Tackling wicked problems: Through the transdisciplinary imagination.* Earthscan.

Bureau of European Policy Advisers (BEPA). (2011). *Empowering people, driving change: SI in the European Union.* Available at https://ec.europa.eu/migrant-integration/librarydoc/empowering-people-driving-change-social-innovation-in-the-european-union. Accessed July 2020.

Crepaldi, C., De Rosa, E., & Pesce, F. (2012). *Literature review on innovation in social services in Europe: Sectors of health, education and welfare services.* INNOSERV Work Package, 1.

Engeström, Y., Virkkunen, J., Helle, M., Pihlaja, J., & Poikela, R. (1996). The change laboratory as a tool for transforming work. *Lifelong Learning in Europe, 1*(2), 10–17.

Frenk, J., et al. (2010). Health professionals for a new century: Transforming education to strengthen health systems in an interdependent world. *Lancet, 376*(9756), 1923–1958.

Hean, S. (2016). *Improving collaborative working between correctional and mental health services.* EU proposal, Proposal number: 734536, MSCA-RISE-2016, CO-LAB.

Hean, S., Staddon, S., Fenge, L., Clapper, A., Oxon, M. A., Heaslip, V., & Jack, E. (2015a). Improving collaborative practice to address offender mental health : Criminal justice and mental health service professionals' attitudes toward interagency training, current training needs, and constraints. *Journal of Research in Interprofessional Practice and Education, 5,* 1–17.

Hean, S., Willumsen, E., Ødegård, A., & Bjørkly, S. (2015b). Using social innovation as a theoretical framework to guide future thinking on facilitating collaboration between mental health and criminal justice services. *International Journal of Forensic Mental Health, 14*(4), 280–289.

Hean, S., Willumsen, E., & Ødegård, A. (2018). Making sense of interactions between mental health and criminal justice services: The utility of cultural historical activity systems theory. *International Journal of Prisoner Health, 14*(2), 124–141.

Iversen, H. P., & Johannessen, S. O. (2020). Et kompleksitetsteoretisk perspektiv på tverrprofesjonell organisasjonspraksis og innovasjonsprosesser [A complexity theoretical perspective on interprofessional organizational practices and innovation processes]. In E. Willumsen & A. Ødegård (Eds.), *Samskaping* [Co-creation] (pp. 247–259). Oslo: Universitetsforlaget.

Murray, R. Caulier-Grice, J. and Mulgan, G. (2010) *The open book of social innovation: London:* Young Foundation. Accessed July 2020. Available at https://youngfoundation.org/wp-content/uploads/2012/10/The-Open-Book-of-Social-Innovationg.pdf.

Norwegian Research Council (NRC). (2012). *Innovasjon i offentlig sektor* [Innovation in the public sector]. Oslo. NRC

Røiseland, A., & Lo, C. (2019). Samskaping—nyttig begrep for norske forskere og praktikere? [Co-creation—useful term for Norwegian researchers and practitioners?]. *Norsk Statsvitenskapelig Tidsskrift, 35*(1), 51–58.

Star, S. L., & Greisemer, J. R. (1989). Institutional ecology, 'Translations' and boundary objects: Amateurs and professionals in Berkeley's museum of vertebrate zoology. *Social Studies of Science, 19*(3), 1907–1939.

Torfing, J., Sørensen, E., & Aagaard, P. (2014). Samarbeidsdrevet innovasjon i praksis: en introduksjon [Collaborative innovation in practice: An introduction.]. In P. Aagaard, E. Sørensen, & J. Torfing (Eds.), *Samarbejdsdrevet innovation i praksis.* København: Jurist- og økonomforbundets forlag.

UNESCO. (1998). *The world declaration on higher education for the twenty-first century: Vision and action.* Paris: UNESCO. Accessed July 2020, Available at https://unesdoc.unesco.org/ark:/48223/pf0000141952.

Voorberg, W. H., Bekkers, V. J. J. M., & Tummers, L. G. (2015). A systematic review of co-creation and co-production: Embarking on the social innovation journey. *Public Management Review, 17*(9), 1333–1357.

Wenger, E. (1998). *Communities of practice.* Cambridge University Press.

White Paper no 4 (2018–2019). *Langtidsplan for forskning og høyere utdanning 2019–2028.* (Long-term plan for research and higher education 2019–2028). Oslo: Kunnskapsdepartementet/Ministry of Education and Research.

Willumsen, E., & Ødegård, A. (2015). *Sosial innovasjon—fra politikk til tjenesteutvikling* [Social innovation—from politics to service development]. Bergen: Fagbokforlaget.

Willumsen, E., & Ødegård, A. (2020). *Samskaping* [Co-creation]. Oslo: Universitetsforlaget.

World Health Organisation (2010) *Framework for action on interprofessional education & collaborative practice*. Geneva: WHO. Accessed July 2020. Available at https://apps.who.int/iris/bitstream/handle/10665/70185/WHO_HRH_HPN_10.3_eng.pdf;jsessionid=6877DCD5E97EFE81E3B1C1399BCA73B3?sequence=1.

Ødegård, A. (2006, December 18). Exploring perceptions of interprofessional collaboration in child mental health care. *International Journal of Integrated Care, 6*. https://www.ijic.org/

Index

S. Hean et al. (eds.), *Improving Interagency Collaboration, Innovation and Learning in Criminal Justice Systems*,
https://doi.org/10.1007/978-3-030-70661-6

The manufacturer's authorised representative in the EU is Springer Nature Customer Service Centre GmbH, Europaplatz 3, 69115 Heidelberg, Germany. If you have any concerns regarding our products, please contact ProductSafety@springernature.com

Printed and bound by CPI Group (UK) Ltd, Croydon, CR0 4YY
30/09/2026
02225453-0009